THE YALE-HOOVER SERIES ON AUTHORITARIAN REGIMES

ILLNESS AND INHUMANITY IN STALIN'S GULAG

GOLFO ALEXOPOULOS

Hoover Institution
Stanford University
Stanford, California

Yale UNIVERSITY PRESS
New Haven and London

Published with assistance from the foundation established in memory of Philip Hamilton McMillan of the Class of 1894, Yale College.

Yale University Press books may be purchased in quantity for educational, business, or promotional use. For information, please e-mail sales.press@yale.edu (U.S. office) or sales@yaleup.co.uk (U.K. office).

Set in Sabon type by Newgen North America.
Printed in the United States of America.

Library of Congress Control Number: 2016951586
ISBN 978-0-300-17941-5 (hardcover : alk. paper)

A catalogue record for this book is available from the British Library.

This paper meets the requirements of ANSI/NISO Z39.48–1992 (Permanence of Paper).

10 9 8 7 6 5 4 3 2 1

To Thomas, Athena, and Sophia with love

Contents

Acknowledgments

Most of the archival research for this book took place in 2007–2008, when I was a W. Glenn Campbell and Rita Ricardo-Campbell National Fellow and the William C. Bark National Fellow at the Hoover Institution. During that memorable year in Palo Alto, I worked with the microfilm collection of Soviet state and party archives at the Hoover Institution Library and Archives, spending most of my time on Gulag records. The remarkable collection made this book possible. I would like to thank especially Paul Gregory for his support of the project, as well as Eric Wakin and the Hoover Institution Library and Archives directors. Over the years, I have benefited greatly from conversations with a brilliant group of scholars at the Hoover Institution's Workshop on Authoritarian Regimes, especially Mark Harrison, Oleg Khlevniuk, Mark Kramer, Anne Applebaum, Norman Naimark, and Amir Weiner, as well as Jörg Baberowski, Evgenia Belova, Leonid Borodkin, John Dunlop, Michael Ellman, Simon Ertz, Catherine Gousseff, James Heinzen, Emily Johnson, Katherine Jolluck, Deborah Kaple, Stephen Kotkin, Valery Lazarev, Andrei Markevich, David Sadder, Robert Service, and David Shearer. I am very grateful to Carol Leadenham, Lora Soroka, David Jacobs, and Linda Bernard of the Hoover Institution Library and Archives, who facilitated my research in innumerable ways. This book is very much a product of the Hoover Institution's exceptional resources, scholarly community, and generosity.

Many people have helped me with this project over the years. It gives me great pleasure to acknowledge them here, beginning with William Frucht, my editor at Yale University Press, for his support of the manuscript, as well as Karen Olson, Mary Pasti, and Jaya Chatterjee for their help at various stages of production. The external reviewers of my manuscript for the Press and my copyeditor, Beverly Michaels, made this book so much better. I also thank Nanci Adler, Patty Apostolos, Alan Barenberg, Steven Barnes, Jenna Bednar, Kees Boterbloem, Shawn Coyne, Michael David-Fox, Michael Decker, Chelsea Esposito, Marcie Finkelstein, Sheila Fitzpatrick, Klaus Gestwa, Jehanne Gheith, Maria Gough, Patricia Gorman, Jana Howlett, David Joravsky, Cheryl Kirstein, Diane Koenker, Judy Morachnik, Adriana Novoa, Victor Peppard, Judith Pallot, Darrell Slider, Peter Solomon, Sofia Somonova, Nikolai Ssorin-Chaikov, Vadim Staklo, Mariana Stavig, and Stephen Turner. I am very grateful to Irina Flige, Tatiana Morgacheva, Evgeniya Kulakova, Ira Suslova, and the archivists at Memorial in St. Petersburg for their generous assistance. I also wish to thank Sam Diener for his important editing and feedback, as well as Ronald Grigor Suny and Valerie Sperling for their encouragement, support, and invaluable insights. My former students at the University of South Florida, Lydia Greiner and Ivana Lam, provided excellent research assistance.

I am forever grateful to my family, whose love, support, and patience enabled me to complete this difficult project, especially George and Pola Alexopoulos, Lia Alexopoulos (whose help has been truly immeasurable), Greg and Kimberly Alexopoulos, and James and Cornelia Smith. This book is dedicated with deep love and gratitude to my husband, Thomas Wright Smith, and to our daughters, Athena Alexopoulos Smith and Sophia Panayiota Smith. I could not have done it without you.

My research and writing have been supported by the Hoover Institution, the National Endowment for the Humanities (NEH), the National Council for East European and Eurasian Research (NCEEER), and the College of Arts and Sciences at the University of South Florida. Parts of this book appeared in my article "Destructive-Labor Camps: Rethinking Solzhenitsyn's Play on Words," in *Kritika: Explorations in Russian and Eurasian History* 16:3 (Summer 2015): 499–526, and are reprinted here with the journal's permission.

A Note on Archives and Language

The archival documents cited in this book overwhelmingly derive from the microfilm collection of the Archives of the Soviet Communist Party and Soviet State at the Hoover Institution Library and Archives, Stanford University. The Hoover microfilm collection includes the archival records of the Gulag administration, which are located in the State Archive of the Russian Federation (*Gosudarstvennyi Arkhiv Rossiiskoi Federatsii*), herein abbreviated as GARF.

Quotations from the original Russian follow the Library of Congress transliteration system. However, consistent with accepted practice, I write Dalstroi instead of Dal'stroi and Norillag instead of Noril'lag, and I use a *y* rather than *ii* at the end of Russian names—for example, Primorsky instead of Primorskii. Unless otherwise indicated, all translations of Russian sources are my own.

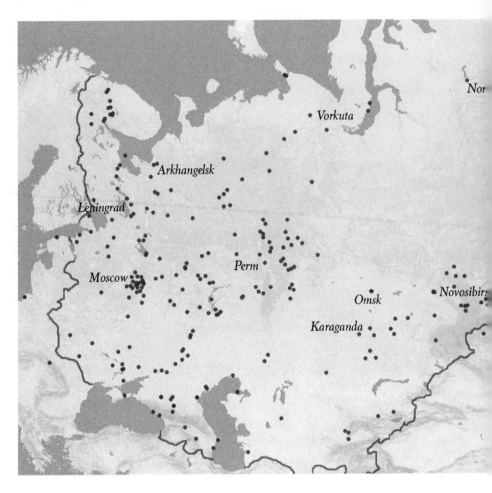

Locations of forced labor camps and colonies during the Stalin years. This map provides only a rough overview, as Gulag sites shifted frequently. I thank Judith Pallot, Sofia Gavrilova, and the Economic and Social Research Council (ESRC) for providing the data and Chelsea Esposito for creating the map.

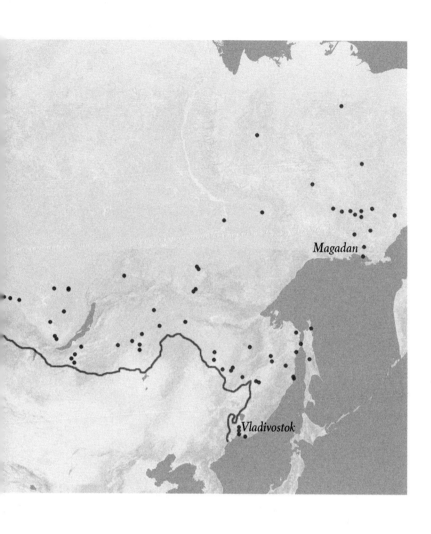

Magadan

Vladivostok

ILLNESS AND INHUMANITY IN STALIN'S GULAG

Introduction

Exploiting "Human Raw Material"

JOSEPH STALIN'S FORCED labor camp system constituted an enormous penal-industrial complex that lasted for nearly a quarter of a century in the Soviet Union. It has been less than two decades since the declassification of the Gulag archive, and new scholarship is only beginning to shed light on this dark corner of twentieth-century European history. Although Gulag survivors often spoke of these as death camps, historians' initial archival findings revealed high-level concerns for labor productivity, condemnations of prisoner abuse, frequent prisoner releases, and low mortality rates. Thus the prevailing view among Gulag scholars has been that these were not camps where prisoners were destroyed by design. In the course of my own research, however, a very different picture emerged. My investigation into health and medicine in the Gulag, a largely neglected area of study, led me to a broad range of material on prisoners' physical exploitation. What I discovered in the archives surprised me. Stalin's Gulag constituted a highly coordinated and lethal system of human exploitation. Viewed as mere inputs in an industrial process, prisoners were supposed to be thoroughly exploited and totally depleted. To be sure, not all inmates faced certain death. Total extermination was not Stalin's goal, but total exploitation was. The present work demonstrates that the Gulag represented a willfully destructive institution to a degree not previously documented, and that the Stalinist regime systematically concealed the Gulag's destructive capacity.

What was the Gulag? In the archival record, it appears as GULAG, an acronym for the Main Administration of Corrective Labor Camps (*glavnoe upravlenie ispravitel'no-trudovykh lagerei*), a bureaucratic entity of the Soviet security police. Stalin's security police went by various acronyms over the years, from the Unified State Political Administration (OGPU) to the People's Commissariat of Internal Affairs (NKVD) and the Ministry of Internal Affairs (MVD). The Gulag administration managed various penal institutions, from prisoner of war camps, filtration camps, and prisons, to so-called special camps, special settlements, corrective labor camps, and corrective labor colonies. Following the 1973 publication in the West of Alexander Solzhenitsyn's *Gulag Archipelago,* the term became synonymous with the Soviet forced labor camp system. Scholars generally use the word to refer to the exile settlements as well, but in the present work, I do not. By the mid-1930s, the labor camps and colonies had emerged as the core institutions of the Gulag.[1] Moreover, the settlements were unlike the camps in important ways. Settlements detained entire families, whether deported kulaks or "enemy nations." Women and children represented the majority, whereas the camps and colonies incarcerated largely male heads of households.[2] Settlers did not live within barbed wire, they interacted more freely among the civilian population, and they were not generally subjected to the same degree of punitive physical exploitation as camp prisoners. The focus of the present work is the Stalinist system of forced labor camps and colonies. I use the term *Gulag* in the same way as Solzhenitsyn and many other writers, to refer to both the administration that managed the camp system and the system itself.

Gulag studies is a relatively new field, given the recent declassification of the Soviet archives. At the present time, historical debate has largely centered around the purpose of the camps, their role within Soviet society, and whether they represented primarily penal or economic institutions. In general, historians have argued that the Gulag "was not in the first instance an economic institution" and have underscored "the limitations of the economic understanding of the Soviet penal system."[3] This view reflected the security police's own ranking of the

Gulag's functions. The OGPU-NKVD-MVD and Gulag leadership consistently maintained that policing state enemies constituted the most important function of the camps. Both before and after the war, Gulag officials described the purpose of the camps as "primarily" the "isolation of especially dangerous counterrevolutionaries and other criminal offenders from the rest of society," while "the utilization of prisoners' labor" and "reeducation through highly productive socially useful labor" represented the Gulag's "second basic function."[4] The mandate of the security police focused primarily on punishing deviants and state enemies, so it is not surprising that policemen identified most with this role. Gulag officials also stressed the menacing profile of inmates because it was in their interest to do so. But separating the Gulag's main functions and ranking them has not helped us to better understand the nature of Stalin's forced labor camp system.

Having once ranked the economic versus penal functions myself, I now believe that it is more useful to think of these two elements as integrated and mutually reinforcing. For Stalin, there was little distinction between the political and the economic. The economic *was* political. As Stalin told the party in 1937: "In life . . . in practice, politics and economics are indivisible."[5] I begin this book with a chapter on rations. The rationing system in the Stalinist camps has received little attention and yet it represents, in many ways, the essential inhumanity of the system. Within the rationing system, the penal and economic motives were fundamentally linked. The Stalinist regime fed its camp prisoners according to their economic output, and organized food distribution both as an economic incentive (to encourage labor productivity) and as a penalty (to punish the so-called slackers and saboteurs who failed to fulfill their work quota). In its pursuit of noncapitalist industrial development, the party employed a vast system of brutal human exploitation, one that framed various classes of prisoners as dangerous enemies. The economic and penal elements of the camps were often indistinguishable.

New research on the Stalinist forced labor camp system has shed light on various aspects of this long-lasting, diverse, and complex enterprise, although a great deal remains to be learned. Scholars have examined the emergence and development of the system of labor camps and settlements in the 1930s.[6] Some have focused on the Gulag economy, including the microeconomics of individual camps and industries, and the local implementation of central policy.[7] Research has explored the ideological underpinnings of the Stalinist camps, which was to reeducate or rehabilitate criminal offenders and protect Soviet society and state against "harmful elements."[8] Scholars are beginning to examine the Gulag's "biopolitics" as well as prisoners' cultural practices like letter-writing.[9] Historians have focused on particular penal institutions or eras, such as POW camps or the Gulag in World War II, or certain populations, such as women, children, and ethnic minorities in the camps.[10] Recent work has examined the transformation of the Gulag from the Stalin to the Khrushchev years, and the dismantling of the forced labor camp system.[11] Much of the work has focused on Stalin and the ruling elite, the security police that operated the penal labor system, and the waves of terror targeting "counterrevolutionaries" or perceived state enemies.[12] My work differs from the current scholarship, but it is deeply indebted to it and builds upon it in fundamental ways. This book does not deal with the origins or dismantling of Stalin's Gulag, nor do I offer a new interpretation of the role of the Gulag in Soviet society. Rather, I use the lens of camp medicine to examine the Gulag as a system of physical exploitation.

I argue that violent human exploitation constituted the essential purpose of Stalin's Gulag. One cannot understand the Gulag fully without appreciating the centrality of its exploitative function. Over the course of the Stalin years, this system of exploitation was unrelenting, punitive, and increasingly brutal. Under Stalin, camp prisoners had to be maximally "utilized" and worked to the point of utter depletion. As Alexander Solzhenitsyn noted, "the supreme law of the Archipelago" was "to squeeze everything out of a prisoner."[13] The Stalinist leadership may not have planned to exterminate all camp prisoners, but it intended to extract all available energy, to physically exploit prisoners to the maximum degree possible. One Gulag administrator stated in the early 1930s: "We have to squeeze everything out of a prisoner in the first three months—after that we don't need him anymore."[14] In a 1941 letter to NKVD chief Lavrenty Beria, another camp official explained: "Our task is to wring out (*vyzhat'*) of the camp population the maximum quantity of marketable commodities."[15] One of the most basic functions of the camps throughout the Stalin years was the total exploitation of prisoners' labor. As Oleg Khlevniuk explained, "The possibility of [prison labor's] unlimited exploitation, including working people to death, was highly valued by the top political leaders and economic managers."[16] This destructive system of human exploitation in the Stalinist camps has not received as much attention in the scholarly literature as other forms of violence, such as inmate strikes, clashes between social and ethnic groups, child abuse, and rape. Yet human exploitation represents the Gulag's systemic violence, which was not episodic but relentless, and arguably more consequential in its impact on human suffering.

The Gulag represented less a "state of exception" according to Giorgio Agamben, involving the suspension of juridical order, than an expression of the Soviet order itself.[17] The striking feature of Gulag violence is not its existence outside the law, but the degree to which violence resided wholly within the norms and structures of the institution. It was, as Slavoj Zizek described, an objective, anonymous, systemic violence, "inherent in the normal state of things."[18] The Gulag constituted a violent order. Its system of rules governing the extreme physical exploitation and systemic starvation of prisoners is documented in the archival records of the Gulag medical-sanitation department or health service.[19] Once prisoners were in the camps, their health status often mattered more than other markers of identity, such as class background, alleged crime, ethnicity, and gender. Inmates constituted the regime's workhorses. At the highest levels of Gulag administration, prisoners were thought of as cheap implements.[20] Stalin's Gulag was, in many ways, less a concentration camp than a forced labor camp and less a prison system than a system of slavery. The image of the slave appears often in Gulag memoir literature. As Varlam Shalamov wrote: "Hungry and exhausted, we leaned into a horse collar, raising blood blisters on our chests and pulling a stone-filled cart up the slanted mine floor. The collar was the same device used long ago by the ancient Egyptians."[21] Thoughtful and rigorous historical comparisons of Soviet forced labor and other forms of slave labor would be worthy of scholarly attention, in my view. For as in the case of global slavery, the Gulag found legitimacy in an elaborate narrative of difference that involved the presumption of dangerousness and guilt.[22] This ideology of difference and the violence of human exploitation have left lasting legacies in contemporary Russia.[23]

"DESTRUCTIVE-LABOR CAMPS": HIERARCHY, REDISTRIBUTION, AND SYSTEMIC VIOLENCE

In Stalin's Gulag, the OGPU-NKVD-MVD deployed what Katherine Verdery called the socialist state's "redistributive power." According to Verdery, the socialist state derived its legitimacy from its capacity to monopolize resources and control their redistribution, to decide who got more and who got less.[24] The Gulag represented the most extreme expression of the Stalinist state's redistributive power. Resources went from low-priority camps and colonies to high-priority sites, and food was transferred from the weakest to the strongest prisoners. Timothy Snyder stressed the lethal nature of Stalinist redistribution in the case of the 1932–1933 Ukrainian famine, when he wrote: "It was not food shortages but food distribution that killed millions in Soviet Ukraine, and it was Stalin who decided who was entitled to what."[25] The same can be said for the Gulag. Food shortages and nutritional imbalances certainly killed, but arguably more lethal was the Gulag's punitive food distribution system.

Stalin's vast pyramid of camps formed a highly coordinated network of slave labor. My research reveals that at the base of the pyramid were the labor colonies, where the Gulag concentrated its sickest and most disabled prisoners. The Stalinist regime claimed that its labor colonies were reserved for short-term offenders, and scholars have long assumed this was the case. But as I demonstrate here, the colonies and regional camps became the dumping ground for the system's most wrung-out and emaciated inmates. As historians have focused their attention on the major camp complexes of the Gulag, we have largely neglected to study the regional labor camps and colonies. Further research is needed here, as there is much to learn. By the late 1940s, the colonies detained as many prisoners as the camps. As inmates grew frail and emaciated, they were transferred from higher-priority industrial locations to lower-priority sites at the bottom tier of the Gulag pyramid where they worked in agriculture and light manufacturing. Priority camps were located at the pinnacle of the redistribution chain, followed by ordinary camps. The most resources and the healthiest prisoners were directed to Stalin's highly valued sites, such as Norilsk.[26] Historical scholarship has shed light on the nature of the Soviet centrally planned economy's "hierarchy of consumption."[27] The same redistributive mechanism existed in the Gulag, and had a punishing impact on the lives of prisoners who occupied the enormous base of the Gulag pyramid.

Stalin's policy of brutal redistribution and physical exploitation reveals that the Gulag was destructive by design. This explains why Solzhenitsyn rejected the benign Stalinist term for the slave labor system, corrective-labor camps (*ispravitel'no-trudovye lageria*), in favor of his own term: destructive-labor camps (*istrebitel'no-trudovye lageria*).[28] His pun or play on Soviet words stressed that Gulag labor was more lethal than corrective. According to Solzhenitsyn, "the camps were designed for destruction" (*izobreteny lageria—na istreblenie*).[29] Recently declassified Gulag archival documents, especially those related to inmate health and the Stalinist system of human exploitation, provide evidence to support this striking assertion. In the course of my own research, I arrived at the realization that human exploitation in the Gulag was, indeed, destructive by design. Soviet scholars have tended to disregard Solzhenitsyn's analysis, as if the writer exaggerated purposefully, perhaps for dramatic effect, in his "experiment in literary investigation." Yet the newly opened archives reveal the Gulag's systemic violence and destructive design.

The Gulag literature has catalogued the causes of human suffering and mortality, but scholars do not generally argue that the Stalinist camps were designed for destruction. Steven Barnes wrote, "Soviet authorities had the know-how, experience, facilities, and will to violence to exterminate every one of the millions who passed through the Gulag, but they chose not to create a truly genocidal institution."[30] More common was the view that the Gulag represented an institution of mass death, but not mass murder. Oleg Khlevniuk wrote that "the conditions prevailing in labor camps at times made them indistinguishable from death camps."[31] According to Anne Applebaum, "The Soviet camp system as a whole was not deliberately organized to mass produce corpses—even if, at times, it did."[32] Scholars have generally characterized mass killing in the Gulag as the result of camp conditions rather than high-level motives. The Soviet security police that managed the arrest, imprisonment, deportation, and detention of millions was distinctly uninterested in preserving human life. Nonetheless, no plan of destruction had emerged from our initial reading of declassified state and party documents. Thus, while historians emphasized the brutality of the Gulag, few argued that the Stalinist labor camp system was at its core intentionally lethal.[33] Before writing this book, I agreed with my colleagues and the general consensus in the field. I now believe that recently declassified documents on prisoners' health and the system of physical exploitation compel us to rethink our current assumptions about the Gulag.

In the scholarly literature, Gulag violence generally appears dispersed and fragmented rather than systemic and centrally coordinated. Scholars have demonstrated that people died from the brutal journey in sealed railcars to their remote camps and the hostile Arctic environment, as well as the neglect, incompetence, and cruelty of camp administrators, guards, and fellow inmates. Gulag memoirs and historical literature often underscore the nonsystemic causes of Gulag mortality, for example, deaths resulting from underdevelopment such as poor sanitation and infrastructure, violent criminal gangs, shortages and theft of food, the chaos of policy implementation, negligent and cruel security police, or factors external to the system, such as the harsh climate and the war.[34] Taken together, these do not generate an image of a labor camp system that was destructive by design. Moreover, no statement from the Stalinist leadership has emerged that expressed a high-level intention or state-sponsored plan to destroy prisoners. Quite the contrary, we found many official complaints concerning elevated rates of illness and mortality, and attempts by party leaders to incentivize forced labor and improve productivity through material rewards. Historians have interpreted this as evidence that high-level intentions did not involve mass killing and that, on balance, Soviet authorities more often sought to improve prisoners' conditions.[35]

For historians of the Stalin era, the Nazi-Soviet comparison looms large. There exists a legitimate desire on behalf of many scholars to avoid false equivalencies between the Nazi extermination camps and Stalin's Gulag. Although a number of Soviet writers, dissidents, and Gulag survivors have highlighted similarities between the two camp systems, the Soviets operated no extermination camps as such.[36] There is little consensus concerning the genocidal nature of Stalinist state violence, and even scholars who admit the applicability of the term in certain cases largely reject analogies between the Nazi and Soviet camps.[37] The Nazi extermination camps remain exceptional, to be sure, yet comparisons between Nazi and Soviet labor camps might advance our understanding of each.[38] There is also survivors' testimony that reads very differently in the Soviet case. Gulag memoirs, predominately authored by political or "counterrevolutionary" offenders, appear to demonstrate the survivability of the Soviet camps.[39] Personal accounts by former prisoners represent testimonies of survival.[40] The Gulag maintained hospitals and clinics, and camp doctors were not assigned the role of "an alert biological soldier" or tasked with experimental and direct medical killing, as in the Nazi case.[41] Rather, camp doctors often viewed themselves as healers and struggled to improve prisoners' chances of survival. The OGPU-NKVD-MVD and Gulag leaders often criticized camp administrators when illness and mortality rates exceeded mandated norms. The serious economic functions of the Stalinist camps also seem to belie any notion that these institutions were designed for destruction. Why would an economic system deliberately destroy its own capital?

In my view, the above paradoxes of the Gulag regime do not necessarily challenge the notion that these were "destructive-labor camps." The OGPU-NKVD-MVD and Gulag leaders pressured camps to preserve their human capital, but the Stalinist leadership exerted much stronger countervailing pressures. One former Gulag prisoner noted, "For [the camp administration] only one thing mattered: that the mine produced gold, as much gold as possible."[42] As Gulag survivor Antoni Ekart explained, regulations governing the length of the work day and the rights of prisoners hardly mattered: "No camp commandant takes any notice of that because his personal liability for getting the work completed is far greater than that for breaking prison regulations."[43] Moreover, there was little incentive for camp administrators to preserve life given the constant influx of prison labor. In the early 1930s, as Lynne Viola demonstrates, kulak settlers were viewed as a "muscle force" and "infinitely replenishable," as commandants focused on plan fulfillment with little incentive to preserve human life given the steady stream of newly deported peasants.[44] Similarly, camp officials thought little about preserving the lives of the sick and disabled when they were constantly assured a transport of new prisoners. Moreover, the Gulag medical-sanitation department, grossly understaffed and relatively powerless in the camp hierarchy, was highly constrained by quotas on the number of allowable sick and nonworking prisoners. In addition, memoirists who survived years in the Gulag attributed their survival to indoor jobs. They worked as doctors, nurses, artists, and accountants.

For extended periods of time, they did not experience heavy physical labor or the "basic work" of the camp, which they uniformly describe as lethal.

Harsh physical exploitation and punitive starvation rations represented the most fundamental features of everyday life in the camps. As Timothy Snyder notes, the Bolsheviks learned in their first few years in power that "food was a weapon" and, in the Stalin years, the Soviet Union "starved by policy."[45] It did so in the Gulag. Hunger represented the Gulag's fundamental labor incentive and food was insufficient by design. Alexander Etkind asserted that the Stalinist camps operated not according to a logic of production or extermination, but "the logic of torture."[46] There was a logic of torture, and starvation was the method used. Even the largest of the so-called differentiated food rations, meant for the prisoners who exceeded their production targets, did not compensate for the energy prisoners expended doing a full day's work mining gold, laying railroad tracks, or felling trees, often in subzero temperatures. The Gulag allocated food to prisoners according to whether they met production norms. As prisoners grew physically weak and failed to meet their work quotas, they earned less food and grew weaker still. The smallest food rations in Stalin's Gulag went to nonworking invalids and weakened prisoners who failed to meet their production norms, and these rations were on par with those allocated to prisoners in the punishment cell.[47] The equivalency was not coincidental. Gulag authorities routinely condemned those too weak to work as willful work refusers. Thus they justified their power, as Giorgio Agamben explained—"to let die."[48]

EXPLOITATION AND INHUMANITY IN THE STALIN YEARS

Forced labor and penal exile had a long history in Tsarist Russia, and the Bolsheviks continued the practice after the Russian Revolution.[49] In 1918, Vladimir Lenin established concentration camps that largely detained political opponents of the new regime, many sentenced by revolutionary tribunals under the security police. Stalin renamed Lenin's "concentration camps" to "corrective-labor camps" and charged them with "the utilization of the labor of criminal inmates."[50] The Soviet leader made an important break with the past by situating the exploitation of human labor at the center of his camp system. Beginning in 1929, Stalin's forced collectivization drive and campaign "to liquidate the kulaks as a class" resulted in the deportation of millions of so-called capitalist peasants. These dekulakized peasants became the Gulag's first mass penal labor force.[51] Stalin's forced labor camp system steadily expanded over more than two decades, drawing in not only peasants but industrial workers, artists, and intellectuals. Throughout its existence, the Gulag possessed several interlocking functions: penal isolation, punishment, and torture; economic production, exploitation, and colonization; population control, discipline, and reeducation. These operations were intimately linked and mutually reinforcing, and they were united under a single logic of maximum human exploitation. Although prisoners were exploited for their intellect and knowledge as well, the present work focuses on the Gulag's system of physical exploitation.[52]

Hundreds of labor camps and colonies stretched across the Soviet Union's enormous territory. They represented an integral part of the Stalinist state, as the Gulag and non-Gulag worlds interacted in important ways.[53] Like other Soviet civilians, prisoners were mobilized to advance noncapitalist industrial expansion and "socialist construction," and they experienced the effects of famine, terror, and war. Party leaders sought to exploit the Soviet Union's rich natural resources for industrial expansion, to profit from gold, copper, platinum, nickel, timber, and coal reserves. As Paul Gregory noted, "Stalin presumed that surpluses could be extracted from Gulag labor," and his goal was to achieve economic "surpluses" similar to Marx's surplus value.[54] Prisoners were expected to cover the cost of their detention through productive labor, as Stalin demanded that the camps be self-supporting and profit generating. This imperative to extract surplus value, reduce costs and maximize output and profit had lethal consequences. When prisoners could no longer work, the system would no longer support them. This is especially evident during the war, when the population of weak and emaciated prisoners grew tremendously, and the Stalinist leadership sought ways to manage a prison workforce that was "not work capable." A burgeoning population of crippled and sick inmates during the war compelled Gulag officials to begin asking serious questions about the efficiency and costs of the forced labor camp system. A re-thinking of the Gulag enterprise that contributed to the dismantlement of the system after Stalin's death originated in the war years.

Despite its paradoxical elements, the Gulag represented a modern more than a premodern institution.[55] The Stalinist leadership justified the exploitation of even the most severely ill and emaciated prisoners because such "labor utilization" illustrated that the security police operated camps in a rational and efficient way. Although the Gulag proved highly inefficient and wasteful, Stalin believed in forced labor, and with his support the OGPU-NKVD-MVD eventually grew to become one of the country's largest economic ministries. The Gulag played an important role in "socialist construction." In March 1934, Gulag chief Matvei Berman praised the ability of the camps to build "at times in uninhabitable places, the greatest economic projects of significance to the state." In addition, the camps isolated dangerous political offenders from the rest of Soviet society. For less dangerous criminal offenders, penal labor was supposed to "reeducate" and "rehabilitate," thus Berman noted the prisoners' "honest labor" as a means of atonement for their crimes before Soviet power.[56] The Stalinist regime touted their "corrective-labor camps," and invested greatly in the message of rehabilitation through labor or reforging (*perekovka*). However, by the late Stalin years, this rhetoric had diminished sharply. In March 1949, the Gulag chief, Dobrynin, hardly mentioned reeducation when he described the new draft of the "MVD USSR instructions on corrective labor camps and colonies." Rather, he stressed the need "to improve the regime and maintenance of prisoners, to raise prisoners' labor productivity, and to strengthen their detention and isolation."[57] Nonetheless, the narrative of corrective labor remained powerful and significant because rehabilitation did not exist apart from physical exploitation. "Reeducation through socially usefully labor" constituted the standard Stalinist slogan.[58]

In the course of the 1940s and into the early 1950s, Stalin's Gulag became larger, more regularized, and more violent. The goal of the Stalinist state was to catch up with and overtake the capitalist West, both economically and militarily.[59] In the rush to achieve this goal, especially during the Cold War, the MVD took on an ever-larger role in the Soviet economy. In the late Stalin years, prisoners built railroads, highways, airfields, dams, shipyards and canals. They mined coal and oil, gold, tin, copper, and nickel, and extracted timber from Russia's dense forests. They worked in chemical factories, docks, fisheries, and dairy farms. During the war, they produced ammunition, designed planes, and sewed uniforms. Gulag labor accounted for about 40 percent of laborers in nickel and copper mining, roughly 70 percent in tin mining, and a staggering 85–100 percent of Soviet labor in gold, diamond, and platinum mining. One in five construction workers in the Soviet Union in 1940 and 1951 were Gulag prisoners.[60] The OGPU-NKVD-MVD lobbied heavily for greater economic responsibilities, and by 1952, the MVD controlled more capital investment in Russia than any other ministry.[61] From the end of the war to the death of Stalin, 1945–1953, the Gulag administration doubled in size.[62] Stalin's appetite for forced labor increased over time, as did the Gulag population of sick and emaciated prisoners.

The Gulag population rose sharply and physical exploitation intensified in the postwar years. The inmate population had reached over two and a half million prisoners on the eve of Stalin's death in 1953. New inmates flooded into the Gulag in the late 1940s, resulting in severe overcrowding, deteriorating living conditions, and staffing shortages, all of which worsened prisoners' health. In the late 1940s, according to Yoram Gorlizki and Oleg Khlevniuk, "the cumulative impact of Stalin's penal policies threatened to push the scale of the Gulag beyond sustainable limits."[63] Moreover, memoirists describe how the camps in the 1940s "began to take on a mass character . . . things became harsher . . . as the camps grew bigger, the regime grew crueler."[64] As this book demonstrates, the system of human exploitation intensified greatly in the late Stalin years. In 1948, a new system of rations reduced the center's obligation to supply food to the camps and placed greater responsibility on individual camps to feed prisoners using local resources. That same year, a system of severely exploitative and brutal "special camps" was created that, like the harsh-regime or *katorga* sites, made physical exploitation explicitly lethal. Detention grew longer for both political and criminal offenders, as the twenty-five year sentence became common. In 1949, new instructions on the "utilization of prisoners' labor" forced greater numbers of weakened prisoners into heavy physical labor and provided fewer resources for their survival. Data on the physical exploitation of prisoners indicates that as many as 60 percent of prisoners were severely ill and emaciated, capable of only light forms of physical labor.

Human exploitation in Stalin's Gulag peaked in the years before the Soviet leader's death. Nonetheless, the Gulag reported its lowest rates of mortality in the late 1940s and early 1950s. Even Stalin's notoriously brutal "special camps" reported mortality rates under 1 percent in 1950, which appears implausible given the especially harsh detention regime at these sites. How did the Gulag generate such low mortality figures?

UNLOADING THE NEARLY DEAD TO "ELIMINATE THE DEATH RATE"

In Vladimir Voinovich's dystopian novel, *Moscow 2042*, the future Soviet state of Moscowrep has managed to "eliminate the death rate" through "reliable and economic means." One of the so-called Communites explained: "It was simply that critically ill people, as well as pensioners and invalids . . . were resettled to the First Ring and lived out their days there."[65] Stalin's Gulag eliminated much of its death rate in a similar way, by moving dying prisoners out of the system. The Gulag maintained low mortality through falsification and deceptive accounting practices but, more importantly, through mass releases. Under Stalin, routine discharges of severely ill and dying prisoners constituted one of the Gulag's principal tools for managing costs and suppressing mortality rates. Although Gulag historians have noted the practice, the present work is the first to demonstrate the enormous scale of these medical discharges and the critical use of prisoner releases for controlling costs and concealing illness and mortality.

Not only was Stalin's Gulag destructive, but it systematically concealed its destructive capacity. Official mortality rates appear largely in the area of 1–6 percent of the total inmate population, with significant fluctuations in certain years. For example, the Gulag recorded high mortality during the 1933 famine and the worst years of the war, 1942–1943. However, some of the lowest rates of mortality were recorded in years when camp conditions were known to have worsened dramatically, such as during the 1936–1937 purges, the 1947 famine, and the late Stalin years, 1950–1953.[66] In addition, declassified Gulag archives reveal that roughly 20–40 percent of prisoners were released annually in 1934–1953.[67] A number of historians, myself included, initially misinterpreted this archival data on Gulag releases, viewing the large numbers of freed prisoners as evidence that the institution was less lethal than previously imagined.[68] In the course of my research for this book, however, a different picture emerged. Gulag documents on inmate health demonstrate that routine mass releases, far from revealing the benign side of Gulag operations, actually expose the institution's destructive capacity. The discharged were often inmates who had become physically depleted or thoroughly "wrung out." The Gulag system exhaustively depleted and inhumanely discarded its prison laborers.

To be sure, there was variation across camps and among prisoners. The historical and memoir literature suggests that the lives of Gulag prisoners could vary greatly. Within the Gulag's hierarchy of camps, different prisoners could have vastly different camp experiences.[69] Prisoners' fate might be determined by the geography and economy of their camp, the personalities of their camp officials, their alleged crime and length of sentence, their health and skills, the kind of work they performed, and other factors. A number of variables determined the distribution of jobs, from a prisoner's sentence and "class category," to their education or willingness to act as an informer. Prisoners also secured more favorable conditions by employing common practices of Soviet everyday life, such as bribery, the black market, informal networks (*blat*), and personal connections.[70] Many prisoners did better because they received regular parcels from home. There were certainly ameliorating factors that enabled some prisoners to survive the camps. Yet there was another, more widely shared experience of the camps, one that few have chronicled because few survived to tell the story.

Roughly eighteen million people are believed to have passed through Stalin's labor camps and colonies, and the official Gulag mortality figure is estimated at around 1.6 million.[71] As this book demonstrates, the Gulag's data on mortality can only be interpreted as inadequate, for it does not include the millions of thoroughly exploited prisoners who died outside the accounting system of the camps and beyond the barbed wire. It is impossible to arrive at a precise figure on mortality in Stalin's labor camps and colonies, given the high degree of deception and false accounting, and the Gulag's failure to record all releases and transfers. Nonetheless, the Gulag's own statistics on prisoners' health, which overstated the physical capacity of the workforce, present a very bleak picture. From the 1930s to the early 1950s, anywhere from 15 to 60 percent of prisoners in Stalin's forced labor camps and colonies were deemed severely incapacitated, that is, labeled "invalids" or only "capable of light labor."[72] In the 1940s, this population of inmates constituted a sizable majority. A conservative estimate, in my view, would place Gulag mortality in the range of six million at a minimum. I believe that it is reasonable to conclude from the Gulag's own health records that no fewer than one-third of all individuals who passed through Stalin's labor camps and colonies died as a result of their detention.

DEHUMANIZATION, *DOKHODIAGI*, AND THE RIGHT "TO LET DIE"

The Gulag system generated tons of raw materials and vast construction projects, yet no less systematically, the camp regime turned out a population of semicorpses, people utterly destroyed from exhaustive labor. Stalinist exploitation generated a massive population of severely ill, disabled, and starving prisoners. Fellow inmates referred to an emaciated and dying inmate as a goner (*dokhodiaga*) or a wick (*fitil'*), suggesting that these prisoners were on their last legs or experiencing the last flickers of life.[73] They were the Soviet camp equivalent of the *Muselmänner* of Auschwitz.[74] Soviet historians have long known about the Gulag's walking corpses, the *dokhodiagi,* from the memoir literature, and studies of these emaciated inmates is only now emerging in the scholarly literature.[75] The history of the goners is especially difficult to capture because, as Alexander Etkind explains, unlike the survivors of the camps, the goners "were desperate and exhausted to the point that they did not express their pain, did not communicate with their peers, and did not tell their stories."[76] This book attempts to tell their story.

Mass killing is made possible by the dehumanization of victims, and this process is plainly evident in Stalin's Gulag. Prisoners represented mere inputs in a production process. Anne Applebaum captured this Stalinist view of Gulag prisoners: "Within the system, prisoners were treated as cattle, or rather as lumps of iron ore. Guards shuttled them around at will, loading and unloading them into cattle cars, weighing and measuring them, feeding them if it seemed they might be useful, starving them if they were not. They were, to use Marxist language, exploited, reified, and commodified. Unless they were productive, their lives were worthless to their masters."[77] Steven Barnes described how camp authorities "often treated their prisoners with the complete disregard of the subhuman."[78] In his *Gulag Archipelago*, Solzhenitsyn revealed to his countrymen and the world the inhumanity of the Soviet penal labor system, and drew attention to the dehumanization of prisoners. He cited the language of Maxim Gorky, who referred to labor camp prisoners of the White Sea-Baltic Sea Canal project as "human raw material" (*chelovecheskoe syr'e*).[79] According to Solzhenitsyn, camp authorities viewed prisoners as a "commodity" (*tovar*) to be exploited to the maximum degree possible, and then discarded, like waste.[80] Many memoirs of camp survivors underscore the degrading objectification of Gulag prisoners. Yehoshua Gilboa, wrote, "The world of prisoners is in constant motion, like barter merchandise."[81]

The present study examines the ways that prisoners were constituted, managed, and discarded as "human raw material." I demonstrate that Stalin's labor camp system worked prisoners to the point of near death, willfully starved the frail and less productive, and then discarded its emaciated and dying workforce en masse. Gulag authorities criminalized illness in the camps and regularly punished weakened prisoners as shirkers and "work refusers." In this way, they justified the power they possessed to let prisoners die. They exerted this power routinely because a prisoner incapable of working was worthless. This book draws attention to the systematic commodification and dehumanization of Gulag prisoners. Historian Viktor Berdinskikh argues that Gulag officials possessed a unique mentality and way of thinking, and often described the most inhumane events "in the calm, routine [language] of a chancellery."[82] I have tried to highlight the Gulag's degrading and dehumanizing language, rather than employ and normalize Stalinist terminology. For example, this work does not reproduce the euphemistic Stalinist term for the Gulag, "corrective-labor camps," but refers simply to Stalin's forced labor camps. The Gulag constituted not only a network of camps and colonies but also a distinct conceptual universe.

This book is organized thematically, and within each chapter I have tried to highlight the increasing brutality of the Gulag regime over the course of the Stalin years. The ordering of the chapters is generally chronological, as I have placed the wartime discussions in the middle and the treatment of the "special camps" and the 1950s crisis at the end. Each chapter deals with some aspect of the Gulag's elaborate, secretive, and lethal regime of human exploitation. I have constructed each chapter around a term or phrase of Gulag-speak, in order to showcase the mentality of the Stalinist leadership.[83] The official language of the camps, as revealed by recently declassified Gulag archival sources, illustrates the degree to which prisoners were constituted, exploited, and discarded as "human raw material." Stalin's Gulag constituted one of the twentieth century's worst crimes against humanity.

1 Food

"Whoever Does Not Work, Shall Not Eat"

THE FIRST SOVIET constitution declared that "labor is the obligation of all citizens of the republic" and trumpeted the warning: "Whoever does not work, shall not eat!"[1] According to Solzhenitsyn, this "great evangelical and Communist slogan" was placed in the camp mess hall, "on wall-paper in the favorite red letters."[2] The slogan remained relevant for decades. In the 1950s, MVD chief Kruglov praised the idea: "V.I. Lenin stressed that one of the decisive factors in the reeducation of people into the spirit of communist morality is high-productivity labor. Article 12 of the Constitution of the Soviet Union states: 'Work in the USSR is an obligation and a matter of honor for each work-capable citizen, according to the principle: "He who does not work, does not eat (*kto ne rabotaet, tot ne est*).""'[3] The Stalinist regime made hunger both an incentive in the Gulag and a punishment, and withdrew food from less productive prisoners. The most productive earned more food, but they had to exert themselves more to receive more, and the Gulag ration was not sufficient to compensate for energy expended. The Stalinist leadership created a punitive and inadequate feeding system by design, which willfully starved less productive prisoners. As Gulag survivor Antoni Ekart explained, "Less work equals less food, less food equals less energy, less energy equals less work, and so on until the final collapse."[4]

The Gulag's feeding regime illustrates the systemic violence and destructive nature of the Stalinist camps. In recent years, scholars have shed light on the Gulag's work incentives, such as early release, rehabilitation, and bonuses for high performers.[5] I focus here on the ways in which the regime willfully denied food to many prisoners and created an institution of mass starvation. Prisoners who failed to meet the regime's demanding production quotas were systematically denied sufficient nourishment. The Stalinist leadership barred local camp officials from feeding prisoners over and above the official quota. In the course of the Stalin years, camps were increasingly expected to find local sources of food to feed their prisoners and to expect less from central supply organs. This proved especially difficult for the Arctic camps. There was never enough food to feed all prisoners in adequate amounts, given the insufficient provisions and chronic theft. In the course of the Stalin years, the quantity of food for most Gulag prisoners declined, and rations became increasingly differentiated. The MVD routinely transferred food from the weakest to the strongest. As one Gulag survivor noted, "if I am alive today, it means that I got those extra seven ounces of bread which the dying man went without."[6] The Gulag food system constituted a violent zero-sum game.

SYSTEMIC MALNOURISHMENT AND THE "DIFFERENTIATED FOOD RATIONS"

The Stalinist leadership did not allocate sufficient quantities of food for its Gulag prisoners. The Council of People's Commissars (*Sovnarkom*) and later the Council of Ministers allocated resources quarterly to the Soviet security police according to the number of Gulag prisoners. The OGPU-NKVD-MVD released funding for food rations based on the Gulag's reporting of prisoners. Although each camp and colony issued regular reports on its inmate population, these figures proved highly imperfect. The NKVD leadership regularly complained that the party's food allocations were based on low estimates of the Gulag population, while individual camps complained that they were not issued enough food rations for all their prisoners.[7] As Paul Gregory explained, economic planners consistently failed to factor in a rise in inmates, even at the start of the Great Terror, which meant that, "attempts at advance planning grossly underestimated the influx of prisoners."[8]

Food provisions proved chronically insufficient for the number of prisoners detained, and the Stalinist leadership did little to address the problem. In a 1933 note to Stalin and V.V. Molotov, who chose not to approve Gulag requests for increased food allocations, OGPU chief Genrikh Yagoda strengthened his appeal. He underscored (the emphasis here is his own) that the industrial tasks of the camps "required improved labor productivity, *the maximum utilization of the labor force,* and a minimum percentage of *sick and weakened* [prisoners] . . . The existing food rations for prisoners are *significantly lower* than they were in 1932."[9] Yagoda insisted that insufficient supplies "may lead" to widespread emaciation and illness among prisoners and the poor utilization of the Gulag work force. He did not say that the current shortages had led to such conditions already, for Soviet officials reluctantly reported bad news to the party leadership. Stalin was a tough sell. He did not easily approve increased allocations, especially since he expected the camps to be self-sufficient. Knowing this, Yagoda underscored the Gulag's efforts at self-sufficiency. He stressed that the camps were doing "everything possible to meet their needs using their own resources," such as growing their own food in agricultural camps, fishing, and maintaining livestock.[10] Yagoda even issued the highly exaggerated claim that "in a year to a year-and-a-half the government will be entirely free from having to supply camps with meat," and that the potatoes and vegetables grown in their gardens "meet 70 percent of demand."[11] Stalin encouraged such claims by his subordinates, for he insisted that the camps maximize productive output and minimize costs. The problem of prisoners' malnourishment, however, did not derive solely from insufficient provisions.

The Stalinist leadership created a camp system that distributed food unequally among prisoners. The Gulag's "differentiated food rations" (*differentsirovannye normy*) represented an elaborate "hierarchy of provisioning," as Wendy Goldman characterized the Soviet Union's wartime rationing regime.[12] In the Gulag, however, food was not just allocated unequally among prisoners but punitively withdrawn, too. Gulag prisoners were fed based on their camp, the kind of work they performed, and the degree to which they fulfilled the camp's plan. Prisoners worked in brigades and their rations depended on how well the entire group worked.[13] The difference between the ration of high-performing prisoners and other prisoners was especially large in the

1930s. In the first decade of Stalin's Gulag, inmates generally received 1000 grams (2.2 lbs.) of bread, while those who exceed their production plan, the so-called Stakhanovites, received twice as much.[14] Nonetheless, the rations were inadequate. In April 1939, NKVD chief Beria argued that the standard 2000-calorie Gulag ration was insufficient and "designed for someone sitting in prison and not for a working person. Plus, in reality, the supply organizations dispense only 65–70 percent of this low food ration."[15] Beria's criticism of the official Gulag food rations was itself striking, given that future rations would fall far below the 1939 level.

New ration schedules followed Beria's call for better food in the camps, the largest prescribed rations in the history of Stalin's Gulag. In August 1939, the NKVD issued upwards of thirteen different ration schedules, some of them further differentiated for specified subgroups, so the actual number of official ration formulas reached well over twenty. For example, the ration for prisoners who did not meet their production targets was differentiated further for varying degrees of plan fulfillment (under 60 percent, 60–79 percent, 80–99 percent), and for categories of confinement (*razriad*).[16] The rations for sick prisoners included a pellagra ration for those without and with diarrhea (the latter representing the advanced stage of the disease), and an anti-scurvy supplement. Prisoners who met or exceeded their output norms received higher rations. The Stalinist regime also gave more food to technical specialists and to highly productive prisoners in the camps who worked in "critical and demanding jobs."[17] The strict allocation of food according to each prisoner's productive output was no simple matter. Camps drew up elaborate charts and kept detailed records on how much prisoners earned and how much they could eat.[18]

The official menu suggests abundance and variety, and Gulag officials were keen to give this impression, yet the reality was quite different. Gulag rations greatly exaggerated the amount of food actually being provided, and both memoir accounts and archival sources indicate that food shortages persisted across decades. For months at a time, prisoners lacked entire food groups. Only the bread appears to have been consistently available, yet prisoners often failed to receive the requisite amount. The Gulag food ration consisted primarily of bread and soup. The itemized list of food in a typical ration schedule was long, and included rye bread, wheat flour, grains, meat, fish, vegetable oil, pasta, sugar, tea, potatoes, vegetables, tomato puree, pepper, bay leaf, and salt. There was some variation. More productive prisoners were supposed to receive pasta and "animal fat," sick prisoners could get dried fruit, milk, and potato flour; some prisoners could purchase up to 155 grams (0.34 lb) of herring per day. However, the sheer uniformity is striking, for the list of foods was almost entirely the same across multiple rations. Moreover, most of the food items were provided in very small amounts and served in soup. Prisoners called the camp soup "balanda," and former prisoners such as Jacques Rossi described it as "very thin and watery."[19] The non-bread portion of the rations reads like a soup recipe: half an ounce of tomato puree, half a cup of flour, about an ounce of meat and pasta, about half a cup of grains, some salt, pepper, and bay leaf.[20]

Gulag prisoners largely consumed carbohydrates. Rye bread represented over half of a prisoner's food in grams, followed by "potatoes and vegetables" which consisted largely of potatoes given that vegetables were in very short supply. For prisoners who fulfilled their norms in basic industrial jobs, the two categories "rye bread" and "potatoes and vegetables" constituted 80 percent of their food in grams. Camp health officials complained about the imbalanced diet and attributed prisoners' health problems to nutritional as well as caloric deficiencies. As one official commented, "the food variety is terrible."[21] Gulag prisoners experienced various health problems because their diet lacked fat, protein, and other essential nutrients.

Bread constituted the staple food item for prisoners, yet it remained inferior. Memoirs reveal that bakery workers used a lot of water when baking, put water on the bread slicer, and served bread that was raw, heavy and wet.[22] The Gulag leadership was aware of the poor quality of prisoners' bread. Two camp investigations in 1942 revealed that prisoners' bread was not fully baked and mostly consisted of water.[23] More water made the bread heavier, and allowed camps to cheat prisoners of their full ration in grams, thereby saving money and flour. In July 1945, the Gulag chief, Nasedkin, characterized the camps' methods of baking bread as "barbaric," yet Gulag policy permitted the production of inferior bread.[24] The OGPU-NKVD-MVD issued flour in weight and determined how much bread could be baked from the flour allocated. Normally, water is added in the process of baking bread, and the weight of bread produced is about 25 percent greater than the weight of the flour used. However, Stalinist leaders insisted on stretching their ruble, and allowed a 48 percent increase in the weight of bread over the weight of flour. The Gulag permitted the production of highly diluted bread, even while warning that those guilty of reducing bread quality and maximizing the weight of bread "for purposes of greed" would be prosecuted.[25]

Although Beria convinced Stalin in 1939 to increase the Gulag food rations to their highest level, the newly increased rations were scaled back shortly after they were introduced. In September 1939, the Red Army invaded Eastern Poland as part of the nonaggression pact between Nazi Germany and the Soviet Union. The Soviet occupation of Poland resulted in waves of arrests and a new influx of prisoners. At the same time, the NKVD leadership cut rations for all categories of inmates in March 1940 and again in February 1941.[26] Prisoners now had to produce much more in order to receive the same quantity of bread.[27] NKVD leaders also insisted that all camps, construction sites, and colonies had to "take the most energetic measures to find additional local food resources," whether this involved buying or growing food locally.[28] On the eve of the Nazi invasion, both camps and prisoners were being forced to do more with less.

WARTIME RATIONS

The war strained the Gulag's meager resources, and prisoners experienced long periods without food, often due to the disruption of transportation lines. Yet Gulag policy, no less than the external shock of war, produced mass starvation. Prisoners had to work harder for less food, and they were punished more severely for failures to meet production targets.[29] Following the Nazi invasion in June 1941, the NKVD issued new food guidelines for prisoners in camps and colonies "given the need for the strictest economizing on food expenditures."[30] Although the Gulag ration contained more than bread, I focus here on fluctuations in the bread ration as the best indicator of how the Stalinist regime rewarded and punished different categories of prisoners. The official Gulag rations gave less productive prisoners, including so-called weakened inmates (*slabosil'nye*) as well as breastfeeding mothers, only 700 grams (1.5 lbs.) of rye bread. Weakened nonworking prisoners, agronomists, accountants, medical and supply personnel, and prisoners in transit camps received 600 grams (1.3 lbs.) of bread, estimated at roughly 1500 calories.[31] Only 500 grams (1.1 lbs.) went to people in service jobs around the camp, such as attendants in cultural and sanitation work (jobs typically reserved for invalids or prisoners with connections), and nonworking inmates under investigation. Nonworking invalids received a meager 450 grams (0.99 lb.), not much more than the 350 grams (0.77 lb.) given to nonworking prisoners in the penalty cell.[32] The wartime rations were streamlined as well, with three principal rations for prisoners in NKVD labor camps and colonies. Ration 1 or cauldron 1 applied to those who failed to meet their production norms, plus invalids and people in low-level service jobs around the camp. Camp rations grouped invalids together with poor workers, and fed them the same. Ration 2 or cauldron 2 applied to workers in industrial jobs who met their output target, and ration 3 represented a supplementary allotment for Stakhanovites and technical workers.[33] In 1941, a camp official reported that the difference between the food in cauldrons 1, 2, and 3 was "purely theoretical" at many camps.[34] According to memoir accounts, most workers ate from cauldron 1. Gulag survivor Antoni Ekart wrote, "The work of moving heavy tree trunks, sawing thick logs, loading railway trucks was becoming past endurance. Most of us were on the lowest scale of rations."[35]

Gulag policy focused on rewarding more productive prisoners and denying food to underperformers. Revisions to the Gulag food rations in December 1941 and April 1942 signaled that prisoners would be starved to death if they failed to meet production targets. All prisoners in NKVD USSR camps and colonies who did not fulfill their production norms, plus invalids and domestic servants, were supposed to receive only 400 grams (0.88 lb.) of bread.[36] Prisoners employed in key industrial jobs who met their norms received 700 grams (1.5 lbs.) of bread.[37] Stakhanovite prisoners, as well as engineers and technical workers, earned an additional allotment of 200 grams (0.44 lb.) of bread.[38] Even the highest food rations remained insufficient and failed to compensate for the calories burned in heavy physical labor. Thus, as Donald Filtzer demonstrated, male industrial workers in the rear, who received the highest rations among the Soviet civilian population during the war, also experienced the highest rates of mortality.[39] Soviet wartime rations, even among civilians, did not compensate for energy expended in heavy physical labor. Varlam Shalamov described how

Gulag prisoners used to say: "In camp a large ration kills, not a small one."[40] Lev Razgon described how peasants, who "made up the majority in the camp," tried to earn the highest bread ration of one and a half kilos (3.3 lbs.): "For peasants who had lived in semi-starvation for years this appeared an enormous quantity, even without any cooked food . . . In fact, it was impossible to survive if you were felling timber. Our wise old doctor, Alexander Stefanov, told me that the discrepancy between the energy expended in work and that provided by the 'big ration' was so great that the healthiest forest worker was doomed to death by starvation within several months. Quite literally he would starve to death while eating one and a half kilos of bread a day."[41]

During the war, the official ration starved prisoners no less than war-time interruptions in food deliveries. In 1942, only 400 grams of bread (0.88 lb.) were allotted to invalids and underperforming prisoners in heavy labor who fulfilled less than half of their production quota. Prisoners in the penalty cell and those in nonindustrial jobs who failed to meet half of their production quota received only 300 grams (0.66 lb.) of bread. Other prisoners did only slightly better. Inmates doing heavy physical labor earned 500 grams of bread if they met their norms by 50–70 percent; 600 grams if they met their norms by 70–90 percent; and 700 grams if they met their production targets by 90–100 percent. Only those whose output was 100–125 percent of targets could earn 800 grams in heavy labor. Prisoners who exceeded their target by 125 percent and more received 900 grams in heavy labor. For prisoners not doing heavy physical labor, as in the case of many sick and ailing prisoners, the allotment in each category was 100 grams less. In the bleak year of 1942, Gulag prisoners had to achieve 125 percent of their production norms in order to earn the same quantity of bread that they received before the war for meeting 80–100 percent of quota.[42] It is important to note, too, that while wartime bread rations for soldiers and civilians did not far exceed the highest-level Gulag rations, non-prisoners could more easily supplement their rations. Plus they were not subjected to steep and punitive ration reductions for underperformance.[43] During the war, the average prisoner received 30 percent fewer calories. Gulag authorities even prohibited packages from relatives, a lifeline for many prisoners.[44]

There were a few changes to the bread ration during the war. Soap eventually appeared as a component of the food ration, which suggests a desire by the camp leadership to reduce infections and epidemics, such as typhus.[45] Bread rations of 1000 grams and over, which were not uncommon in the 1930s, ceased to exist. In the course of the war, as the fortunes of the Red Army and conditions of Soviet civilians improved, Gulag rations nonetheless declined. By 1944, prisoners were allotted 750–800 grams (1.65–1.76 lbs.) of bread in basic heavy labor (*na osnovnykh tiazhelykh rabotakh*), only if they achieved 125–200 percent—or more—of their production quota.[46] These modest rations, reserved for prisoners who greatly over-fulfilled their work norms, went to only about a third of working prisoners.[47] Prisoners in heavy physical labor who fulfilled their production quotas at 100–125 percent earned 650 grams (1.4 lbs.); for 80–100 percent of quota they earned 550 grams (1.2 lbs.) of bread; and for 50–80 percent of quota they received 500 grams (1.1 lbs.). Inmates in heavy physical labor who could only manage to fulfill less than half of their production quota earned roughly the same as inmates in the penalty cells, just 400 grams (0.88 lb.) of bread. Prisoners who did not work in heavy physical labor, typically the sick and frail, received even less.[48] Gulag exploitation became increasingly severe in the course of the war, as prisoners were fed less for the same amount of work. In a letter to Stalin in October 1943, Beria indicated that, "prisoners' food rations declined—the main foods almost by half—as compared with the prewar period."[49]

Finally, it must be stressed that the Stalinist leadership prohibited camps from feeding prisoners over the ration levels. Inmates could not eat more than the Gulag's draconian rules allowed. Even those who had money to buy themselves extra bread could not do so if their labor productivity had not earned them the right to additional food. When bread rations were cut in February 1941, the NKVD instructions stressed that, "the sale of bread to those who do not fulfill their production norm is prohibited." The deputy NKVD chief Chernyshev told the camps that they could not give more food than the official ration dictated.[50] During the war, administrators at camps and colonies were told repeatedly that prisoners were limited to the food they earned through work. The NKVD stressed that it was "categorically forbidden" to give food beyond the stated rations or to diverge from the ration system, and foremen were to be punished for "distributing food or bread not in accordance with the output of the members of the brigade."[51] In 1942, Gulag inspectors criticized one camp for giving prisoners more food than their official ration allowed.[52] Another camp official was criticized when he touted the fact that his prisoners were getting additional food. His inmates who were contracted out to regional economic organs obtained over 3000 calories per day because they received camp food plus lunch at the enterprise. He thought that he was doing a good job, but the Gulag medical-sanitation department chief condemned him for deviating from the official ration.[53] The Gulag chief Nasedkin stated: "I categorically forbid the directors of regional camps and colonies (UITLK-OITK) to make any changes in the food rations without the approval of the GULAG NKVD USSR."[54] The Stalinist leadership was committed to the fundamental principle of the camps, which dictated that prisoners should receive food in accordance with their productive output.

POSTWAR RATIONS

By the late 1940s, the official food rations were even lower than during the war. Highly productive prisoners at top-priority camps could earn more bread, but other prisoners received much less. Moreover, the Stalinist leadership, promising far fewer provisions from central supply organs, transferred greater responsibility for feeding prisoners onto individual camps and colonies. In the late 1940s, for reasons discussed in the following chapter, the population of Gulag prisoners expanded greatly. In May 1948, the security police or MVD issued new food rations.[55] It developed the two-tiered system that began to be implemented toward the end of the war, in which prisoners were fed differently depending on their economic sector. One ration applied to prisoners who performed high-priority work in the coal, metallurgical, and energy sectors, and another applied to inmates in all other MVD camps and colonies. For the former group in priority industries, prisoners who fulfilled and over-fulfilled their quotas were allotted 900 grams (almost 2 lbs.) of bread. Those in mining could get 100 grams more, and prisoners who failed to meet their production targets received 100 grams less. Thus the gap between the bread rations of the most and least productive prisoners narrowed at the priority camps. In non-priority industries, prisoners were supposed to receive 700 grams (1.5 lbs.) of bread, and those doing heavy labor could get 100 grams more.

Thus the May 1948 bread rations involved less differentiation, and they also transferred greater responsibility for feeding prisoners from the central authorities to the individual camps and colonies. The new ration regulations stated that, "potatoes and vegetables, tomato puree, pepper, and bay leaf will be provided when resources are available."[56] The MVD apparently no longer guaranteed "potatoes and vegetables," the second-largest category of food in the prisoner's diet behind bread. Bread was to be provided to prisoners who met their norms fully, and those who exceeded their norms would receive a flat bonus. The bread ration for non-priority-sector prisoners who failed to meet their production targets was not indicated, which suggests that responsibility fell to the camps for feeding these prisoners.[57] Prohibitions on issuing food above the official rations, which were present in previous iterations, were abandoned only for high-performing prisoners. If camps and colonies wanted to "encourage prisoners to work well by feeding them above the basic and supplementary rations," they could do so. Camps could feed their top performers more, but they would assume the extra cost without help from MVD suppliers. Camps and colonies could acquire more food for these highly productive prisoners by using any unused funds from the food budget, or by hunting, fishing, farming, or selling food to prisoners in kiosks within the camp zone.[58] At the same time, central authorities continued to oppose giving more food to those who failed to meet their production quotas.

The following year, the MVD issued new food rations that widened the gap between the best and worst fed prisoners. In August 1949, the MVD issued new "differentiated rations" that explicitly transferred food from the weakest to the strongest prisoners.[59] The zero-sum nature of the Gulag's feeding system was made explicit. The MVD declared that bread rations would be cut for nonworking invalids and prisoners who failed to fulfill their production targets, in order to increase the supplementary rations for highly productive prisoners. The MVD released no additional funds for these supplementary rations. They represented not an enhancement of the food budget but an accounting manipulation, a mere transfer of food from one population of prisoners to another. Similar to the injunction the previous year, the MVD's directive allowed directors of the camps and colonies to provide more food in order "to encourage prisoners to work well."[60] The MVD only approved of giving more food as a reward to prisoners who exceeded their production quotas or as a work incentive, but not to prevent prisoners' physical decline or to strengthen weaker prisoners.[61] The decree also allowed the directors of the camps and colonies to create new supplementary rations beyond the quota established by the MVD, but only for the best workers. Again, these supplementary rations would come at the expense of other prisoners. The MVD instructed camp directors to generate these additional supplementary rations by using the food saved when a prisoner was sent to the penalty isolator. The differential between prisoners' basic food ration and the meager punishment ration could be considerable.[62] This MVD instruction created an incentive for camp officials to send some prisoners to the penalty cell. Not coincidentally, after 1949, the Gulag witnessed a dramatic increase in the number of prisoners condemned to the isolation cell.

The 1949 instructions allocated the highest rations to the party's priority industries. More bread went to prisoners at high-priority projects and economic sectors, such as designated "special" construction projects under Glavpromstoi, camps of the Volga-Don construction administration, the "special list" of camps, including Norillag and Vorkutlag, and mining and metallurgy camps. These prisoners were supposed to receive 800 grams (1.76 lbs.) of bread, and those who met or exceeded their targets were supposed to receive 900 grams of bread.[63] At the "special" construction projects under Glavpromstoi or the Volga-Don construction administration, if inmates met or exceeded their production targets they were supposed to receive 875 grams of bread. Additional food went to prisoners who exceeded their targets by 110–130 percent, 131–150 percent, and over 150 percent. The Gulag continued to push for higher and higher levels of production. Those working on the construction of the northern railway line were supposed to get 1000 grams (2.2 lbs.) of bread, the highest level of any prisoners in this 1949 iteration of the food rations.

In the late 1940s, as the number of inmates increased sharply, the Gulag leadership insisted that camps maintain strict adherence to the food rations. In 1949, the Gulag chief, Dobrynin, complained that some camps had lowered the ration for nonworking invalids, or distributed 50 grams less bread than the ration called for, or provided supplementary rations to prisoners who did not fulfill their norms, or routinely gave more food to sick prisoners or prisoners who served in positions around the camp (likely invalids).[64] In the years before Stalin died, the MVD reduced its obligation to feed prisoners and transferred more of that responsibility onto the camps. It reduced the maximum amount of bread that prisoners could receive and told the camps that if they wanted to feed prisoners more, they would have to find ways to do it themselves. This trend reached its logical conclusion in MVD Order No. 00273 of April 29, 1950 "On improving labor productivity and more rationally utilizing the labor of prisoners in MVD USSR corrective-labor camps and colonies," which called for transitioning prisoners to a work-for-pay system.[65] The order introduced a system of wages for Gulag prisoners, where prisoners could use money to purchase goods and food.

The transition from a rationing system to a wage system transferred responsibility for feeding prisoners from MVD suppliers to camps and prisoners. Camps were required to establish a network of retail outlets (stores, stalls, kiosks) where prisoners could purchase items they needed, and communal kitchens (cafeterias, buffets) where prisoners could even prepare their own food. Camps apparently transitioned slowly, and prisoners were left without much to buy with their wages.[66] In many ways, the pay-for-work system represented the MVD's answer to the problem of feeding Gulag prisoners. It had always been the prisoners' job to work in order to eat, and it had always been the camps' responsibility to locally procure additional food supplies for their prisoners. The MVD intensified both imperatives in the late 1940s and early 1950s.

FEEDING SICK AND DISABLED PRISONERS

Special food rations for ailing prisoners existed from the inception of the Stalinist labor camp system. In the early 1930s, sick prisoners could be placed on a special diet or a hospital ration, or they might receive an "anti-scurvy" ration.[67] Yet these rations were distributed according to strict quotas, and camps often had far fewer than needed. In March 1932, Gulag chief Matvei Berman refused to issue more anti-scurvy rations, and insisted that the average monthly anti-scurvy ration would remain at a mere 5 percent of the prisoner population. He told camp administrators that if they wanted more anti-scurvy rations, they would have to cut overall rations for prisoners.[68] Berman, who is often considered the least inhumane of the Gulag chiefs, nevertheless refused to allocate more resources to combat malnutrition. Like later Gulag bosses, he maintained severe limits on all rations for sick inmates. In 1945, a camp health official complained that her camp had been allocated too few supplementary rations for hospitalized prisoners: "We have such a negligible number that we don't even know how to give them out."[69]

Sick prisoners did not necessarily receive more food. In 1939, four basic rations were established for sick prisoners in NKVD camps and colonies. These included rations for hospitalized inmates, and a supplementary anti-scurvy allotment for inmates with the disease. Hospitalized prisoners were supposed to receive 700 grams (1.5 lbs.) of bread, plus a greater variety of food, including rye and wheat bread, eggs, meat, dried fruit, cottage cheese, sour cream, and milk. However, such goods were difficult to acquire for patients, as they were in short supply and desirable to potential thieves. The supplementary anti-scurvy allotment largely consisted of more potatoes and vegetables.[70] There were also rations for prisoners with pellagra and diarrhea, and for prisoners with pellagra but no diarrhea. The two groups represented the different stages of the disease, as pellagra with diarrhea signaled acute malnutrition and end of life. The ration for patients with non-diarrhea pellagra included only 400 grams (0.88 lbs.) of bread, while pellagra patients with diarrhea received only 100 grams (0.22 lbs.) of bread, the smallest official bread ration of any Gulag prisoner. Although these prisoners were supposed to be allocated more meat, the exceptionally high meat ration for pellagra patients (200 grams or 0.44 lbs.) appears unrealistic, given the chronic shortage of meat.[71] Pellagra with diarrhea represented the advanced stage of the disease, and no other carbohydrate source was included to compensate for the severe decline in the bread ration. Prisoners who suffered from pellagra with diarrhea also received half the amount of fish given to the other pellagra patients, less butter, and fewer potatoes and vegetables. The Gulag's pellagra rations appear to be signaling to camp officials that food need not be wasted on prisoners with acute starvation.

In 1941–1944, the Gulag reduced food rations for physically weakened prisoners and those in hospitals and clinics.[72] Prisoners in camp hospitals and clinics and in NKVD USSR colonies received 600 grams (1.3 lbs.) of bread. The pellagra and anti-scurvy rations were supposed to remain unchanged from their August 1939 levels, consistent with NKVD Order No. 0943, but the non-bread component of these rations eventually declined.[73] The wartime rations for sick prisoners maintained the same bread allotments but reduced other foods, such as potatoes, fish, meat, and vegetables. In 1944, the general ration for hospital patients was reduced slightly to 550 grams (1.2 lbs.), but the pellagra rations remained the same. The NKVD demanded that hospital rations be administered on the recommendation of the medical-labor commission. Doctors would not have sole authority over their distribution, and prisoners considered more valuable workers would get priority.[74] As I demonstrate in chapter 4, prisoners were only fed and treated if doctors determined that they could be restored to health and returned to work. Otherwise, inmates were effectively left to die. The Stalinist system represented an economy of shortage.[75] These shortages were not benign, certainly not in the Gulag. They involved choices about who deserved to receive goods and who did not.

The NKVD issued new food rations throughout the war, cutting many foods that were supposed to go to sick prisoners. In 1942 the NKVD warned camps not to use the anti-scurvy food allotment to supplement the food rations of prisoners who did not have scurvy.[76] Yet in 1944, the NKVD instructed directors of camps and colonies to derive their anti-scurvy ration from their general fund for food, and not to expect additional funds from the center.[77] The category "potatoes and vegetables" represented the largest component of the anti-scurvy allotment, and it declined from 400 grams in 1939, to 200 grams in 1942, to 150 grams in 1944.[78] Nonetheless, bread rations for sick prisoners during the war remained relatively consistent with 1939 levels. By 1944, the Gulag rationing system had become more differentiated, and higher rations were given to prisoners in priority economic sectors, such as Vorkutlag, Norillag, Intlag, Pechorlag, Construction Site No. 500, and the oil fields of Ukhtizhemlag.[79] Yet the bread ration for all sick prisoners, including those with nutritional disorders and tuberculosis, was not significantly higher. One camp medical official noted that the condition of camp hospital patients "doesn't change because hospital food does not produce a quick and effective recovery."[80]

In 1945, many regional camp medical-sanitation department directors met with the Gulag medical-sanitation department chief, D.M. Loidin, and discussed the difficulties associated with treating sick prisoners without adequate food rations.[81] They argued that they lacked the resources and the ability to provide rations at prescribed levels, and complained that the food distribution system unfairly advantaged camps that were more centrally located. Moreover, they protested that the Gulag did not give them the authority to feed ailing prisoners more than the official rations dictated. They pleaded for the right to determine the appropriate food for any given ailment.[82] The Stalinist leadership reprimanded camp officials for diverging from the official rations or giving prisoners more than the prescribed amount of food. They chastised one camp medical-sanitation department director for placing weakened prisoners in desk jobs consistent with the inmates' training, as a way to give them a higher ration. The medical-sanitation department director for the Krasnoiarsk regional labor camps and colonies noted that, "For the weakened contingent, food plays a key role, so we devote all of our attention to food, alongside everyday life issues. Several groups of category 3 [light labor, weakened] prisoners have asked us to put them in work consistent with their professional training and in factories where they would receive their norm plus an additional meal." Although his Gulag boss, Loidin, condemned this practice, the camp official defended the need "to compromise in order to advance the general mission." He asserted, rather courageously, that in order to improve the physical condition of weakened prisoners and prevent further "degradation" or health decline, one could not adhere to the official food rations.[83] He and other camp officials stressed the need to feed prisoners more. Although mid-level camp officials often tried to increase food to prisoners, the Gulag medical-sanitation department chief rejected any actions that would circumvent the system's rigid feeding rules.

In May 1948, the Gulag again issued new rations. Camps and colonies were now forced to shoulder part of the burden of feeding their inmate population in hospitals, clinics, and convalescent camps. The May 1948 revision of the food rations was the first to divide sick prisoners into two groups. The rations for prisoners in hospitals and clinics were divided into "general" and "for patients with tuberculosis, dystrophy, hernias (*iazvennoi bolezn'iu*), and vitamin deficiency."[84] They both received 500 grams (1.1 lbs.) of bread, slightly less than even the wartime bread ration, and varying amounts of other items, such as potatoes, vegetables, meat, cheese, and milk. Not only were bread rations cut for sick prisoners in the late 1940s, but the camps and colonies had to provide the milk and cottage cheese from their own farms. In addition, all prisoners in these recovery camps, hospitals, and clinics, and weakened prisoners who were workers but not in the care of any convalescent institutions, were supposed to get a one-time enhanced supplementary ration or UDP (*usilennyi dopolnitel'nyi paiok*). The UDPs had to be authorized by the camp or camp division's medical-sanitation department, and prisoners could not receive more than one per day. These supplementary rations were not generous, and included only 100 grams (0.22 lb.) of bread, plus some meat and fish. The bread portion was not provided centrally. Camps had to generate funds for this bread themselves.[85]

By the late 1940s, the MVD required camps and colonies to assume most of the burden for feeding their sick inmates, while continuing to highly restrict the amount of food such prisoners received. In June 1949, the MVD instructed camps and colonies that special food rations for patients in clinics could only be given to prisoners with permission of the medical-labor expert commission, and that such rations would be limited by quota. The number of sick rations issued could not exceed a mere 1.5 percent of the camp labor pool.[86] The MVD also urged camps and colonies to acquire additional food through local supply sources, from their own farms, and from gathering berries, mushrooms, and wild plants. It instructed camp officials to set up stalls where prisoners could buy food cheaply, and establish camp sections devoted to fishing. It stressed that officials should "utilize on all these jobs the weakened contingent and the defective workforce."[87] This constituted a typical NKVD-MVD refrain, yet camp efforts in this area were often thwarted by the Gulag requirement that prisoners move under armed escort. One medical-sanitation department official complained that his camp leadership made it difficult for him to employ severely weakened prisoners to fish or gather wild plants.[88] Camp authorities, applying Gulag rules, would not allow most prisoners to go outside the camp without armed escort, yet guards were in short supply.

The 1949 revision of the food rations involved greater differentiation. It divided prisoners in hospitals and clinics into two groups: prisoners in the priority sectors, which consisted of the camps on the "special list," the construction sites of Glavpromstroi (the main administration of camps for industrial construction), and Volgodonstroi (the camps of the Volga-Don construction administration); and prisoners at all other MVD camps and colonies.[89] As in the 1948 version, prisoners in hospitals and clinics were fed according to two different rations, one for all sick prisoners, and one specifically for "patients with tuberculosis, dystrophy, hernias, and vitamin deficiency." Rations were set at only 500 grams of bread for sick prisoners at non-priority camps, and 550 grams (1.2 lbs.) for those at priority camps. As in the May 1948 rations, all patients in hospitals, clinics, and convalescent camps were supposed to get a one-time enhanced supplementary ration of 100 grams (0.22 lb.) of bread, but camps were largely required to fund these UDP rations.[90] The center would provide only a small fraction of the meat ration for sick prisoners.

In the late Stalin years, as this book demonstrates, Gulag brutality intensified. The MVD focused attention and resources on economic priority sectors, and transferred the burden of supporting the sickest prisoners onto individual camps. It increasingly abandoned its responsibility for sick prisoners, just as it had for working prisoners. This responsibility often proved impossible for individual camps. In 1952, MVD USSR agricultural camps, where the system's weakest and ailing prisoners were concentrated, produced enough potatoes and vegetables to meet only 60 percent of their needs.[91] MVD policy only worsened the problem of starvation in the Gulag.

BARELY FEEDING THE PUNISHED

The Stalinist leadership deliberately starved those who violated camp rules, refused to work, harmed themselves, or were believed to have induced or faked illness. In fact, the Gulag criminalized low labor productivity. Many were punished with a starvation ration simply because they proved too weak or disabled to fulfill their production targets. The mother-in-law of former NKVD chief Yagoda was detained in a women's camp in Tomsk where prisoners sewed uniforms for the Red Army. Yagoda and his entire family had been arrested in the Great Terror. A woman with poor eyesight, she could barely meet half of the required production target at her textile factory. As a result, she received the penalty ration of just 300 grams (0.66 lbs.) of bread.[92]

Camp authorities were inclined to perceive ailing prisoners as willful shirkers and fakers of illness or injury. At the camp of the White Sea Canal in the early 1930s, the penalty ration often went to weakened prisoners who were too sick to work.[93] One camp official noted that prisoners who did not entirely fulfill their daily work norms received only 300 grams (0.66 lb.) of bread.[94] A former prisoner described how, "Only those who completed the whole norm received the full bread ration of 700 grams. Those who could not, or who were unable to work at all, got 300."[95]

The MVD consistently assigned the lowest official food ration to prisoners who served time in the punishment blocks, the sturdy and damp cells that prisoners often described as torture chambers.[96] In 1939, inmates in these camp prisons were allocated only 400 grams of bread, and this paltry amount was cut further to 350 grams in 1941 and 300 grams in 1942.[97] In the postwar years, prisoners in the penalty isolator were supposed to receive 350 grams of bread.[98] In 1949, bread rations for prisoners in the penalty cells increased slightly to 450 grams at priority camps and 400 grams at all other camps and colonies.[99] Gulag survivors have even reported smaller rations—200 or 250 grams of bread—for prisoners in the penalty cells.[100] According to Gulag instructions, penalty rations applied not only to work refusers and malingerers (*simulianty*), but to prisoners who fulfilled less than 50 percent of their production targets.[101] Thus the smallest bread rations in the Gulag went to punished prisoners in the camp cell block, and to those with acute starvation disease or pellagra. Considered a financial burden on the camp, such prisoners were often left to die.

LOSSES: THEFT, SPOILAGE, AND SHORTAGES

Many factors contributed to the systematic malnourishment of Gulag prisoners, including the fact that inmates often did not receive even the mandated amount of food. Food shipments often failed to reach prisoners. In April 1942, the NKVD chief, Beria, together with the USSR Procurator and Justice Commissar, addressed a long letter to Stalin and Molotov, in which they wrote: "There are issues in the supply of camps located mainly in distant areas of the USSR. Particular difficulties are encountered in transporting significant quantities of food cargos there."[102] Such difficulties were not limited to wartime. In 1947–1948, the camps and colonies received only about 70 percent of their planned allocation of potatoes and vegetables.[103] Central authorities promised food that was never delivered.

The Stalinist leadership blamed camp administrators for not providing requisite food rations to prisoners. In 1933, the Gulag deputy chief criticized some camps for failing to give prisoners their entire allocated ration, and for not replacing absent foods with other foods on hand.[104] Camp health officials, in turn, complained that central Gulag authorities failed to deliver the promised quantities of food. Interruptions in food supply and food shortages were endemic. The medical-sanitation department chief for the Turkmen SSR camps and colonies described his system's food situation as "extremely unsatisfactory," due in part to the fact that his camps and colonies failed to receive tons of meat, fish, fats, sugar, and vegetables the previous year. He insisted that under such conditions, "we medical workers alone cannot eliminate vitamin deficiency. I disbursed about eight kilograms of vitamin supplements without thinking about the cost, yet these can hardly be helpful without a corresponding assortment of food."[105] Another camp medical-sanitation department director told her Gulag boss: "You can increase rations all you want, but if everything isn't always regularly available, of course, food will remain unsatisfactory. Even if the doctors are geniuses, it makes no difference. It is surely impossible to improve prisoners' [physical] condition under such circumstances."[106]

Theft of food constituted another major problem. As James Heinzen explains, both Gulag officials and civilian workers in the camps engaged in various forms of corruption, such as theft, embezzlement, and bribery. Tens of millions of rubles allocated to the system were siphoned away, depriving prisoners of resources.[107] Camp supply officials and prisoners who worked in the storerooms brazenly stole food, often in enormous quantities, which they consumed or resold. Some camp officials stole cash from the accounts intended for prisoners' food, others raided the food budget to pay for goods in short supply, such as clothing and shoes. Fellow inmates also stole prisoners' food rations. Gulag authorities investigated food problems, and sometimes punished camp officials. The MVD adopted the Stalinist approach of framing all problems as willful deviations, but the camps existed within the Soviet economy of shortage. As two Gulag investigators put it, "Acutely scarce and rationed food items and goods are the ones that are mainly subject to theft, embezzlement."[108] Goods were stolen because they were in such short supply.

There were many other reasons why prisoners did not receive their full ration. Camps failed to maintain food inventories, making it difficult to determine how much food was supposed to be on hand and how much had been siphoned away. Bakeries kept no inventory of flour, and there was no consistent accounting concerning the processing of flour and baking of bread. Enormous food losses occurred due to poor storage, as tons of food rotted in damp warehouses. Warehouses were poorly constructed and overrun with mold, insects, and rodents. Storerooms had leaky roofs so food spoiled, and flour spoiled when it was not shipped in sacks (due to a shortage of sacks). In 1933, the OGPU described how prisoners were contracting bacterial infections and other illnesses due to the lack of proper food sanitation. Prisoners were getting sick from drinking unclean water and from water that was not boiled before being added to the cauldron.[109] Lack of proper hygiene plagued the food system. Medical workers were not supervising sanitary conditions in the kitchens. Kitchens, bakeries, and pantries were dirty and unsanitary. Prisoners lacked bowls and utensils. Weights at some camps were off by as much as 250 grams, and camps lacking scales measured rations "by sight." Administrators often economized on food, diverted funds from the prisoners' food budget to other purposes, replaced one food item with a cheaper one, or gave prisoners in the penalty isolator even less than mandated. In the prisoners' dense and soggy bread, one would often find shells from oats and barley grains; sand got mixed into the bread, as well as nails, twigs, soap, and wood chips.[110] In Siblag the state confiscated a significant portion of the camp's agricultural output during the war, leaving less food for prisoners.[111] By the early 1950s, the Gulag's general budgetary problems contributed to the underfunding of agriculture, which made food shortages even more acute.[112]

FIND YOUR OWN, GROW YOUR OWN

The OGPU-NKVD-MVD leadership repeatedly demanded that camps and colonies do more to feed their own prisoners, and the mandate only intensified from the 1930s to the 1950s. The Stalinist forced labor camp system was supposed to be self-supporting. Camp officials had to acquire food locally at markets, grow their own vegetables, gather wild plants and greens, go fishing, and try to get more food into the camps through packages sent to prisoners from relatives.[113] Local efforts often fell short of expectations. In 1934, Yagoda asked for thousands of tons of flour to compensate for shortages in the grain harvest in the Far East.[114] Camps also had to find local sources of meat, which was no easy task. Solzhenitsyn indicated that camps "used to give [the prisoners] horse meat from exhausted horses driven to death at work, and, even though it was quite impossible to chew it, it was a feast."[115] A 1939 Gulag memo to camp directors offered instructions on how to properly use "meat from horses who are sick with chronically infectious anemia" in food served to people.[116]

Once the war began, the imperative to be self-sufficient intensified as regional camps became entirely cut off from central food supplies. In August 1941, the Gulag leadership told the regional labor colonies (OITK UNKVD) that they had to be self-sufficient with respect to food, for Stalin was directing all resources to the front. The colonies had to "maximize the mobilization of internal resources," in order "to preserve state funds for especially important needs of the government." The Gulag leadership demanded that agricultural products be strictly accounted for and distributed only within the Gulag system and according to established food rations.[117] In 1943, Nasedkin informed his subordinates that they could no longer utilize camp funds to feed their dogs, but instead had "to utilize local resources to the maximum," or provide the dogs food acquired through hunting, fishing, and local agriculture.[118] Camp officials often relied on food packages sent by prisoners' relatives. In 1945, the medical-sanitation department chief of the Sverdlovsk regional labor camps and colonies described how food allocations from the Gulag supply department arrived late when ordered from distant regions (meat from Arkhangelsk and Georgia, sugar from Odessa), so they had to compensate. He explained: "The situation was very difficult. We did a lot of work to find food locally . . . using the prisoners' own money [to buy food] from vendors, and by economizing on food. We did a lot of work with care packages sent to prisoners."[119]

To feed their prisoners, camp officials had to be creative and resourceful. In 1942, one camp reported collecting over 17,000 kilograms of sorrel and over 11,000 kilograms of mushrooms.[120] In 1945, the medical-sanitation department director for the Molotov regional labor camps and colonies described the practice of sprouting whole grain wheat, rye, oat, and even sprouting peas, which, she said, "rescued us to a large degree, at the end of 1942 and in 1943, as a substitute for the absence of vegetables."[121] Camps also reported feeding prisoners scraps from the slaughterhouse. The medical-sanitation department director of the Novosibirsk regional labor camps and colonies explained: "We now administer blood sausage (krovianaia kolbasa). True, it's hard to make. A good deal of control is required because the sanitation inspectors don't allow its use. But we have established strict controls for administering this sausage. It's only used fresh, immediately after it arrives from the meat factory. Whatever remains the next day is destroyed. Thus we have fed prisoners without any infections."[122]

HOW MANY CALORIES?

In his Kolyma Tales, Shalamov told the story of a prisoner who before his arrest had worked as a stable hand, where physically larger horses were given more oats than the smaller horses because their bodies required more. "This was the practice everywhere," recalled the prisoner, and it struck him "as being only fair. What he could not understand was the camp's rationing system for people . . . If human beings were to be equated with livestock, then one ought to be more consistent and not hold to some arithmetical average invented by the office."[123] In Stalin's Gulag, human beings were indeed equated with livestock, but the camp food ration, as Shalamov noted, "had no relation to the weight of the human body."[124] The Gulag allocated rations without regard for individual dietary requirements. Although prisoners engaged in heavy physical labor were supposed to receive slightly more bread, the ration amount was established with little account for the physiological needs of individual prisoners. Gulag survivors describe how a prisoner's physical size often determined his chances of survival. Yehoshua Gilboa wrote, "The husky, muscular, and corpulent men were struck down by diseases, infirmity, and death more often than the naturally weak and thin ones," because the bodies of "the rugged types . . . demanded more and collapsed more quickly in times of want."[125] Similarly, Shalamov noted, "the lightweight convicts" actually "survived longer than the others."[126] The writer explained, "the larger men die first—whether or not they were accustomed to heavy labor. A scrawny intellectual lasted longer than some country giant, even when the latter had formerly been a manual laborer, if the two were fed on an equal basis in accordance with the camp ration."[127] Some former inmates remarked that women were less susceptible to vitamin deficiency diseases like pellagra because they were physically smaller and could survive longer on fewer calories.[128]

The Gulag leadership was not primarily interested in prisoners' caloric needs. An average-sized male prisoner engaged in vigorous physical activity would require over 3,000 calories daily, far above the maximum Gulag ration.[129] In 1939, Beria indicated that prisoners received a 2000-calorie ration, and during the war, they earned even less. At Ukhtizhemlag, prisoners recalled how even the larger food rations for the shock workers were not enough, and few could hope to exceed the exceptionally high production targets.[130] Camps reported well under 1500 calories for the basic Gulag ration or cauldron 1, and under 2300 calories for cauldron 2, which, as one official noted, "does not cover energy expended, not even [at a person's] basic metabolic rate."[131] In a 1941 letter to Beria, an official from the Arkhangelsk region argued that the camp soup might be adequate "if one sat in a room, but not if he moved meters of timber, tons of coal, and other products."[132]

The Gulag leadership and camp officials well understood this, too. The fact that prisoners received food that did not replenish nutrients lost in heavy physical labor constituted, according to Gulag survivor Antoni Ekart, a "deliberate NKVD policy of undernourishment."[133] At the same time, Stalinist officials obscured this fact. They did not use the Russian words for hunger and starvation (*golod, golodanie*), but instead employed Gulag-speak when addressing such issues. One camp official noted that prisoners "on the second and especially on the first cauldron survive, to a significant degree, by depleting their body's reserves."[134] Another told the Gulag health chief that food rations in 1943–1944 provided 1900–2000 calories, and added: "Of course, this is the reason why prisoners began to drop out of the system."[135] Officials spoke euphemistically, yet they described a process in which prisoners were being starved to death. In a wartime report to Beria, the NKVD and Gulag chiefs stated: "The food allotted to the Gulag NKVD and food rations established for prisoners do not completely restore the energy that is expended by inmates doing heavy labor in the NKVD camps . . .

Even for prisoners doing basic work, the established food ration, set at 2500 calories, compensates for no more than fifty percent of expended energy, especially when one considers that [absent] fatty and protein-rich foods must be replaced systematically with carbohydrates."[136]

CONCLUSION

Gulag food rations were designed not to sustain life, but to coerce labor. The central government set rations that were below subsistence levels, and failed to provide even the prescribed level of support. To be sure, Gulag ration policy often diverged from its local implementation, sometimes to the benefit of prisoners. Some inmates survived on care packages from relatives or by bribing camp officials for extra food. Nonetheless, the regime's intentions are revealed in the policy, which involved the deliberate starvation of perceived underperforming and deviant prisoners. From the 1930s to the 1950s, the Gulag regime became increasingly brutal, as prisoners were forced to produce more for the same quantity of food or less. Weakened prisoners, unable to meet elevated production targets, received increasingly less food. Stalin's OGPU-NKVD-MVD leaders from Yagoda to Beria complained that they could not fulfill their daunting economic tasks with an emaciated inmate population. Yet resources did not improve. Instead, the Stalinist leadership produced a more differentiated system whereby some prisoners ate at the expense of others. The Gulag increasingly withdrew responsibility for feeding prisoners, forcing camps to secure more food from local sources. The Stalinist leadership chose to starve millions of prisoners and replace them with new arrestees rather than allocate the resources required to keep prisoners alive.

2 Prisoners
"The Contingent"

THE GULAG'S ESSENTIAL nature as a system of exploitation is illustrated, in part, by the kinds of people who were hauled into the camps. As Nicolas Werth noted shortly after the declassification of Gulag records, most Gulag prisoners "were simply ordinary citizens who were victims of particularly harsh laws in the workplace and a growing number of regulations regarding social behavior."[1] Contrary to popular belief, the majority of prisoners in Stalin's labor camps and colonies were not intellectuals, former communists, perceived spies and saboteurs, or other "counterrevolutionaries." Most were ordinary workers and peasants, largely ethnic Russian and less educated, who had been arrested for routine Soviet crimes, such as workplace infractions, speculation, theft, or internal passport violations.[2] Moreover, from the 1930s to the 1950s, Stalin's prison labor force consisted mainly of people who had been condemned to Gulag detention by Soviet courts rather than the security police. For example, in 1936–1937, at the height of Stalin's Great Terror, as many as two-thirds of camp prisoners were sentenced by civilian courts and one-third by the security police.[3] Stalinist terror extended well beyond the acts of the OGPU-NKVD-MVD and its arrests of perceived state enemies. It involved regular civilian courts, routine criminal offenses, and ordinary workers and peasants. Camp prisoners came from various ethnic and social groups, Soviet republics, and foreign countries, but throughout the Stalin years, the principal Gulag labor force consisted of ethnic Russian men under 40. The Stalinist leadership wanted Gulag prisoners with a capacity for heavy physical labor. Thus the Gulag's undesirable population consisted of women, children, the sick and disabled, and the elderly. Stalin's Gulag drew in "human raw material" with sufficient "physical labor capability" to be profitably "utilized" in strenuous manual labor.

THE GULAG LITERATURE: POLITICAL PRISONERS AND CRIMINAL RECIDIVISTS

The current scholarly and memoir literature on the camps devotes most attention to political prisoners. There is good reason for this. Lenin established the country's first concentration camps to isolate and punish "class enemies" and other opponents of the fledgling Bolshevik regime. Stalin's first mass arrest involved the so-called kulaks, who were attacked as the rural bourgeoisie and anti-Soviet elements. These peasants became the initial labor force of the Stalinist Gulag, but they were joined by many other "counterrevolutionaries," who were sent to the camps as saboteurs, wreckers, and spies. During the 1936–1938 Great Terror, the Stalinist regime executed over three-quarters of a million people and many more were sent to camps, colonies, and settlements as "enemies of the people" and "family members of enemies of the people." Mass arrests continued during the war, as Soviet civilians were charged with defeatism, collaboration, and anti-Soviet agitation. Political repression that in the 1930s focused on "class enemies," by the 1940s targeted "enemy nations," although arrests of perceived "bourgeois elements" persisted, especially in the conquered territories of the Baltic states. In the postwar years, Ukrainian nationalist guerrillas and others were sent to the camps on anti-Soviet charges. During Stalin's anti-Semitic campaigns of the late 1940s and early 1950s, many Jewish citizens were arrested under political statutes, on the suspicion of being anti-Soviet, foreign spies, and agents of the Americans.[4] Political repression under Stalin was relentless, and mass arrests of various "counterrevolutionaries" sent millions to the Gulag.

Much has been written about political prisoners in the Soviet Union. Western attention has tended to focus on prisoners of conscience and the ways in which the regime attacked its citizens as "anti-Soviet."

Moreover, Gulag survivors who wrote memoirs about their camp experience were largely intellectuals drawn into the camps during one of Stalin's campaigns against "counterrevolutionaries." Workers and peasants were also condemned under political statutes, rounded up for "anti-Soviet" actions such as telling a joke or deserting their army unit. In the war and postwar years, many political offenders were not intellectuals. In October 1942, politicals constituted only one-third of the inmate population, and the vast majority of these were not sentenced as traitors, spies, saboteurs, or terrorists. Rather, they fell under the softer headings of "various anti-Soviet statements," and "miscellaneous counterrevolutionary crimes."[5] After the war, the Gulag population grew immensely, reaching its peak in the early 1950s, just prior to Stalin's death. New kinds of prisoners entered the camps in these years: foreign nationals, Ukrainian and Baltic partisans, Japanese and German POWs, former Red Army soldiers, and persons sentenced for treason and desertion. Again, many of these individuals came from the working classes. In 1946–1947, "counterrevolutionary" offenders continued to represent about a third of Gulag prisoners, even as the inmate population rose steadily, but "traitors to the motherland" (*izmena rodine*) represented the largest single group of politicals.[6] These included POWs, and individuals who had lived on Nazi-occupied territory and were suspected of collaboration. Many were also arrested as nationalist "bandits" and resistance fighters.[7] These mass arrests of ordinary civilians brought millions into the camps who were not necessarily intellectuals or prisoners of conscience.

Memoirists often spoke of political prisoners in the camps, and the Stalinist regime did, too. Gulag instructions and memoranda focused especially on those prisoners considered to be the most threatening or dangerous. The first regulations on the corrective labor camps from April 1930 specified that prisoners would be classified according to their "social origin," the nature of their offense, and the length of their sentence.[8] The regulations suggest that working-class criminal offenders had an easier time in the camps than former-bourgeois political offenders. Coveted administrative jobs could not be performed by "nonlaboring elements and persons sentenced for counterrevolutionary offenses," at least in the early years of Stalin's Gulag.[9] Moreover, political offenders were often detained separately, in special barracks and later in "special camps" where the labor regime was especially severe. Prisoners sentenced for counterrevolutionary offenses and "especially dangerous crimes" had to be housed separately from prisoners sentenced "for white-collar, workplace, and other so-called everyday crimes" (*bytovye prestupleniia*)." Gulag instructions focused especially on distinctions of age, gender, and sentence, and drew attention to the need to secure the most dangerous prisoners, namely, "bandit elements and recidivists,"[10] and counterrevolutionary offenders, who had to occupy a separate zone.[11] Varlam Shalamov wrote, "first name, surname, crime, sentence. These were the four questions that a prisoner had to answer thirty times a day."[12]

Despite Stalin's unrelenting arrests of various "counterrevolutionaries," political offenders represented a distinct minority in the Gulag. In Stalin's labor camps, persons sentenced for political charges typically constituted anywhere from one-quarter to one-third of the Gulag population. In 1935, just 13 percent of prisoners were identified as counterrevolutionary offenders, and the Great Terror caused their numbers to jump to 34 percent by 1939.[13] During the war, politicals accounted for 30–40 percent of Gulag prisoners.[14] Many political prisoners were sentenced under Article 58–10 on counterrevolutionary agitation or anti-Soviet agitation. In 1936, over 80 percent of all counterrevolutionary cases in the Russian republic or RSFSR were for agitation. The vast majority of those sentenced were members of the working class, and many had been accused due to "mundane chatter, grumbling . . . and the singing of anti-Soviet ditties or songs."[15] According to Solzhenitsyn: "The wave [of repression] of Section 10 was perhaps the most constant of all" and "was universally accessible," in that it applied to "aged old women and twelve-year-old schoolboys."[16] In 1946–1947, only "traitors to the motherland" surpassed political prisoners sentenced under Article 58 Section 10, apparently the older category of "various anti-Soviet statements" with a new name: "anti-Soviet agitation."[17] Of all the political offenders in the camps, these Article 58 prisoners apparently received the greatest leniency and were not sent to the special camps.[18] In the last years of Stalin's Gulag, 1948–1953, the percentage of counterrevolutionary offenders dropped sharply to under one-quarter of all prisoners in labor camps and colonies, and most were sentenced for treason and for anti-Soviet agitation.[19] Many who had been arrested as "enemies of the people" in the late 1930s were rearrested in 1948–1949.[20] The expansion of the camps in the late 1940s, however, was not largely due to this renewed political repression, but rather was the result of Stalin's draconian criminal legislation.

In addition to political offenders, the Gulag literature devotes a good deal of attention to the habitual criminals or *ugolovniki*—the "thieves in law" or criminal bandits. In *Kolyma Tales,* Shalamov wrote extensively about the professional criminals and their "criminal world," men who were railroad thieves, rapists, and murderers, and who had their own unique customs, foul language, tattoos, and long fingernails. They hardly worked at all, received better food and other goods, and served as petty guards who beat and tormented the political prisoners.[21] Gulag officials established a social hierarchy in the camps, and assigned the hardened criminals to manage the other inmates. Memoirists, largely political prisoners from the intelligentsia, intensely loathed the criminals and, as Adi Kuntsman shows, viewed their sexual practices as disgusting and discounted their humanity.[22] According to Shalamov, "The criminals are not human," and Solzhenitsyn similarly asserted, "They are not people."[23] Although the hardened criminal recidivists appear prominently in the memoir literature, they constituted a minority of criminal offenders in the camps. Gulag historian Galina Ivanova estimates that, "the number of criminal recidivists was no greater than 10 to 15 percent on average."[24] Camp inmates who had been sentenced for banditism or as socially dangerous and socially harmful elements reached 17.6 percent in 1935, and peaked at 23 percent in 1939.[25] Thereafter, their numbers would drop markedly as a percentage of total inmates. In 1942, only about 8 percent of prisoners were doing time for armed robbery, murder, banditism, or as "thieves, recidivists" (*vory retsidivisty*). In the postwar years, their numbers climbed to 12 percent in 1947 but then steadily declined to about 5 percent in 1952.[26] These hardened criminals have received much attention in the memoir literature because they wreaked havoc in the camps, yet their numbers were relatively small.

THE GULAG MAJORITY: STALIN'S EVERYDAY CRIMINAL

In his *Gulag Archipelago,* Solzhenitsyn confessed that he did "not attempt by any means to list *all* the waves which fertilized Gulag—but only those which had a political coloration."[27] Thus Solzhenitsyn's magisterial work left the impression that the Gulag represented political camps primarily, and this view was reinforced by the fact that the book was published in the West in the 1970s, a time when the Soviet regime was sending many prisoners of conscience to labor camps. Recently declassified Gulag documents reveal that this popular conception is incorrect, especially for the late Stalin years, when the Soviet forced labor camp system reached its zenith in terms of size and brutality. Petty criminal offenders represented the majority of prisoners in Stalin's Gulag.

To be sure, Stalin's many criminal arrests were distinctly political in nature, reflecting the party's ideological conceptions of labor and property. Soviet decrees against shirking, violating passport laws, speculation, and "theft of socialist property" cannot be viewed as strictly criminal laws.[28] During the campaign against the kulaks, the Soviet courts were involved in the party's class war, sentencing many so-called rich peasants or kulaks as traders, exploiters, and speculators. As Oleg Khlevniuk has argued, "It is difficult to consider criminal all those millions convicted under the prewar decrees for being late to work or absent from work without leave. The same can be said for the victims of the economic campaigns who were sentenced for a failure to fulfill the plan."[29] Moreover, various waves of political repression punished people for such "anti-Soviet behavior" as speculation, the use of hired labor, trading, and other "non-laboring activity."[30] During the height of the Great Terror, Stalin focused much of his attack against a rural population of "former kulaks, criminals, and other anti-Soviet elements."[31] There was no clear line separating the political and the criminal in the Stalin years. Nonetheless, within the Stalinist system of justice it remained significant whether one were classified as a political or criminal offender. The courts largely sentenced criminal offenders, while the OGPU-NKVD-MVD sentenced people on political or counterrevolutionary charges. The two categories of offenders were treated differently in the camps as well.

The majority of Gulag prisoners were neither professional thieves nor intellectuals, but poorly educated workers and peasants, who were condemned to Gulag detention by the courts, and not the OGPU-NKVD-MVD special tribunals.[32] They included people who stole grain, potatoes, boots, or bread and, unlike the intellectuals who were sentenced under political statutes, they did not leave memoirs of their camp experience. The petty criminals and short-term offenders constituted the backbone of the Gulag's labor force and, as such, they appear to have been the most likely to die. As one camp official explained: "[M]ost of those who die on us are short-term offenders and petty thieves (*ukaza-niki i melkie vorishki*) with sentences of under a year."[33] Gulag survivor Lev Razgon wrote: "Timber-felling work as it was then, was simply murderous: there were no chain-saws, no timber-haulage tractors and no mechanical loaders. With good reason people in the camps referred to such work as 'slow' or 'green execution.' It was not the consumptive intellectuals who died fastest in the camps, because they had certain skills and knowledge to offer. No, it was the sturdy peasants who were accustomed to hard physical labor."[34] Ordinary workers and peasants labored the hardest in the camps. Shalamov told the story of a work-gang leader who "never thought of anything other than his men's capacity to work," so "he selected a work gang exclusively of peasants" because "he knew that peasants worked hard in the camps." The writer claimed that the Soviet leadership reasoned similarly, and made sure that peasants were among the camp prisoners: "Yezhov and Beria . . . understood that the intelligentsia's value in terms of physical labor was not very high."[35] Not only were petty criminal offenders placed in the most strenuous jobs, but they often lacked the kind of support system that aided the survival of other groups. According to Anne Applebaum, "the criminal gangs, the more militant national groups, the true communists, and the religious sects provided instant communities, networks of support, and companionship" in the camps, and "most 'ordinary' criminals—the vast majority of the Gulag's inhabitants—did not fit so easily with one or another of these groups."[36]

The population of petty criminal offenders grew steadily in the Stalin years. In the early 1930s, at the vast gold mining camps of Dalstroi, the overwhelming majority of inmates were common criminals and peasants swept up in the campaign against kulaks.[37] In the mid-1930s, more than half of Gulag prisoners had been sentenced for white-collar crimes, theft of socialist property, passport violations, and other everyday offenses (*bytovye prestupleniia*).[38] As David Shearer explains, "the scale of civil and political police operations against social marginals in the mid-1930s was significant," and involved mass police sweeps of perceived "undesirables," "parasitic and itinerant elements" and "socially dangerous elements."[39] By 1939–1943, inmates sentenced "for white-collar and other everyday offenses" constituted roughly two-thirds to three-quarters of all Gulag prisoners.[40] In the 1940s and 1950s, the largest population of prisoners was classified under the following ten offenses: stealing livestock, property crimes, hooliganism, passport violations, white-collar crimes, theft of socialist property (law of August 7, 1932), speculation, violations of labor discipline (decrees of December 26, 1941 and August 10, 1940), and "miscellaneous criminal offenses." In the postwar Stalin years, this inmate population grew from a plurality into a substantial majority. In October 1942, they constituted over 40 percent of all Gulag prisoners, compared to roughly one-third of inmates who were sentenced under counterrevolutionary statutes.[41] In 1946–1947, their numbers grew from 40 percent to over half of all prisoners in labor camps and colonies, and over two-thirds in the colonies alone.[42] These prisoners were considered especially strong and fit for heavy physical labor. Gulag health workers, whose job was to keep prisoners working in the most strenuous labor possible, often focused on improving the health of the petty criminal offenders. One Gulag medical-sanitation department official described how his employees conducted "an experiment" to improve the physical profile of prisoners. They decided to select the hardy Ukrainian peasants who were short-term offenders, and to place them in a convalescent camp or OP (*ozdorovitel'nyi punkt*): "We took the Ukrainians from the hospital [and placed them in the OP]. Most of them reached category 2 [medium physical labor] . . . 92.8 percent of those from category 3 [light labor] reached categories 1 [heavy physical labor] and 2 [medium physical labor] . . . We mostly selected short-term offenders (*ukazniki*)."[43]

In the late 1940s, the Gulag's population of petty criminal offenders increased sharply. In just two years, 1939–1941, the population in labor camps and colonies rose markedly as a result of the June 26, 1940 decree on labor discipline and the August 10, 1940 decree against petty theft and hooliganism.[44] Many were short-term offenders. In the 1930s, persons with sentences of under three years were supposed to be directed to special agricultural camps and industrial colonies, yet by 1941, the camps were getting many prisoners sentenced to as little as ten months under the June 26 and August 10 decrees. According to Oleg Khlevniuk, "The short-term prisoners thus became an important source of forced labor."[45] Later in the decade, Stalin's harsh laws of June 4, 1947 concerning the theft of state and personal property condemned peasants and workers to camp sentences from five to as high as twenty-five years.[46] "As a result of this decree [on the theft of state property]," wrote Ivanova, "a typical—if not the typical—inhabitant of the Gulag became 'the collective farmer who stole a sack of potatoes.'" Ivanova also stressed that Stalin's MVD "chose to begin its active struggle against theft during the famine of 1946–1947 . . . Of the number of people arrested for theft, over half (52.5 percent) were peasants, that is, direct producers of grain, whom the severe government policies left essentially without the means for subsistence."[47] By 1951, nearly twice as many people were in the Gulag for violating the June 4, 1947 laws on the theft of state and personal property as were incarcerated for all counterrevolutionary offenses.[48] Solzhenitsyn described the edict of June 4, 1947 as "one of the most grandiose of Stalin's decrees . . . In the years immediately following this decree, whole 'divisions' from the countryside and the cities were sent off to cultivate the islands of Gulag in place of the natives who had died there."[49]

It is important to consider the context for this large shift in the proportion of criminal inmates in the Gulag. In the late 1940s, Stalinist political repression intensified not only at home but in the Soviet bloc as well. According to Mark Kramer, Stalin sought to solidify his political control at home, shield Soviet society from "hostile Western contamination," and crush underground nationalist movements in the borderlands. He also feared a war with Yugoslavia and began political repression against potential "fifth columnists."[50] Thus it is striking that even in the context of renewed political purges against "hostile elements," ordinary criminal offenders continued to vastly outnumber so-called counterrevolutionary offenders in the camps. In 1948–1949, over two-thirds of all Gulag prisoners, and over three-quarters in the colonies alone, had been convicted of ordinary criminal offenses such as theft, hooliganism, speculation, and violations of labor discipline and internal passport laws.[51] In 1950–1953, such offenders comprised roughly 70 percent of all prisoners in camps and colonies, and over 80 percent in the colonies alone.[52] These *bytoviki* and *ukazniki* were often women and juveniles. The experience of this cruel environment in their formative years drew many young people into a life of crime.

Throughout the existence of Stalin's labor camp system, the vast majority of prisoners in the Gulag were male, ethnic Russian, and relatively young and uneducated. In the 1930s, over 90 percent were men, over 60 percent ethnic Russian (followed by Ukrainians at 14 percent); over 85 percent between the ages of 18 and 40 (over half were 18–30 years old); and over 90 percent were either illiterate, semiliterate, or had only some elementary school education.[53] During the war, these proportions remained relatively constant, except that the proportion of women increased, as did the percentages of older prisoners.[54] In the immediate postwar period, ethnic Russians as a percentage of total prisoners dropped briefly to under half, but then increased again. Even in the postwar era, with the influx of ethnic minorities from the Western borderlands, Russians remained a majority. In 1946–1949, as the Gulag population nearly doubled, most continued to be ethnic Russian men, ages 18–40. Ukrainians constituted the next largest ethnic group at 15–20 percent.[55] With the exception of Russians and Ukrainians, no other ethnic minority made up more than 4 percent of the camp population. Similarly, in 1950–1952, most of the roughly 2.5 million prisoners in MVD labor camps and colonies were ethnic Russians, one fifth were ethnic Ukrainians, and men under forty constituted, as usual, the overwhelming majority.[56] With the introduction of the draconian 1947 theft decrees, the proportion of younger prisoners increased. In the late 1940s, the overwhelming number of young people in MVD children's labor colonies had been arrested and sentenced for theft; once they reached 17 years of age, they were moved into regular labor camps and colonies.[57] Despite the vast diversity of Gulag prisoners, Stalin's core prison labor force appears to have been relatively homogenous over the course of over two decades.

THE LESS PROFITABLE: WOMEN, CHILDREN, AND THE ELDERLY

Given the Gulag's priority on heavy physical labor, certain prisoners—women, invalids, the elderly, and children—were considered unproductive and a costly burden. As Nicolas Werth notes, the security police did not want many women, children, or elderly prisoners, as they were believed to have "no value in terms of economic development."[58] Nonetheless, the Gulag detained many of these less productive prisoners, and often grouped them together.[59] There were women's camps and camps that held women with children, as well as children's homes or nurseries. Children, in particular, represented a net loss to the camps because they demanded resources without generating income. Camp officials did not want children born in the camps, and tried to keep women separated from the men to avoid pregnancies.[60] Children in the camps were especially vulnerable to illness and disease, neglect, hunger, and abuse.[61] In 1948, roughly a third of all children in the children's homes (*doma mladentsa*) of the Gulag died, mostly of pneumonia, dysentery, and tuberculosis.[62] At times, food supplies for children were simply cut and children were left to starve.[63] For the camps and colonies, children cost money, so officials preferred to move them out.[64]

In addition to children, camp authorities sought to release women, invalids, and the elderly. They were of limited use to camp officials who needed to meet production targets. Party leaders treated this disparate group of prisoners as a single population of unproductive and less valuable inmates, and in the 1940s, they regularly benefited from early release.[65] A number of amnesties in 1945–1947 released women convicted of everyday crimes, women who were pregnant, and mothers with young children.[66] In 1946 and 1947, the MVD issued orders aimed at the "maximum release of invalids and those with incurable illnesses," especially as new inmates were flooding into the system.[67] In August 1950, decrees of the USSR Supreme Soviet, MVD and Procuracy called for the early release of pregnant women and women with children, resulting in the release of over 114,000 prisoners.[68]

No less than men, women in the Gulag experienced harsh physical exploitation. Women were often excluded from priority camps, such as mining and construction, and Gulag officials preferred to use female labor in light industry, agriculture, and textiles. In 1937, M.K. Sandratskaia was arrested as the wife of an enemy of the people and traitor to the motherland, and received a sentence of eight years in a camp. She journeyed eighteen days in a train, and eventually arrived at a Tomsk women's labor camp that was largely for female relatives of so-called traitors to the motherland. There they sewed army uniforms. Sandratskaia was proud of her work in support of the war effort, yet she feared the supervisor. He inspected their work and always found fault with it, and women whose output was deemed defective were punished with time in the penalty cell and 300 grams (0.66 lbs.) of bread daily. The Stakhanovites who overfulfilled their plan by 150–250 percent received the best food ration—600 grams (1.3 lbs.) of bread, plus soup and kasha with vegetable oil. "Yet the Stakhanovite rations became harder

and harder to reach," she testified, "because we were completely depleted of all strength. Overworked and famished, we developed pellagra or stage three dystrophy. Many of the women died, and even I got
it. I was in the hospital for a long time, nearly a corpse, skin on bones.
I'm surprised that I survived."[69] The USSR labor code of 1932 prohibited the use of women in heavy labor, but apparently this provision was
often violated. Camps placed women in heavy labor such as forestry,
where they often failed to meet their quotas.[70] Eugenia Ginzburg described how she was removed from work in the quarry when her health
declined sharply, and placed in "light labor" felling trees: "In that camp
tree felling was considered light work. And indeed, everything is relative. After the lime quarry I myself felt that working in the taiga was
almost like being on vacation."[71]

It was the hope of release from harsh physical labor that prompted
some women to get pregnant. According to Jacques Rossi, "some female camp inmates strive to get pregnant in order to avoid exhaustive
gang labor for a period of time prior to and after the birth."[72] A pregnancy could be advantageous, as one Gulag boss, Fyodor Mochulsky,
explained: "[I]f a female prisoner managed, despite the rules, to get
pregnant, then all the same she could lighten her load. (She would see a
decrease in the amount of physical labor, an increase in food, however
meager, for the time she was breastfeeding, and so on)."[73] If women
employed these strategies, they often did so reluctantly. One Gulag
survivor, who gave birth to her stillborn child in the camp morgue,
said: "I gave birth in this way so that they would be merciful to me."
As Jehanne Gheith and Katherine Jolluck explain, this was a complicated statement: "She gave birth so they would stop beating her, she
gave birth, perhaps in part out of the complicated desire—conscious or
unconscious—for life that many women had in the camps."[74]

According to Solzhenitsyn, women sought to get pregnant due to
the harsher Gulag conditions in the postwar years. The Gulag was
made up of mixed, coeducational camps until the end of the war, when
the leadership decreed that men and women should be housed in separate camps. By 1948, women either went to women's camps or lived
in the women's section of a general camp. In any mixed brigade or
mixed camp, the women were assigned the easier work, while in the
all-women brigades and all-women camps, women performed the labor of men, often working as lumberjacks, ditch-diggers, bricklayers,

and loaders, even hauling bags of 175–200 pounds.[75] Solzhenitsyn asserted that in the postwar period, as "women were driven out to general work," they began to pursue pregnancy: "To get off general work for at least a while became a question of life and death."[76] The testimonies of women in the camps confirms this view that pregnancy and maternity were sought by some women as a way of gaining early release, as temporary relief from hard labor, or just to replace a family that had been lost.[77] Nonetheless, relatively few women got pregnant and had children in the camps. In 1949, when the Gulag detained over half a million women, roughly 9000 were pregnant and 24,000 were mothers of young children in the camps.[78] Pregnancy generated what the Gulag called "lost labor days" (which I explain further in chapter 4), so camps required women to quickly return to work. Many women tried to end their pregnancies, and some died from dangerous camp abortions.[79]

Women were often sent to the Gulag as counterrevolutionaries or political offenders; imprisoned for their "social origin" or religion; or arrested as "wives of enemies of the people" or "family members of traitors to the motherland."[80] Yet like men, women were also arrested in large numbers under Stalin's severe criminal decrees, for offenses such as theft of socialist property and violations of labor discipline. In the 1930s, women constituted roughly 8 percent of prisoners, even following the mass arrests of wives and kulaks during the Great Terror. However, the percentage of female prisoners jumped sharply following Stalin's 1940 decrees concerning violations of labor discipline. Throughout the war years, the proportion of female prisoners in NKVD labor camps and colonies rose steadily, reaching over 23 percent in 1943, and the vast majority of these women, like the men, were relatively young. In part, the large percentage of female prisoners during the war was due to the release of draft-age men. No less significant were the mass criminal arrests of women during the war, for the number of women increased nearly 30 percent in the camps and almost quadrupled in the colonies. Stalin's draconian labor laws during the war subjected many women to Gulag detention, and his 1947 theft decrees also victimized women in large numbers. In early 1948, the number of female prisoners in the Gulag jumped by nearly 50,000 prisoners in just three months.[81]

Female *bytoviki* and *ukazniki* occasionally appear in Gulag memoirs. When Eugenia Ginzburg worked in the Elgen children's home, her favorite among the children was a Yakut boy. She wrote: "His mother had done time in a camp on a charge of 'deer stealing' (like so many Yakuts), and she was now working as a truck driver, ferrying equipment to the gold mines."[82] Memoirists described how young women who entered the Gulag for petty theft, shirking, and similar crimes, were forced into prostitution: "Hundreds of young girls between the ages of eighteen and twenty were sent to Kolyma for running away to their villages because they could no longer endure the starvation in the cities where they had been forced to work. Some had only gone back home for a few days to visit a sick mother, but the factory manager would not give them any days off and when they returned they were arrested. They came as adolescents and were instantly transformed by Kolyma into full-fledged prostitutes. Thousands of workers were sent into the Kolyma camps as *ukazniki,* for some petty misdemeanour."[83] The abuse of young women who entered the Gulag for petty offenses convinced former camp official Mochulsky of the injustice of Stalin's mass criminal arrests: "One of the most scandalous cruelties of our judicial system, I am convinced, was handing a prison term in the camps to a young girl, for some, small, insignificant crime."[84] Solzhenitsyn promised that his *Gulag Archipelago* would make public the brutal treatment of these working class women: "During and after the war, who crowded all the factories full? Women and girls. And who had to feed the family? They. And what were they to feed the family with? Need knows no law. And so they would pilfer: they used to put sour cream in their pockets . . . [and] . . . stick a spool of thread between their breasts . . . And then the guard would jump in and there would be a body search—and it was ten years for that shitty spool! The same as for treason!"[85] He announced, "to you, girl, I promise: the whole wide world will read about you."[86]

WERE ARRESTS USED TO GENERATE GULAG LABOR?

Gulag prisoner Yehoshua Gilboa wondered, "why were there so many criminal offenders, corrupt petty thieves like the ones caught misappropriating apples in collective farms here?"[87] Historians have asked the same question, although scholars have largely argued against a link between mass arrests and the Gulag economy. During the Great Terror, Stalin chose to execute over three-quarters of a million people whose labor and skills could have been exploited in the Gulag. The OGPU-NKVD-MVD did not necessarily pressure the party leadership for more inmates.[88] Indeed, camps experienced periods of severe overcrowding that made shortages of food and clothing more acute. As we will see in later chapters, some Soviet leaders preferred to manage a smaller Gulag operation. In the late 1940s, the Gulag did not expect the massive influx of prison laborers, just as it was taken by surprise by the large influx of prisoners during dekulakization in the early 1930s. The NKVD's fourth Five-Year Plan (1946–1950) anticipated a reduction in prisoner labor, but the agency quickly witnessed a sharp increase in prisoners as a result of the 1947 theft decrees.[89] Mass political repression, in fact, often caused the OGPU-NKVD-MVD to generate useless and inefficient capital construction projects as it scrambled to exploit all prisoners.[90] While a glut of Gulag labor appears highly inefficient, especially given the chronic food shortages, the question of whether there existed any link between arrests and the Gulag economy remains unsettled.

Stalin valued the Gulag's economic role, and key sectors of the Soviet Union's national economy, such as gold mining and railroad construction, depended greatly on Gulag labor. A 1930 report from the Gulag administration to the OGPU leadership noted the shortage of skilled labor for the White Sea-Baltic Sea Canal project, and suggested that, "a few skilled workers be arrested."[91] Historians acknowledge that there is some evidence to suggest that arrests of engineers and specialists, in particular, were economically motivated.[92] Yet with Gulag labor accounting for 85–100 percent of workers in key export industries such as gold, diamond, and platinum mining, it is highly likely that economic factors had an impact on the arrest of non-skilled workers as well. The Gulag economy required a constant influx of new prisoners. Heavy industry, military enterprises, and the state's export sectors all relied on prisoners. Whether it was metals production (gold, nickel, tin, copper, aluminum, and magnesium) or the construction of new hydroelectric stations and railroads, the labor of Gulag prisoners proved essential. The Gulag often experienced acute labor shortages, as there were never enough prisoners to fulfill NKVD production plans. Demand for prison laborers also came from the Soviet industrial sector that contracted workers from the Gulag.[93] Individual camps often issued requests for additional laborers and hoarded prisoners when they feared they lacked the manpower to fulfill their production plan.

In December 1949, the Gulag administration reported on its investigation of a rapidly growing camp in the Bashkir ASSR that was engaged in the construction and exploitation of oil fields. The camp had detained about 3600 prisoners in May 1949, and had an astounding 15,000 just eight months later. Apparently, the camp's director and chief engineer had submitted elevated and premature requests for more laborers to the Gulag "with the goal of playing it safe and maintaining a surplus of labor that they could keep for future use."[94]

Stalin may have used the criminal code, in part, to draw working class and peasant laborers into the Gulag, for the camp population of *bytoviki* and *ukazniki* increased during periods of labor shortage. In April 1939, Beria argued that the Gulag was experiencing a labor shortage and required increased mechanization in order to attain the same levels of productivity. He stated: "The leadership of the people's commissariat, spoiled in the past by the abundance of workers, did not address the questions of rationalization and mechanization of work. A double and even triple number of workers compensated for the machines. Today, when the number of available workforce is 20–25 percent below that required, and will decrease in the future, the camps cannot complete their tasks without a high level of mechanization at work."[95] The NKVD apparently explored the possibility of increased mechanization but, in the end, the Gulag economy resorted to the usual method for improving productivity—additional workers. Just a few months after Beria issued his warning, a series of laws sent many people to the Gulag. On June 26, 1940, the Presidium of the USSR Supreme Soviet issued a decree, "On the transition to an eight-hour work day, a seven-day work week and on the prohibition of voluntary departures by workers at enterprises and factories," which tied workers to their factories and criminalized poor labor discipline and tardiness.[96]

The impact of the June 26, 1940 decree on labor discipline was staggering. In 1940 alone, it condemned over two million people, or 61.5 percent of persons sentenced that year.[97] In the war years 1940–1944, over half of all sentences were attributed to this singular decree alone.[98] The party leadership used the war as justification for these severe sanctions on workers, yet arrests continued long after the war ended. In 1940–1952, ordinary courts and military tribunals sentenced nearly fourteen million people under the June 1940 law.[99] Most received their punishment in the form of workplace sanctions, reduced pay, and 25 percent lower food rations, but many of these petty offenders were sent to the Gulag.[100] In addition, an August 1940 law severely punished workers for drunkenness, hooliganism, petty theft, and other minor workplace offenses.[101] In the first months of the war, the party leadership also issued the December 26, 1941 law directed at unauthorized departures by workers in the defense sector. Absences and "malicious idleness" became interpreted as "desertion from the labor front" and punishable by Gulag sentences of five to eight years. Applied by military judges rather than the ordinary courts, the law sent over 600,000 workers to the Gulag during the war.[102] The correlation between Beria's bleak assessment of Gulag labor shortages in 1939 and the draconian criminal decrees a few months later may not have been coincidental.

Many Gulag observers believed that there was a connection between the Gulag's labor needs and mass arrests. Gulag survivor Antoni Ekart described a conversation he had after the war with a fellow prisoner, Grigori Roginsky, who had worked under Stalin's chief prosecutor. He told Ekart that Stalin's criminal code was used to transfer workers to locations and industries that could not attract free laborers. "Prisoners," he said, "can be disposed of arbitrarily. One can get as many as one wants on any conditions, and one can waste as many people as one wants too without loss to the State. In fact, the State gains politically. Planned enterprise requires mobilization of labor. And it is our labor camps that keep this immense machinery going."[103] Gulag boss Mochulsky wondered: "Why did they send small-time criminals off to camp for long prison sentences? Was it just to have a huge army of workers who would, with the stroke of a pen, be sent to labor-intensive construction work in far-flung remote regions with terrible climatic conditions?"[104] High-priority sectors of Stalin's economy relied on Gulag labor, which the petty criminal offenders, the *ukazniki* and *bytoviki*, provided in large numbers. Solzhenitsyn believed that arrests were proportionate to economic plans, while admitting that the calculation existed "perhaps in Stalin's head alone."[105]

CONCLUSION

From the 1930s to the 1950s, the most significant spikes in the number of Gulag inmates occurred following periods of mass criminal arrests, and these arrests largely condemned ordinary workers and peasants.

This prisoner profile satisfied the Gulag's need for prisoners who could perform heavy physical labor. Bolshevik ideology made productive labor the defining feature of the Soviet citizen. This produced a system of values wherein the stronger represented the morally superior. In this worldview, frail and sick individuals constituted an inferior population. According to Shalamov, "in the eyes of the state and its representatives, a physically strong person was better—yes, better—more moral, more valuable than a weak person, who couldn't shovel twenty cubic meters of dirt out of a trench in a day. The former was more moral than the latter. He fulfilled his 'quota,' that is, carried out his chief duty to the state and society and was therefore respected by all . . . Thanks to his physical advantages, such a person was transformed into a moral force in the resolution of the numerous everyday questions of camp life. Of course, he remained a moral force only as long as he remained a physical force. When Ivan Ivanovich was first brought to camp he was an excellent 'worker.' Now that he had become weak from hunger, he was unable to understand why everyone beat him in passing."[106] Stalin's Gulag valued prisoners according to their capacity for physical labor. The healthy and strong appeared superior, while the sick and emaciated were vilified as lazy shirkers and malingerers.

3 Health
"Physical Labor Capability"

THE RUSSIAN WORD for health (*zdorov'e*) almost never appears in Gulag records. Nor does the word for people (*liudi*) or the word for life (*zhizn'*). The Stalinist leadership was not interested in prisoners' health per se, but in their ability to perform physical labor. Camp officials spoke not of people's life and health, but of their "physical labor capability." The Gulag sought "the maximum labor utilization of prisoners" and, to that end, classified inmates according to categories of physical labor capability (*kategoriia fizicheskoi trudosposobnosti*). Gulag administrators needed people who could perform hard manual labor in logging, mining, and construction, so they examined and documented the bodies of prisoners to determine who was "fit for physical labor." Inside the barbed wire, individuals constituted simply bodies, either "fit" or "weakened." Varlam Shalamov wrote, "All convicts were divided, like horses, into categories of labor . . . To give a man an 'easy' labor category often meant saving him from death."[1]

Yet few got off easy. Even prisoners in very poor health were forced to perform strenuous labor. As Simon Ertz noted in his work on the Norilsk camp: "Prisoners were assigned to work without consideration for their physical state or qualifications. Some of the weakest and oldest prisoners were assigned to the hardest form of manual labor."[2] The Gulag's system of exploitation intensified from the 1930s to the 1950s, forcing a larger population of ailing prisoners into heavy physical labor. According to the Gulag's own statistics, which likely understate the health crisis in the camps, prisoners were overwhelmingly sick and emaciated. Even in the late 1940s, long after the hardships of war had ended, only a minority of prisoners was deemed "fit for heavy physical labor." Nonetheless, the Gulag continued to violently exploit them, to the point where they could no longer be "utilized."

MEDICAL EXAMINATIONS AND WORK ASSIGNMENTS

At the Gulag's inception, official guidelines specified that labor in the Stalinist camps would be manual, heavy, and physical. If an engineer appeared fit to perform heavy labor, he would not be given work as an engineer. Once prisoners had become physically depleted from brutal manual labor, they might be used in skilled work. Only prisoners limited in their capacity to do physical labor could be placed in their area of expertise as doctors, engineers, economists, accountants, or technicians.[3] This requirement, which was modified later, as camps required more skilled workers, represented one of the great inefficiencies of the Gulag economy.[4]

Over the long history of Stalin's Gulag, the medical-sanitation department possessed a range of responsibilities, from general sanitation, cleanliness, and disinfection to general health care and medical inspections. New camp prisoners (both men and women) arriving from prisons and transports were routinely subjected to a whole-body shave and placed under quarantine. The process served not only to protect the camps against lice infestations and infectious diseases, but to humiliate prisoners.[5] At Bamlag in the Far North, a memo of January 1934 stressed the importance of regular haircuts for prisoners, and prisoners admitted to camp medical facilities had to have all their bodily hair shaved.[6] As soon as they entered the camp, prisoners were subjected to a search, bath, and medical examination (*meditsinskoe osvidetel'stvovanie*).[7] The initial documentation of prisoners' physical state occurred at the point of entry, and was repeated at regular intervals thereafter. A prisoner's category of physical labor capability, disinfection, and other health information was recorded on his or her camp medical card (*sanitarnaia kartochka*) or health passport (*sanitarnyi passport*).[8] Camp prisoners had to be reexamined in May and November, and some every three months, since their category of physical labor capability was always subject to revision—preferably upward, to more heavy physical labor.[9] The process of physical evaluation was explained only in internal Gulag documents, and received hardly any mention in published camp regulations.[10]

With the emergence of the Stalinist camps, the task of determining prisoners' physical labor capability ceased being the sole responsibility of physicians. This represents a powerful symbol of Stalin's break with the past. In the 1920s, the civilian health ministry managed prisoners' health and doctors were in charge of assessing prisoners' physical labor capability.[11] But according to 1931 guidelines, a medical-labor commission (*vrachebno-trudovaia komissiia*) determined a prisoner's category of physical labor ability. Each camp division (*lagotdelenie*) and camp section (*lagpunkt*) was supposed to have a medical-labor commission. It was the industrial managers and not the doctors or the medical-sanitation department officials who ran the medical-labor commissions. In MVD Order No. 0418 of June 1949, the medical-labor commissions were renamed medical-labor expert commissions. Although now the director of the medical-sanitation department was supposed to serve as chair of the commission, this individual remained subordinate to the camp production administrators.[12] The medical-labor commissions, and later the medical-labor expert commissions, were monitored by a central camp commission, whose job it was to oversee their work. The head of the central medical-labor commission was the chief of the accounting and distribution department or URO (*uchetno-raspredelitel'nyi otdel*), which managed the prisoner workforce.[13] In Stalin's Gulag, medicine served production.

DEHUMANIZATION, HUMILIATION, AND THE MEDICAL EXAMINATIONS

Gulag survivors say relatively little about the general medical examination and the assignment of categories of physical labor capability. These constituted not only routines of camp life, but everyday degradations as well. Scholars have called attention to such omissions in the testimonies of those who experienced trauma. According to Leona Toker, Gulag survivors did not describe the worst of their experiences: "Though Gulag memoirists have witnessed atrocities that they could never have imagined, there usually remains some 'untidy spot' where they fear to tread, some Orwellian room 'one-oh-one.' Each author is reluctant to face some special type of suffering, depravity, or horror . . . This is one of the reasons Gulag memoirs are never felt to be self-sufficient, finished, works."[14] Memoirists may have avoided discussing the routine medical examinations, given their deeply humiliating quality. A former Gulag prisoner described his experience of the medical examination in 1946: "Everyone was ordered to the courtyard and told to strip. When your name was called you appeared before a medical team for a health inspection. The exam consisted of pulling the skin of your buttocks to determine the amount of muscle."[15] Similarly, Solzhenitsyn described how camp authorities would "examine [the prisoners] naked to determine their fitness for labor from the condition of their buttocks."[16]

For prisoners, medical examinations and physical labor assessments constituted everyday humiliations. In his reminiscences, a prisoner who worked as a camp doctor described the dehumanizing nature of the physical exam and likened the process to a slave market: "The GULAG system sought to maintain a veneer of legality, so a prisoner's labor capability depended on a medical examination . . . They conducted the examination without any medical devices . . . only visually and by probing. Among the deciding factors in the examination was skin elasticity and the layer of fat under the skin. Therefore they always pinched our buttocks . . . an inhumane and humiliating spectacle . . . The prisoners stripped naked and lined up in long rows. From this mass of people, an officer would call out one person at a time. It was the scene of a slave market, and sometimes it appeared as if they were driving us like cattle to the slaughterhouse."[17] Another Gulag survivor described the selection of prisoners for work as tantamount to a "slave market," where "unknown officials, both uniformed and in civilian clothes," walked among prisoners, "feeling their arms, their legs, looking over the palms, commanding others to bend over. Sometimes they would order a prisoner to open his mouth and peered at his teeth, like horse traders at a county fair . . . all were always in need of physically strong men for work as lumberjacks, in agriculture, in coal-mining, and in the oil wells."[18]

Memoirists offer only brief references to the medical exam, yet when they do, they characterize it as tantamount to the selection of slaves.

Gustaw Herling described both the degrading nature of the physical labor assessments and the violence of heavy labor: "Forest work was considered to be one of the heaviest forms of labor in the camp . . . I never came across a prisoner who had worked in the forest for more than two years. As a rule they left after a year, with incurable disease of the heart, and were transferred to brigades engaged in lighter work; from these they soon 'retired'—to the mortuary. Whenever a fresh transport of prisoners arrived in Yercevo, the youngest and strongest were always picked to be 'put through the forest.' This selection of slaves was sometimes similar even in the details of its décor to the illustrations of books about negro slavery, when the chief of the Yercevo camp section, Samsonov, honored the medical examination with his presence, and with a smile of satisfaction felt the biceps, shoulders and backs of the new arrivals."[19] According to Solzhenitsyn, camp officials ("the buyers") selected prisoners ("the natives on the islands") like merchandise at a slave market: "During the years when the prisoners' cases didn't carry any indication of their final destination, the transit prisons turned into slave markets . . . the natives on the islands kept dying off; and even though they cost not one ruble, a count was kept of them, and one had to worry about getting more of them for oneself so there wouldn't be any failure in fulfilling the plan. The *buyers* had to be sharp, have good eyes, and look carefully to see what they were taking so that last-leggers and invalids didn't get shoved on them . . . The conscientious merchants demanded that the *merchandise* be displayed alive and bare-skinned for them to inspect. And that was just what they used to say—without smiling—*merchandise.*"[20]

PHYSICAL LABOR CAPABILITY AND THE LIST OF ILLNESSES

Early Gulag records refer to several categories of physical labor capability, and over the years these categories were frequently revised. On February 3, 1931, Lazar Kogan, chief of the Gulag and director of the White Sea-Baltic Sea canal project, announced that category 1 physical labor capability referred to prisoners who were "of full value (*polnotsennyi*), fit to perform any kind of productive physical labor."[21] Category 2 physical labor applied to the "inferior or defective workforce (*nepolnotsennaia rabochaia sila*) with reduced capacity for unskilled physical labor; fit for skilled physical labor according to his profession." Category 3 designated "invalids who are fit for light forms of physical labor and complete invalids who are not capable of any kind of work."[22] Lynne Viola describes a similar system of labor classification in the early 1930s for so-called kulaks living in the special settlements.[23] In Stalin's labor camps and colonies, this three-tiered system of physical labor classification largely persisted throughout the 1930s, but not without modification. In 1933, the category of "the weak" was added for "able-bodied prisoners who are unable to work immediately upon arrival owing to emaciation."[24] The physical labor classifications were again revised and expanded in the 1940s. "The doctor's most important job," wrote Shalamov, "was to determine 'labor categories,' the degree to which a prisoner was capable of working."[25]

The Gulag medical-sanitation department's "List of Illnesses" (*raspisanie boleznei*) accompanied the three classifications of physical labor ability. Occasionally revised, the important List of Illnesses offered instructions on assigning prisoners, often with severe ailments and disabilities, to the various categories of physical labor capability. The List of Illnesses also identified which sick and emaciated prisoners could be released as invalids (the release process for invalid prisoners is detailed in chapter 6). The List of Illnesses is a creation of the Stalinist camps, and provides the clearest evidence of the brutal system of exploitation established at the Gulag's inception.[26] According to the February 1931 version of the List of Illnesses, produced by the Gulag's medical-sanitation department chief, Isaak Ginzburg, inmates considered "of-full-value" were capable of performing all forms of physical labor. However, these prisoners were not necessarily healthy. They might suffer from milder forms of bronchial asthma, heart trouble, tuberculosis, benign tumors, and many other ailments.[27] Category 2, the "inferior workforce" that Gulag officials considered to have only "reduced capacity for unskilled physical labor," referred to persons with very severe ailments.[28] These included profound and incurable nutritional disorders, heart disease, acute emphysema, anemia, tuberculosis, severe forms of gonorrhea, and progressive muscular atrophy, as well as inmates who experienced "movement impeded by malformations, chronic disease, or a curvature or other changes in the shape of the pelvis." This second category of physical labor capability also applied to persons with the following: "incurable illnesses, significant damage to and defects of the bones and soft tissue of the face, of the tongue, palate, nose, larynx, windpipe, throat, or esophagus, accompanied by impaired functions that are important for life."

In general, illnesses described as "treatable" would qualify someone for category 2 or a "reduced capacity for unskilled physical labor." More severe ailments would cause a prisoner to be designated category 3, which was reserved for "invalids who are fit for light forms of physical labor and complete invalids who are not capable of any kind of work." For example, prisoners with severe malnutrition such as pellagra, a starvation illness that the OGPU benignly characterized as a general eating disorder (rastroistvo obshchego pitaniia), were classified as "inferior workforce" if their illness was "significant but curable."[29] Prisoners blind in only one eye were considered "inferior," while the completely blind were classified as "invalids." Epileptic prisoners could be "inferior" or "invalids," depending on the frequency of their seizures, just as those with tuberculosis could be either, depending on the progression of the illness. Prisoners with anemia were "inferior workforce," but those with severe anemia and leukemia were "invalids." Many of the weakest prisoners were assigned to do "work for invalids," despite their severe disabilities and illnesses.[30] The Gulag forced even the most sick and disabled prisoners to continue working. A former Gulag boss, Fyodor Mochulsky, recalled that, for the central administration of his camp: "The plan for constructing the rail line was a sacred matter . . . The feeling was: You can do it all. Just work each and every prisoner as hard as you can."[31]

In 1939, the Red Army invaded eastern Poland and the Baltic states, and Stalin began a wave of arrests that drew new prisoners into the camps. The Gulag population also expanded as a result of Stalin's draconian criminal laws against violators of labor discipline. As more people entered the camps, living conditions deteriorated and prisoners' health declined sharply. An NKVD order of August 1940 identified six distinct categories of physical labor capability: capable of physical labor (godnye k fiztrudu); limited labor capability; weakened (slabosil'nye); sick; invalid; prisoners requiring constant assistance.[32] After the Nazis invaded the USSR in June 1941, Gulag authorities developed even more categories to capture the growing numbers of weakened prisoners. In 1942–1943, the physical profile of prisoners appeared in seven categories: capable of heavy physical labor; capable of medium physical labor; capable of light physical labor; certified invalids, working; certified invalids, nonworking; noncommissioned workers; without designation.[33] At Siblag in 1942, the camp's population of over 33,000 inmates appeared overwhelmingly emaciated. Less than 20 percent could be described as capable of heavy or medium labor, while over 80 percent were characterized as follows: capable of light labor, 37.8 percent; certified working invalids, 31.5 percent; certified nonworking invalids, 13 percent.[34] In 1942, the Northern railroad camp (*Sevzheldorlag*), which was building part of the Northern Pechora mainline, had 46,000 prisoners of whom 16,000 or 35 percent were classified as weakened, sick, or invalid.[35] Another NKVD wartime memo divided invalids and chronically ill prisoners in NKVD camps into five categories: "invalids-hospitalized"; "invalids requiring constant care"; "invalids who are completely unfit for labor"; "invalids with limited work capability of up to 25 percent"; and the mentally ill.[36] More categories had to be generated, as large numbers of prisoners experienced various stages of severe illness. In the course of the revisions, the first category of labor capability did not change, while the last categories, to which the most disabled prisoners were assigned, proliferated in number and description.

Toward the end of the war, the multiple descriptors for prisoners' physical labor capability were streamlined into four simple categories. In a June 1944 report to NKVD chief Lavrenty Beria, the Gulag leader, V.G. Nasedkin, divided prisoners into four physical labor classifications: category 1: capable of heavy work; category 2: capable of medium work; category 3: capable of light work; category 4: invalids and weakened prisoners.[37] A new List of Illnesses accompanied the new categories of physical labor capability. The lengthy document, produced by the chief of the Gulag's medical-sanitation department, D.M. Loidin, was titled: "The list of main illnesses, physical disabilities, and defects for determining prisoners' category of labor capability or classifying them as invalids." The 1944 List of Illnesses was lengthier and more systematic than the 1931 version. It paired over a hundred ailments with a corresponding labor category, and specified in detail which prisoners to classify as invalids.[38] Highlighting the Gulag's interest in medical training and expertise (which intensified during the war), illnesses were organized according to formal medical specializations: internal medicine; surgery; dermatology; ear, nose, and throat;

gynecology; ophthalmology; psychiatry. At the same time, it appears that the Gulag leadership failed to offer adequate instructions on what jobs corresponded to the different categories. As the medical-sanitation department director of the Altai camp system complained: "We have no specific listing of professions, so I often don't know what constitutes heavy labor or medium labor. This makes our work difficult."[39]

Like the 1930s version, the 1944 List of Illnesses illustrates the ways in which sick prisoners were physically exploited at each stage of their debilitating illnesses. The question was not whether someone with heart disease, asthma, or tuberculosis should work, for they must. Medium physical labor applied to prisoners with some forms of bronchial asthma, cancer, and tuberculosis, as well as deaf prisoners and those having "clearly pronounced degeneration of the heart muscle; neurosis of the heart and other functional disorders of the cardiovascular system."[40] Light physical labor was assigned to those with more serious forms of tuberculosis, cancer, bronchial asthma, emphysema, or heart disease, plus amputees who had lost "both lower or one upper extremity," and inmates with "a goiter whose size makes it hard to wear clothes or disturbs nearby organs."[41] The invalid category referred to persons with "significantly pronounced senile decrepitude" or "the absence of both upper extremities," as well as schizophrenia and "an affliction of the central nervous system with sustained, progressive, and profound functional disruption."[42]

Prisoners' category of physical labor depended on how far their developing illness had advanced. Someone with a "general nutritional disorder (pellagra, acute dystrophy or malnutrition)" that was subject to treatment was assigned to "light labor," but the same nutritional disorder considered incurable or requiring months of treatment would classify someone as an "invalid." Prisoners with malignant tumors that had not metastasized were "light labor," while "invalids" were those with malignant tumors considered to be at an advanced stage or inoperable.

Each category was flagged by particular words and phrases. Medium labor illnesses often included phrases like: "without changes in pathology" and "lacking marked objective signs and dysfunctions." Light labor included notations such as "moderate impairment" and "subject to treatment." The invalid category was associated with a grim prognosis: "incurable," "requiring long-term specialized treatment," "sustained loss of labor capability," "severely limited or complete loss of labor strength," "sustained and profound functional disruption," "complete loss of movement," and "clearly pronounced dysfunction." Medical assessments were concerned with prisoners' functionality rather than health, and they constituted matters of perception.

Comparing the 1931 and 1944 Lists of Illnesses, it is evident that sick and disabled prisoners continued to be severely exploited. In 1931, for example, whether or not malnutrition was identified as "significant but treatable" or "profound and incurable," the prisoner was placed in category 2 or the "inferior workforce (*nepolnotsennaia rabochaia sila*) with reduced capacity for unskilled physical labor; fit for skilled physical labor according to his profession."[43] The 1944 List of Illnesses assigned the treatable prisoners to "light physical labor" and the incurables to the "invalid" category.[44] These criteria were also used for prisoners with Addison's or Basedow disease, anemia, emphysema, epilepsy, or heart disease, and for disabilities such as "the absence of all extremities, hands or feet, as well as defective hands or feet that hinder functioning of the extremities."[45] Nevertheless, weakened prisoners were not entirely protected from the most strenuous forms of work. In the 1940s, the guidelines on labor utilization allowed camps and colonies to place sick prisoners in arduous physical labor if production targets were reduced. Work quotas were supposed to be cut by up to 50 percent when "light labor" prisoners were used in medium labor and "medium labor" prisoners in heavy physical labor. The 1931 and 1944 Lists of Illnesses appear to be equally harsh in their work requirements for ailing prisoners.

Prisoners' categories of physical labor ability were supposed to be continuously reassessed, for there was pressure built into the system to always revise prisoner classifications upward, in favor of more strenuous classifications of physical labor ability. Shalamov told the story of prisoner Andreev who "had been classified only for 'light physical labor,' but he knew how abruptly such a classification could be changed."[46] Yet in practice commissions often assessed prisoners' health only infrequently, leaving sick prisoners in strenuous physical labor. One Gulag health official recalled a group of invalids and sick prisoners, many of them severely weakened with nutritional dystrophy, who remained classified under "light physical labor," because the commission that reviewed inmates' labor capability had not convened for a long time. One of the prisoners complained that he was unable to work, the hospital would not take him in, and reclassification by the commission appeared unlikely.[47] Doctors could not necessarily offset Gulag pressures to keep weakened prisoners in brutalizing work. As Donald Filtzer explains, in Stalin's civilian health care system, there existed "a strong punitive dimension" that required doctors to be "extremely stringent when deciding whether or not to grant a sick note." Still, many civilian doctors chose to treat workers more mildly than the regime would have preferred.[48] In the Gulag, doctors faced much greater risks for such leniency. Doctors experienced great pressure to push the limits of prisoners' physical capacities and to keep all prisoners working in industry, for they were held responsible for physical labor classifications.[49] Solzhenitsyn argued that the doctors and the medical-sanitation department only served the production chiefs: "When quarterly commissioning took place—that comedy known as the general medical examination of the camp population, where prisoners were assigned to categories TFT, SFT, LFT, and IFT (that is, heavy, medium, light, or individualized physical labor)—were there many good doctors who opposed the evil chief of the medical-sanitation department, who was kept in his job only because he supplied columns for heavy labor?"[50]

"THE INVERSE RATIO BETWEEN SOCIAL POSITION AND HUMANENESS"

To those who actually worked with the List of Illnesses, the new 1944 law appeared more severe. In a September 1945 meeting, the Gulag sanitation chief, D.M. Loidin, met with the medical-sanitation department directors for the regional camps and colonies. The director of the medical-sanitation department for the Cheliabinsk regional system of labor camps and colonies stated simply: "I underline my remarks with red pen. I think that the categories are defined rather harshly."[51] A certain Prokhorov from the Novosibirsk region likewise criticized the severity of the new List of Illnesses. He cited the fact that prisoners with "extensive scars that are inclined to be ulcerations or grow into tissue that inhibit free movement or putting on clothes and shoes" were assigned to "light individualized labor."[52] Prokhorov said that most of these prisoners were not work-capable but "practically invalids, practically bedridden" who should be certified as invalids. He also disagreed with the assignment of "light labor" for prisoners whose ailments included "complete immobility or inactivity of the large joints, significantly limited movement of the limbs that is inherent and also the result of traumatic injury or chronic illness of the bones, muscles, tendons, or joints."[53] Prokhorov said that in most cases these prisoners too "aren't able to do anything."[54] Loidin pushed back, and suggested that the new List of Illnesses was actually too lenient: "Take the collective farms. You'll find the elderly there with [acute] hernias, and they're working."[55] Prokhorov persisted. He cited another article that designated "medium labor" for prisoners with "the absence of, complete reduction of, or immobility of, two fingers or one thumb or the index finger on the right hand. The absence of phalanx bones on two or more fingers on the right hand without eliminating the functions of the extremities."[56] Prokhorov argued that prisoners were severely limited without a thumb and could not necessarily perform medium physical labor.[57]

Despite criticism from his subordinates, the Gulag health chief refused to accept the argument that the new List of Illness represented a more severe revision of earlier practice. Loidin's defense reveals the mentality of the Stalinist leadership. On illnesses related to vitamin deficiency and malnutrition, he said that it would be very easy to place someone with "pronounced nutritional decline" in light labor instead of medium labor, as the List of Illnesses dictates. But he cautioned his "comrades who are panicking" to consider the ramifications of such a change: "We thought about this, comrades. But think of how many people experience nutritional decline. I'm telling you, this change can be made easily, but if we do it we'll be making a big mistake . . . We'll turn our contingent upside-down. Our entire [category] of useful (*polnotsennyi*) contingent would fall into the inferior [category]. It was so much work to draw up these instructions. You yourselves know that we lived without instructions . . . A [change in the List of Illnesses] might have little impact on your own contingent but for another contingent, like one in a forestry camp, it would be a big deal."[58] Loidin's comment is striking, for it represents an admission that classifying prisoners according to the true metrics of their ill health would deny the Gulag its labor force. One medical-sanitation department director stated that Gulag instructions were forcing camps to work their prisoners to death: "Why do we have such [high] mortality rates? I think that here, there's a big error in the definition of the categories. If the categories were defined correctly, there wouldn't be such [high] mortality."[59]

Moreover, the 1944 List of Illnesses made it more difficult for camps to classify ailing prisoners as invalids, a classification that would have qualified these inmates for release. According to the medical-sanitation department director for the Altai regional labor camps and colonies, prisoners who had qualified for release as invalids were now kept in the camps doing some form of physical labor. He cited specific examples: "Regarding the List of Illnesses, the first point states, 'pronounced decline in appetite without pathological changes in the body . . .' and this corresponds to the second category [medium physical labor]. We used to put these prisoners in category 3 [light labor], if we didn't have to hospitalize them. Before we got the new List of Illnesses, we used to certify for early release inmates with 'subcompensated pulmonary tuberculosis and a decline in appetite.' Now I don't know whether we can do that. Yet in this List of Illnesses they correspond to category 3 [light labor]. Of course, I won't be certifying them for early release anymore. I think that 'subcompensated pulmonary tuberculosis' is not all that different from active pulmonary tuberculosis. We must treat this patient and, depending on his condition, decide the issue of what to do next. In addition, I'm concerned about the completely blind prisoners who are also designated as category 3 [light] individualized labor. We have six of them. Then there are the prisoners who are missing both legs or one arm. They also have been designated category 3 individualized labor, whereas they used to fall under certification for early [medical] release."[60]

If camp officials considered the 1944 List of Illnesses to be a harsh revision of existing practice, the Gulag leadership disagreed. Later, the Gulag top brass would, in Orwellian fashion, characterize the List of Illnesses as a humane document that improved the physical condition of prisoners. In 1945, the chief of the Gulag medical-sanitation department, Loidin, claimed that the List of Illnesses "introduced a degree of clarity in determining the category composition of prisoners and to a large degree enabled the elimination of the vagueness and confusion that existed in this area. This document, which the sanitation organization created in the course of many years, has played an enormous role in improving and preserving the physical condition of the contingents."[61]

Similarly, in May 1947, Nasedkin claimed that the order reduced illness and mortality, and fundamentally improved the physical profile of prisoners. For the Gulag chief, the decree brought about a "radical change" in camp conditions, and improved the physical profile and labor utilization of prisoners.[62] Nasedkin noted that the order prohibited the existing practice of assigning physically weakened "light labor" prisoners to do heavy physical labor, and it required that work norms should be reduced up to 50 percent when "light labor" prisoners were used in medium labor and "medium labor" prisoners in heavy physical labor. He touted these changes specifically for their economic impact, which represented his principal concern: "Improvements in prisoners' . . . physical condition played a decisive role in the successful fulfillment of production plans by MVD camps and colonies."[63] The Stalinist leadership insisted that its instructions improved the health of prisoners and, more importantly, the economic output of the camps. Low-level officials, who were more qualified to judge, believed that the 1944 List of Illnesses represented a harsh revision. Loidin rejected such assertions from his subordinates. Solzhenitsyn called this attitude "the universal law of the inverse ratio between social position and humaneness."[64]

PHYSICAL EXPLOITATION AND THE EMACIATED GULAG LABOR FORCE

According to the Gulag's own internal records, the Stalinist labor camp system destroyed its prisoners. According to Oleg Khlevniuk, "by August 1, 1930, the estimated number of exhausted, sick, disabled, infirm, and elderly inmates was 30,000–50,000 out of 180,000 prisoners overall."[65] In 1939, Beria stated that the number of prisoners "who are weakened and useless for production" was so large that "no more than 60–65 percent of the workforce is being utilized."[66] As of January 1, 1939, in the colonies alone, 40 percent of prisoners were considered so sick and disabled that they could not work at all, or they possessed only limited labor capability and could perform only light labor.[67] When the categories of physical labor capability expanded to include light, medium, and heavy physical labor, prisoners' health profiles remained exceptionally poor. Gulag chief Nasedkin noted that in 1940, over 39 percent of prisoners were either invalids, weakened, or fit only for light labor, and that figure nearly doubled to roughly 64 percent in

1942.[68] In 1942–1943, roughly half of all labor camp prisoners were considered either invalid or capable of only light physical labor.[69] Individual camps often reported even higher proportions of ailing prisoners. In May–July 1938, some camps reported 16–19 percent of prisoners who were not work-capable.[70] In March 1942, over two-thirds of the roughly 18,000 prisoners at the logging camp Berezlag were classified as either fit for light labor, invalids, weakened prisoners, or hospitalized.[71] A May 1942 report on the Usollag camp noted that over 75 percent of the nearly 6000 prisoners there were classified as either invalids or capable of only light labor. Many had starvation disease or pellagra. These figures are especially dire in light of the fact that more than half of the prisoners had been in the camp for less than a year, 40 percent were under the age of 40, and 72 percent were under 50, yet even this relatively young contingent had been swiftly destroyed.[72] In December 1945, the Gulag chief reported that in mining and metallurgy camps, nearly 40 percent of prisoners were classified as either invalids or capable of only light labor.[73] The Gulag exploited prisoners so brutally that production targets could hardly be met. As one camp boss told his colleagues, "Of my 900 people, 300 are sick, 300 are invalids and 150 are juvenile offenders. Who's going to fulfill the plan?"[74]

World War II is often cited as the worst period for Gulag prisoners, yet camp statistics indicate that prisoners' health remained abysmal and even worsened in the postwar years. In 1946–1947, as the number of prisoners in NKVD labor camps and colonies grew from over one million to over two million, half of all prisoners were classified as either invalids or capable of only light physical labor.[75] In July 1947, the "light labor" and "invalid" categories constituted 53 percent in the camps and as many as 64.3 percent in the colonies; in October 1947, these categories made up 52.4 percent in the camps, and had reached 66.7 percent in the colonies.[76] In other words, over two-thirds of the one million prisoners in the colonies were extremely sick and disabled. This data reflects the fact that the Gulag transferred its weakest inmates to the colonies. In September 1947, the Gulag leadership reported to its MVD bosses that only 40 percent of prisoners were healthy enough to perform heavy or medium physical labor—the principal work of the Gulag—while nearly 60 percent of prisoners in Gulag camps and colonies were classified as either invalids or capable of only light physical labor.[77] As bleak as these statistics appear, they likely understate the health crisis in the Gulag, since this data was generated by an agency that sought to maximize the number of prisoners in heavy physical labor.

Data on physical labor capability appeared increasingly dismal in the late 1940s. A January 1946 report indicated that of all prisoners in NKVD camps and colonies, over half were classified as either invalids or capable of only light labor, while fewer than 15 percent were deemed capable of heavy physical labor.[78] This data is especially striking given that it reflects the composition of inmates following the 1945 amnesty, when many sick and invalid prisoners were released.[79] By late 1946, the situation had not changed significantly, with a mere 14 percent of Stalin's labor camp prisoners deemed capable of heavy physical labor. Again, half of all labor camp prisoners were determined to be either capable of only light labor or invalid.[80] Into the late 1940s, the health of Gulag prisoners continued to decline. By July–October 1947, roughly 60 percent of prisoners in MVD camps and colonies were classified as either invalids or capable of only light physical labor, while fewer than 10 percent could do heavy labor.[81] The physical profile of prisoners in the colonies was evidently worse than in the camps. Central MVD authorities unloaded sick and invalid prisoners onto the MVD organs of the union republics that operated the colonies. Thus prisoners classified as either invalids or capable of only light labor made up 67 percent of prisoners in the labor colonies. Again, the official data likely understates the poor health of prisoners. According to one Gulag medical worker, many inmates classified as capable of heavy and medium physical labor were in such poor health that they proved incapable of meeting their production targets at the stone quarry, while those with a light physical labor classification "could hardly move their legs."[82]

Typically in the Soviet Union, officials would stop reporting social statistics when they appeared unfavorable, and this happened in the case of prisoners' physical profile data. For the years 1942–1947, quarterly reports on the composition of Gulag prisoners routinely included data on their physical labor capability.[83] These reports, likely produced by Gulag leaders for their MVD bosses, included various statistics, such as the gender, nationality, sentence, and physical profile of camp inmates. As data on the physical profile of prisoners worsened and reflected poorly on the Gulag, that component of the reports was simply dropped. In 1948–1952, the handwritten quarterly reports "on the composition of prisoners detained in camps and colonies of the USSR MVD" no longer included any data on the physical profile or labor capability of prisoners.[84] This sensitive data continued to be compiled by the individual camps and reported to Gulag authorities for internal use, but the Gulag chose not to share it with MVD leaders or with Stalin.

The poor health of Gulag prisoners represented highly classified information. It exposed the consequences of severe physical exploitation and the impossibility of achieving utopian production goals with depleted and emaciated workers. Even before 1948, Gulag administrators, under pressure to demonstrate maximum "utilization" of all inmate labor, often withheld data from their OGPU-NKVD-MVD bosses on the poor physical state of prisoners. A one-hundred-plus-page report to NKVD chiefs Beria and Kruglov in March 1940, "On the Work of the Gulag," offered no breakdown of prisoners by physical labor capability and, in fact, skirted the issue.[85] A 1944 statistical report on "the number and composition of prisoners" in the regional colonies gave no breakdown of prisoners by physical profile or labor capability.[86] Gulag administrators were reluctant to share physical profile data with their bosses in part because the Stalinist leadership insisted on interpreting prisoners' poor health as a failure of camp administrators, rather than the logical consequence of severe physical exploitation. OGPU-NKVD-MVD bosses constantly criticized the Gulag leadership for failing to preserve the physical labor capability of prisoners. In December 1947, the MVD minister, S.N. Kruglov, chastised the then Gulag chief, G.P. Dobrynin, for "a series of failures" in Gulag operations, including the shortage of armed guards and surveillance personnel, as well as problems with food rations and prisoners' physical condition.[87] The OGPU-NKVD-MVD leadership often criticized Gulag officials for failing to maintain the physical profile of prisoners, yet it wrote the very rules that destroyed prisoners' health.

REVISIONS TO THE CATEGORIES OF PHYSICAL LABOR CAPABILITY

MVD Order No. 0418 on June 25, 1949 again revised the categories of physical labor capability and intensified the Gulag's system of physical exploitation. The order began by cynically praising the 1944 revision for improving the physical condition and labor utilization of Gulag prisoners. MVD chief Kruglov stated that Order No. 00640 of 1944 "made it possible for camps and colonies in the difficult conditions of the war and postwar period to preserve the physical condition of contingents and to gradually improve the basic level of prisoners' labor utilization."[88] With the introduction of new instructions, the older guidelines were characterized as lenient and appropriate only to wartime and immediate postwar conditions. Kruglov defended the need to introduce a new system: "At the present time . . . the condition of prisoner detention has improved overall." He even claimed that the supply of food, clothing, and other goods to prisoners takes place "without interruption."[89] Such assertions were blatantly false, yet consistent with the Gulag-MVD leadership's manner of speaking. Kruglov argued (contrary to the evidence) that the older List of Illness was no longer needed given the improved condition and care of prisoners, so it was time to reduce the number and definition of the categories of physical labor capability. The 1949 MVD order returned to the older three-tiered system, but the three categories were more harshly defined than they had been in 1931.[90] Now, category 1 pertained to "all prisoners who are basically fit for physical labor." The second category applied to "physically inferior prisoners who could work in light labor with a 15 percent reduction [in their production quotas], or in medium labor with the application of a 30 percent reduction, or in special forms of work without any kind of reduction."[91] Category 3 was for "invalids." The new List of Illnesses reveals the escalating brutality of the Gulag regime in the late Stalin years.

The 1949 revision intensified the regime of exploitation in the Gulag. Category 2 of 1949 appears to be commensurate with the earlier categories concerning light labor and light individualized labor. The 1949 List of Illnesses essentially collapsed the older categories of heavy and medium labor into a single category, and reserved category 2 for the severely weakened prisoners previously classified as light-labor, who were still a notch above the invalid category. Like the light-labor prisoners in the previous list, the 1949 category 2 prisoners were prohibited from doing heavy physical labor.[92] The category 3 or invalid category was reserved for "prisoners suffering from severe chronic illnesses or physical limitations that do not give them the ability to work, or who can be utilized in work consistent with their remaining labor capability."[93]

As in earlier practice, weaker prisoners (category 2 and invalid) were supposed to undergo a quarterly medical reexamination to have their physical labor classification reassessed, while prisoners in category 1 remained stuck in physical labor for six months.[94]

In the late Stalin years, the party leadership pressured the Gulag to improve labor utilization rates. The 1949 List of Illnesses stressed labor exploitation, even in the title: "The list of main illnesses, physical deficiencies, and defects in development that prevent the assignment of prisoners to category 1 labor." The order stressed that camps could not easily excuse prisoners from physical labor. Earlier editions of the List of Illnesses had different titles, which drew attention to the invalid classification and early release. In previous years, the Stalinist leadership had focused on minimizing the number of prisoners classified as invalids and thereby entitled to medical discharge. Now the goal of keeping prisoners in heavy labor appears paramount. Heavy physical labor was to be the assignment for all but the most emaciated and disabled prisoners. The 1949 List of Illnesses aimed at increasing labor utilization rates by forcing a larger population of weakened prisoners into heavy physical labor. For example, in order for prisoners with tuberculosis to be removed from physical labor and classified as "physically inferior," they must have had the disease for over a year. To be classified as an invalid, someone with tuberculosis would have to display "significant disorders of the respiratory and cardiovascular systems."[95]

The 1949 List of Illnesses offered instructions on how to classify prisoners with nearly one hundred different ailments and disabilities. As in earlier iterations, categories were determined by disease progression. The invalid category was marked by such descriptors as "severe and incurable," "not responsive to treatment," and "pronounced loss of function." For example, the list included guidelines for prisoners with chronic respiratory diseases such as emphysema, pneumosclerosis (the result of chronic pneumonia, bronchitis, asthma, influenza), as well as silicosis, caused by inhaling crystalline silica dust in jobs such as sandblasting, rock drilling, mining, building, and road construction. Such inmates would only drop down to category 2 if they suffered "moderate" damage to the lungs, and to the invalid category only if lung damage was "severe." Prisoners with severe neurodegenerative diseases could be classified as category 2 if their disease was thought to be progressing slowly and had not produced "profound loss of movement or sensation." They would be "invalids" only if their disability was considered "persistent and profound." Those with malignant tumors that had not metastasized would be in category 2, but they could be classified as invalids if their malignant tumors were "in advanced and inoperable forms." Category 2 or "physically defective prisoners" would include those with "nutritional disorders" when "obvious and pronounced," but such prisoners would be classified as invalids if their ailments proved "deep and incurable." The following ailments would classify prisoners as "inferior" and limit their physical exploitation: "benign tumors that make it hard to wear clothing or impair organ functions," "extremely large hernias," "goiter that impairs the functions of nearby organs," and loss of vision in one eye.[96] The MVD used these instructions to send a strong message to camp officials that only the most disabled prisoners could be excused from heavy physical labor. The invalid category, as usual, was reserved for severely diseased and debilitated prisoners. To be classified as an invalid, a prisoner had to be completely blind or have stage three silicosis. The invalid category also included those with "disfiguring inflammation" and chronic illness of the tendons, muscles, and joints that resulted in "the complete loss of movement," as well as inmates who demonstrated "pronounced effects of senile decrepitude." When the 1949 list was issued, the MVD chief instructed camps and colonies to conduct medical examinations of all their prisoners within the next month for the purpose of reclassification under the new rubric.

Just as party leaders intensified Gulag exploitation, they blamed local officials for prisoners' declining health. The Stalinist leadership was responsible for Gulag overcrowding, ambitious production plans, and brutalizing rules governing the physical exploitation of prisoners. Yet the MVD routinely imposed unrealistic demands on camp officials. Kruglov insisted that prisoners get the required two-square-meters minimum of living space, eight hours of sleep per night, regular baths, full rations, and four days off of work per month, plus heated barracks and proper clothing in the winter. The lack of clothing, he asserted, "is one of the main reasons why prisoners get sick and drop out of the system."[97] The phrase "drop out of the system" was Gulag-speak for mortality and the routine release of dying invalid prisoners. Kruglov also demanded that the supply of food, shoes, and clothing had to improve sharply, especially at newly established and distant camps, where living conditions for prisoners were notoriously poor. Camps and colonies had to solicit more packages from inmates' relatives.[98] The MVD chief blamed the poor living conditions on the medical-sanitation departments, who were responsible for the proper labor utilization of prisoners, health care and sanitation, medical examinations, and physical labor assignments, as well as the prevention of illnesses and epidemics.[99] Kruglov stressed repeatedly that persons responsible for the poor physical labor capacity of prisoners would be severely punished. The theme of punishing the guilty for the deterioration of prisoners' physical labor capability runs throughout the entire 1949 order. For example: "The MVD USSR warns directors of labor camps and colonies that henceforth the guilty will be severely punished for the worsening physical profile of prisoners, and for a rise in illness and mortality . . . the role and responsibility of the medical-sanitation departments in camps and colonies for the physical condition of prisoners should increase; sanitation workers are obligated to immediately inform the GULAG MVD USSR of all cases where the leadership of camps and colonies violate basic sanitation requirements."[100] In the same decree that intensified the system of exploitation, the MVD leader stressed the need to improve prisoners' health. Soviet authorities established a labor camp system that was fundamentally destructive, yet they criticized local camp officials for the Gulag's crippled workforce.

As a result of the new 1949 List of Illnesses, prisoners were administratively relabeled and physically exploited more severely. A report on prisoners' physical profile at the Borsky railroad camp reflected this abrupt change from five physical labor categories to three between August and September 1949. The Borsky camp report demonstrates that Order No. 0418 made life harder for prisoners, as now they were reclassified into higher categories of physical labor capability. In September, prisoners who had been classified for medium physical labor were now included in category 1 "basically fit for physical labor." Prisoners who had been in category 3 or category 3-individualized labor were now category 2 "physically inferior prisoners."[101]

The 1949 revision to the categories of physical labor capability did more than intensify the level of physical exploitation in the Gulag. It also effectively masked the ill health of the Gulag labor force. Under the new system, the health of prisoners appeared less bleak.

The majority of prisoners were now deemed "basically fit for physical labor." With the reclassification, the Gulag population roughly went from 60 percent either invalids or in light labor to 60 percent "basically fit for physical labor." In the years 1949–1953, the physical profile of prisoners across the Gulag system of camps and colonies was roughly 60 percent in category 1 "all prisoners who are basically fit for physical labor," 30 percent in category 2 "physically defective prisoners," and 10 percent in category 3 "invalids."[102] Prisoners' health appeared worse at some individual camps and in the Gulag's labor colonies, where the system concentrated its emaciated prisoners (see chapter 8). For example, in March 1950, camps and colonies operated by the Khabarovsk regional MVD detained 24,235 prisoners, and roughly 55 percent were classified as either "invalids" or "physically inferior prisoners."[103] At the time of Stalin's death in March 1953, one-third of prisoners in the camps were classified as "invalids" or "physically inferior" compared with nearly two-thirds in the colonies.[104] In Stalin's Gulag, an enormous segment of labor camp prisoners was so brutalized by severe exploitation and starvation rations that they could hardly work at all.

CONCLUSION

The Gulag survivor Yehoshua Gilboa described his own inexorable physical decline, as he dropped from one physical labor category to the next. He noted that the actual work that one had to perform under "heavy," "medium," and "light" labor did not vary greatly, as prisoners in these different classifications were forced to work under similarly difficult conditions. Gilboa wrote: "I began my career in the North at 'heavy hard labor,' quickly passed to 'medium hard labor,' and then proceeded to 'light hard labor.' In all these categories, the variations are still small and you go out to 'production,' which means you work outside the camp and not on service jobs inside. Later I was assigned to 'weak units' numbers one, two, and three. Shortly after that, I was transferred to a sort of small hospital, then to a 'recovery center,' and finally back to the top again quickly to descend the whole gamut once more."[105] In later chapters, we will discuss the weak units and recovery centers or convalescent camps, which (like the "invalid" category) were limited by strict quotas. For the purposes of this chapter, however, the circular image that Gilboa presents must be acknowledged. Gulag officials touted the accommodations they offered sick prisoners, and for some, like Gilboa, these may have been life saving.

For many others, however, the process of physical exploitation was not circular but linear, as very few prisoners were granted leniency. In Stalin's Gulag, the system of exploitation dictated that prisoners be worked to the point of utter depletion. The Stalinist leadership may not have planned to exterminate its camp prisoners, but it intended to physically exploit them to the maximum degree possible. As Mark Mazower wrote regarding Nazi prison laborers: "Like Hitler himself, German business never saw them as a scarce or valuable resource . . . Rather they were cheap commodities to be worked until they were worn out."[106] Stalin, no less than Hitler, believed in exhaustive labor. Labor camp violence did not result from a breakdown of order, nor was this violence derived largely from "excesses" of camp officials that Soviet leaders tried to combat. Rather, Gulag violence emerged from the order itself. Official Gulag documents and instructions reveal the lethal nature of Stalin's system of human exploitation, and also the fact that some camp health officials complained about and sought to mitigate its effects. Nonetheless, brutalizing Gulag exploitation intensified over time, and reached its apex in the late 1940s and early 1950s, the years of High Stalinism.

4   Illness and Mortality

"Lost Labor Days"

THE OGPU-NKVD-MVD did not routinely gather and maintain basic health information, such as prisoners' weight, body temperature, or blood pressure. The Gulag weighed prisoners or took their temperature only in a camp hospital that was lucky enough to have a thermometer or scale. "The orderlies lifted me off the scales," Varlam Shalamov wrote, "but their cold, powerful hands would not let me touch the ground. 'How much?' the doctor shouted, dipping his pen into the ink-well with a click. 'One hundred and six pounds.' They put me on the stretcher. My height was six feet, and my normal weight was 177 pounds. Bones constitute forty-two percent of a man's total weight, seventy-four pounds in my case. On that icy evening I had only thirty-two pounds of skin, organs, and brain. I was unable to make this calculation at the time, but I vaguely realized that the doctor peering at me from under his eyebrows was doing precisely that."[1] Shalamov's doctor made that calculation, but the Gulag's medical establishment routinely did not.

The task of the Gulag medical-sanitation department was not necessarily to keep prisoners healthy, but to maximize exploitation and minimize "labor losses." The Gulag routinely reported health data under the heading "illness and lost labor" (*zabolevaemost' i trudopoteri*). From the 1930s to the 1950s, Gulag internal data concerning prisoners' medical visits, hospitalizations, illnesses, and deaths concluded with a column on the far right: "total loss of labor days." Inmate health was only relevant as it impacted production.

The Stalinist leadership established quotas on illnesses and deaths, and would not tolerate large numbers of non-working prisoners. Severely weakened non-hospitalized inmates had to find a camp job, for only through work would they be fed. The Stalinist leadership called this "labor therapy," and believed in work as the key to convalescence. Although sickness, emaciation, and disability were widespread, Gulag officials concealed their existence. They minimized the appearance of mass starvation in the camps by artificially maintaining rates of illness within quota and skillfully misclassifying vitamin deficiency diseases. Camp officials also obscured widespread emaciation and disease (and reduced the burden on hospitals) by classifying sick prisoners as willful shirkers. Many prisoners deliberately harmed themselves in order to put an end to the exploitation, but they were treated harshly, as self-mutilation constituted the destruction of state property or an act of sabotage. In the Gulag, illness was widespread, yet it remained largely untreated, concealed, and even criminalized.

DOCTORS, SHORTAGES, AND DIFFERENTIATION

In the memoir literature, one encounters a generally positive portrayal of camp doctors, nurses, and medical assistants. This perspective may be partly explained by the fact that many of the most noted Gulag memoirists worked within the camp medical establishment— Eugenia Ginzburg, Varlam Shalamov, Alexander Dolgun, Gustaw Herling, Joseph Scholmer, and Janusz Bardach, to name just a few. One former prisoner and doctor stated, "The doctor and his assistant in the camps are, if not gods, then demi-gods. Upon them hangs the possibility of a few days' freedom from killing work."[2] Shalamov claimed that, "the convict's only defender in any real sense was the camp doctor."[3] Solzhenitsyn rejected such benign characterizations of camp medicine, and asked: "Was there ever a time when the Medical Section excused from work all the prisoners genuinely ill on a given day? Or when it didn't drive a given number of seriously ill people out of the camp compound to work?"[4] Indeed, camp doctors functioned within a highly constrained medical environment. Many were themselves prisoners, and since work in the infirmary spared them from felling timber or mining gold, they were likely to obey orders to keep the maximum number of prisoners working. Few would have wanted to risk losing their life-saving positions in a clinic or hospital. The Gulag medical staff did not necessarily have to keep prisoners healthy, only to maintain the required statistics on illness and mortality. Most of all, they were tasked with supporting the system of exploitation by keeping prisoners in heavy physical labor.

The number of doctors, nurses, medical assistants, dentists, pharmacists, and even hospital beds varied according to the size of the camp. On August 29, 1933, the Gulag established firm target figures for medical workers at each of the major camps.[5] Camps had to establish medical facilities, enable the transport of sick prisoners to hospitals, make pharmacies and dentists available, and recruit trained medical staff from among the prison population. Prisoners often had mixed feelings about the camp doctors. On the one hand, doctors could release an inmate from heavy physical labor. On the other hand, they represented camp officialdom, whose goal was to maintain the maximum exploitation of prisoners. Many lacked formal medical training, and camps hastily trained prisoners and non-specialists for jobs as nurses and medical assistants.[6] In May 1934, the Gulag newspaper, *Perekovka*, published a letter from prisoner Gelberg in which he described his experience at the camp infirmary: "They fed me delicious food, and treated my condition carefully and attentively. I recovered in five days and I rested wonderfully too. I just had to write to *Perekovka* about this. Only malingerers and evil rumor-mongers could accuse our infirmary of treating sick prisoners poorly. Don't believe them!"[7] Although the Gulag used this scripted testimony to praise its clinics, the fact that it was published suggests that many prisoners did not view camp medicine favorably.

Nonetheless, prisoners overwhelmed the Gulag's medical facilities, when healthcare was available. In the early 1930s, over 40 percent of all prisoners spent nearly three weeks in the hospital, but many prisoners did not receive any medical attention or care at all.[8] In 1935–1936, several camps reported an average of two to three visits to a health facility per inmate in any given month.[9] At the same time, the Stalinist leadership sharply limited the health care available to prisoners. In 1939, there were enough hospital beds for only 3 percent of the camp population and 2 percent of inmates in prisons and colonies.[10] In the first half of 1940, Bamlag was granted enough hospital beds for only 3.34 percent of its inmate population.[11] In the first quarter of 1948, medical-sanitation department workers had over 12.5 million visits throughout the entire Gulag system (camps, colonies, main administrations), of which over three million were by first-time patients.[12] In that same time period, visits to a medical-sanitation department outpatient facility averaged nearly six times per Gulag prisoner, and roughly half of all prisoners were registered as sick.[13] These figures represent official Gulag data.

In the late 1930s, shortages of doctors became especially acute, with a large influx of prisoners as a result of the Great Terror and a corresponding increase in sick prisoners. NKVD camps, prisons, and colonies experienced what Gulag chief Izrail Pliner characterized as a chronic shortage of camp medical personnel.[14] Camp doctors earned roughly a median civilian health department salary yet were burdened with a far greater caseload. Pliner told the deputy NKVD commissar that whereas the target had been one doctor for thirty-five prisoners, in some camps there was only one doctor for up to 200 hospital patients. Not surprisingly, the NKVD had a problem with widespread labor turnover among the civilian medical staff throughout the penitentiary system. Pliner asked his bosses to approve a 20 percent increase in salaries for healthcare personnel, but he was careful not to request additional funds. The Gulag system, after all, was supposed to be self-supporting. Mindful of this fact, Pliner informed the deputy NKVD commissar that he would initiate the salary increase while not exceeding the budgetary allowances for salaries.[15] Apparently, his strategy involved reducing the number of civilian doctors but increasing their salary, while relying more on prisoners to staff clinics and hospitals. As civilian medical specialists proved hard to retain, the Gulag came to rely more on prisoners to staff camp hospitals and clinics.

The Gulag tried various ways to remedy the shortages. It recruited prisoners with medical training. It also worked through the civilian health care institutions to attract newly trained doctors and nurses. In 1937–1938, the camps tried to remedy the severe shortage in medical personnel (doctors, nurses, pharmacists, dentists, medical assistants) by placing ads in local papers and medical journals. To maintain the secrecy of the camps, the civilian health department served as the proxy that placed the ads and fielded the responses.[16] The Gulag maintained a list of prisoners with medical training, and often prohibited their use in non-medical jobs. Gulag authorities routinely moved highly qualified doctors into the priority camps, rather than allow them to remain "in the least important places."[17] Administrators at low-priority camps often felt resentful at having to give up their doctors. After the war, one health official from Irkutsk complained that the Gulag leadership was constantly sending telegrams asking his camps to supply medical specialists, when it knew they had a shortage of cadres—just eight civilian and twelve prisoner doctors for 8100 inmates dispersed over a large territory. He refused to respond to more of these directives: "We sent out as many [doctors] as we could. We cannot lose any more."[18]

The living conditions for prisoner doctors varied, depending on the status of the camp. Consistent with the Gulag's hierarchy, the priority camps were able to pay civilian doctors more and provide better living conditions, and their medical facilities were much better equipped. In April 1938, the Gulag stated that higher salaries were supposed to go to medical personnel working in more distant camps; those in camps of the Irkutsk region and the Far East had 20 percent added to the base salary, and medical staff working in the Norilsk camp received 50 percent more salary.[19] As a doctor, Antoni Ekart lived better than the other prisoners. At the Pechorlag hospital after the war, he "belonged to the elite of the camp. My room was cleaned by the hospital attendants, who also brought my food, cleaned my shoes, and washed my linens."[20] For prisoners with skills in high demand, survival and even upward mobility became a real possibility. E.I. Kharechko, a medical researcher at the Soviet Institute for Experimental Medicine in Leningrad, was arrested on a political charge in 1936 and given a five-year sentence. After grueling general work in the Northern camps, he became too weak to do more than assemble coffins for dead prisoners and repair locks. A fellow prisoner and doctor learned of Kharechko's medical training, nursed him back to health, and took him on as a medical-sanitation inspector. Eventually, Kharechko became director of a camp medical-sanitation department after completing his sentence during the war, and deputy director of a new camp hospital in the postwar years.[21]

Camp physicians often lacked training and acquired medical knowledge on the job. One prisoner doctor described how his surgical training involved "three practice appendectomies on cadavers."[22] Many learned about human anatomy by performing autopsies. One medical-sanitation department director stressed that the knowledge and training of his doctors had been greatly improved by "regular conferences for doctors and medical personnel" as well as "mandatory autopsies of all the dead."[23] By the 1940s, autopsies of all the dead and scientific scrutiny of severely ill prisoners had become routine throughout the Gulag system. In his reminiscences, a former Gulag prisoner and medical assistant in the camps wrote that, in addition to administering medicines and treatments to patients, his tasks included performing autopsies of the dead. He recalled, "There was an order that all dead prisoners had to be autopsied. This introduced an unexpected difficulty, for in the winter the corpses quickly froze and became hard. I would place bodies near a well-heated stove in the corner of the room. The corpses would thaw and fall on the floor, and I would immediately begin opening them up, without gloves—at that time, we had enough formaldehyde."[24]

PRACTICING MEDICINE: RISKS, DANGERS, AND INHUMANITY

Jobs in the camp health service were highly coveted because prisoners preferred to work in a hospital or clinic rather than do exhaustive heavy physical labor. As one former prisoner doctor explained, "who wouldn't rather work with thermometers and pills than with shovels and wheelbarrows?"[25] In 1934, Gulag chief Matvei Berman stated that prisoners on the medical staff experience "no doubt better conditions than the majority of other prisoners," so these highly coveted jobs should be reserved for those who are well trained and politically loyal. He described the case of one prisoner who had a long stint as a doctor in the camps but was exposed as a quack.[26] In the 1930s, camp regulations barred political prisoners from the most coveted indoor jobs, including those in health care. For example, Yagoda's mother-in-law, an experienced pediatrician, was prohibited from working as a doctor in the camp.[27] Yet camps routinely violated this rule, and it was abandoned in later years because many political prisoners were doctors, scientists, engineers, and other specialists with desirable skills. Working in a clinic was certainly easier than laying tracks in Arctic temperatures, but the job was not without risk. Doctors were held personally responsible for their medical decisions. Following the medical examination, the name of the doctor whose assessment was responsible for a prisoner's physical labor classification had to be noted on all medical-labor commission protocols of inspection, next to the name of the prisoner.[28]

Doctors were under pressure to keep prisoners working. Ekart described going to the camp hospital when he felt on the verge of death: "The doctor looked at me, pinched my flesh, and said: 'Too early. If people like you are admitted to hospital, then nobody will be left to do the work.' I tried to explain that in my present state I was of no use to the camp, and that I had no strength left even to march to my task, let alone do it. He seemed to believe what I said, but assured me that he could do nothing. He continued: 'It does not depend on me; I have my instructions and I am responsible for seeing that they are carried out. I am a prisoner, just as you are.'"[29] Thus many doctors diligently served the system of exploitation. They executed their primary task of maximizing workers, and did not necessarily represent humane counterweights to a brutal system. Gulag survivor Eugenia Ginzburg believed that "it was harder for doctors than for anyone else to keep a clear conscience and avoid selling for a mess of pottage the lives of thousands of their comrades."[30]

Medical personnel were vulnerable to various forms of criticism from Gulag bosses. They were accused of not doing enough to extend prisoners' work life, going too easy on prisoners and letting them miss work, being gullible in the face of inmates' fakery, not hospitalizing sick prisoners in a timely manner, and incorrectly placing prisoners in a lighter labor category. One camp supervisor entered the infirmary and yelled at a prisoner doctor: "What is this—a sanitarium, a health resort? Eighteen sick leaves in one day! Some medic! So scared he unloads in his pants and signs sick leaves for every faker in sight. Or maybe they grease your palm, eh? You want to be sent to the pit yourself or have your sentence extended?"[31] Health officials were blamed for illnesses and deaths, and they were vulnerable to accusations of sabotage. One medical-sanitation department director described how two of her doctors had been arrested and accused of confusing pellagra, dysentery, and gastrointestinal disorders. Eager to avoid blame for health problems at the camp, she scapegoated the arrested doctors, and told her boss that the misdiagnosis of the censured doctors was "the main reason for the high mortality rates."[32] The Gulag leadership was quick to blame camp administrators for epidemics and high mortality, and these officials in turn blamed the prisoners who worked as health care providers. In April 1941, a group of doctors at the Oneglag camp was accused of committing sabotage, and blamed for contributing to the high mortality rate and epidemics of influenza, pneumonia, and typhus at the camp. This case attracted the attention of the Gulag leadership because the camp's massive typhus epidemic passed beyond the barbed wire and affected the civilian population nearby.[33] During the war, when mortality rates soared at Karlag, the camp director blamed his medical-sanitation department chief, charging him with "using narcotics with prisoners."[34]

The job of a medical-sanitation department worker in the camps was far from ideal, especially for non-prisoners. Civilian doctors wrote letters to the central Gulag administration complaining about poor living and work conditions, problems with remuneration, lack of uniforms, frequent transfers from one camp section to another, interruptions in the supply of firewood and other necessities, and the failure to receive transportation when they attended to sick prisoners in different camp locations.[35] Civilian medical personnel were often treated poorly—insulted, mocked, and abused by prisoners. Many lived in silent fear of persecution.[36] The deputy head of the NKVD, Chernyshev, described this "intolerable situation" in a memo to all camps.[37] Letters from young medical workers had detailed their difficult work and life conditions. One prisoner poured boiling water over a doctor's head; others stabbed a medical-sanitation department director in the chest and stabbed a doctor through the arm. Another doctor had carbolic acid poured over her by a prisoner. Although hospital staff largely lived in barracks that were slightly better than the overcrowded quarters for prisoners on general work, some medical workers were eating from the same cauldron as the prisoners and sleeping in the same barracks. A number even attempted suicide. They were scorned and derided by other camp officials. With knife in hand, prisoners would threaten doctors to give them drugs or to free them from work.[38] Solzhenitsyn told the story of his own camp physician who lived in fear and with a guilty conscience, and was eventually murdered "with a plasterer's mallet while he still slept."[39]

Despite the risks, prisoners viewed jobs within the camp medical establishment as tickets to survival. Antoni Ekart worked in a camp hospital in Kotlas during the war, and wrote, "The only hope of saving my life, without risking the disfavor of the NKVD, was to extend my knowledge of medicine, for there would always be work for a medical assistant in any camp."[40] To that end, he worked hard to acquire medical textbooks and further his education: "I used to go to the dissecting room where dead bodies were examined almost every day and sometimes dissected. (This was done by order of the senior physician whenever there was a doubt as to the cause of death. The doctor who had treated the patient was present, with the uneasy feeling that if he had made a mistake he would be put in the kartser, sent back to general work, or even sent to the Northern camps.)"[41] Camp authorities increasingly relied on prisoners like Ekart to be camp doctors and medical researchers.

ILLNESS, DISEASE, AND MASS STARVATION

Prisoners not only grew sick in the camps, but they often arrived already severely weakened. Many had endured months in prisons, and experienced lengthy journeys on overcrowded railcars and boats to their distant camps. In transport, inmates received little food and water, and epidemics of typhus and dysentery were common. Once they arrived at their destination, detainees were housed in overcrowded barracks, if proper barracks existed, and many slept in tents or temporary structures near construction sites. At one of the better-supplied camps, the prisoners slept on solid plank beds (*sploshnye nary*).[42] Inadequate food, housing, clothing, medical care, and other basic life necessities, as well as hazardous work conditions, made prisoners vulnerable to disability, food- and water-borne illnesses, diseases and epidemics. Illnesses raged in the Gulag, including scurvy, cholera, tuberculosis, and pellagra. The strenuous physical labor, harsh living conditions, and insufficient food and medical attention made prisoners especially vulnerable to illness and disease.

Vitamin deficiency represented prisoners' most fundamental, underlying ailment. As noted in an earlier chapter, camp food rations were severely inadequate in both quantity and quality, and this deficient diet produced widespread illness. Prisoners received very little fat, which they would have needed to properly absorb the fat-soluble vitamins, such as A, D, K, and E. They subsisted largely on bread of little nutritional value. Malnourished prisoners suffered from various diseases: pellagra from a lack of niacin or vitamin B3, scurvy caused by vitamin C deficiency, beriberi from thiamine or B1 deficiency, rickets due to vitamin D deficiency, night blindness from lack of vitamin A, and goiter from iodine deficiency. As historian Oleg Khlevniuk explains, the "exploitation of prisoners was constantly on the rise due to high production plans," resulting in "the physical exhaustion of prisoners, the spread of disease, and high mortality. Typhus, tuberculosis, and scurvy became normal for camp dwellers."[43] Memoirists catalogued various illnesses as well. Varlam Shalamov described his frequent bouts of frostbite and his "legs that were festering with scurvy sores."[44] Another Gulag survivor recounted the effects of malnutrition: "Literally within several months of logging, I had acute signs of vitamin deficiency, and a few months after that, the obvious indicator of camp life—scurvy. We grew thin, our muscles sagged and our legs became swollen. Some of our teeth loosened and then fell out. I suffered from diarrhea, inflammation, and increasingly intolerable skin irritation. Black spots appeared first on my legs and then spread."[45] Prisoners got frostbite on their feet because of inadequate boots, or on their wrists where skin was exposed between their gloves and jackets. Severely weakened prisoners with diarrhea got frostbite on their scrotum from frequently squatting at the toilet in temperatures of minus 30–40 degrees Fahrenheit.[46]

According to a Gulag survivor and camp medical assistant, Bela Irani, prisoners were "tortured by starvation." Many had scurvy and night blindness, as well as pneumonia, heart disease, and intestinal disorders. Health care workers rarely had access to antibiotics, so they relied on primitive treatments—baths, lotions, herbal remedies, and vitamin supplements such as vitamin A from fish oil, and vitamin C in the form of ascorbic acid. Prisoners with tuberculosis were transferred to the central city hospital because the camp had no laboratory or x-ray machine. Irani detailed how heavy physical labor quickly transformed inmates into dystrophy patients (distrofiki). The Latin term, distrophia alimentaris, refers to "pathological changes in the body that are the result of starvation." In the last stages of the disease, "the pelvic muscles and hips hang over the bones and inhibit walking." Irani catalogued the effects of the persistent lack of adequate food: "First the body uses up its own reserves of fats and carbohydrates, and then proteins. The normal functions of the body's internal organs are progressively destroyed, producing digestive disorders and tumors, and even damaging the person's central nervous system . . . A person who is tortured by starvation simply wants to sleep, for all his sensations and feelings have been snuffed out. He is governed only by apathy and indifference . . . In the end, for the dying person, nothing matters, and he quietly and imperceptibly leaves this world."[47]

Survivor testimonies confirm that prisoners were, indeed, tortured by starvation. According to one account from Vorkuta, "Scurvy, pellagra, and nutritional dystrophy mercilessly mowed down prisoners. Given the constant malnutrition, the body ate away at itself . . . The person became a skeleton with dark, dry skin, and covered with sores."[48] Doctors who examined such prisoners, turning to the prisoner's back and pulling down his pants, would say crudely, "The ass knows" (*anus znaet*). That is, "There were no buttocks. The torso rested on two sticks. Our doctors typically wrote the diagnosis using only letter codes—three *d*'s plus *p*—which signified nutritional dystrophy, diarrhea, dementia (memory loss) and pellagra."[49] Pellagra, a disease of malnutrition and starvation, was one of the main killers of Gulag prisoners. Anatoly Chernusov, a party member in Leningrad, died of pellagra in October 1944 in a camp in the Arkhangelsk region, at the age of 39. His wife managed to acquire a formal death certificate for her husband only in 1947.[50] A Gulag prisoner and doctor described the horror of attending to pellagra patients. They all looked alike: "In place of eyes, they had cavities or depressions, their faces gaunt and wrinkled, their cheeks sunken, and instead of a stomach—a pit. Across their whole body, but especially on their arms and legs, the skin sagged from the bones, as if there was no meat on them at all."[51]

In the Komi republic, where prisoners worked in Arctic temperatures to extract coal and oil, Iakov Zultan was diagnosed with pellagra and tuberculosis. The prisoner wrote many letters to his daughter, including one from the camp infirmary in May 1943, where he told her: "I have grown very thin and weak because of my illness. My legs are skinny and it's hard to walk." In another letter, he told her never to lose hope, and gave her fatherly counsel: "Most of all, be a *human being* in the deepest sense. I wish you health and happiness. I send you a big, big kiss and hug you close to my lonely heart." The camp nurse was clearly moved by Iakov's love for his daughter, and wrote a letter to her when he died, four months after he was first admitted to the infirmary. Signing the letter simply "nurse," she enclosed the daughter's photograph that the prisoner always kept with him, and wrote: "The nurse is writing to you with sad and very shocking news, but I have decided to inform you that your father, Zultan Iakov Davidovich, died in the infirmary sick with severe diarrhea. Despite all our efforts and care and every good intention, we were unable to revive him. He died at six o'clock in the morning on June 29th. You won't be able to see him, so honor his memory. I'm sending you the photograph that was with him . . . He missed you greatly. He wanted to see you. Don't despair. Goodbye."[52] The nurse was careful not to mention Zultan's diagnosis of pellagra, but suggested that it was best that the daughter did not see her emaciated father in his final days. The case of prisoner Zultan reveals that genuine human connections did occur in the camps. The nurse's courageous effort to introduce normalcy and humanity, in notifying family about the death of a loved one, challenged the anonymity of death in the Gulag.

In addition to vitamin deficiency diseases such as scurvy and pellagra, many prisoners contracted tuberculosis. Medical-sanitation department officials asserted that "tuberculosis is the greatest scourge in the work of our camp divisions," and that three-quarters of all deaths were attributed to tuberculosis.[53] The medical-sanitation department director for the Norosibirsk regional camps and colonies told the Gulag medical-sanitation department chief, D.M. Loidin, in 1945 that despite their best efforts, deaths from tuberculosis remained high—42 percent of all deaths in March and 73.2 percent of all deaths in July. They were using x-ray machines to diagnose early, testing the saliva of patients suspected of having tuberculosis, and inviting specialists to regularly meet with camp doctors and patients. Nonetheless, their tuberculosis cases continued to increase.[54] Camp doctors sometimes refused to be trained to treat tuberculosis patients, fearing that they might be infected themselves.[55] According to the Gulag medical-sanitation department chief, tuberculosis represented the second most deadly illness in the camps during the war, and it was "closely linked to vitamin deficiency."[56] Emaciated prisoners were particularly susceptible to infectious diseases.

Camps often lacked proper water and sewage facilities, so bacterial infections were widespread. Across the Gulag system, camps lacked quality drinking water, effective sewage disposal, and toilets. Toilets consisted of buckets or pails, or outhouses, and even, according to one prisoner's account, "the pole with a white rag tied to the top."[57] In the Molotov regional system of labor camps and colonies, the inadequate disposal of human waste produced what one official called "fecal burial sites within the zone" that resulted in bacterial infections and gastrointestinal illnesses.[58] Other illnesses common to camp life included typhus and pneumonia. In 1929–1930, the Solovetsky camps recorded 25,552 cases of typhus.[59] After the war, roughly a third of hospital patients were dying from pneumonia in many camps.[60] Camp officials pleaded for assistance from central Gulag authorities in order to stave off major epidemics. They wanted disinfecting agents, extra linens, razors to cut hair, drugs, and herbal medicines, as well as x-ray machines.[61] In 1945, one camp official told his Gulag boss: "Without a better supply of medicines, I don't know how we can improve health care."[62] Those who managed illnesses on the ground complained about the lack of support from the Gulag leadership and from local hospitals and clinics. In Omsk, there were many cases of malaria, particularly in camp divisions surrounded by lakes, yet malaria specialists at the local civilian hospital offered no assistance.[63]

The Gulag leadership urged camps and colonies to approach state health institutions for medical advice and training, but not for resources. Some camp officials described useful collaboration with state health departments. In the Molotov region, camps invited civilian doctors to give lectures on tuberculosis, and the Soviet health department helped the camp to x-ray many prisoners and examine their saliva for tuberculosis.[64] The Altai regional system of labor camps and colonies received certain drugs through the civilian pharmacy and paid local doctors to examine camp prisoners.[65] But other camps received no help from state health authorities. In the Yakut autonomous republic, the People's Commissariat of Health issued a wartime order to confiscate drugs and medical supplies from the camps and colonies, which left prisoners with nothing, according to Yakut camp officials.[66] In 1945, many medical-sanitation department officials complained that Gulag authorities, as well as state health institutions, refused to supply camps with necessary drugs, bandages, and medicine containers.[67] The chief of the Gulag medical-sanitation department, Loidin, showed little sympathy for such complaints. When one camp health official stressed that her staff needed sulfur to combat bedbugs, Loidin replied angrily: "There won't be any sulfur and there shouldn't be any bedbugs."[68] When she complained that there was only one x-ray machine in the regional hospital, he responded: "You're not getting another one."[69] The Gulag leadership wanted camps to solve their own problems, and not expect recourses from central Gulag agencies or state health departments. Loidin criticized the directors of camp medical-sanitation departments who described acquiring medicine from their local health departments, and cynically insisted that camps had always been adequately supplied with medicine, even during the war. "So when I hear you say that you're doing well with medicine because you get supplies both from the Gulag and also from the state pharmacy, I don't agree with it. I'm against your taking medicine from the state pharmacy. This corrupts you, and discourages you from saving a kopek. It depletes the Health Ministry's fund for medicines, and adds to your own funds which are already entirely sufficient."[70]

The party leadership expected the OGPU-NKVD-MVD to maintain low mortality rates in the camps, and used high rates of illness and mortality to punish camp officials for failing to maintain state capital. Camp authorities were held personally responsible for perceived failures, whether high mortality, epidemics, or wrongful medical releases.[71] Especially during the war years, the Gulag leadership repeatedly ordered camp officials to improve the health of prisoners, and often meted out punishments, especially when camp epidemics threatened neighboring civilian populations.[72] A 1942 NKVD directive argued that prisoners must sleep no fewer than eight hours per night because sleep-deprived inmates worked poorly and thus fell into the category of "weakened prisoners, invalids, etc."[73] A 1943 NKVD order required that prisoners get three rest days per month, eight hours of sleep, three meals per day, two square meters of living space, an individual bunk bed, timely medical care and hospitalization, plus a shortened work day when the temperatures were extremely cold and prisoners had a long walk to the worksite.[74] High-level orders to improve the treatment of camp inmates appear to reflect a rational calculation on the part of the Stalinist leadership to preserve capital. Yet such directives must be viewed within the larger Gulag context, which starved and criminalized prisoners for underperformance.

THE CRIMINALIZATION OF ILLNESS

The Stalinist labor camp system distorted medical practice and turned doctors into policemen, a Soviet practice that continued after Stalin when political dissidence became medicalized.[75] Gulag officials spoke extensively about the crimes of false illness, such as self-mutilation (*chlenovreditsel'stvo*) and malingering (*simuliatsiia*). As a result, the sick prisoner and the shirker often became indistinguishable. In 1931, the OGPU stressed that medical-labor commissions "must always consider the possibility of simulation or aggravation, that is, symptoms of illness that have been artificially provoked," and warned that such prisoners would be subjected to "harsh punishments."[76] Doctors had to be medical skeptics. Health officials and prisoners alike recall the harsh punishments, including additional sentences, meted out to prisoners suspected of injuring themselves.[77] Doctors perceived as lenient in releasing prisoners from work were also punished severely. In 1934, Berman alerted his subordinates that a doctor-prisoner at Bamlag had been executed after being accused of making false assessments in medical examinations so that prisoners could be released as invalids.[78] Like all Gulag bosses, Berman maintained a deep suspicion of ailing prisoners, viewing them as possible saboteurs, and warned that prisoners were using "fictitious illnesses" to get out of work or to secure release as invalids. Even during the severe famine of the early 1930s, he insisted that prisoners who were poisoned after eating wild plants and garbage from the dump could have been motivated not by hunger but by a desire to make themselves sick and avoid work.[79]

To the Stalinist leadership, the bodies of prisoners constituted state property. If there is one piece of evidence to suggest a comparison between slavery and the Gulag, it was this. Prisoners did not own their bodies. According to Jacques Rossi, a person who feigned illness was considered a criminal, and placed in the penalty isolator as a wrecker or someone who damaged state property. Rossi described the many ways prisoners tried to deceive doctors or manufacture illness, for example: "drinking an infusion of tobacco, which causes intensified heartbeat"; "burning the head of the penis or the labia with a cigarette. The resultant wounds are very similar to the symptoms of syphilis, which rules out dispatching the individual to remote camps"; grinding an indelible pencil up into a powder and putting it beneath the eyelids, causing eye infection"; "exposing the fingers or toes to the frost in wintertime. Depending on the severity of the frostbite, it is possible to cadge a couple of days off or, in the event several fingers or toes must be amputated, it is possible to be transferred to the "light work" category"; "ingesting accessible objects such as aluminum spoons and the like to get into the prison hospital, where the food and living conditions are better."[80] Prisoners would drink soapy water or smear dirt, salt, and feces on open wounds. Many prisoners harmed themselves in order to be removed from heavy physical labor or to obtain early release as invalids.[81] Solzhenitsyn expressed empathy for such prisoners, but warned that "you had to be careful not to overdo, hurting yourself so badly that you leapfrogged invalidism into the grave."[82]

The fact that so many prisoners resorted to self-mutilation only testifies to the severity of physical exploitation in the Stalinist camps. In a 1935 case from Dmitlag, several prisoners, largely petty criminal offenders, were accused of self-mutilation. Almost all had been classified as fit for heavy physical labor, but they grew sick, failed to meet production norms, and consequently received little food. Camp officials refused the ailing prisoners work releases. Thus the inmates committed desperate acts, such as using axes and knives to chop off their own fingers, feet, and hands. One of the prisoners testified: "I went to the doctor, but they would not release me from work, so I decided to chop off my foot with a knife I found in the barracks." Another explained: "I was completely exhausted because they were giving me little bread, given my output. So I could not fulfill my production norm. I decided to cut off my own hand so that I would be placed among the weak to whom they give more bread."[83] Memoirists expressed compassion for such desperate prisoners who tried to preserve their lives. According to Solzhenitsyn, self-mutilation constituted "an act indicating love of life—a straightforward calculation of sacrificing a portion to save the whole."[84] Their fellow prisoners may have sympathized, but these inmates elicited no mercy from camp officials.

Gulag authorities routinely suspected prisoners of lying about their ill health. In 1939, the Gulag leadership instructed directors of all camps and colonies to aggressively combat prisoners' attempts to mutilate themselves and artificially induce illness or delay recovery. Not a single instance should go unpunished; perpetrators as well as their instigators and accomplices should be brought to justice; all cases should be recorded and documented; medical workers (whether free laborers or prisoners) must be protected against threats and violence if they refuse to release someone from work.[85] Accompanying the directive was a listing of the most common tactics: artificially provoking the symptoms of heart trouble or kidney malfunction; faking gastrointestinal illness or colitis; artificially infecting or irritating a wound; artificially raising one's body temperature, lowering one's blood pressure, or provoking weakness; simulating venereal disease, epilepsy, blindness, and other disorders; delaying one's recovery by not adhering to the prescriptions of the medical staff. The most common methods of self-mutilation included cutting off fingers and extremities, provoking gangrene of the extremities, and chemically burning the skin.[86] For Stalinist leaders, any illness could be construed as an act of sabotage. Many genuinely sick prisoners were accused of fakery. One Gulag physician was remembered fondly for exonerating a prisoner with pellagra who had been suspected of self-mutilation.[87]

Self-mutilation and refusing to work were considered, in the eyes of the Stalinist leadership, especially serious state crimes. Beria condemned wartime unrest among Chechen special settlers who had been deported by Stalin in 1944, calling them, among other things, "shirkers and malingerers."[88] Reproducing the common trope of the Soviet state enemy as pretender, camp authorities were often quick to accuse sick and weakened Gulag inmates of sabotage or refusing to work.[89] In a May 1947 report, Gulag leaders catalogued various forms of antigovernmental activities that had been discovered in the camps, including plans for armed uprisings and escapes, and theft of socialist property.[90] This very menacing list of threats to camp order and discipline included "systematic refusal to work." The report profiled three cases under the heading "the struggle against criminality," and all involved the charge that prisoners refused to work. Gulag officials characterized these prisoners as groups of "saboteurs" and "bandits" who came up with various schemes to induce illness. In one case, a group of "counter-revolutionary saboteurs" used syringes to insert milk and saliva under their skin in order to generate "fake illness."[91] To the Gulag leadership, simulation constituted one of the worst state offenses, no less serious than armed uprisings, planned escapes, and theft of socialist property. As one camp doctor noted, "the authorities severely punished those prisoners who injured themselves."[92]

The Gulag leadership was obsessed with self-mutilation and fakery. Camp doctors warned medical-sanitation department workers to be vigilant against prisoners who harmed themselves or pretended to be ill. In 1948, prisoner-doctor K.P. Bogolepov produced a clinical report entitled, "A Description of the Methods of Self-Mutilation among the Criminal Underworld."[93] Bogolepov, who had to speak the language of his captors, strongly condemned prisoners who injured themselves, calling them members of the "criminal underworld." He stated that his purpose in writing was to share his experiences and observations with other medical workers so that they would not make the same mistakes that he did in his first years as a Gulag doctor. When a doctor realizes that he failed to recognize self-mutilation and malingering, wrote Bogolepov, "that awareness gives rise to self-flagellation," a sense that one has failed to do his work, that these scoundrels have taken advantage of you and abused your trust, and "they consider you a stupid simpleton and in some cases even a coward."[94] Bogolepov believed it was easy for prisoners to find ways to harm themselves or to fake an illness, using items that were readily available to them in the camps. He reproduced the assertions of the Gulag leadership that acts like self-mutilation and the feigning of illness wasted resources and capital, and harmed other inmates. Bogolepov claimed that a larger pool of sick and disabled prisoners effectively reduced the number of additional rations that would be available for the brigade, which in turn worsened everyone's physical condition.[95] Self-mutilation, the doctor asserted, should be viewed as a social evil, and such cases should be reported in the camp newspapers.

Bogolepov's report reveals how Gulag doctors were being forced to think about simulation. According to Bogolepov, "every incorrect work exemption for a scoundrel reduces the labor productivity of the entire collective, disrupts the fulfillment of production tasks, leads to lower food rations for all honest workers, infringes upon those who are truly sick and need rest, and serves as a bad example for the slackers who seek to avoid work."[96] He asserted that "the job of a medical-sanitation department worker in the camps is very important" because "preservation of the labor force is crucial for the country, especially in this period of reconstruction following the devastation of German fascism's rapacious attack on the country."[97] He concluded by asserting that the idler or slacker needs to abandon the goal "work less, but eat more."[98] Doctors remained under pressure to see self-mutilation even where it did not exist, for medical care could be denied to malingerers. As one survivor recalled, Gulag prisoners landed multiple times in either the hospital or the penalty isolator.[99] A prisoner at Ustvymlag insisted that he was too sick to work, yet, according to an investigation of his case, "The medical workers paid no attention to his protest, and he was sent to work. Not being in a condition to work, he refused to work, for which he was shut up in the punishment cell. There he was kept for four days, after which he was taken in very poor condition to the hospital, where he died."[100] At one camp in 1940, the overflow of sick prisoners was left to lie outside the hospital door. Thus camp administrators could give them reduced rations as "shirkers" rather than register them as hospital patients, where they would be fed a hospital ration.[101] In the Gulag, emaciated inmates were often classified as self-mutilators and work-refusers.

PHYSICAL EXPLOITATION AS "LABOR THERAPY"

Alexander Solzhenitsyn's fictional character, Ivan Denisovich, described one of the camp doctors as an accessory to the crime of working prisoners to death: "He'd had the bright idea of putting all the walking cases to work around the hospital, making fences and paths and carrying earth to the flowerbeds. And in the winter there was always snow to clear. He kept saying that work was the best cure for illness."[102] This constituted no fictitious scene. Solzhenitsyn was not portraying a quirky individual doctor, but rather referencing an official policy of Stalin's Gulag, which went by the name "labor therapy" (*trudovaia terapiia*). The OGPU-NKVD-MVD heavily promoted labor therapy and insisted that camp medical staff find work for ailing prisoners. In 1945, the Gulag medical-sanitation department chief touted the positive results of labor therapy, and stressed "the need for comprehensive development of labor therapy for hospital patients as well as groups of weakened contingents."[103] Labor therapy served the goal of maximum exploitation and minimal "lost labor days." It also enabled ailing prisoners to continue to earn rations through work.

Illness and disability challenged the most fundamental tenet of the Gulag—that only those who work shall eat. What about prisoners who were too sick or disabled to mine gold or fell timber, or those too weakened to meet production targets in heavy physical labor? If suspected of being fakers or willful work resisters, these prisoners could be dispatched to the camp prison or penalty isolator, where they would receive starvation rations. However, the Gulag's population of weakened prisoners was much too vast for camp prisons, and many classified invalids could not be released or discarded. The Stalinist leadership believed in total labor utilization or the maximum exploitation of the Gulag workforce. The Gulag medical chief stressed the importance of labor therapy for generating "material profit" and criticized his subordinates for insufficient "labor therapy measures."[104] Work for the sick was considered therapeutic and beneficial, as if to justify the thorough exploitation of prisoners. One camp director replied to a prisoner who asked why the sick were being marched out to work: "You don't cure scurvy with bed rest. Scurvy cases need as much movement as they can get."[105]

Sick and ailing prisoners had to work, however menial the task. Camp medical-sanitation department directors boasted of keeping weakened prisoners working and earning food.[106] Labor therapy enabled camp officials to improve the diet of feeble prisoners, since as working inmates they received more food. In 1945, one camp health official described how hospital patients had been put to work knitting in order to generate income to supplement their hospital rations: "We have two barracks where patients with [nutritional] dystrophy are concentrated. A knitting shop has been organized with no attention to output norms. In the course of a month, these patients earned 10–12 thousand rubles. All of this money went to buying additional food, which improved the quality of food in the hospital. Now, the work is suspended because there's no yarn, but they're promising that yarn will come and that patients will be doing this work once again."[107] Medical-sanitation departments lobbied for resources that would enable them to utilize weakened prisoners and improve their rations. At one camp, money generated through labor therapy went to the purchase of blood, which was used to fortify hospital food and strengthen sick prisoners.[108] For years, Soviet scientists had been investigating the therapeutic effects of blood transfusions from animals, other human beings, and even cadavers, and this research influenced camp medical practices.[109] Many weakened prisoners were put to work in subsistence agriculture.[110]

At the same time, medical-sanitation departments questioned whether their own bosses in the camps and even the Gulag leadership wanted to provide work and food to weakened prisoners. As one health director stated: "I agree with my colleagues who said that the camp leadership sometimes does not want to think about the complete utilization of the defective contingent."[111]

Prisoners were not supposed to be fed for lying around and doing nothing to generate income, at least not for very long. They had to be returned to work in short order. Labor therapy could appear as a form of medical treatment, as a way to give prisoners more food and improve their health. But there was a distinct cruelty in this policy as well, as in much of the Gulag's perverse health care system, where ailing prisoners could be criminalized for willful shirking or faking their illness, and where sickness threatened to produce "lost labor days." According to the medical-sanitation department director for the Chkalov regional camps and colonies, anyone alive should work: "If a person cannot work, that doesn't mean that he should lie around and occupy a [hospital] bed for 24 hours a day. We call it labor therapy when anyone who can move can work."[112]

THE MANY DECEPTIONS OF GULAG HEALTH STATISTICS

The Stalinist leadership concealed the mass starvation in the camps. The Gulag required that camps maintain certain quotas on illnesses, hospitalizations and mortality, in order to minimize "lost labor days." Camps made sure that their health data appeared favorable, that illnesses were low and hospitalizations brief. The resulting health data appears improbable and distorted, given what other sources reveal about "physical labor capability." For example, the Gulag medical-sanitation department chief boasted that the wartime data on pellagra and nutritional dystrophy was only about 2.7 percent of prisoners in 1944–1945, and that as a proportion of labor days lost, pellagra and nutritional dystrophy declined to 30 percent in 1945.[113] It appears highly unlikely, given the data on physical labor capability and the Gulag's feeding policy, that only a third of ailing prisoners suffered from nutritional disorders in the last year of the war, or that fewer than 3 percent of all prisoners experienced starvation disease. The Gulag leadership forced camps to meet exceptionally low quotas concerning lost labor days, and the camps largely reported what was required of them.

Moreover, the Stalinist leadership pressured camps to reduce hospitalizations, and to move prisoners quickly through the clinics. Gulag survivor Antoni Ekart described how the priority of the Pechorlag hospital after the war was to minimize the number of days that prisoners spent in the hospital. Ekart explained: "A doctor was now threatened with punishment unless he cured his patients within a fixed time. Competitions developed between the different sections, the goal being the highest possible number of discharged patients."[114] Gulag leaders used the unit "days in bed" to measure the length of time that prisoners were out of work, and pressured the camps to reduce this number. In 1948 the Gulag medical-sanitation department reported the average length of time that sick prisoners were out of work at 24 to 35 days throughout the entire Gulag system, and the longest hospital stays were reported in the Main Administrations for railroad construction (GULZhDS) and forestry (GULGPP).[115] Medical-sanitation department officials complained that it was the terminally ill who occupied their hospital beds. One confessed: "Our hospital patients are mainly those with tuberculosis and [nutritional] dystrophy, and they lie there for no less than a year."[116] Officials reduced hospitalization stays in various ways. They sent prisoners off to work before they had fully recovered, moved inmates from hospitals to convalescent facilities, and discharged severely ill prisoners from the camp.

The violence of the Stalinist camps was concealed in various ways, including strict quotas on illness, mortality, and hospitalizations, and the practice of classifying starving prisoners as shirkers and malingerers or as having only minor ailments. Gulag officials often recorded starvation illnesses as mild disorders. Nutritional deficiency produced a variety of symptoms, from skin ailments to digestive problems. Rather than report a large number of inmates with starvation diseases, the Gulag registered this enormous population of vitamin deficient prisoners under more benign headings. Starving prisoners were reclassified in order to create the appearance of a small population that suffered from nutritional deficiency diseases. During the war, the Gulag kept records on five categories of illness: pellagra and nutritional dystrophy, diseases of the skin and subcutaneous tissue, industrial accidents, gastrointestinal illnesses, and tuberculosis. Remarkably, diseases of the skin and subcutaneous tissue had more than three times the number of average monthly cases than the other four categories in 1944, and twice as many in 1945.[117] In 1948, the Gulag collected prisoners' health data for the following illnesses: nutritional dystrophy, skin disorders, gastrointestinal disorders, malaria, flu, pneumonia, tuberculosis, industrial accidents, and "illnesses of the circulatory organs." For the first quarter of 1948, the medical-sanitation department reported that only 2.9 percent of prisoners had nutritional dystrophy while as many as 21 percent had skin disorders.[118] Gulag officials deliberately concealed mass starvation in the camps by classifying starving inmates as dermatology patients.

Similarly, camp officials routinely characterized prisoners with acute vitamin deficiency diseases such as pellagra as suffering from skin or digestive ailments. Nutritional deficiency was in fact the underlying cause of various medical conditions, for starvation weakened the immune system. Starvation was manifested in various ways. This grim portrait of a female prisoner appears in Solzhenitsyn: "She has become ageless; her shoulders stick out at sharp angles, her breasts hang down in little dried-out sacs; superfluous folds of skin form wrinkles on her flat buttocks; there is so little flesh above her knees that a big enough gap has opened up for a sheep's head to stick through or even a soccer ball; her voice has become hoarse and rough and her face is tanned by pellagra."[119] This starving woman suffered from a series of ailments related to her underlying condition of nutritional dystrophy. Yet camp officials often classified people like her as suffering from skin disorders, and thereby concealed the reality of mass starvation in the camps.

CONCLUSION

In 1945, Gulag medical-sanitation department chief Loidin declared: "The urgent task of health care is to maintain a major capital base."[120] However, investment in maintaining this capital base remained exceptionally meager. Medical facilities in the camps and colonies suffered from chronic shortages of doctors, hospitals, medicines, and equipment. Although illness and death were widespread in the camps, to the Gulag they represented not problems of health but matters of production. Health care was instrumentalized and aimed at keeping prisoners working. The ultimate goal assigned to the camps was "maximum labor utilization" or a minimum of "lost labor days." Camp officials had to produce health statistics that were consistent with Gulag quotas or face the consequences. A culture of personal blame framed common sickness as shortcomings or errors of camp officials who failed to implement Gulag orders. Camps concealed the underlying causes of ailments, camouflaged mass starvation, criminalized the sick, and underreported illness and death. In his story about the typhoid quarantine, Varlam Shalamov exposed the Gulag's narrow productivist outlook that reduced human life to workdays: "Every day the camps lost twenty thousand workdays, one hundred and sixty thousand hours, perhaps even three hundred and twenty thousand hours; workdays vary. Or a thousand days of life were saved. Twenty thousand days of life."[121]

5 Invalids
"Inferior Workforce"

FOR OGPU-NKVD-MVD OFFICIALS, the *dokhodiagi* or goners represented a contingent that was useless or lacking value. Gulag officials referred to these severely ill and disabled prisoners as physically inferior (*fizicheski nepolnotsennye*), the defective labor force (*nepolnotsennye rabsily*), and the not-work-capable elements (*netrudosposobnye elementy*). They were unable to do the camp's basic work, which involved heavy physical labor in such sectors as construction, mining, and forestry. The so-called inferior workforce included both prisoners classified as invalids and those assigned to light labor. This segment of the Gulag labor force represented an enormous population of prisoners, and it grew significantly over the Stalin years. Prisoners whose health placed them in the "light labor" or "invalid" categories of physical labor capability constituted roughly 30 percent of prisoners in 1930, 40 percent in 1940, and a stunning 60 percent of inmates in 1947. Even more sobering is the fact that such figures are likely understated, given that camps were reprimanded for reporting high numbers of weakened prisoners.[1] The archives reveal that the *dokhodiagi* in many ways symbolized the Stalinist Gulag.

An ailing and disabled workforce could hardly meet the enormous tasks of Stalinist industrialization and postwar reconstruction. Given that one-third to two-thirds of the prison labor force was severely ill and disabled, the Gulag leadership sought ways to manage, conceal, and discard this enormous emaciated population. In Stalin's Gulag, prisoners had to be thoroughly "wrung out," that is, all prisoners, even the very frail, had to be exploited or "utilized" in some way. For most of the Gulag's existence, those classified as capable of light labor or light individualized labor corresponded to category 3. These severely weakened prisoners were separated from industrial laborers and concentrated into distinct camp compounds where they were given easier forms of labor, typically in agriculture and manufacturing. Separation and isolation also applied to category 4 prisoners or "invalids," those with "incurable" and "untreatable" illnesses and disabilities. Sickened prisoners were forced to keep working and meet output targets in order to earn their food and survival. The destructive nature of Gulag exploitation forced the Stalinist leadership to continuously find new ways to manage its ever-growing population of starving and debilitated prisoners.

REMOVING AND ISOLATING THE DISABLED

According to Varlam Shalamov, camp authorities "raked the human rejects" into brigades for weakened prisoners.[2] The Gulag concentrated the most severely disabled and ailing prisoners in invalid barracks and invalid camp sections, or assigned them to so-called brigades for the weak (*komandy slabosil'nykh*). Many were dispatched outside the Gulag system, to invalid communities in the special settlements or to so-called sanatorium-towns (*sangorodki*).[3] Invalid prisoners were segregated for many reasons. Special camp sections and brigades concentrated the weakest prisoners where they could still be put to use in light industry and agriculture. They helped reduce the burden on camp hospitals and doctors, since they did not require special facilities or physicians. Such camp facilities functioned as a system of long-term care and recovery, whose purpose was ideally to return prisoners to heavy physical labor in industry or, minimally, isolate them from work-capable prisoners. Finally, isolating the weakest prisoners in separate camp sections and units helped to improve camp production figures. As Anne Applebaum noted, one goal of the invalid camp sections was "to prevent the invalids from dragging down the camp production statistics . . . When these weak prisoners were removed from the significant work sites and replaced with brigades of 'fresh' new workers, the camp's production figures magically rose much higher."[4]

Brigades for weakened prisoners and for prisoners requiring long-term care appear in the earliest records of the Stalinist camps. They were tightly regulated and could not exceed 1–1.5 percent of all prisoners.[5] In 1931, the OGPU instructions noted that one of the purposes of prisoners' medical examinations was for doctors to assign certain prisoners "to brigades for the weak and convalescing."[6] The brigades for the weak served primarily an economic purpose. They relieved hospitals of the burden of prisoners requiring long-term care. In August 1933, the Gulag leadership encouraged camps to reach their targets for medical personnel by reducing the amount of medical attention allotted to sick prisoners. Hospitals should not be burdened with invalids, the chronically ill, and prisoners in long-term recovery. Rather than have such inmates occupy beds in the camps' medical facilities, the Gulag ordered camps to establish ways to detain such prisoners that would require "the minimal amount of medical staff," for example, by organizing sanatorium-towns or brigades for the weak.[7] The separation and isolation of invalids effectively reduced camp expenditures.

Within the Gulag's hierarchical system of labor camps and colonies, certain sites were designated for invalids. Agricultural camps and colonies became the typical destination for invalid prisoners, although these sick and disabled inmates were ill-suited for the heavy physical labor that sowing often requires.[8] Reflecting the broader priorities of the Stalinist leadership, the Gulag undervalued its agricultural sector. Emaciated prisoners were also often directed to regional camps and colonies to work in light industry.[9] In 1938, Gulag chief Izrail Pliner told camp administrators, including the heads of the medical, financial, and production sectors, to organize additional, separate camp sections for invalid prisoners. Directors of large agricultural enterprises had to accept invalid prisoners capable of light labor, who were to be transported from their current place of detention to these agricultural camps.[10] The Siberian camp, Siblag, appears to have been one such camp, for its proportion of invalid and ailing prisoners remained among the highest in the Gulag system. In 1940–1941, for example, more than a third of the 63,000 prisoners at Siblag were classified as "invalid" or "half-invalid."[11] In December 1951, roughly 20 percent of prisoners at Siblag were classified as invalids.[12] Many invalid camps were located in southern Russia and Central Asia. By far, the most invalids were located in the Central Asian Camp, Sazlag, whose 11,945 invalids represented 38 percent of its prisoner population and over 20 percent of all the invalids in the entire NKVD labor camp system. Based in Tashkent, Uzbekistan, the camp specialized in agriculture and cotton production, but prisoners there also worked in consumer goods production.[13] The second largest population of invalid prisoners behind Sazlag's nearly twelve thousand was only half this number. Karlag in the Karaganda region of Kazakhstan had 5739 invalids, who represented 18 percent of the camp's prisoner population. Work at Karlag included animal husbandry, light industry (metalworking, woodworking, sewing), consumer goods production, fishing, agriculture, sugar production, glassworks, and drying fruit.[14] Many infirm prisoners were sent there because they were not physically able to perform work in camps devoted to mining, logging, and construction.[15] Karlag's population of invalids would reach over 150,000 during the war.[16]

The outbreak of the war turned the Gulag's invalid problem into a crisis. During wartime, camp directors were confronted with new strains on the system and were even less inclined to devote their inadequate resources to invalid prisoners. On June 28, 1941, days after the Nazi invasion, the director of Soroklag, in the Karelia autonomous republic, tried to convince Gulag chief Nasedkin that a separate section for invalids should *not* be built at the camp, as previously planned. In a lengthy memo, complete with itemized lists and expenses, he argued in favor of suspending the project, noting that the cost would represent an enormous burden for the camp. His calculations indicated that the camp would be spending twice as much per capita on the 200 invalids who were unable to work as it would on the 800 work-capable invalids.[17] Invalids were costly. The NKVD had a powerful incentive to abandon them, especially in wartime when resources were in short supply. In July 1941, the NKVD moved large populations of prisoners from Latvia, Lithuania, Estonia, Poland, plus many other Soviet citizens, from the war zone in the West to the camps in the East. "They shot the sick people and the invalids," according to one account.[18] Instructed to move people quickly, the NKVD made no accommodations for weakened prisoners. In a November 1941 memo, a Gulag official described the total neglect of very weak and infirm prisoners at the Vytegorsky camp. Following the temporary closing of the camp days after the Nazi assault, sick prisoners were shunted off to "a separate area" where they were given insufficient food and housed in buildings lacking heat. As a result, prisoners were dying daily and corpses piled up.[19] Another wartime memo indicated that, in many camps, elderly and invalid prisoners "were not given any attention or necessary medical care, and mortality among this group was viewed as inevitable."[20]

During the war, the Gulag's population of sick and invalid prisoners soared, and the Gulag chief openly acknowledged the system's inability to feed them. In a February 1942 memo to his boss, the deputy head of the NKVD, S.N. Kruglov, Nasedkin described the problem of 15,000 invalids and persons incapable of work who were located in the combat zone, at camps and military enterprises located in the Murmansk, Arkhangelsk, and Vologoda regions and parts of the Karelo-Finnish republic.[21] These prisoners did not qualify for release under the November 24, 1941 amnesty decree (described in the next chapter), but they had to be immediately transferred out, so that camps would no longer have to deal with "the tremendous difficulties involved in supplying food for this group of prisoners." The prisons were already burdened with 23,000 invalid and not-work-capable inmates, so they could not accommodate this population. Nasedkin believed that the director at the Karaganda camp should be "forced" to create "a special invalid camp" for 15,000–20,000 persons. He acknowledged the difficulty of finding work for these prisoners (so they could eat), but stressed the need "to free NKVD industrial camps and construction projects from having to support prisoners who were incapable of working."[22]

Camp authorities were not convinced that it was in their interest to invest in the health of prisoners, and perceived their frail population as a costly burden. Such prisoners were incapable of performing heavy or medium physical labor, and they overwhelmed the system's meager health care services. Labor camp administrators complained that the maintenance of sick and invalid prisoners was exacting a heavy toll on the Gulag budget.[23] Stalin and the party leadership responded to the growing number of emaciated and disabled prisoners by insisting on a system of independent invalid camps. NKVD chief Beria and his colleagues at the Procuracy and the Commissariat of Justice opposed the idea, arguing that these new camps would introduce additional problems and expenses into an already overtaxed system. They stressed that the transfer of weakened, sick, and invalid prisoners from industrial and construction camps to special invalid camps would be a burden for railway transportation. Moreover, "large quantities of deficit building materials" and other resources would be spent to equip these invalid camps and to maintain frail prisoners.[24] The NKVD-Gulag leadership preferred to simply "unload" its "inferior work force," as we will see in the next chapter.

Yet the NKVD lost this argument with Stalin. In July 1942 it issued a decree "On the establishment of a system of corrective-labor camps under the NKVD Main Administration of Camps for the detention of prisoners who are invalids."[25] Since the start of the war, numerous criminal offenders who were severely ill or invalid had been released under special amnesties, but sick and disabled political offenders were barred from release. Thus the party created "independent invalid camps" under the Gulag's main administrations for forestry, industrial and railroad construction, and the administration of corrective-labor colonies. These new entities would house all prisoners sentenced for counterrevolutionary offenders who were declared invalids, who had severe and incurable illnesses (but were barred from release), or who were completely incapable of working. The number of inmates who fit this description at the time was estimated at roughly 59,000.[26] Many of the newly created invalid camps were to be located in segregated areas belonging to former and existing agricultural and other camps, labor colonies, or existing invalid camp sections. Invalid camps already existed within larger camps, but the proposed network of independent invalid camps was a way of further marginalizing severely ill, starving, and unprofitable prisoners. Beria designated the location and capacity of the camps, the kind of work that invalids were supposed to perform there, and the precise date when the camps needed to be operational. He created a procedure whereby larger feeder camps would send their emaciated prisoners to specified invalid camps. Emaciated prisoners in invalid camps would be "utilized" in agriculture, gardening, the "simplest kinds of woodworking," and animal husbandry. They would also labor in consumer goods production using local materials and industrial scraps, weaving sandals, working in the local glass factory, gathering mushrooms and berries, fishing, or making objects for internal camp use.[27] However, the NKVD did not allocate additional resources for the network of independent invalid camps.[28] According to Dan Healey, by the postwar period this network of discrete invalid camps was funded separately, and "excluded from the general accounts that supposedly furnished the MVD with arguments for the profitability of forced labor."[29]

Some Gulag survivors considered conditions in the invalid camps an improvement over ordinary camps.[30] Invalid labor appears easy by Gulag standards. However, overall conditions for weak and ailing prisoners were often worse than in regular camps.[31] Camp officials repeatedly asked the Gulag for resources for their weakened and disabled population, so as to create separate camp divisions or "special colonies."[32] However, the party leadership failed to fund the maintenance of disabled and nonworking prisoners.[33] One Gulag survivor characterized the brigades for the weak as "hell," since weakened prisoners from all the camp sections were concentrated there and left to die.[34] In 1932, Siblag had an outpost in the village of Yaia where 1,350 invalids lived and worked in various shops. A contract worker who visited the camp wrote the following in a letter to Molotov: "There are those who are completely blind, with eyes burnt by mine drilling cartridges, as well as those who are paralyzed, disfigured, and completely mutilated, without hands or legs, and those dying of consumption. In other words, it is awful. The food is very bad; those who are sick and do not work receive meatless pickled-cabbage soup twice a day and 400 grams of bread. They are thin, dark, exhausted . . . There is no one to take care of them, and they are scolded, to say nothing about medical treatment or food . . . Invalids and old men mutilated by work in the camp, sick people unable to work, continue to suffer in the Yaia camp of the Siblag, where they were brought from all places. They are dying here of exhaustion and camp mutilations." This remarkable letter resulted in an inspection of the camp, yet the inspection was carried out by Siblag's own administration, and camp officials flatly refuted the contractor's claims. The heads of Siblag's production and medical departments spuriously asserted: "All disabled [. . .] are working with passion and receive workers' rations" and "Medical assistance is adequate. Food is provided according to existing standards."[35]

Invalids were often left to die. The medical-sanitation department director for the Molotov regional camps and colonies spoke openly about the general neglect of sick and disabled prisoners in the contracting camp sections where "living conditions were nonexistent." She described the misery: "A process of degradation occurs because of these prisoners—it's horrible. Tuberculosis primarily affects these weakened prisoners."[36] Another location where the Gulag concentrated a large population of invalids and those designated for light labor, the Taishet camp in the Irkutsk region was known by many as "the camp of death."[37] In the mid-1940s, the camp held POWs, accused Nazi collaborators, and other wartime criminals who were sentenced to strict-regime hard labor. In 1945, although prisoners whose health improved were moved out of Taishet, the camp still held nearly five thousand terminally ill prisoners who were "not-transportable."[38] A former prisoner at the camp wrote a poem entitled, "Ballad on the Uprising of Invalids in the Norilsk camp." The voice in the poem belongs to an invalid prisoner who urges others like him to refuse to surrender to death, and even to "grab a knife in desperation" and rise up "to take revenge for the insults" because "we have nothing to lose, invalids; we have no hope and no salvation."[39]

EXPLOITING THE WEAK: "MAXIMUM LABOR UTILIZATION"

In Stalin's Gulag, human exploitation extended to all prisoners, regardless of their health. Weak and disabled prisoners, no less than healthier inmates, had to be "utilized" to the greatest degree possible. In a December 1933 note to Stalin and Molotov, OGPU chief Yagoda described how camps were manufacturing their own shoes (laptei) "using prisoners that are not engaged in heavy labor (na zemlianykh rabotakh)."[40] In July 1933, Gulag chief Berman ordered his subordinates to identify all blind prisoners and to concentrate them in a single camp for the blind. Many prisoners had become blind from exposure to harsh industrial chemicals and other hazardous camp work, and Berman wanted to keep them "utilized." In these new camps for the blind, he imagined that "several hundred people who have lost their eyesight will be drawn into a life of labor."[41] Even severely incapacitated prisoners had to do some form of physical labor. According to Solzhenitsyn, "Multitudes of 'goners,' unable to walk by themselves, were dragged to work on sledges by other 'goners' who had not yet become quite so weak."[42]

The Gulag leadership valued the "rational utilization of labor," which meant allocating tasks according to prisoners' physical labor capability.

Able-bodied prisoners would be assigned to heavy physical labor and the weakest inmates to light labor or work under reduced quotas. In August 1933, Semyon Firin, the deputy head of the Gulag, infamously guided a group of Soviet writers on a Potemkin tour of the White Sea Canal labor camp. That same month, he issued a directive to all camp administrators on the problem of invalids. He indicated that although many invalids, chronically ill prisoners, and other "not-work-capable elements" had been "unloaded," the camps still had "a large number of weak, exhausted, and emaciated prisoners" and generally experienced "a rise in illness, invalidity, and mortality."[43] Firin blamed camp directors for placing weak and emaciated prisoners in physically demanding jobs, in which they were unable to meet production targets. As a result, these prisoners received lower rations and their health deteriorated further.[44] Such admonitions give the impression that the goal of the Gulag leadership was to preserve labor. Yet it sent opposite messages as well. Firin spoke of "unloading" weakened prisoners and adhering to the Gulag's punitive system of differentiated food rations. The Stalinist leadership pressured camps to "utilize" its frail workforce. In October 1938, during the Great Terror and only a month before he too was arrested, I.I. Pliner, the head of the Gulag, complained: "Most camps have a significant number of defective workers . . . who are not being utilized in jobs."[45] In May 1939, the new, post-purge Gulag leadership reiterated that, "All invalids in the camps or colonies who are able to work in some sort of job must be utilized."[46] In January 1941, the head of the Gulag's medical-sanitation department informed camps that they had to report quarterly "on invalids and the measures being taken for their labor utilization."[47] In April 1943, the deputy NKVD chief, Sergei Kruglov, instructed the camps to use nonworking, sick, and invalid prisoners to gather wild plants, like sorrel and nettles, to be used as substitutes for vegetables, which were in short supply.[48]

Officials experienced great difficulty finding jobs for non-hospitalized but exceptionally frail prisoners, many of them classified as invalids or fit for light labor.[49] The problem of how to use such prisoners was, according to one medical-sanitation department director, "without a doubt, a real and serious issue."[50] In 1945, she expected to face new challenges finding jobs for weakened prisoners, since large military orders to sew uniforms would likely diminish.[51] The medical-sanitation department director of the Sverdlovsk regional system of labor camps and colonies likewise admitted difficulty finding work for emaciated and exhausted prisoners, especially given that work in the Urals consisted largely of hard physical labor in mining and construction. He described the camps' frustrating efforts to find light industrial work for these prisoners or to reduce their output norm, but admitted that very weak prisoners often went to work with the others. "Sometimes," he said, "when a heavy-labor brigade would be formed, it would be allocated category 3 [light labor] prisoners. For example, a brigade of loggers—that's heavy labor. But it's light labor to gather twigs and that's what the category 3 [light labor] prisoners are included to do."[52]

The medical-sanitation department director for the Novosibirsk region also addressed the problem of prisoners classified for light labor. He said that in April 1945, only a third of their prisoners were deemed capable of heavy or medium physical labor, yet the camp was required to maintain the "complete utilization of prisoners" and "not allow degradation." He stated: "The situation in the camps in April was such that we couldn't fulfill the NKVD order about using category 3 [light labor] prisoners [in basic, heavy labor] only in exceptional cases. For us, it wasn't the exception. It was practically the norm."[53] Camps lacked adequate light labor jobs, but officials were required to keep all prisoners "utilized," including weakened inmates. Thus officials kept frail inmates in the basic work of the camp, whether this involved logging, constructing, mining, or other strenuous physical labor. At the Chita labor camps and colonies, prisoners classified for light physical labor constituted one-third of the inmate population, and remained assigned to basic work. Production quotas for these inmates were reduced 25 percent per Gulag instruction, an insufficient accommodation. The medical-sanitation department official admitted that, "we occasionally have to make some compromises." Not all category 3 prisoners can be used in [light work], she said, but "we're required to utilize their labor."[54]

Camp officials found various ways to exploit the Gulag's large population of emaciated and disabled prisoners. They were systematically "utilized" in light manufacturing, including the textiles and consumer goods industries.[55] Sick and frail prisoners were sometimes assigned to work in camp fire brigades or as armed guards.[56] Weakened prisoners were forced to work making children's toys such as dolls, sewing garments, producing shoes and linens, and painting around the camp compound.[57] Some of the women were forced to knit mittens. During the war, the weakest prisoners were concentrated in special colonies where they worked making dominos and checkers and repairing army supplies.[58] Shalamov described how "one-armed men were forced to spend the entire working day in deep, loose, crystal snow, tramping down a path for people and tractors at the timber-clearing sites."[59] In the best of circumstances, weakened prisoners would be removed from heavy physical labor and placed in lighter work behind a desk at the camp compound, cleaning around the barracks, sewing uniforms for soldiers, or making toys for local sale. An elderly woman who was no longer work-capable "cleaned and looked after the barracks during the day."[60] One Gulag survivor described how the camp administration assigned physically weakened female prisoners to do jobs involving stitching and embroidery.[61] Like other prisoners, sick and disabled inmates had to meet their production quotas or their food rations would be reduced.[62]

Many sick and disabled prisoners were allowed to live or work outside the camp zone. De-convoyed prisoners (*bezkonvoinye*) were allowed to leave the area of the camp without a guard convoy, and de-zoned prisoners (*zazonniki*) could live outside the camp zone. Camps often flouted Gulag regulations that limited the use of both these categories, and some camp complexes recorded over a third of all prisoners unguarded. Scholars have attributed the widespread use of both categories to a shortage of guards, economic necessity, or the demands of certain jobs, as well as the desire to offer incentives to productive laborers.[63] The extremely poor health of the Gulag workforce also played a major role in categorizing prisoners as de-convoyed or de-zoned, as the sick and disabled presented a low risk of escape. During the war, when the number of sick and invalid prisoners soared, the Gulag sanctioned the use of emaciated prisoners in work beyond the zone and without armed escort, thereby improving the prospects of finding work for the weakest, and saving money on guards and surveillance.[64] De-zoned prisoners could do such jobs as fishing or collecting berries. A former Gulag boss described his plan to supplement prisoners' food by snaring northern partridges, using the least work-capable prisoners: "I proposed that we give the sick and weak prisoners a pass to leave the camp, and teach them how to set traps for partridges around the zone."[65] Memoirist Shalamov writes that one year after he arrived in

Kolyma, he suffered from the starvation disease pellagra. "More dead than alive," he was transferred out of the gold mine and given light work in a vitamin outpost collecting dwarf-cedar needles as a nutritional supplement.[66] Needle-picking, Shalamov wrote, "was considered not just an easy job, but the easiest of all" and "it didn't require the presence of a guard."[67] The writer asserted that, "Only the real 'goners' were used for needle-picking."[68] In such memoir accounts, light labor in the Gulag is described as life-saving. Like Shalamov, many found themselves on the verge of death, but were saved by a light labor assignment or an extended hospital stay."[69]

In fact, the life of a camp invalid or a severely weakened prisoner was highly precarious. Light labor was not widely available. The Gulag imposed quotas on the number of classified invalids and prisoners on light labor, and camps in certain sectors, like mining, could not easily generate lighter work for their emaciated prisoners. Persons classified for light physical labor who worked outdoors were still expected to put in an eight-hour workday. They would still receive a paltry ration if they failed to meet their production quotas.[70] In the eyes of camp administrators, sick and emaciated inmates represented an enormous burden. They took resources away from stronger prisoners, for whom investments in food and clothing would yield greater economic returns. It was difficult to place them in physical labor and hard to find other suitable jobs. Yet camp officials had to keep all prisoners working, regardless. Not only were they obligated to achieve "maximum labor utilization," but they were reprimanded for high rates of illness and mortality among prisoners. The way to keep inmates healthy was to keep them fed, and the only way to keep them fed was to keep them working. Thus the persistent quest to find work for the weakest, so they could eat.

Both camp administrators and contractors of Gulag labor ignored the health of weakened prisoners. Medical-sanitation department officials, who were blamed for high rates of illness and mortality, had little power to challenge their superiors. The director of the medical-sanitation department for the Cheliabinsk regional system of labor camps and colonies described how the regional economic organs fed working prisoners at the worksite, but worked them very hard, and reported that weakened prisoners did not fare well: "It must be said that economic

organs are not interested at all in finding work for the weakened contingent. They give our workers the most strenuous jobs. They don't
treat our workers as well as they treat their own cadres. They give
[their own cadres] the easy jobs." He suggested that the Gulag issue an
order mandating that a certain percentage of people had to be placed in
light work, "otherwise we have nowhere to put them." He continued:
"We can't organize independent colonies and provide appropriate work
for this category of prisoners. You require that we place even chronically ill and convalescent prisoners in some kind of work. But for this,
we would have to organize many independent camp sections. We have
been supplied no resources for this, and we have none ourselves."[71]

Outside the hospitals and clinics, camp officials could feed only
working prisoners. At one camp on the Pacific coast, a Polish woman
recalled that, "prisoners begged to work" in order to be fed: "They feed
only those who work, but because there are more prisoners than work,
some die of hunger."[72] The Gulag wanted the camps and colonies to do
more "labor therapy" with their weakened population. The medical-
sanitation department directors engaged in a desperate struggle to find
jobs for their weakest inmate population. "He who does not work,
shall not eat" applied to even the most sick and disabled inmates, yet
work appropriate to their weakened state was seldom available. Camp
officials often chose either to leave these prisoners without work and
without food, or to place them in labor that would only hasten their
physical decline. Extended hospitalization was not an option, as hospitals had very few beds to accommodate the large population of ailing
prisoners. The medical-sanitation department director for the Omsk
regional system of labor camps and colonies complained about a group
of 200–300 prisoners in her system of camps and colonies who were
classified for light individualized labor, just one notch above the invalid
category. Demonstrating little compassion toward such prisoners, she
expressed outrage that they were freeloading and "not doing any kind
of work." It was difficult to push them out of the hospitals and into
light labor, she complained. Like other camp officials, she believed that
the chronically ill and frail Gulag population represented free riders
and a drain on hospitals and resources: "I think that this is the core
mass of prisoners that is feeding off of our hospitals. We have to address the problem of their labor utilization."[73]

BRIGADES FOR THE WEAK AND CONVALESCENT CAMPS

Weakened prisoners were supposed to be isolated and employed in light forms of work, with the goal of returning them to heavy physical labor. In addition to separate invalid camps and camp divisions, the Gulag established various recovery facilities, including brigades for the weak, sanatorium-towns, convalescent camp sections and convalescent brigades. Only a few prisoners were allowed into these facilities, despite the enormous population of weak and emaciated prisoners. Moreover, they were intended for prisoners who held the promise of returning to heavy physical labor. The point of these recovery or convalescent institutions was to reduce the burden on hospitals, and improve the physical labor capability of weakened prisoners.

Convalescent institutions did not represent an accommodation for ailing prisoners, but a method of continued exploitation. In assigning prisoners to these institutions, Gulag officials considered their chances of recovery—the likelihood that their physical condition could improve and they could be returned to heavy physical labor. In 1931, the Gulag declared that sick and weak prisoners could be granted a break of two weeks to three months if the prisoner's condition "was expected to improve."[74] However, the message from above was often contradictory. On the one hand, weakened prisoners could be in convalescent facilities under a lighter regimen, and the Gulag leadership often accused camp officials of not sending weakened prisoners to invalid camps in a timely manner, discharging these prisoners too soon from convalescent brigades, and returning them to physical labor prematurely.[75] On the other hand, the Gulag leadership stressed that convalescent assignments should be temporary, result in the restoration of the prisoners' physical labor capability, and still involve work governed by production targets and punitive food rations. Like other inmates, ailing prisoners on lighter work regimes would receive smaller rations for failing to meet production targets.[76] Although the Gulag leadership offered certain accommodations for weaker prisoners, it also warned camp officials not to be too soft on them. Camps had to be vigilant against malingerers.

Attention to the Gulag's ailing workforce increased following the Nazi-Soviet pact and the Red Army's invasion of eastern Poland and the Baltic states. The subsequent political repression generated a large population of weakened prisoners. In 1940–1941, Gulag leaders called for longer convalescent periods of five months, and urged subordinates to improve the physical labor capability of prisoners.[77] At the same time, the Gulag leadership urged labor colonies, where the Stalinist labor camp system concentrated its weakest prisoners, to keep frail prisoners working. It criticized the medical-sanitation department directors of the regional colonies for the fact that brigades for weakened prisoners demonstrated low labor productivity.[78] The Stalinist leadership consistently blamed camp officials for the poor health of prisoners, insisting that they failed to adequately calibrate when prisoners should be shifted to light work and when they could return to heavy physical labor.

The evidence suggests that as camp officials responded more to Gulag pressures to maximally exploit prisoners, they often neglected to use the convalescent facilities. In May 1941, the Gulag chief Nasedkin admonished camps and colonies for "clearly failing to appreciate the significance" of the brigades for the weak as "one of the most effective means for improving the health of the labor pool."[79] Nasedkin condemned the camps for failing to restore the physical labor productivity of prisoners in these brigades and instead providing such inmates with poor living conditions and insufficient food and medical care.[80] He also criticized a number of camps and colonies for having mostly "second group" or nonworking weakened brigades, and very few weakened prisoners in the "first group" of working prisoners; and he attributed this to the fact that camps were allowing prisoners to become so severely exhausted that they could only be assigned to a nonworking "group 2" brigade.[81]

In March 1942, the Stalinist leadership established a system of convalescent-prophylactic camp units or OPPs (ozdorovitel'no-profilakticheskie punkty). The OPPs were designated their own ration, which was lower than in brigades for the weak. In 1941, prisoners in the brigades for the weak received 700 grams (1.5 lbs.) of bread if they worked, and 600 grams (1.3 lbs.) if they did not work.[82] By comparison, working invalids in the OPPs who met their production quotas could earn only 600 grams of bread, and only 500 grams (1.1 lbs.) if they failed to meet their quota.[83] Nonworking invalids received only 400 grams (0.88 lbs.) of bread, not much more than inmates in the punishment cell. Unlike prisoners classified as invalids, those in brigades for the weak and the OPPs were expected to get better and return to heavy physical labor. During the war, the large population of sick and disabled prisoners forced the Gulag leadership to create more convalescent arrangements for prisoners. At the same time, the NKVD-Gulag leadership stressed that only those prisoners whose health could be restored should be "selected" for temporary transfer to a weakened brigade or convalescent camp. Resources were scarce. The Stalinist leadership wanted to support only productive prisoners. In September 1943, the NKVD issued an order that reorganized the previous system of convalescent camps (OPP), and created in its place two institutions for sick prisoners in long-term recovery, the convalescent camp sections or OPs (ozdorovitel'nye punkty) and convalescent brigades or OKs (ozdorovitel'nye komandy).[84] The NKVD consistently sought to create hierarchies. The Gulag dealt with the growing number of weakened and sick prisoners by dividing them into finer subgroups depending on their degree of ill health and potential for work. Weakened prisoners whose recovery appeared more likely were directed to the convalescent camps, and fed more than the others. The least promising workers were denied food and resources, as was the case across the system.

The convalescent brigades were intended for prisoners with the most severe illnesses who were the least likely to return to physical labor. In the convalescent brigades, food and other resources were woefully lacking. In 1944, the NKVD instructed camps to give 750 grams of bread (1.65 lbs.) to prisoners in the OPs, but only 550 grams (1.2 lbs.) to prisoners in the OKs.[85] Many medical-sanitation department officials considered the OKs useless in restoring the health of prisoners, given the lack of food. The Gulag leadership largely rejected this view. In September 1945, the chief of the Gulag's medical-sanitation department, D.M. Loidin, stated that, "the main task of the OK is to improve the physical condition of category 3 [light labor prisoners] and not allow their degradation."[86] He considered it "totally unacceptable to ignore the OK," given that 69 percent of prisoners released from the OKs in recent months had gained 1–3 kilograms (2.2–6.6 lbs.), and 5 percent gained 3–5 kilograms (6.6–11 lbs.).[87] Loidin demanded that his subordinates end the "harmful talk" about whether the OKs served a purpose.[88] The Gulag medical-sanitation department chief indicated that 23,000 people passed through the OKs every month in 1944, and roughly 93,000 in the five months April–August 1945 alone; of these, 2 percent were reclassified as category 1 heavy physical labor, and more than 14 percent as category 2 medium physical labor. He praised such results.

Convalescent institutions served the exploitation function of the Gulag, and were created to improve prisoners' physical labor capability. The OPs were intended for prisoners whose health could be improved within a fixed period of time.[89] Prisoners in convalescent facilities were typically those classified for light labor and who, following a temporary lighter regimen, were expected to return to more strenuous work.[90] The Gulag measured the success of convalescent institutions based on how many prisoners they discharged into physical labor. Camps with well-functioning OPs returned more prisoners to work in heavy or medium physical labor, while the camps criticized for poor performing OPs returned too many prisoners to light physical labor.[91] Camp officials reported on their OPs accordingly. In 1945, the medical-sanitation department director for the Primorsky regional system of labor camps and colonies described the success of his OPs: "In the first half of the year, 1626 people recovered, of them 947 were category 1 or 2 [heavy and medium physical labor], and their average weight gain was between 3 and 5 kilograms" (6.6–11 lbs.).[92] Other medical-sanitation departments lacked scales and could not report on improvements in prisoners' weight, as the medical-sanitation department director for the Krasnoiarsk regional system of labor camps and colonies complained: "Scales for weighing the human body are urgently needed in all the camp divisions."[93]

Gulag bosses told their subordinates that food and medical care should not be wasted on inmates unlikely to recover. In 1945, Loidin, the Gulag medical-sanitation department chief, complained that poorly performing OPs were costing the state a lot of money: "Naturally, in those camps where the OP results are unsatisfactory, a lot of money is being wasted. The negligence of some of our sanitation services produces unacceptable results for the costs incurred."[94] Convalescent camps had to produce healthier inmates ready for productive labor.[95] According to Loidin, the failure to make prisoners work-capable again represented "a critical distortion of [our task to provide] daily assistance to production."[96] For their part, camps often refused to allow prisoners to stay in the OPs for an extended period of time due to "an acute need for labor."[97] Despite the problems with convalescent facilities, the Gulag leadership continued to believe that these institutions could effectively restore prisoners' physical labor capability. In May 1947, MVD and Gulag leaders again urged camps to "take measures to restore the physical condition of contingents, in particular, by organizing special convalescent camp sections and convalescent brigades."[98] In 1944–1947, the bread ration for prisoners in the OPs improved to 800 grams (1.76 lbs.) of bread, and 850 grams (1.87 lbs.) for prisoners in the OPs of the high-priority industrial regions of the north, including Vorkuta, Pechora, and Norilsk.[99] Later, OP prisoners would receive less, especially if they did not reside in one of the Gulag's high-priority camps. In 1948–1949, changes to the food rations still granted prisoners in the OPs of high-priority camps 800 grams of bread, but prisoners in the OPs of other MVD camps and colonies received 700 grams (1.54 lbs.).[100]

Many prisoners passed through the OPs, but not as many prisoners as needed recovery. The Gulag maintained a very low quota on the number of inmates allowed into the convalescent camps. As of January 1946, the NKVD reported that a meager 1.9 percent of camp prisoners, or just over eleven thousand, were in the OPs.[101] The following year Gulag chief Nasedkin reported that 271,000 prisoners or 16 percent of Gulag prisoners had passed through convalescent camp sections in the first seven months of 1947.[102] In 1948, the Gulag reported having roughly 100,000 prisoners in OPs per quarter, yet this represented just a small fraction of the Gulag's population of roughly two million prisoners.[103] In the late 1940s, when roughly two-thirds of prisoners were classified as either invalids or only fit for light labor, the Gulag's highly constrained convalescent institutions hardly made a difference.

SEPARATION, SECRECY, AND INHUMANITY

As the Gulag's population of weak, disabled, and diseased prisoners increased, the system of convalescent institutions grew accordingly. The brigades for the weak and sanatorium-towns of the 1930s gave way to convalescent brigades and convalescent camp sections in the 1940s. By the postwar period, the Gulag designated entire camps and camp divisions to housing its burgeoning population of infirm inmates. In May 1946, MVD Order No. 0154 "on the organization of special camp sections for restoring the physical condition of prisoners being detained in MVD corrective-labor camps and colonies" called for the creation of larger recovery institutions or entire convalescent camp divisions (*ozdorovitel'nye podrazdeleniia*). The new convalescent camp divisions or OPs were to be established at existing agricultural colonies or camp sections (*lagpunkty*) that were "most suitable" for improving health. They had to provide prisoners with medical care and food "according to special norms." In addition, NKVD chief Kruglov ordered Nasedkin to establish independent convalescent camps directly subordinate to the Gulag MVD USSR. He named three such camps that should be created for 20,000 prisoners, including one for 12,000 prisoners on the site of the Stalingrad agricultural labor colony. Administrators at these convalescent camps, colonies, and camp sections were told that they would receive awards for successfully restoring the health of their prisoners. At the same time, information on the new camps was highly classified. Their identity was concealed, suggesting that these sites of starving prisoners were too dreadful to speak of. The Gulag assigned the three new convalescent camps mysterious acronyms—AE, AIu, and AIa—which had no reference to their name or location.[104] The letters represented mere codes or symbols, intended to protect the secrecy of these institutions, similar to the names that would be assigned to the special camps two years later.

It was not just the secret code names for the convalescent camps that indicated that MVD Order No. 0154 was far from benign. The order also stressed that not all sick prisoners in need of recovery could go to a convalescent camp. Prisoners who violated labor discipline, refused to work, or were negligent workers were barred from going to these camps. Thus it was not just the counterrevolutionaries or traitors that were excluded from the convalescent camps, but those who refused to work. The only prisoners who were supposed to be sent to the OPs were "enfeebled prisoners from prisons and transit camp sections (*peresyl'nye punkty*), as well as prisoners whose labor capability had been reduced in industry, whose physical condition can be restored." Kruglov stressed at officials in these new convalescent camps had to restore prisoners' labor capability within a period of three to five months.[105] In effect, prisoners who could not be made well enough to return to work within this time should not be sent to a convalescent camp. Something else had to be done with such prisoners, but what exactly, Kruglov did not specify. Still, a reader of this decree would understand that the Gulag was not going to waste its resources on lodging, feeding, and attending to prisoners who were too sick to be returned to work in short order. The incentive for staff of the convalescent camps (for whom Kruglov now promised rewards) was to accept only those prisoners who could conceivably return to physical labor in a few months.

As before, ailing prisoners in the new convalescent camps had to work in some capacity. MVD Order No. 0154 made clear that the new convalescent camps did not represent sanatoria where prisoners went to rest. Kruglov spoke of "the production program" and "the labor utilization of prisoners held in the convalescent camp sections." He gave directors of the regional administrations of labor camps and colonies permission to establish reduced work norms and shorter workdays for different groups of prisoners consistent with inmates' physical condition and medical treatment. He also mentioned "labor therapy" as one way that the new convalescent camps could restore the health of prisoners, listing it first.[106] In 1947, the Gulag chief insisted that medical-labor commissions, or VTK, in the camps, which were headed by production managers, had to formally approve work releases that exceeded ten days, and that the VTK should classify as invalids prisoners who had been deemed incapable of work for over three months.[107]

As convalescent institutions proliferated, the Gulag still specified that only a narrow segment of prison laborers would be admitted. In June 1949, as part of MVD Order No.0418, the MVD directed every camp and colony to organize camp sections for prophylactic rest (punkty profilakticheskogo otdykha) as well as convalescent camp sections. The camp sections for prophylactic rest would be for prisoners who "systematically fulfill production targets but who need a rest," and these inmates would be recorded as part of the inmate population "working in production." The quota for the camp sections for prophylactic rest or "Rest Points" was set at only 1 percent of the labor pool. Prisoners could only stay there for two weeks, and each prisoner could go only once a year. Solzhenitsyn expressed his unfavorable view of the Rest Points in the following: "Tens of years the zcks bend their backs, don't get vacations, so they have Rest Points—for two weeks. They feed much better there and they're not driven outside the camp compound to work, and in the compound they only put in three, four hours of real easy work: pounding rocks to pave roads, cleaning up the compound, or making repairs. And if there were half a thousand people in the camp—they'd open a Rest Point for fifteen. And then if everything had been divided up honestly, everyone would have gotten Rest Point in just over a year. But just as there was no justice in anything in camp, there was especially none with Rest Points."[108] Indeed, many prisoners were probably assigned to these convalescent or recovery sites as a result of bribery, corruption, or connections.

In 1949, the MVD also established different rules for the new OPs. In contrast to the Rest Points, the OPs would be for a weaker contingent, including prisoners coming from prisons, whose health was often very poor, and "prisoners whose labor capability declined in industrial work, and whose physical condition can be restored with time in the OP." The OPs were for prisoners who could be made work capable again, and these prisoners would be recorded in internal Gulag data as sick inmates. The MVD established a limit on spaces in the OPs too, but this quota would vary, and would be determined for each individual camp and colony by the Gulag and the corresponding production division.[109] These recovery institutions were for prisoners who worked in industrial labor and needed a short break or those who experienced temporary illness and could be returned to industrial work. For the vast majority of frail and starving prisoners, there was only permanent isolation and separation in invalid camps and camp sections for weakened prisoners.

On the surface, the Gulag's convalescent or recovery organs appear better than they often were, in fact. Only a small percentage of the large ailing Gulag population spent time in convalescent camps and convalescent brigades. Moreover, not only did the Gulag enforce quotas on these facilities, but it did not fund them adequately. Camp officials felt greater pressure to keep prisoners in heavy labor than to give them a break from strenuous work. Camp medical-sanitation department officials had a low opinion of these facilities, as they remained poorly supplied. The director of the medical-sanitation department for the Buriat-Mongolia regional system of labor camps and colonies noted ironically: "If there were no interruptions in the supply of food, then one could say that the food is good in the OP and OK [convalescent camps and convalescent brigades]."[110] Many camp administrators either chose not to form OPs or used them only for sick and invalid prisoners who could not be accommodated in overcrowded hospitals and clinics. At Siblag during the war, one observer noted that, "The OP was typically the most filthy section of the barracks, with overcrowded two-level bunks without any bedding or linens, and no defined regimen or health care for prisoners."[111]

The medical-sanitation department director for the Molotov regional system of labor camps and colonies characterized the workshops for disabled prisoners as tantamount to prison cells. Although weakened prisoners did better when employed because they earned food, they were also confined without proper hygiene, and in conditions that spread disease. She described camp sections for weakened prisoners as centers of tuberculosis: "I think that handicraft production has played an enormous role in improving the health of the prisoners, but in 1944, it turned into a grave danger for our inmates. We saw how handicraft shops became places for the widespread dissemination of tuberculosis."[112] According to this official, camp administrators came into close contact with prisoners infected with tuberculosis when they visited and "carried away profits" from the shops. The handicraft shops in 1944 "created prison conditions" for inmates, as the shops lacked ventilation and prisoners could not walk around. She concluded: "I think that control over the handicraft shops must be exceptionally strict now. The selection [of inmates] for the handicraft shops has to be perfect. Not a single person with obvious signs of tuberculosis can be in these shops."[113]

The convalescent facilities served the larger purpose of human exploitation by preparing weak and emaciated prisoners to return to physical labor. The Gulag leadership often rebuked local officials for neglecting these recovery facilities, but their criticism did not reflect an interest in preserving the health of prisoners. Rather, the Stalinist leadership wanted the maximum number of prisoners to be engaged in heavy physical labor, and believed that temporary respite for a select number of "the more promising" exhausted prisoners would serve this purpose. In the late Stalin years, MVD-Gulag bosses often criticized camp officials for not using these facilities. In January 1950, Gulag officials complained about the "unsatisfactory" convalescent work at several camps, calling the underutilization of the OPs "an extremely serious defect."[114] The Gulag criticized camps for waiting too long before transferring emaciated and exhausted prisoners into convalescent institutions, and for failing to select those sick inmates who held the

greatest promise of returning to heavy labor. For example, a Gulag sanitation inspection of the labor camps and colonies of the Khabarovsk
region determined that convalescent camp divisions were underutilized
and ineffective. Of the 762 prisoners who were discharged in the fourth
quarter of 1949, only 306 were classified as category 1 or basically fit
for physical labor. According to Gulag inspectors, this failure to return
more ailing prisoners to physical labor was "evidence of the fact that
an unpromising contingent (*neperspektivnyi kontingent*) was improp-
erly selected and directed into the convalescent camp sections."[115] In
other words, convalescent facilities were intended not to restore the
health of weakened prisoners, but to return more "promising" inmates
to strenuous labor.

Weakened prisoners were treated poorly, both by camp officials and
their fellow inmates. The Gulag's *dokhodiaga* was not unlike the dying prisoner of the Auschwitz labor camp, the *Muselmann*, who, as
Giorgio Agamben writes, was "universally avoided because everyone
in the camp recognizes himself in his disfigured face."[116] The Gulag's
"physically inferior workforce" appeared grotesque and inhuman to
the other prisoners, and a frightful reminder of what they might become. Weakened prisoners also became the targets of their comrades'
anger for failing to meet their production quotas and suppressing the
productivity of the group. They endured the "shoves and fists of the
orderly" and beatings from their foremen and comrades who blamed
them for reducing the output of the brigade.[117]

CONCLUSION

Stalinist exploitation produced invalids and disabled inmates on a
massive scale—even according to the Gulag's own data, which must
be reasonably interpreted as an underestimate. Camps underreported
their numbers of sick and invalid prisoners in order to stay within the
quotas set by the party leadership. The Gulag coped with the continuous loss of prisoners capable of heavy physical labor by relying on the
constant inflow of new inmates, although these new prisoners often arrived at the camps in very poor health themselves. The easiest way for
officials to improve their camp's overall health profile was to receive an
influx of newer and healthier prisoners. As one camp official explained,
his population of prisoners capable of heavy and medium physical

labor increased sharply when weakened prisoners were discharged and stronger prisoners were admitted.[118] The unrelenting flow of prisoners through the camp system allowed camp officials to temporarily improve the appearance and productivity of their prison labor force.

Gulag scholars have examined the MVD's approach to the problem of labor productivity, and the use of a system of labor days, prisoner salaries, and other incentives (see chapter 9). Yet these measures targeted the healthier prisoners. For the large population of weakened and disabled inmates, there were few incentives. From the 1930s to the 1950s, the Gulag separated out and isolated its least productive prisoners. Some of them were transferred to recovery or convalescent institutions, such as brigades, settlements, camp sections, and camp divisions. The most sick and disabled were directed to invalid camp sections or camp divisions, even to separate camps designated for invalids. Thus the Gulag managed its large population of weakened prisoners through separation and isolation. Evidence also suggests that the Gulag abandoned and starved its weakest prisoners, those who could not work or had the least hope of surviving. Once prisoners could no longer be physically exploited, the camps systematically "unloaded" them. As Solzhenitsyn explained, "the Archipelago could not keep swirling about without precipitating to the bottom its principal form of waste— the *last-leggers*."[119] We turn now to the Gulag's method of unloading its waste.

6 Releases
"Unloading the Ballast"

THE OGPU-NKVD-MVD RELIED greatly on its ability to unload the Gulag's "inferior workforce," which camp officials referred to informally as their "ballast." Prisoners deemed terminally ill, with severe and incurable ailments, were formally discharged from Stalin's labor camps and colonies. Camp officials referred to this process as "unloading" (*razgruzka*), and it involved many types of releases, including medical discharges and special amnesties. Just as Stalin selected German POWs for repatriation who were invalids, and whose labor could no longer be exploited in camps, he unloaded sick and emaciated Gulag prisoners.[1] Terminally ill prisoners who had been fully exploited were callously discarded, and many died shortly after their release. As Michael Ellman explains, "The policy of releasing 'unfit for work ballast' was a cost-cutting measure which was intended to save on food consumption and on guards and other personnel, and hence reduce the deficit and improve productivity in the Gulag."[2] Medical releases and amnesties of dying prisoners constituted a fundamental Gulag practice applied on a massive scale. It effectively kept official mortality rates low, and thus concealed the destructive nature of the Gulag. Stalin touted his policy of reforging (*perekovka*) that rewarded productive convict laborers with early release, yet in reality his Gulag more often granted early release to women, minors, and the elderly, and sick, invalid, and dying prisoners.

Following the Nazi invasion of the USSR, the Gulag faced a crisis as its population of severely ill and emaciated prisoners rose sharply. At that time, various bans on prisoner releases limited the Gulag's ability to "unload ballast," as it had been doing for most of the 1930s. The Soviet Union's leaders in charge of penal policy, including Beria and the heads of the Procuracy and the Commissariat of Justice, sought ways to dramatically reduce the size of the Gulag. They argued that many prisoners would be more productive and less costly if they worked as civilian laborers. Wartime conditions prompted the NKVD-Gulag leadership to advocate for a more modest enterprise, one that focused on detaining only the most dangerous offenders. Many high-ranking Soviet leaders believed that the system could not afford to maintain a large population of sick and disabled prisoners, and that it did not need to because many of these inmates "posed no threat to state security." Thus we see that the arguments for fundamentally restructuring Stalin's Gulag, which surfaced shortly after the Soviet leader's death in March 1953, were first articulated during the war.

CERTIFICATION OF THE NEARLY DEAD

The Soviet Union's famous bard Vladimir Vysotsky often inserted references to the Gulag into his own compositions. According to Alexander Etkind, "From 1961, the earliest songs that Vysotsky wrote himself were all stylizations of camp songs, *blatnye pesni*."[3] One of these compositions, "In Kolyma," included the following lines: "Through certification, the escape path offered by doctors, I left my native camp."[4] Vysotsky's song drew attention to the process of certification or medical discharge (*aktirovanie*), the Gulag's routine release of sick and disabled prisoners. Medical discharge was largely reserved for prisoners who had been sentenced under routine criminal statutes. Political prisoners were generally barred from medical release, as were criminal recidivists. According to Articles 457–458 of the RSFSR Code of Criminal Procedure, courts had the authority to grant early release to prisoners "in cases of grave incurable disease or mental illness."[5] The word "incurable" is key here, for it was used in Gulag documents to flag the invalid category of physical labor capability.

From the beginning of Stalin's labor camp system, prisoners classified as invalids were eligible for release. The List of Illnesses, as discussed in chapter 3, instructed camp officials on how to classify prisoners according to "physical labor capability," and specified which ailments and disabilities qualified someone for medical discharge or *aktirovanie*. Routine medical examinations would determine whether prisoners' poor health qualified them for early release. In the 1930s, medical discharge applied to prisoners classified as "invalid, fit to perform light forms of physical labor, or complete invalid, unable to do any kind of work."[6] The Gulag leadership strictly limited medical release to the incurables— prisoners who were dying and no longer work-capable.[7] The Gulag's general quota on invalids tended to be around 10 percent. Thus in the second quarter of 1931, the Gulag planned to release over 11 percent of its chronically ill and disabled prisoners.[8] In January 1935, the deputy head of the Gulag, Izrail Pliner, called the "List of Illnesses for Early Release" the most important Gulag directive on the subject of early release, but he warned camp officials against granting early release too hastily.[9] Distrustful Gulag officials were also quick to suspect prisoners of acquiring their invalid classification through bribery or deception. In November 1935, Gulag chief Matvei Berman noted that, "the practice of releasing prisoners from the camps for reasons of illness and invalidity is systematic and has been expanded recently, such that the medical and unloading commissions are not operating secretly." He expressed concern that because prisoners were aware of such releases, they had stepped up their efforts at self-mutilation and fakery in order to get classified as invalids.[10]

There were millions of certified invalids in the camps, and their numbers rose especially during periods of war and overcrowding. In just two years, 1933–1935, as a result of Stalin's harsh criminal statutes and campaigns against marginals, the Gulag population tripled, to nearly a million prisoners. Inmate health declined sharply, as the system lacked clothing, food, and barracks to accommodate the large influx of prisoners. The Gulag sought to release this ailing population. According to Gulag instructions, invalids were to be released into the care of relatives.[11] This would relieve the NKVD of the transportation costs associated with relocating ailing prisoners. The Stalinist leadership preferred not to transfer the cost of these prisoners from the Gulag to the civilian health department. Many released prisoners were restricted in where they could live.[12] Stalinist exploitation involved the maximum "utilization" of prisoners at each stage of their deteriorating health, plus the discharge of prisoners who could be utilized no longer. Gulag survivor, Oleg Volkov, described this policy: "So many prisoners without strength and worn out from work accumulated—the elderly with joints that could no longer bend, with crooked fingers and many hernias, inmates who developed dementia, deafness, and blindness. They had to be disposed of. The Gulag's creaky laboring body had to be freed of this ballast . . . Let them find themselves a hole they can crawl into like old dogs sensing imminent death, and where they can await the Great Redeemer. I saw how camps released and sent beyond the zone the veterans of Gulag labor."[13]

AMNESTIES AND THE BAN ON RELEASES

In April 1939, Lavrenty Beria argued in favor of abolishing early release for Gulag prisoners.[14] The NKVD chief believed that prisoners who worked well should no longer earn workday credits towards early release, which had been a Gulag policy since as early as 1931.[15] Instead, the Gulag should offer these prisoners other incentives—better food, direct payments, and improved living conditions. The change reflected Stalin's own view that rewarding productive prisoners with early release harmed the state economy. The Soviet leader argued: "The best people would leave [the camps], and the worst would stay."[16] The worst people, according to Stalin, were the least productive laborers, the group that the Gulag released early on health grounds. The June 1939 Politburo resolution that abolished early release made no mention of medical discharge for sick prisoners, and neither did the subsequent decree of the Presidium of the USSR Supreme Court that formalized the party's new policy.[17] The initial ambiguity prompted Gulag officials to panic at the prospect of losing the right to release emaciated prisoners. They petitioned the Soviet leadership and argued that Article 457 of the Criminal Code "is necessary for deciding the question of invalids."[18] But they lost the argument. Stalin's 1939 ban on early releases even extended to medical discharge.[19] Denied the right to routinely unload its sick and invalid prisoners, the Gulag had to rely on other methods, such as special amnesties.

With the Nazi invasion of the USSR in June 1941, conditions in many camps, especially those along the front, worsened sharply and the number of weak and emaciated prisoners soared. Moreover, the NKVD banned any releases of prisoners sentenced for "serious state crimes," which included betraying the motherland, espionage, terror, sabotage, Trotskyism, and banditism. It also prohibited many other categories of "dangerous elements," including "anti-Soviet agitators" and "family members of traitors," from leaving the camps even upon completion of their sentence.[20] Paradoxically, just when conditions in the camps worsened, the ban on releases tightened. One month later, the deputy head of the NKVD, V.V. Chernyshev, and the head of the Gulag, V.G. Nasedkin, wrote to NKVD chief Beria about the release of 100,000 prisoners.[21] The men focused on camps and colonies near the front, and requested the release of "prisoners who do not pose a threat to state security" so that the Gulag could focus on detaining "counterrevolutionaries, bandits, recidivists, and other dangerous [state] criminals." They urged the release of many prisoners, including petty criminal offenders, women, juveniles, and "chronically ill prisoners, mainly the elderly, who can be transferred to the care of relatives (except for counterrevolutionary and especially dangerous criminals)."[22] The July 1941 amnesty was motivated, in part, by problems associated with moving prisoners away from the front. In total, Soviet authorities moved three-quarters of a million prisoners from nearly 250 camps and colonies.[23]

In the crisis of wartime, Gulag leaders expressed their desire to manage fewer prisoners and to detain only the most dangerous state enemies. As soon as the July 1941 decree was issued, the Gulag sought to expand its scope. In subsequent months, as the wartime situation worsened conditions in the camps, Gulag leaders requested the release of more invalids, even including certain counterrevolutionary offenders. In August 1941, Chernyshev and Nasedkin wrote to Beria again for permission to release an additional 80,000 prisoners from camps and colonies, "for the purpose of unloading camps and colonies of invalid prisoners who do not pose a threat to state security."[24] These included prisoners convicted of white-collar and economic crimes with less than three years left on their sentence, plus "socially dangerous" and "socially harmful elements," as well as those sentenced for counterrevolutionary offenses, banditism, and "other especially dangerous crimes" who had no more than three years left to serve. Thus in the first weeks of the war, the Gulag leadership succeeded in lobbying the NKVD to release a large population of sick and emaciated prisoners who did not benefit the industrial mission of the camps.

In their August 1941 memo to Beria, Chernyshev and Nasedkin suggested expanding the scope of an earlier July 12, 1941 decree of the Presidium of the USSR Supreme Soviet "On releasing prisoners sentenced for several categories of offenses." The original decree extended only to prisoners located in areas under martial law, but just weeks later Chernyshev and Nasedkin wanted the decree to apply to sick and invalid prisoners in other locations as well, and to be extended to women, children, and juvenile offenders.[25] In November 1941, the July decree was formally applied to the above categories of prisoners in all camps, not just those located in areas under martial law.[26] By that time the total number of prisoners detained in NKVD camps and colonies who had been identified as invalids, sick, or of "limited fitness for work" had reached staggering proportions.[27] The Gulag wanted to release hundreds of thousands of invalids and sick prisoners, including "persons of limited physical ability" who likely fell into the physical labor categories of light labor and light-individualized labor. By the Gulag's own reporting, this invalid, disabled, and sick population had reached 594,395 prisoners, or well over one-third (perhaps 36–39 percent) of all prisoners in NKVD labor camps and colonies.[28]

Following the 1939 ban on early releases, the Gulag had to rely on periodic amnesties to unload its emaciated and disabled workforce. But the Gulag leadership wanted more ways to unload prisoners. The catastrophic wartime situation generated large numbers of sick and disabled prisoners and necessitated a return to the more regularized system for releasing invalids. In September 1941, the NKVD, Commissariat of Justice, and Procuracy produced a draft decree stating that prisoners who were "sick with mental illness or severe incurable illness" could be "released from detention, according to Article 457 of the RSFSR Criminal Procedural Code, by a decision of a court in the district where the sentence is being served."[29] This decree represented not just a return to an earlier practice, but an expansion of it, as the civilian courts located near the camps, rather than the court that handed down the original sentence, could now process the prisoner's medical release.[30] The effort to convince the party leadership to grant the Gulag this right continued for months. NKVD-Gulag leadership stressed that police organs needed to systematically release certain categories of prisoners because "maintaining them in the camps diverts considerable resources and funds for food."[31]

The two major amnesties in the weeks after the Nazi invasion of the Soviet Union had targeted petty criminal offenders who, as discussed in chapter 2, constituted the majority of Gulag prisoners. The decrees of the Presidium of the USSR Supreme Soviet dated July 12 and November 24, 1941 called for the release of prisoners with short-term sentences who had been convicted of everyday white-collar and economic crimes as well as absenteeism.[32] The November 24, 1941 secret decree of the presidium of the USSR Supreme Soviet, "On releasing certain categories of prisoners from detention," extended the work of the July 12 decree.[33] This release applied to the usual population of petty criminal offenders and prisoners least capable of heavy physical labor, and focused on those with a few years remaining on their sentence. They included: persons sentenced for shirking, absenteeism, and other violations of labor discipline (under the June 26 and August 10, 1940 decrees of the USSR Supreme Soviet); pregnant women and women with small children; former soldiers sentenced for minor offenses; and the elderly and invalids who were not work-capable and could be released into the care of relatives. Criminal recidivists, political prisoners, and counterrevolutionary offenders, and those sentenced for banditism, were barred from release. Many national groups were also excluded, including Germans, Finns, Romanians, Hungarians, and Italians, as well as Latvians, Estonians, and Lithuanians.

The Gulag leadership portrayed the fall releases in the most positive way, as a transfer of prisoners from the camps to the army. Indeed, in the course of the war, the Soviet leadership released many Gulag prisoners into military service, including former kulaks.[34] Yet the vast majority of those released from the camps following the Nazi invasion hardly constituted able-bodied soldiers. In November 1941, when the Procuracy urged the party leadership to expand the scope of the July 1941 decree, the USSR Procurator boasted that many released by the July 1941 decree had been conscripted into the Red Army. He also noted that mortality rates in the camps had increased threefold since July due to problems with clothing, food, and housing.[35] In their petition to party leaders, both the Procuracy and the Gulag leadership stressed that mortality rates were increasing and that prisoners should be released to aid the war effort. In many cases, according to the Procurator's letter to Stalin, "former prisoners whom the medical commission determined to be unfit to serve in the Red Army for health reasons insisted on enlisting."[36]

However the early wartime releases were sold to the party leadership, they were primarily motivated by the desire to unload the Gulag's "ballast." The November 24, 1941 decree alone released 279,068 prisoners of whom only 82,014 went into military service. Together, the decrees of July 12 and November 24, 1941 resulted in the release of as many as 650,000 prisoners, but only 110,000 were actually conscripted into the Red Army.[37] During World War II, the NKVD-Gulag leadership convinced Stalin of the need to release prisoners in order to aid the war effort. However, recently declassified Gulag documents reveal that most of those released in the wartime amnesties were disabled and emaciated prisoners. The Gulag was not mainly unloading prisoners for the Red Army, but unloading its invalids.

RETHINKING THE GULAG

The highest rates of mortality that the Gulag ever recorded were in the years 1942 and 1943, due not only to the deprivations of wartime but also to Stalin's ban on releases. The Gulag had always been able to keep camp mortality rates low by releasing dying prisoners. During the war, however, the population of sick and disabled prisoners in the camps soared, and the Gulag was limited to releasing them through special amnesties. The NKVD-Gulag leadership lacked the ability to routinely and systematically release its "inferior workforce," whether criminal offenders or politicals. On the very day of the Nazi invasion of the Soviet Union, June 22, 1941, a NKVD and Procuracy directive prohibited the release of any counterrevolutionary offenders, bandits, recidivists, and "other dangerous criminals" from camps, colonies, and prisons. Such prisoners could not leave the camps once they completed their sentence, but had to stay on as wage laborers.[38] Many of them were emaciated and severely ill.

The increasing population of dying inmates, and the fact that the NKVD-Gulag leadership could no longer "unload the ballast," resulted in a crisis in the camps. This situation prompted high-ranking Soviet officials to question a number of Stalin's penal policies. The Gulag archives have preserved many draft decrees and letters to Stalin and other party leaders from spring 1942 seeking the authorization of additional large releases of sick and invalid prisoners. The flurry of letters and decrees, all making similar arguments in slightly different forms, can be interpreted in a number of ways. On the one hand, it appears that the leaders of the NKVD, Procuracy, and Commissariat of Justice were trying to convince Stalin and other party leaders to permit additional releases of ailing prisoners, above and beyond the enormous amnesties in fall 1941. The various iterations of letters and draft decrees suggest that Stalin was opposed to such releases, and that his subordinates had to make the case repeatedly using various arguments. This interpretation appears consistent with the Soviet leader's own views. Not only did he favor the 1939 ban on releases, but he refused to release counterrevolutionary offenders after the Nazi invasion. On the other hand, it is possible that the numerous revisions were part of an internal discussion among the NKVD, Procuracy, and Commissariat of Justice, and that the plans were never presented to the party leadership. Whatever the purpose or outcome of these draft letters and decrees, one thing is clear. More than a decade before the Gulag was dismantled, a number of high-ranking Soviet officials were convinced of the need to significantly restructure the Soviet forced labor camp system. The enormous wartime population of sick and emaciated prisoners prompted this discussion.

By the first half of 1942, weakened and invalid prisoners had reached 30–40 percent in most camps, and many camps reported over 50 percent.[39] The NKVD-Gulag leadership warned the party that in these circumstances high mortality rates would be unavoidable, and that it was necessary to take immediate action to release prisoners, even certain counterrevolutionary offenders. They wrote, for example: "At the present time there are 1,565,000 prisoners in the NKVD labor camps and colonies and of those, 142,000 prisoners, as of April 1, 1942, represented documented invalids removed from the labor rolls. They are entirely supported by the camps. At the same time, there are also 150,000 sick prisoners and prisoners with severe incurable ailments in NKVD camps and corrective-labor colonies. Most of them are bedridden and entirely unable to work. It would be impossible to restore their labor capability under camp conditions. This large number of prisoners who are invalids, sick, and not-work-capable produces high rates of mortality. The maintenance of this contingent in NKVD camps and colonies negatively impacts construction and industrial activities. It makes it difficult to create normal everyday conditions for the main labor pool. Housing prisoners becomes complicated and significant material resources (food and supplies) are being diverted."[40] Under Beria's proposal, persons sentenced for treason, terror, spying, sabotage, counterrevolutionary rightist-Trotskyist crimes, wrecking, and banditism would still be barred from release.[41] Beria argued that, "it would be expedient (*tselesoobrazno*) to give the NKVD an additional opportunity to release invalids, not-work-capable, women, and first-time offenders sentenced for petty crimes who do not represent a threat to state security."[42] Invoking the language used to justify the July 1941 release, Beria asserted that another large unloading of prisoners would enable the NKVD "to focus its attention and strength on securing the isolation of state criminals sentenced for counterrevolutionary activities, banditism, and other especially dangerous crimes."[43]

The hardships of war convinced many high-ranking Soviet officials, including Beria, that the camps should be limited to the most dangerous offenders. They asserted that discharging invalids would reduce pressure on the Gulag's limited resources and improve conditions for the work-capable prisoners. They also wanted fewer people to be sentenced to Gulag detention. They urged a greater reliance on the sentence of "corrective-labor without deprivation of freedom," which would not require that offenders be transported and detained in distant camps.[44] Leaders of the Gulag, NKVD, Commissariat of Justice, and Procuracy acknowledged as early as 1942 that citizens were more valuable to the state as free workers rather than penal laborers. Sending fewer people to the camps would save on the high cost of food, guards, and housing. Included among the draft letters was a one-page cost accounting of the 800 million rubles that the Gulag claimed it was spending annually to support hundreds of thousands of nonworking sick, weak, hospitalized, and invalid prisoners.[45] In 1940, Beria told Stalin that the Gulag was entirely self-supporting, but he could no longer offer such assurances. In a 1942 draft letter to Stalin and Molotov, NKVD chief Beria, the USSR Procurator, and the Commissar of Justice stressed that of the Gulag's 1.6 million prisoners, more than a third could no longer work for their upkeep: "400,000, or 25 percent of the total contingent, are sick or weakened, and another 180,000, or more than 10 percent, are invalids." They argued that the resources going to support this enormous population of ailing prisoners could otherwise be spent on work-capable inmates.[46]

Beria and his allies advocated a major reduction in the size of the Gulag population, by limiting Gulag detention to serious offenders. They believed that for crimes punishable with less than two years' deprivation of freedom, the courts should limit the sentence to corrective-labor without deprivation of freedom. The point of this, they said, would be to reduce the number of labor camp prisoners with short-term sentences. In 1941, as many as 28 percent of labor camp prisoners were serving terms of under three years.[47] On November 12, 1941, prompted by the growing labor shortage, Beria had signed an order transferring short-term offenders to the camps.[48] Now, however, the large number of emaciated prisoners caused him to advocate a different policy, the expanded use of non-custodial corrective labor, which involved penalties and fines. A non-custodial sentence of corrective labor without deprivation of freedom included a 25 percent deduction in wages.[49] Thus, proponents reasoned, persons sentenced would have to be highly productive in order to be able to support themselves and their family, and labor productivity would rise. To further illustrate the benefits of this non-custodial sanction, Beria noted that the NKVD had transferred as much as 474 million rubles into the state budget in 1941 from the wages of people sentenced to corrective labor at their place of work.[50] Moreover, the NKVD would no longer have to transport and accommodate large numbers of prisoners who had been sentenced for petty crimes.[51] This amounted to a fundamental rethinking of penal policy.

In several letters to Stalin and the party leadership (which included draft decrees of the Presidium of the Supreme Soviet), Beria and the heads of the Procuracy and the USSR Commissariat of Justice presented a number of radical ideas. First, they argued for the release of larger segments of the sick and invalid population, including many counterrevolutionary offenders.[52] Also released would be many women, juveniles, and former soldiers.[53] Second, Beria wanted to restore the Gulag's ability to routinely release sick and disabled prisoners according to Article

457 of the RSFSR Criminal Procedural Code and corresponding articles of the Criminal Procedural Codes of the other union republics. Judicial organs located in the areas where prisoners were serving their sentence would decide cases. It appears that the party leadership did restore the Gulag's right to routinely release sick prisoners through legal channels, a process that had been banned in 1939, sometime between April and August 1942. Nevertheless, the Gulag continued to deal with the problem of emaciated political prisoners, who were not eligible for release. The third proposal from Beria and his allies was to restore the practice of conditional-early release (*uslovno-dosrochnoe osvobozhdenie*) as an incentive for improving labor productivity, which had also been banned in 1939. They believed that prisoners should be allowed, once again, to earn workday credits for good behavior and productivity.[54] Workday credits were gradually reintroduced only after the war.[55]

It appears likely that at least some of the draft letters and decrees were presented to the party leadership. The arguments seem to have had little impact initially, as the NKVD was forced to establish a system of "independent invalid camps," for emaciated counterrevolutionary offenders, as noted in the previous chapter.[56] Beria had opposed the creation of such a system, arguing that it only added costs to an already overstretched Gulag. Nonetheless, a number of the ideas presented in the letters and draft decrees were eventually adopted. On April 29, 1942, camp directors were granted the right to release many counterrevolutionary offenders who had completed their sentences, including "complete invalids, not-work-capable prisoners (*netrudosposobnye*), the elderly, and women with children." Only counterrevolutionaries who had served out their sentences were included, and only "if they could not be utilized in the camps at all." Prisoners sentenced for "treason, terror, spying, diversion, Trotskyism, Rightists and bandits" were not to be released.[57] Stalin only granted an exception to the ban on camp departures for certain categories of political prisoners, and only if they were not work-capable and had completed their sentence. The April 1942 directive also partially reversed the ban on early release as an incentive for increasing labor productivity, a right that the Gulag had been lobbying hard to restore. It allowed camp directors, with the approval of the NKVD, to release "the more conscientious workers who fulfill their production targets and have not violated camp rules," all "in order to stimulate high labor productivity of prisoners."[58]

As the Stalinist leadership debated the release of greater numbers of prisoners who had grown sick and emaciated in the camps, they cracked down on so-called fakers. On April 8, 1943, the NKVD issued a circular entitled "On the battle against prisoners' willful self-exhaustion (*samoistishchenie*) and self-mutilation." The NKVD claimed that it had identified groups of prisoners at various camps, many of them Germans, who engaged in self-exhaustion and self-mutilation in order to obtain release from work and early release as invalids. The NKVD instructed camp officials "to expose every case of organized refusal to work, self-mutilation, the simulation of illnesses, and self-exhaustion." It identified several ways in which prisoners might commit such acts of "counterrevolutionary sabotage," including such benign acts as "selling their ration bread in exchange for tobacco." One of the accused was quoted as offering the following confession: "I tried to get released from work, to come before [the medical] commission as unfit for labor, and then to be certified [as an invalid] and sent home."[59]

In the course of the war, some of the policy changes advocated by Beria and his allies in the Procuracy and the Commissariat of Justice were gradually implemented. The ban on releases for political offenders continued to be enforced, but exemptions also widened. A May 7, 1942 directive allowed the release of persons sentenced for counterrevolutionary activity and anti-Soviet activity, as well as so-called socially dangerous elements. If these individuals were too sick and emaciated to be utilized in the camps, then they could be released, but only if they had completed their sentence.[60] A decree of the USSR Supreme Court plenum of August 1, 1942 authorized the courts to grant early release to one category of political prisoners, "family members of traitors to the Motherland," who were severely ill with incurable ailments.[61] In October 1942 and July 1943, circulars of the NKVD, Commissariat of Justice, and the USSR Procuracy allowed camps to proceed cautiously with the release of certain categories of counterrevolutionary offenders who had "mental illness or severe incurable ailments."[62] A NKVD and Procuracy directive of August 3, 1943 definitively lifted the ban on the early release of invalid prisoners who were sentenced for many "counterrevolutionary and especially dangerous crimes." The directive allowed for the early release of these prisoners in cases where inmates are "sick with severe incurable ailments or have completely lost their labor capability." By September 1, 1943, the Gulag reported that

205,297 invalids had been freed by court rulings. A NKVD, Procuracy and Commissariat of Justice directive of September 9, 1943 called for the early release of prisoners with "serious and incurable ailments."[63]

In the last quarter of 1943, the Gulag unloaded an enormous population of weakened and disabled prisoners. The archives contain evidence of new letters from Beria to Stalin at the USSR State Committee of Defense in September–October 1943, in which the NKVD chief requested a large release of invalid prisoners.[64] The language here repeats the earlier 1942 correspondence in a tired, bureaucratic way, suggesting a routine petition. Perhaps by now wartime releases of sick and disabled prisoners had become a frequent and regular occurrence. As Gulag chief Nasedkin briefly reported in August 1944, many prisoners were released from labor camps and colonies "by special decisions of the State Committee of Defense" in 1942–1943.[65] In late 1943, Beria indicated that the number of sick and disabled Gulag prisoners had reached staggering proportions. He now argued that the release of invalids, the elderly, the physically not-work-capable and chronically ill prisoners, regardless of the length of their sentence and the time of their arrest, would be "efficient." In NKVD camps and colonies, there were "200,000 invalids, elderly, persons physically unable to work, and sick with severe incurable ailments." Many were hospitalized and entirely unable to work, and Beria stressed that "their labor capability cannot be restored in conditions of detention."[66] Beria also asked for the right to release sick prisoners who had been sentenced for counter-revolutionary and other especially dangerous crimes, as well as recidivists.[67] He excluded from release only prisoners sentenced for "spying, sabotage, terror, treason, betrayal (*predatel'stvo*), collaboration, and self-mutilation."[68] Beria proposed that such prisoners would have the remainder of their term converted to a conditional sentence. Thus they would be removed from the Gulag system, but transferred to other places of detention, most likely to internal exile or a special settlement. Indeed, starting in the early 1930s, many sick, elderly and invalid prisoners who lacked relatives willing to take them in were systematically transferred into exile communities.[69]

Like the Gulag officials in 1941, Beria boasted that these releases largely freed men to enlist in the Red Army—an argument he knew would appeal to Stalin. However, most were severely emaciated. Solzhenitsyn described this population when he told the story of men released from camp in the winter of 1943–1944 who were huddled on the floor of the Cheliabinsk railroad station when the temperature outside was minus 13 degrees. Solzhenitsyn wrote: "Even to call them threadbare would be rank flattery. These were young fellows—emaciated, swollen, with sores on their lips. One of them, evidently in a fever, lay with bare chest on the snow, groaning . . . One of them had served out his term in camp, another had been released for illness . . . they could not get tickets to go home on the train. And they had no strength left to return to camp either—they were totally fagged out with diarrhea." A policeman shouted at a woman who tried to give them bread: "What's going on, auntie, have you recognized your relatives? You better get out of here."[70]

CAMP OFFICIALS ON "UNLOADING THE BALLAST"

To commemorate the Soviet victory in World War II, Stalin announced an enormous amnesty of prisoners in June 1945. The amnesty freed nearly half of the Gulag population. Yet this time it was Beria who objected, on the grounds that the amnesty freed many able-bodied prisoners and thereby undermined the ability of camps and colonies to meet production targets.[71] The NKVD chief wanted to "unload the ballast," not free work-capable inmates.

For many Gulag officials, however, Stalin's 1945 amnesty was welcome news. Gulag chief Nasedkin was relieved to have fewer prisoners competing for the system's limited resources. In July 1945, he stated: "A nearly 50 percent reduction in the contingent. That represents an enormous and great easing of our work both centrally and locally." He praised the amnesty for improving conditions in the camps. Nasedkin considered it a great accomplishment that the State Planning Agency (*Gosplan*) maintained the Gulag's bread and grain allocations at the levels of the third quarter, despite the enormous reduction in prisoners resulting from the amnesty. This, he said, would allow the Gulag to increase the average bread ration from 650 to 800 grams, or from 270–280 calories.[72] Similarly, many camp officials welcomed the amnesty "with extreme joy," as it helped relieve overcrowding and improve problems with inadequate supplies.[73]

While Gulag officials generally appreciated the 1945 unloading of emaciated prisoners, the camps and colonies continued to be burdened by sick and invalid prisoners who were barred from release.[74] Prisoners sentenced under the worst counterrevolutionary statutes, such as treason, spying, and sabotage, "can't go anywhere," noted one camp official. "They're sick but the civilian health departments (*oblzdrav, raizdravy*) won't take a single one of these sick people, so we keep them. All we managed to do is send our mentally ill inmates to the hospitals in Birobidzhan."[75] Large populations of emaciated political prisoners continued to burden camps, and officials complained about delays and difficulties with medical discharges. Camp health officials asked that the process of certifying invalids for release (*poriadok aktatsii*) be expedited because doctors were spending too much time on such releases. They needed more doctors to accelerate the process, but the Gulag medical-sanitation department chief, D.M. Loidin, refused. "We have enough doctors assigned to this task," he insisted.[76] Camp medical-sanitation department directors also continued to advocate for the right to medically discharge many counterrevolutionary offenders. Behind the scenes, the central Gulag leadership pushed this right with its NKVD-MVD superiors as well, but when speaking to camp subordinates, it took a tough line. Releases were considered too easy. Camps need to be pressured to do more with less.

Gulag officials admitted that a large population of prisoners were starving to death. The camps had no resources to support them, and prisoners were too emaciated to work and earn a ration. In a December 1945 report to Gulag chief Nasedkin, the director of Temlag described the dire condition of the prisoners he had released as invalids in previous years. "We had to release those with limited physical capability," he admitted, "because they could not survive on their own labor, given their weak physical condition. And the camp has no resources to support them."[77] As prisoners grew emaciated, they could not earn a ration to keep themselves alive. Either they starved to death in the camps or the Gulag released them to die elsewhere.

CONCEALING MASS RELEASES OF THE NEARLY DEAD

Even in its internal documents, the Stalinist regime worked hard to disguise the degree to which prisoners were violently exploited and then discarded en masse. In an August 1944 report to NKVD chief Beria entitled "The Work of the GULAG in the War Years (1941–1945)," Gulag chief Nasedkin noted that in the years 1941–1944, roughly 1.8 million prisoners had entered the camps and as many as 2.9 million prisoners were recorded as having left (*ubylo*). He boasted that 975,000 of the 2.9 million prisoners who exited the system were conscripted into the Red Army.[78] Nasedkin deceptively characterized the massive release of prisoners during World War II as a service to the Red Army and to the war effort, as if conscription were the primary purpose of these releases. Yet only one-third of prisoners who left the camps and colonies in the war years were actually conscripted. Nasedkin only briefly mentioned the catastrophic health of the prison labor force, despite the fact that the release of invalid and emaciated prisoners represented one of his primary concerns during the war. Gulag leaders routinely glossed over the problems of mass illness and starvation. In September 1945, the Gulag's medical-sanitation department chief asserted that the camps managed to endure the war "without serious epidemic outbreaks" and that even in 1942–1943 the typhus outbreak "did not pose a serious danger."[79] Such deceptive and Orwellian speech, as we have seen, was not unusual.

Moreover, the Stalinist leadership systematically concealed the Gulag's massive and routine unloading of its "ballast." Just as internal Gulag documents concealed mass starvation by classifying nutritional diseases as skin disorders, the Gulag omitted from its internal reports any specific mention of *aktirovanie* or medical discharge. In 1943, for example, internal reports included a few general "reasons for releases," such as prisoners released at the end of their sentence, released because their case was closed, released following "a review of the case in connection with a reduced sentence," and "other reasons." Most were identified as having been freed after completing their sentence.[80] It appears that the release of emaciated prisoners was accounted for under "other reasons," especially given that more prisoners were recorded under this subheading in the colonies, where most invalids resided. In July 1947, for example, 11 percent of released prisoners in the camps were freed for "other reasons," while in the colonies the figure was over 44 percent.[81] At the same time, emaciated prisoners could have been freed for various reasons. Perhaps the large population of prisoners released at the end of their sentence represented the *ukazniki* or the short-term offenders. Perhaps releases of invalid counterrevolutionaries were recorded under "other reasons." In 1948, the heading "reasons for releases" was replaced with "reasons for quarterly losses." Once again, there was no single entry that captured the release of certified invalids or medical discharge, which is especially striking given the large population of sick and disabled prisoners. Instead, the subcategories for labor "losses" or releases included the following reasons: the end of the prisoner's sentence; the closing of the case; review of the case in connection with a reduced sentence; clemency; directed to other places of detention; deaths; escapes; released and directed to exile and special settlements; and, as usual, the subcategory "other." Officials could have recorded released invalids under any of these subcategories of "losses," and chances are, they did.

The year 1948 represented a critical year in the history of Stalin's Gulag. A massive influx of new prisoners occurred following the draconian 1947 theft decrees. New rations were issued that year, as well as a new List of Illnesses. The number of released prisoners described as having completed their sentences dropped significantly, as did the number in the category "other." In the late 1940s, sentences got longer, and this may partly explain the sharp decline in the number of prisoners released at the end of their sentence. Moreover, an enormous number of prisoners were recorded under "directed to other places of detention." In July 1948, over 35 percent of prisoners released from the camps were "directed to other places of detention" as were 56 percent of prisoners released from the colonies. Most likely, these prisoners were transferred to special settlements, as Stalin introduced permanent exile in 1948 for persons released from the camps.[82] Three-quarters of all releases, an astounding 484,693 inmates for the quarter, were from the colonies, where the Gulag systematically concentrated its weakest and most emaciated prisoner population. This number amounted to nearly a quarter of the entire Gulag population unloaded in a mere three-month period, a truly staggering statistic.[83]

After 1948, the Gulag continued to unload emaciated prisoners on a massive scale, yet it deliberately masked the process in its internal reports. In April 1949, nearly 65 percent of those released were classified as "directed to other places of detention"; for the colonies, it was nearly 53 percent. The colonies accounted for 67 percent of "losses" in that quarter, with the total of all registered "losses" recorded at 386,221 inmates or nearly 16 percent of the Gulag population.[84] The Gulag's annual rate of turnover was well over two-thirds in the late 1940s. Many prisoners themselves petitioned for *aktirovanie*. In the third quarter of 1949, the largest share of prisoner petitions to the Gulag's medical-sanitation department were requests for medical discharge.[85] In 1949, when the MVD-Gulag leadership drafted new corrective labor camp instructions for the Council of Ministers' approval, it emphasized two issues—the need for incentives "to encourage good work by prisoners" and the need to unload sick and invalid prisoners "who need constant care and who do not have relatives and close friends." The latter, "would be placed in institutions of social security following their release from corrective-labor camps and colonies."[86] These prisoners were likely counted among those "directed to other places of detention."

In the 1950s, the Gulag continued to "unload its waste," in Solzhenitsyn's words, or its population of last-leggers—the *dokhodiagi*. In July 1950, the camps recorded 52.4 percent of releases and the colonies 63.7 percent under "directed to other places of detention." Releases from the colonies accounted for over 79 percent of "losses," with total registered "losses" recorded at 490,826 inmates, or nearly 19 percent of a Gulag population that had by now reached nearly 2.6 million.[87] In late 1952, a new subcategory appeared—"released early due to labor day credits," to reflect the reintroduction of an older policy. Many releases were recorded under this new subcategory, yet many more prisoners were released as invalids "to other places of detention." The quarterly report of April 1952 indicated that the camps released 42.3 percent as "directed to other places of detention," 35.6 percent as "released early on labor day credits," and only 9.3 percent as "freed at the end of one's sentence"; for the colonies, it was 67 percent "directed to other places of detention," only 2.8 percent "released early on labor day credits," and 25 percent "freed at the end of one's sentence." The total of "losses" recorded was 339,423, nearly 14 percent of the Gulag population.[88]

In the late Stalin period, the Gulag "unloaded the ballast" on a remarkable scale. In 1953, for the first time, medical discharge or *aktirovanie* was openly recorded under "reasons for losses in the quarter." According to the January 1953 report, over 56 percent of prisoners released from the colonies were freed under Article 457, five times as many as released by the camps. The largest single population of Gulag releases in the last quarter of 1952 (or as of January 1953) were persons freed under Article 457. Such releases accounted for nearly 36 percent of all inmates freed for the quarter, as compared with those released due to labor day credits (29 percent, the vast majority of whom were released from the camps) and releases at the end of one's sentence (24 percent). In total, over 90,000 prisoners were medically discharged or released under Article 457 in the last quarter of 1952, far surpassing all other categories of releases, including early release for labor day credits (over 72,000) and releases at the end of one's sentence (nearly 60,000).[89] Not coincidentally, the Gulag also reported its lowest rates of mortality in the 1950s. Dying prisoners were being released en masse.

The Gulag's own statistics likely underestimate the magnitude of release-to-die. Weak and emaciated prisoners could have been released at the end of their sentence, as many constituted petty criminal offenders. Prisoners who were severely ill but classified for light labor could have been released due to work-day credits. Sick and emaciated prisoners who were sentenced under counterrevolutionary statutes, and thereby barred from medical discharge, may have constituted the largest segment of those "directed to other places of detention." Thus the Article 457 subcategory probably did not capture all prisoners who were released as severely ill and no longer work-capable, but only those in the invalid category who were sentenced for routine criminal offenses. Moreover, when the Article 457 subcategory appeared, it included the wording, "and directed to other places of detention," which suggests that the earlier subcategory of "directed to other places of detention" actually referred to these Article 457 prisoners. The Gulag's internal data on medical discharges or *aktirovanie* was highly opaque, and designed to conceal the destructive nature of human exploitation in the Stalinist camps. Such distortions were not uncommon in the Stalin years, even in classified government documents. During the war, the leader's speeches, as well as official party newspapers, failed to mention hunger and starvation, despite the devastating impact of food shortages on the population.[90] Mainstream medical literature at the time limited its analysis of starvation to Soviet soldiers and citizens in occupied territories, and did not speak of starvation in the rear.[91] Later, during the 1946–1947 famine, use of the word "famine" was prohibited. Even the most secret governmental reports avoided the term, and Soviet doctors were instructed to mask mortality resulting from famine.[92] Thus both during the war and during the postwar famine of 1946–1947, Soviet statistical administrations concealed deaths from starvation in their internal records under "other causes of death."[93]

RELEASES AND MORTALITY RATES

Gulag prisoners died from illnesses and epidemics, insufficient food, housing, and clothing in the Arctic cold, and dangerous work conditions. Many died en route to their distant camps, thrown overboard from ships or out of trains in remote locations.[94] Memoirists describe undocumented and anonymous deaths, as bodies were "hauled away to the cemetery and buried in mass graves without so much as identification tags."[95] Despite the evidence of mass death in the camps, declassified Gulag archives reveal lower than expected mortality. Official mortality rates in the Gulag were generated as monthly or yearly averages. Typically camp officials reported that roughly 1–5 percent of the total inmate population died on their watch, although the figures reached as high as 15 percent following the 1932–1933 famine. In 1938, the final year of the Great Terror, mortality across all camps in the USSR averaged over 5 percent.[96] The Gulag reported the largest numbers of inmate deaths in the two worst years of the war, 1942–1943, when camp mortality climbed to nearly a quarter of all prisoners. Scholars have been justifiably cautious when using this data. Internal Gulag records are often inconsistent. Both the medical-sanitation department and the accounting and distribution department kept records on inmate deaths, and their figures do not coincide. Deaths during transport did not get included in the official record.[97] Sometimes mortality figures include the camps and colonies, other times only the camps or only camps and prisons, and sometimes the mortality data excludes the special camps. The official, yet incomplete and contradictory, Gulag figures for deaths in labor camps and colonies amount to roughly 1.5–1.7 million for the Stalin years, 1930–1953.[98] Given that roughly 18 million people passed through the camps and colonies at that time, the official Soviet statistics would suggest that only about 8–9 percent of prisoners died in Stalin's forced labor camp system. By all other accounts, this appears unlikely.

The Stalinist leadership demanded that camps maintain low mortality rates, and frequently punished officials when morality exceeded

mandated norms. Higher rates of mortality were consistently interpreted as the fault of camp administrators. Under such pressures, officials developed strategies to keep their mortality rates low, just as they
feigned higher production output through padding or deception (*tufta*).
Yet such manipulations of Gulag statistics were not limited to the lower
levels. The Gulag leadership and its OGPU-NKVD-MVD bosses con-
spired to produce camp statistics that would appear favorable. Thus
an accurate accounting of mortality in Stalin's Gulag is enormously
difficult to produce. The mortality rate most used in official documents
captured only deaths that occurred in Gulag medical facilities. In February 1933, Gulag chief Berman and Gulag medical-sanitation department chief Ginzburg complained that camp medical-sanitation depart
ments were failing to record deaths that did not take place in their
facilities.[99] By the mid-1930s, deaths both in- and outside camp clinics
and hospitals were reported. For 1935, Bamlag reported 5954 deaths
in health care facilities and 998 outside them, for a total of 6952,
or roughly 4 percent of its average prisoner population for the year.[100]
The reporting of two mortality rates—one within and one outside camp
medical facilities—persisted into the 1940s.[101] In 1945, a medical-
sanitation department director confessed that her staff believed that
their responsibilities were limited to serving only the hundreds of prisoners in their hospitals and clinics: "All other prisoners were out of the
view of medical workers." She underscored this as a "serious lapse,"
yet it demonstrates that camp health officials who maintained mortality records had little awareness of mortality outside their facilities.[102]

Moreover, the Gulag's culture of personal blame, where problems
were viewed as the result of individual failures, effectively discouraged
the honest reporting of camp deaths. In 1933, the Gulag chief attributed deaths that occurred outside the medical-sanitation department
facilities, in part, to "untimely hospitalization" and "the negligence of
medical workers."[103] Such accusatory memos were commonplace, for
the OGPU-NKVD-MVD and the Gulag leadership denied the destructive nature of Stalin's forced labor camp system, and were not inclined
to attribute deaths to the Gulag regime of severe exploitation and punitive rations. For example, Gulag officials maintained that the significantly higher rates of mortality (from heart, pulmonary, and stomach-
intestinal diseases as well as vitamin deficiency) in the NKVD colonies in
1941 were largely the result of untimely medical attention.[104] In 1949,

MVD instructions noted that hospital deaths constituted potentially punishable offenses: "In cases where death resulted from delayed hospitalization, a special investigation should take place for the purpose of exposing the guilty parties."[105]

Many factors contributed to the production of artificially low official Gulag mortality rates, yet perhaps none of these suppressed the death count more than the routine release of nearly dead prisoners. Camp officials openly acknowledged the direct correlation between releases and mortality rates. They complained that high rates of mortality were attributed to their inability to release prisoners in a timely manner. The medical-sanitation department director for the Molotov regional system of labor camps and colonies described how in the first half of 1945 her camps experienced an increase in the number of invalid and light-labor prisoners, as well as prisoners "off the labor rolls" (*zabalansovoe*). For accounting purposes related to "labor utilization" (as discussed in the final chapter), prisoners "off the labor rolls" included severely ill, disabled, invalid, and not-work-capable inmates. In all likelihood, they were largely political prisoners who could not be released as "incurables" or freed with a conditional sentence and transferred into exile. The medical-sanitation department director explained why this population of weakened and ailing prisoners had increased in the Molotov regional camp system: "Since August 1944, we almost never released people as incurables . . . I think that this explains, on the one hand, the growth in the number of contingents off the labor rolls and, on the other hand, it explains the high mortality figure that we have at present. We would have a lower mortality rate if we had released people a bit earlier than we were able to do with the amnesty."[106] Her camp system of about 20,000 inmates was releasing roughly 5,000 every six months before the sharp drop-off in releases, which suggests that they were unloading half of their prisoners annually. Such an extraordinary rate of turnover may not have been unique to the Molotov camps and colonies.

When officials failed to release terminally ill prisoners "on time" and these prisoners died in the camps, Gulag authorities were quick to reprimand them. In March 1934, Gulag chief Berman denounced a medical worker in Belbaltlag who failed to authorize a sick prisoner's release before that prisoner died at the worksite.[107] In February 1935, the procurator of Dmitlag in the Moscow region asked the USSR

Procuracy about the cases of prisoners who, consistent with the criminal code, were being released early due to illness.[108] He complained that sometimes it took months for these prisoners' cases to be processed, by which time the prisoners often died. He argued that if the local people's court (*narsud*) or regional court (*oblsud*) could handle these cases for Dmitlag, they could be processed in two or three days and "mortality can be avoided."[109] Many prisoners died shortly after their release, for the Gulag reserved the invalid classification for the nearly dead. A former prisoner and nurse in the Gulag told of how the medical staff was under orders to prepare the dying prisoner for release: "Before their exit (*pered exitus*), we had to inject camphor under the skin of the dying person."[110] Camphor injections were commonly used to raise blood pressure and to treat pain and fever.

The system of medical discharge or *aktirovanie* was deliberately employed to suppress mortality rates in the camps. A medical official commented on how one camp had "freed itself of its ballast and thereby improved its statistics."[111] The director of the medical-sanitation department for the Tomsk regional system of labor camps and colonies stated that, "our mortality rates are mostly due to people [with tuberculosis and nutritional dystrophy], who by law are not eligible for early release. I think it would be expedient to organize a local hospital in the Tomsk region for tuberculosis patients." He complained that the civilian health system would not take severely ill ex-prisoners, even when ordered to by the health minister.[112] Camps apparently routinely unloaded dying counterrevolutionary offenders into the civilian hospitals, or created makeshift hospitals that were designated as civilian medical institutions. The director of the medical-sanitation department for the Molotov regional camps and colonies stated: "At one of the subcontracting camp sections, we identified eight barracks where we could place the most severely ill from other camp sections of the region. This primitive institution was called a regional hospital."[113] She not only indicated that they isolated the sickest prisoners in a place they "called" a regional hospital, but noted that these prisoners received little food.[114]

The Gulag kept mortality rates low through deceptive accounting and by transferring severely ill and dying prisoners out of the camps and colonies. Some went to other places of detention such as prisons and settlements. Others were transferred into the civilian health care institutions, or released into the care of family members. Many were simply dumped out into the streets. A look at Gulag death statistics reveals that mortality trends correlated with releases to a certain degree, although more work needs to be done to better understand how the movement of prisoners affected mortality rates. Large and periodic amnesties make the correlation difficult to perceive during the war, when releases did not keep pace with the sharp rise in sick and emaciated prisoners. Nonetheless, the precipitous drop in mortality beginning in 1943 can be partly explained by the large releases of sick prisoners in 1943, and the lifting of the ban on medical discharge under Article 457 of the Criminal Code. In the late 1940s and early 1950s, the number of prisoners increased dramatically, living conditions worsened, and prisoners' physical labor capability plummeted. At the same time, Stalin's Gulag recorded the lowest rates of mortality in its history. Massive and systematic releases no doubt played a significant role in suppressing mortality in these years. Unloading sick and disabled prisoners concealed the Gulag's destructive capacity. As Solzhenitsyn explained, "The higher-ups were sly bastards. They released ahead of time on health grounds those who were going to kick the bucket in a month anyway."[115]

Historians are now looking more closely at this phenomenon. According to Oleg Khlevniuk, "early release for disabled and chronically ill prisoners offered an easy opportunity to tweak the figures . . . Since they did not die in the camps, they did not affect Gulag statistics."[116] Anne Applebaum writes, "both archives and memoirs indicate that it was common practice in many camps to release prisoners who were on the point of dying, thereby lowering camp death statistics."[117] Similarly, V.A. Isupov indicated that Gulag prisoners were released as invalids "in order to die."[118] Recent work by Mikhail Nakonechnyi demonstrates that Gulag mortality figures were highly distorted by the systematic release of *dokhodiagi*. According to Nakonechnyi, "Camp statistics only accounted for those prisoners who died within the confines (gates) of the camp or in camp medical institutions. Those who died shortly after their release as 'complete invalids' or 'seriously ill' did not spoil camp statistics, although their deaths resulted from Gulag detention."[119]

The NKVD preferred that prisoners be released into the care of relatives or to a set location. Relatives often could not even recognize their released family members, who had been utterly transformed by the systemic violence of the camps.[120] Freed invalids and other weakened and emaciated prisoners were often so frail that they could not make their journey home.[121] Indeed, many prisoners, like the former kulak described by historian Orlando Figes, died shortly after their release.[122] Solzhenitsyn described a man who was given a Gulag sentence in 1947: "And in 1950 he was released because he was dying and allowed to return home, where he died five months later."[123] Dr. Anton Walter, whom Eugenia Ginzburg met in the camps and later married, fell ill with scurvy while in the gold mines of Kolyma, and died soon after they left Kolyma when his scurvy sores reopened.[124] Ekaterina Golts was medically discharged (*aktirovana*) in 1944, and returned from her camp in Komi to the home of her brother in Moscow. Her niece recalled Katia's release: "She stayed with us for one night [in Moscow] . . . The next day, Katia went to the home of relatives of a fellow camp prisoner, somewhere about one hundred kilometers outside Moscow. After a few days there, she died suddenly. I think it was a stroke." Less than one week after her release, Katia was dead. Her niece remarked, "Of course, they released her from the camp in order to die at home. Such was the vile custom (*podlyi obychai*)."[125]

CONCLUSION

Gulag inmates were physically exploited to the maximum degree possible at each stage of their declining health, and then released when they were no longer work capable and on the verge of death. Systematic releases of sick and invalid prisoners made it possible for the Gulag to artificially suppress mortality rates, lower costs, and conceal the violence of exploitation. The dual system of "wringing out" and then discarding severely ill and emaciated inmates was temporarily disrupted following Stalin's 1939 ban on releases. The Nazi invasion of the Soviet Union in June 1941 deepened the health crisis in the camps. This provoked the NKVD-Gulag leadership, together with the leaders of the Procuracy and the Commissariat of Justice, to lobby party leaders persistently for the right to release greater and greater numbers of sick and disabled prisoners, including many categories of political prisoners who had previously been excluded from early release. Enormous amnesties and releases ensued. During World War II, millions of prisoners were freed on the pretext that they were being released to join the Red Army. However, only a fraction of them were physically fit for conscription. Most of them were emaciated and dying. At the same time, the wartime crisis forced Stalin's entourage to advocate for a leaner camp system, one that detained and exploited only the state's most dangerous enemies. Several Soviet leaders, including Beria, came to question whether the camps could continue to operate as a vast economic enterprise committed to the exploitation of millions of ordinary workers and peasants "who posed no threat to state security."

7 Power

"We Are Not Doctors but Delousers"

THOSE WHO WORKED within the Gulag's medical-sanitation department, including the prisoner doctors, found themselves in what Robert Jay Lifton called "an atrocity-producing situation." Those who worked within the institution, even the well intentioned, became associated with mass violence.[1] Some diminished and dehumanized their patients, while others tried hard to improve the lives of prisoners. The principal task of the Gulag medical-sanitation department was to maximize the number of working prisoners. Health care workers operated in a highly constrained environment and were forced to serve the system of physical exploitation. The Stalinist leadership established quotas and target figures on the numbers of prisoners that had to perform the basic work (*osnovnaia rabota*) of the camp, be it construction, mining, or forestry. There were also quotas restricting the number of inmates who were sick, hospitalized, in recovery or convalescent camps, invalids and non-working, and even quotas on mortality. Doctors who undermined the camp's mandated quotas often faced punishment, which for prisoner doctors, could mean leaving the relative comfort and survivability of the clinic and returning to the deadly work of the mine. The Gulag's medical-sanitation department had little power relative to the camps' production managers, as their work was often limited to operating the bathhouse and containing epidemics. As a camp medical-sanitation department director lamented after the war, a certain view persisted among Gulag officials, that "we are not doctors but delousers (*my ne vrachi, a vosheboiki*)."[2]

The Gulag medical-sanitation department possessed various functions. It employed civilian and prisoner doctors, medical orderlies, and nonmedically trained staff to provide health care to prisoners in clinics, hospitals, and convalescent institutions. It maintained prisoner health records, and compiled statistics on illness and mortality. The department was tasked with reducing illnesses and preventing and containing epidemics. It conducted disinfections of persons and facilities, and ensured the regularity of prisoners' baths. It inspected camp kitchens and cafeterias, and monitored food preparation.[3] As the Gulag medical-sanitation department chief told his subordinates after the war, they had to "secure real sanitary order in the kitchens, in the cafeterias, and in other food sites."[4] But their job did not end there: "Comrades, you have enormous health care tasks before you—from eliminating lice to maintaining heat in the barracks in the winter, to obtaining clothes [for prisoners]—these and much, much more have to be in your field of vision."[5] Although the department was tasked with a great deal, it possessed little power within the camp hierarchy.

The powerlessness of Gulag's health care workers relative to other camp authorities was put on display at an historic meeting that took place shortly after World War II. In September 1945 in the Siberian city of Novosibirsk, the directors of the medical-sanitation departments for the regional camps and colonies in the Far East, Siberia, the Urals, and Central Asia met with their boss, D.M. Loidin, the Gulag's medical-sanitation department chief.[6] By the 1940s, the NKVD-MVD-Gulag administration supervised an immense network of hundreds of labor camps and colonies. In 1944, there were 56 labor camps directly subordinate to the central or all-Union NKVD-MVD, and 69 labor camps and colonies that operated under republic and regional administrations and departments of so-called corrective-labor camps and colonies (UITLK-OITK). The 69 large complexes of camps and colonies consisted of 910 camp divisions and 424 labor colonies.[7] These locally operated camps and colonies represented the base of the Gulag pyramid. Following the June 26 and August 10, 1940 decrees on labor discipline, petty theft, and hooliganism, the number of prisoners in the camps and colonies rose dramatically, and the colonies began to assume more important economic tasks.[8] They directed their healthier prisoners to priority sites and became the dumping ground for the Gulag's most sick and emaciated prisoners.

The postwar meeting brought the regional medical-sanitation department directors together for the first time in Gulag history. Gulag medical chief Loidin stated that the point of their meeting was to discuss what they had learned from their wartime experience and to find ways to better execute their tasks in the new era of postwar reconstruction.[9] The two-day conference (*soveshchanie*) was captured in verbatim transcripts. These unusual archival artifacts reveal the principal concerns of Gulag medical-sanitation department administrators, as well as the mentality of the officials who managed the system. The transcript captures the exchange between camp health directors and the Gulag medical-sanitation department chief, and exposes their underlying tensions and disagreements. It reveals the worldview of those who worked with ailing prisoners, their hidden assumptions, and their automatic responses to chronic problems. The discussion provides information on a range of issues related to the Gulag's health care system. Finally, it illustrates the systemic subordination of prisoners' health to the economic and production priorities of the camps. The function of the Gulag medical-sanitation departments was to keep prisoners work-capable, and thereby advance the Stalinist system of human exploitation.

The regional camp officials were pleased finally to be gathered together for the first time, and used the opportunity to vent their frustrations. The director of the medical-sanitation department for the Cheliabinsk regional camp system called the meeting "enormously significant." "We boil in our own juice," he said. "We know only our own particular camp, and we don't know how other camps work."[10] The medical-sanitation department director for the Kazakh republic system of camps and colonies described the meeting as "extremely long-awaited" and a chance not only to listen to Loidin's complaints, but "to settle scores (*svesti schety*) of our medical-sanitation departments in the periphery with the Gulag sanitation administration."[11] The group was not pleased with their boss. They complained repeatedly that their requests for help were not heeded, and that camp administrators undervalued their work. The NKVD-Gulag leadership rarely provided assistance, and the civilian health departments could not support their efforts either. According to the medical-sanitation department director for the

Krasnoiarsk UITLK system, camp authorities "don't view [health care] activities as serving the state's interest."[12]

TENSIONS BETWEEN CENTER AND PERIPHERY

The Gulag's was not a typical health care establishment. As previously noted, the Stalinist leadership did not routinely collect basic health data on prisoners, such as blood pressure, temperature, or weight. Rather, the Gulag health care system was tasked with maximizing the number of working prisoners. Rates of exploitation were recorded in the "labor utilization" data. As discussed in more detail in chapter 9, the Gulag created four categories of labor utilization: Group A: labor force working in industry; Group B: occupied in the service and maintenance of camps and colonies; Group C: sick; Group D: not working for various reasons. The Gulag health service had to maximize the number of prisoners engaged in the industrial work of the camps (Group A) and to minimize the number of inmates performing light labor (Group B) or not working at all (Groups C and D). The medical-sanitation department directors routinely communicated with their Gulag superiors via telegram to report their camps' data on "lost labor days" (cases of illness, self-mutilation, mortality, etc.) and "labor utilization."

Responsibility for the physical condition of prisoners rested largely with the camps. In the view of the Gulag medical-sanitation department chief, the camps could be doing a lot better. Although the medical-sanitation department directors were reporting relatively modest mortality figures, Loidin wanted them even lower. He stated that the Gulag leadership is "not satisfied with the current data on Group C [illness] and on mortality."[13] The medical-sanitation department chief demanded that camps maintain impossibly low quotas—mortality under 0.3 percent and illness under 5 percent.[14] On the one hand, Loidin admitted that hospital rations were inadequate, and that camp prisoners largely suffered from nutritional dystrophy (alimentarnaia distrofiia) and vitamin deficiency (avitaminizy). He accepted that many camps lacked undergarments, beds, dishes, and medical equipment.[15] On the other land, Loidin had an aggressive and accusatory style. He condemned "criminal and disgraceful practices" that produced "shameful and unacceptable" mortality rates, and insisted the camp officials who hospitalized prisoners "too late" should be punished.[16]

Loidin appeared annoyed with his staff, and accused them of being weak, lacking initiative, and dealing with problems superficially. He reproached them for their "mood of demobilization" and characterized his less exemplary subordinates as having sin in their soul (*na svoei dushe grekh*).[17] His first instinct was always to blame problems on individual camp administrators who, he insisted, were responsible for their camps' statistics on illness and mortality.[18] For Loidin, it was the incompetency of the camp medical-sanitation departments, rather than the Gulag's system of brutal exploitation, that was responsible for the poor health of prisoners.

When his subordinates complained, the Gulag medical chief hurled accusations at them, and scolded them for their lack of initiative and resourcefulness. He criticized them for complaining about shortages of trained cadres instead of taking the initiative to organize training sessions for doctors at regional hospitals.[19] One official complained that the Gulag refused to give him a doctor who specialized in treating tuberculosis patients, but Loidin asked, "Whose fault is that?" Although the health official rejected any accusation, Loidin told him to simply order his doctors to go through tuberculosis training: "You must order them to do it, and that's it" (*nuzhno prikazat' i vse*).[20] The tense discussion between center and periphery often concerned resources and personnel. One director complained that his camps had only four doctors to serve 5000 prisoners, and that the Gulag refused to provide resources, but Loidin accused him of "connivance."[21] He told officials who complained about the lack of food that their efforts to gather wild plants were "very weak." He condemned them for whining about the shortages of medical literature rather than thinking up ways to better use the medical journals they had.[22] In short, rather than acknowledge his subordinates' grievances, Loidin blamed them for failing to be resourceful and discover solutions to the problems themselves. He scolded his subordinates for their "perverse method of leadership," for working "superficially" and "automatically." He described the quality of their work as unsatisfactory or "on a low level," and told them that they had to work "more intensely" and examine issues more deeply.[23] Nonetheless, Loidin tried to motivate his subordinates. He challenged, rather cynically, the notion that the medical-sanitation departments were relatively powerless and stressed that they have "by right, a leading role to play" in the camps.[24]

Loidin's attitude underscored the industrial mission of the health care system in the camps. The medical-sanitation departments were tasked not just with providing health care, but with maximizing the exploitation of prisoners' labor: "We don't simply represent a health care organization designed to provide medical assistance to a certain population. We are a medical-sanitation organization that is inextricably tied to an industrial organization with specific government plans. The more people participate in production, the better the chance that any given organization's production plan will be fulfilled. The success of production depends on the physical condition of people and how many people are included in production. One of the main tasks of our sanitation service is to facilitate the best execution of the industrial plan."[25]

At the same time, Loidin told the medical-sanitation department directors that they were obligated to report infractions. He told his staff "to avoid appeasement" on matters concerning the everyday sanitary conditions of prisoners "for fear of straining the relationship" with their camp administrators.[26] They must not hide information on camp operations from the Gulag leadership: "Failing to send information to us is tantamount to covering up sanitation problems at the camp."[27] Soviet leaders strongly encouraged "signals from below," but sending such letters and denunciations was often risky for the informant.[28] Loidin assured his subordinates that the Gulag would punish camp administrators who violated sanitation rules.[29] At the same time, he told his staff not to overdo it. Fines for violations of camp rules should be measured and not issued with "unhealthy enthusiasm."[30]

Medical-sanitation department officials experienced a great deal of workplace stress to keep mortality, illness, and labor utilization data close to mandated targets. One health official explained: "A camp is a very shaky thing. If we don't fulfill our role in the camp, if we become the least bit lenient, then it all collapses like a house of cards. D.M. [Loidin] asked me why I'm anxious all the time. I'm used to boiling in a pot. I feel that even if I relax for an hour at home, I might neglect something [at the camp]."[31] The medical-sanitation department directors did not appreciate the fact that their boss was increasing the pressure on them.[32] They expressed frustration that health workers were being asked to do so much, while the Gulag leadership refused to respond to their requests for various forms of assistance. The medical-sanitation department director for the Turkmen republic camps and colonies told

Loidin, "You have given us a whole series of tasks that we must fulfill unconditionally. Yet we need the medical and financial tools to do it. I have submitted my requests in detail, but in reality, I've received nothing so far."[33]

The September 1945 meeting exposed the tensions between the Gulag center and its periphery. The medical-sanitation department directors felt undervalued and neglected, and complained that Gulag leaders did not appreciate the difficulties they faced.[34] The director of the medical-sanitation department in the Yakut autonomous republic told his comrades that conditions in his region were so terrible that "few people can truly comprehend what Yakutia is all about" and "even the Gulag does not understand it sufficiently."[35] He described how mortality rates were "catastrophic" in the first half of 1943, although he received telegrams from Moscow every ten days asking why the high mortality rates. His camps lacked linens, the food was terrible, and simply: "The picture was ugly."[36] Another health official noted that in many of his camp divisions, over a third of the prisoners were "defective."[37] The medical-sanitation department directors of the regional camps and colonies underscored the structural, systemic, and environmental problems that they confronted. In Yakutia, camp units were dispersed and remote, some 3500 kilometers from the center of Yakutsk. In one of these distant camps consisting of 370 prisoners who worked in fishing and coal mining, there was no sanitary regime to speak of; the prisoners, guards, and civilian employees, men and women, all lived under one roof.[38] In the Turkmen republic, some camp subdivisions were 1100 kilometers from the center and one was only reachable by plane.[39] Other officials described camp sections without telephone or telegram connections, where no communications could be sent to the Gulag for weeks.[40] By stressing environmental and systemic constraints, camp officials defended themselves against Loidin's accusations.

Gulag health officials also underscored the difficulty of maintaining work-capable prisoners when basic supplies were severely lacking. The deputy head of the Chita medical-sanitation department complained about the lack of clothing for prisoners, which directly impacted their health. The problem, she said, begins at the moment the prisoner enters the system: "How do the prisoner contingents arrive in our camps and colonies from the prisons? Practically in their birthday suit. One summer, sitting in the medical-sanitation department, I saw a prisoner convoy and I didn't know whether these were prisoners or some kind of athletes because they were walking around town in their underwear." She stressed to Loidin, "Understand, that if people are coming to us naked, we don't have the means to constantly clothe them."[41] She believed that the Gulag "must go to the prisoner's home, get his clothes and shoes, and only then transport him to the camps."[42]

Medical-sanitation department authorities repeatedly stressed to their Gulag boss that they were not responsible for the poor health of prisoners. They catalogued the many systemic obstacles they faced in their attempt to improve inmate health conditions. In particular, officials explained that prisoner overcrowding made it impossible for them to comply with NKVD Order No. 0033 of January 1943 "On preserving and improving the physical condition of prisoners," which mandated a two-square-meter minimum for housing per prisoner.[43] The department director for the Turkmen republic camps and colonies complained, "What is keeping us from creating appropriate living standards for prisoners? A lot. First of all, we're inhibited by the relentless influx of prisoners into our camp sections. How many times have I intervened on this matter? How many times have I reported to the deputy of the NKVD? How many times have I spoken with the head of the regional camps? All with no result."[44] His camps and colonies experienced severe shortages of clothing—only 25 percent of their need for tunics and pants had been met, 65 percent of their need for footwear, and 50 percent for undershirts. He said that the idea of changing all linens to prevent epidemics was just a fantasy, especially for colonies located outside the major city of Ashkhabad.[45]

Camp health officials had to contend with insufficient housing, clothing, and other resources. Prisoners in the camps, whether they were in barracks or hospitals, lacked sheets, towels, and undergarments. The medical-sanitation department director for the Molotov regional system of camps and colonies complained: "We don't think about two shirts anymore, we dream of having just one. We're forced to collect undergarments the night before in order to give prisoners a change of clothes during the sanitation bath."[46] Another health official stated simply: "There are no undergarments, hence the lack of sanitation."[47] Severe overcrowding and poor housing also negatively affected the health of prisoners. The medical-sanitation department director for the Krasnoiarsk regional system of labor camps and colonies described

how many prisoners "lived in a canvas tent all winter."[48] He noted:
"Only the Stakhanovite barracks have bed linens, and they get their
bedding at the expense of the other brigades."[49] The official pleaded:
"Help is absolutely crucial."[50] In the Molotov region, one square me-
ter per prisoner was the norm in many industrial colonies. Given the
lack of beds, many prisoners slept with their clothes on, which in turn
caused an enormous number of skin ailments.[51]

Under such impossible conditions, camp officials resented being held
responsible for the health of prisoners. The medical-sanitation department director for the camps and colonies of the Novosibirsk region
complained about the lack of hair clippers. He said that the 13,000 prisoners who had passed through the transit camp in the past eight months
were infested with lice because the camp lacked even a single pair of
clippers. He expressed frustration with his superiors: "The Gulag has
to take up this issue of haircutting instruments. We have sent letters to
the Gulag, but we received no answer."[52] Camp survivors frequently
mention the intractable problem of lice. Varlam Shalamov described
how prisoners boiled their underwear furiously in large tin cans in order to kill the parasites.[53]

While Moscow issued orders to the camps to maintain the physical labor capability of prisoners, the Stalinist leadership offered little
help to officials who tried to execute these orders. Medical-sanitation
department directors could do little when prisoners emerged from long
transports in dire physical condition. For inmates, these degrading and
painful rail journeys constituted, as Judith Pallot notes, "punitive transportation" an important element of the Soviet penal order.[54] Novosibirsk, which was located on a railway line, received many inmates who
had been transported in such prison boxcars. The health official cried:
"What is the result? The prisoners lack hot food, the journey drags on
for a month and, in the end, once the prisoners arrive and are removed
[from the boxcars], it is hard to restore them to health, they occupy a
[hospital] bed, and it's impossible to do anything with them." Loidin
asked, "What are you suggesting?" The medical-sanitation department
director replied, "That there be no lengthy transport of prisoners in
boxcars. Those prisoners who come to us from boxcars, most of them
are in an irreversible condition."[55]

Many health problems were systemic and chronic, and inherent in
the Gulag's design. As one official stated, "From the comrades' speeches,

it's evident that they cope with a number of defects when it comes to sanitary everyday life conditions, food, and the labor utilization of contingents. Some UITLKs do a bit better, others do a bit worse, but all told, we all suffer from the exact same illness."[56] Health officials struggled with food, clothing, housing, and other resources because the Gulag system was not designed to fully supply all prisoners. The Gulag provided barely enough food to the most productive prisoners, and it expected camp officials to find local resources for additional food and medicine. The medical-sanitation department director for the Kazakh republic camps and colonies put it this way: "The state of health care in many cases depends on things that are beyond our control—the lack of space, the inadequacy of the food ration, the lack of specialized hospitals. And we have complained about this to the Gulag."[57] The director of the Novosibirsk region complained that prisons and transit camps unloaded their sickest prisoners into his labor camp system: "The Tashkent transit camp sends us an especially poor contingent. There wasn't a single prisoner that wasn't infested with lice . . . The Tashkent transit camp took the liberty of sending people who couldn't even move. We had to remove them and put them in a hospital . . . Our camp divisions get clogged with large numbers of sick prisoners from the transit camp. Plus they're severely ill people who are not subject to medical discharge. We have now accumulated many such people."[58] Camp officials underscored the systemic problems that destroyed the health of prisoners, and refused to accept blame from their Gulag boss.

For the doctors and camp officials who were involved in the process of medical discharge or *aktirovanie,* there were certain risks. They could be punished for performing "improper" certifications for release, that is, releasing prisoners who were not completely depleted and could still perform some light labor. The medical-sanitation department directors were required to oversee this process and make sure that no one was being certified who was not truly incurably ill and useless as a laborer. A medical-sanitation department official described how one of his health directors had been arrested for wrongly certifying invalids for release (*za nepravil'noe aktirovanie*) but released following a court review. He complained that doctors are not given the final word in these decisions, that they "have a passive role" while the director of the camp operations department can protest a doctor's decision on certification.[59] The medical-sanitation department director from the

Chkalov region stated: "We need to examine the issue of certification [for medical discharge]. The matter is extremely important. It impacts everyone here today on some level. A doctor was arrested in Chkalov, and another was detained for four months in Kazakhstan . . . I think that this matter [of *aktirovanie*] must be managed better because it's a serious issue. The leaders of the medical-sanitation departments are held personally responsible for it."[60]

To avoid punishment, health officials had to be very careful in their releases. Many were keen to tell their boss Loidin that they were vigilantly supervising the process of *aktirovanie*, and provided examples of their strict oversight. One medical-sanitation department official reported that his staff was verifying the medical discharges, and that they had some cases where they had to protest incorrect certification, although he stressed (to protect his staff) that the doctors were not at fault. Rather, four months had passed and the prisoners' health had improved, such that they were moved to category 3 light labor.[61] Since these prisoners could still do light labor, their certification was cancelled. The head of the medical-sanitation department for the Altai regional system of camps and colonies described how her staff handled medical discharge in order to ensure that no one was being freed who did not meet the Gulag standard of total physical depletion. She said, "There is not a single prisoner whose case I have not personally reviewed. I think that this method is the most appropriate. I can see for myself that a person is, in fact, eligible for release."[62]

As we have seen, OGPU-NKVD-MVD and Gulag chiefs blamed individual camps for high rates of illness and mortality, but camp officials rejected the accusation. Instead, they blamed illness and mortality on systemic problems outside their control, such as overcrowding and insufficient food. In 1945, the medical-sanitation department director for the Omsk regional camps and colonies attributed the high illness and mortality rates largely to severe overcrowding and the lack of a proper transit camp, a problem that "mixes up all the cards on us." She noted that her transit camp building was built to accommodate 500, but it now held 1200–1300 people, and stressed: "Certainly we can't observe the rules of quarantine and labor utilization."[63] Camp officials often complained about overflows of prisoners coming through the transit camps.[64] The medical-sanitation department director for the Turkmen republic camps and colonies described the bleak food situation for prisoners, and noted: "Naturally, mortality among the camp population has increased."[65] He turned to his boss and bluntly insisted: "We need the GULAG's help with food." Yet food was not his only problem. He identified several other causes of high mortality in 1945, beginning with the prisons: "We receive a very emaciated contingent from the prisons." Prison inmates experienced extreme overcrowding, to the point where they were literally deprived of oxygen. To remedy the situation, the NKVD issued an order to unload the prisons and send the contingent to the colonies, yet these prisoners were already in extremely poor health. Prisoners' diet was not balanced and was vitamin deficient, he argued, and even in camps, prisoners were densely crowded together. They lacked adequate supplies of clothing and bedding, and the camp had a shortage of hospital beds and medical staff.[66] Like the other directors, he asserted that medical-sanitation department workers should not be responsible for problems that were outside their control.

SHORTAGES OF DOCTORS, SUPPLIES, AND MEDICAL TRAINING

Loidin indicated that the system experienced a 30 percent shortage of doctors and an even greater deficit of specialists (surgeons, ophthalmologists, x-ray technicians, etc.). He told his subordinates: "Comrades, our [medical] cadres are not bad. The trouble is that we have fewer than we need."[67] Living conditions at many camps remained extremely poor for civilian doctors, and retention proved difficult. According to one medical-sanitation department director, "I have fourteen petitions from medical workers asking for dismissal because they do not have adequate food for their children or clothing or appropriate housing conditions."[68] Similarly, the medical-sanitation department director for the camps and colonies of the Kazakh republic spoke of his inability to accept some civilian doctors because he lacked housing for them.[69] The medical-sanitation department director for the camps and colonies in the Novosibirsk region also lamented the very poor living conditions for civilian medical workers, and said that they were all trying to leave the camp system and get work elsewhere.[70]

Health officials complained that the Gulag leadership ignored their appeals for more doctors. The head of the medical-sanitation department for the Altai region noted, "Someone here said that they had

8000 prisoners and twenty-five doctors. Well, we have 16,000 prisoners and fifteen doctors—eight civilian and seven prisoners. We used to have two camp divisions that didn't have a doctor at all."[71] She pleaded with Loidin to send more doctors. The head of the medical-sanitation department for the Turkmen republic camps and colonies indicated that his system had a shortage of doctors as well, and when he turned to the Gulag for help, he was told that no civilian cadres were available. Although the inmate population at his camp continued to increase, the medical staff remained unchanged at just seven civilian workers for 5000 prisoners.[72] At the Primorsky regional camps and colonies in 1945, there were sixteen civilian and fifteen inmate doctors, which included those staffing the separate clinic for civilian workers.[73]

In addition to shortages of personnel, health directors complained about the lack of medical equipment and access to medical training for their staff. The deputy director of the Chita regional medical-sanitation department stated that doctors in the system had to be generalists and prepared to handle everything from pediatrics to epidemiology. She argued that since young doctors were being trained as specialists in the academic centers of Novosibirsk and Omsk, those in Chita too should be allowed to take leave for more education to acquire additional specialties.[74] Like many of her colleagues, she pleaded for greater access to scientific publications, for "a doctor cannot work by instructions and directives. He needs to have some kind of additional resources."[75] By contrast, another health official said that every Saturday her doctors attended industrial and scientific meetings in the city of Molotov, where they received practical advice from local medical specialists who presented reports and lectures. Professors at the medical institute had also agreed to allow camp doctors to earn additional training and "acquire the title of specialist." One official concluded her remarks with a plea for Loidin to help her staff improve their qualifications and acquire additional training at the regional medical institutes. She complained that prison doctors were given release time for education and training, but camp doctors were not.[76] Many health officials stressed the need to provide for doctors' continuing education, arguing that camp doctors were not keeping up with medical knowledge. One described how there was an outbreak of malaria in a women's barracks because doctors knew very little about malaria prevention.[77] The head of the medical-sanitation department for the Kazakh SSR camps and colonies admitted: "We've been working for decades and have fallen behind [in our knowledge]. No one has ever raised his qualifications or taken any classes for retraining."[78]

In addition to more staff and better training, Gulag health officials wanted equipment, medicines, and access to medical journals and literature. The medical-sanitation department director for the Molotov region said that health care remained "at a low level" for many reasons, including a lack of facilities and equipment. "Our health care institutions have a primitive and temporary character. We don't have a single facility that can be called a real hospital. We completely lack supplies. Most of our patients lie on trestle-beds (*na topchanakh*). There's no medical equipment."[79] At the same time, there was a good deal of variation in the quality of hospitals and equipment across the camps of Stalin's vast archipelago. One official could not believe how well-equipped the hospitals were in the camps of Novosibirsk, especially as compared with the terrible conditions in Yakutia, where there were "only two decent hospitals." Many camp divisions had no hospital at all, and at several others the prisoner barracks, clinic, and hospital were housed together in one building. Given the distant location and overcrowding of the central hospital in Yakutia, prisoners who were not centrally located could not access it.[80]

Despite the dismal state of camp medicine, Loidin demanded that all camps must conduct medical research. He indicated that the NKVD-Gulag leadership wanted camps to maintain laboratories for "bacteriological and medical analysis" in order "to improve their diagnoses and treatments."[81] In the 1930s–1950s, Gulag medical research grew steadily, and certain camps developed their own research facilities.[82] Recently declassified archival documents indicate that doctors may have begun conducting medical research on prisoners during the war. Medical research in the Gulag does not resemble Nazi medicine, where physicians who supported the Nazi's aims conducted lethal experiments on prisoners.[83] It often involved severely ill or dying inmates and, in many cases, the scientists were themselves prisoners. These scientific studies largely focused on starvation diseases, and scientists often merely catalogued the physiological changes that occurred as human bodies slowly deteriorated from starvation.[84] My preliminary analysis of these scientific papers indicates that Gulag medical researchers were highly constrained in their statements, treatments, and subjects of study, and maintained a conspicuous silence concerning the context of penal labor. Gulag medical research concealed or denied the presence of mass starvation and penal exploitation, and often served to sanitize and normalize the labor camp environment.[85]

AT THE BOTTOM OF THE GULAG HIERARCHY

Memoirists offer differing accounts concerning the relative power of Gulag doctors. Shalamov claimed that, although a tension existed between camp health officials and production chiefs, the doctors possessed a degree of control over their decisions to relieve prisoners from work. "Relations were almost inevitably hostile between camp authorities and their medical personnel. The very nature of their duties pulled them in different directions. The authorities always wanted ... as many people as possible working. The doctor, on the other hand, saw that the bounds of good and evil had long since been passed, that people being sent to work were sick, tired and exhausted, and had a right to be freed from work in much greater numbers than the camp authorities desired."[86] At the same time, the medical-sanitation departments faced enormous pressure to keep all prisoners working. Solzhenitsyn characterized the medical-sanitation department as "servile" and significantly less powerful than the production administration.[87] Recently declassified Gulag archival documents demonstrate that health officials in the camps were, in general, considerably disempowered.

Despite the importance of its work, the Gulag medical-sanitation department occupied a very low position within the camp bureaucracy. The director of the medical-sanitation department for the Yakut republic camps and colonies believed his staff had less power than even the camp cultural-education department, whose deputy director, he said, effectively ran the hospital in 1942: "If he didn't like the fact that a doctor admitted a sick person into the hospital, he would verify the history of the person's illness, take their temperature, and if there was no fever, he would discharge the patient."[88] Health officials complained that they were excluded from production meetings, and that economic planning decisions were made without regard for prisoners' physical labor capability.[89] One official complained of "colossal overcrowding in all of our camp sections" because the medical-sanitation department is not involved in decisions related to capacity. He described his attempt to write to the Gulag about the problem. His camp director demanded to see the letter, then crossed out much of the text, and cried: "What kind of garbage are you writing?! You're not sending off a single piece of paper without my signature!"[90] Tired of the camp administration's obstructionism, one medical chief insisted that there be a law making the Gulag medical-sanitation departments subordinate to the civilian health departments. According to Solzhenitsyn, prior to 1932, the Gulag medical-sanitation departments were indeed subordinate to the People's Commissariat of Health, and "the doctors could still be doctors," yet once these departments were handed over to the Gulag, "it became their goal to help the oppressors and to be gravediggers."[91]

Late in the war, the Gulag leadership began issuing directives to the camps and colonies on the need to improve the physical condition of prisoners. According to health officials, these Gulag directives enhanced the authority of the medical-sanitation departments and made their work easier. One official underscored the connection between such signals from above and the behavior of local camp administrators. He noted that camp operations changed dramatically once the NKVD and the Gulag began to stress issues related to prisoners' living conditions late in the war: "Comrades! 1944 and 1945 represented a radical change in our work and life in the camps and colonies. The USSR NKVD orders No. 0033, No. 00640, and other orders, plus a series of other Gulag directives and instructions, played a major role in the dramatic shift in favor of improved conditions in the camps and colonies and especially in preserving the physical condition of prisoners. From the moment these orders were issued, from the time that the NKVD and the Gulag became directly involved and interested in the prisoners' daily life and labor utilization, from that time on, a new era in the life of the camps began, an era of care for prisoners, an era of struggle for human life. The appearance of serious demands from the NKVD and the Gulag to the administrative leadership of the camps and colonies concerning the everyday life of prisoners forced many directors to change their style of work. And this made the job of the medical-sanitation departments much easier and their work more effective."[92] The medical-sanitation department directors stressed the importance of high-level interventions on their behalf, given that camp bosses were typically unresponsive to their needs.

Regional health directors also protested the Gulag's low status relative to Soviet prisons. They complained about how prisons unloaded sick prisoners into the camps and colonies. One official explained:

"Our relationship with the prisons is very difficult. This issue remains unsettled. I have raised this issue numerous times, but still we have no concrete solution. The prisons remain the sons and we, the UITLK, the stepsons. Whatever the prisons do, it's all forgiven. But all we have to do is mistakenly transfer the wrong contingent, and we're severely punished. Here's my request: establish a proper relationship between the prisons and the UITLK. The prisons pass people on to us who are practically corpses. When we object, they tell us that operational measures cannot be disrupted, and they continue to throw us a defective contingent. They free themselves of the burden and dump it all on our shoulders. Often they don't even observe quarantine and [their prisoners] give us infections."[93] Indeed, the terrible condition for inmates in Soviet prisons was due, in part, to severe overcrowding. Many Soviet prisons exceeded their capacity threefold. For example, in 1941, the main Arkhangelsk city prison had between 1661 and 2380 inmates, although it was built for 780 prisoners. In 1940, a prison in eastern Poland with a capacity of 472 contained as many as 1709 inmates.[94]

Other directors agreed with the metaphor of sons and stepsons, and complained that prisons were sending them their sickest inmates.[95] According to the medical-sanitation department director of the Altai regional system of labor camps and colonies, prisons transferred to camps inmates who had been recently discharged from the hospital with advanced-stage pulmonary tuberculosis.[96] The medical-sanitation department director of the Novosibirsk regional camps and colonies complained that the prisons had more powerful supporters than the camps: "The NKVD for some reason always stands up for the Prison Department. If a prison needs to get rid of someone, they always find support. We're then forced to accept these sick people."[97] The poor physical state of prisoners who emerged from months in Soviet prisons is detailed in the memoir literature. Shalamov referred to a man who had just been released from prison as "one of those goners who were so emaciated they were known as 'wicks.'"[98] In the first year of the war, when the Gulag's economy became a top priority, camp officials complained that too many prisoners were arriving from the prisons entirely unfit for heavy physical labor. In May 1942, Beria issued an order to the prisons to maintain "elementary health conditions" for prisoners under interrogation.[99] Yet little changed. The medical-sanitation department director for the Primorsky regional camps and colonies indicated that of the over 3000 inmates who had been recently transferred from the prisons "about 60 percent of them constituted a completely defective labor force," only capable of light labor.[100] The medical-sanitation department director for the Cheliabinsk regional camp system complained that the prisons "often send us seriously ill people," and suggested that prisons be given back their old authority to medically discharge incurably sick prisoners.[101]

Moreover, the health directors described how local supply organs and party officials failed to support their work. The health of prisoners represented a low priority for camp and party leaders.[102] The Gulag undersupplied camps, and help from local economic and supply organs did not materialize.[103] The director of the medical-sanitation department for the Cheliabinsk regional camp system pleaded for a self-financing arrangement (khozraschet), which would afford health officials a degree of control over their own funds.[104] He also expressed his frustration at the Gulag's General Supply Section or OOS (otdel obshchego snabzheniia): "When they speak to us, they say your scurvy patients or your pellagra patients. We can just as easily turn it back on them, and say that the problem of scurvy and pellagra is yours, that is, it's the OOS's illness. The OOS workers are in no small measure responsible for scurvy and pellagra."[105] Camp health officials resented being blamed for prisoners' poor health when various Soviet authorities were responsible. Camp doctors had little power to challenge officials who refused to release critical supplies of food and clothing. The medical-sanitation department director for the Omsk regional camp system complained that the OOS was completely unresponsive to the needs of ailing prisoners: "Our conversations with them are like throwing peas at the wall—nothing sticks. I raise issues at meetings, but nothing ever happens."[106] Another health official said of the supply organs, "They don't consider people and their physical condition."[107] In the Siberian region of Tiumen, the supply organs "systematically" failed to give the labor colonies essential food, such as fats, meats, and vegetables. These food shortages, said the medical-sanitation department director, "produced [physical] degradation and a rise in mortality. Who is to blame for this? The OOS."[108]

Medical-sanitation department directors also asserted that production chiefs and engineers focused narrowly on output and ignored prisoners' safety. These officials assumed no responsibility for industrial accidents, and were rarely punished for safety violations. One medical-sanitation department official testified that camp leaders were not intimidated by safety inspectors and simply refused to enforce tighter safety regulations. He described the tendency to shift blame for accidents onto prisoners, too: "There are cases where the production site caused an obvious injury, but the camp director certifies that the injured prisoner deserves the blame."[109] Another explained that "no one has ever once punished an employer" for workplace injuries.[110] In the Kuzbass region, the director of the Kuznetsk Metallurgical Combine that contracted prisoners' labor dismissed the problem of workplace accidents: "What's important to me is plan fulfillment. I'm not interested in what's being done about injuries."[111] The Gulag system dehumanized prisoners, and camp officials reproduced this degrading view of inmates.

The inferior status of doctors within the camp hierarchy reflects the fact that the Stalinist leadership placed little value on the health of prisoners. Medical-sanitation department staff received lower wages and lacked access to the rewards and incentives given to other camp officials.[112] According to Solzhenitsyn, even prisoners showed contempt for camp medical staff, believing that they deliberately papered over ailments in order to swiftly return prisoners to work. He noted that camp slang for a medical assistant was "plasterer."[113] The medical-sanitation department directors resented their low status and the Gulag's chronic shortages of physicians. They saw themselves as trained medical professionals who deserved greater authority and respect. They wanted to be treated as important medical experts, and not relegated to pest control or hustling undergarments for prisoners. As one official explained to her Gulag boss: "We don't want to have to hear anymore that we are not doctors but delousers. Such [insults] discredit us. You should help us to become doctors and specialists, and help us to make our work real, great and honorable."[114]

LANGUAGE AND MENTAL UNIVERSE

The Gulag's dehumanization of prisoners is revealed in the language of camp officials. As we have seen, camp bureaucrats spoke not of prisoners' health, but of their "physical labor capability," and interpreted illness and mortality as "lost labor days." Severely ill and emaciated prisoners constituted the "defective" and "inferior" contingent, and this "ballast" had to be "unloaded" from the camps. The Gulag lexicon was in full use at the September 1945 meeting of the directors of camp medical-sanitation departments, and sheds light on the mentality of those who administered Stalin's camps.

The degree to which prisoners represented "human raw material" is revealed in many ways, including the fact that very little mention is made of nonphysical markers of inmate identity. In the lengthy conference transcript, officials make almost no reference to prisoners' offenses. These officials do not think of prisoners as counterrevolutionaries or thieves. There is no evidence that they hate the prisoners for who they are or what they did. Rather, they viewed all prisoners as physical bodies to be used in production. They thought of prisoners in terms of groups defined by age and health, as illustrated by the director of the medical-sanitation department for the Chkalov region: "I have to say, from my own experience, that people must be chosen by group—[there should be] colonies for juveniles and colonies for those with tuberculosis. It's necessary to improve the living conditions of category 3 [light] individualized labor. People should be gathered into the colonies according to their status and, when possible, according to whether they can be utilized."[115] Although she refers to a prisoner's "status" or sentence, she views prisoners primarily through the lens of physical labor capability.

Nevertheless, the medical-sanitation department directors express greater compassion for prisoners than the Gulag medical chief, Loidin. Their testimony also reveals that they cared more about the health of prisoners than any other camp authorities, even civilian and party officials. Once again, we see evidence of what Solzhenitsyn called "the universal law of the inverse ratio between social position and humaneness."[116] A few of the medical-sanitation department directors sometimes humanized prisoners in their language. One camp health official occasionally referred to prisoners as people (*liudi, narod*) rather than "contingents," the term of use. She expressed a genuine desire to improve inmates' health or, in Gulag-speak, "to preserve and maintain the physical profile of prisoners."[117] Similarly, the medical-sanitation department director for the Molotov regional camp system referred to inmates not only as "contingents," but as "people."[118] Such language seems to jump off the page because it appears so rarely in Gulag documents. In general, these officials viewed sick prisoners as a distinct burden, and condemned the common practice of one camp unloading its emaciated prisoners on another. Describing this practice as a serious problem, one official complained that many light-labor and invalid prisoners were being sent from Kurgan and Cheliabinsk to Construction Site No. 500 in Omsk, even though the medical evaluation determined that they were unfit for work and should not be transferred: "It is not especially pleasant to hold up a convoy and check inmates' health, only to retain them yourself and fill up your own hospitals."[119]

The medical-sanitation department directors could be both sincere in their desire to improve inmates' health and cruel in their dehumanization of prisoners. The comments of the medical-sanitation department director for the Krasnoiarsk region illustrate how the same Gulag official could embody both qualities. On the one hand, he was the only official at the conference to speak about human love and caring towards prisoners. He described the decent living conditions for weakened prisoners at a colony and a convalescent camp: "The *zemlianki* [earth dugouts] of that camp are enviable. In every little detail, a love and concern for people is evident. Similarly, OP [convalescent camp] No. 1 at the construction of the hydrolytic plant also serves as an example of this care for people. The premises are wonderful. They create comfort in the place."[120] Yet by singling out prisoners' respectable conditions in the OPs and the earth dugouts or *zemlianki*, he is admitting what the other medical-sanitation department directors already know well, namely, that such good conditions are rare. One Gulag survivor who experienced the *zemlianka* reported that it was "a space cleaned of snow, with the upper layer of earth removed. The walls and roof were made of round, rough logs. The whole structure was covered with another layer of earth and snow."[121]

On the other hand, just moments later this same Krasnoiarsk director made one of the most strikingly insensitive remarks at the conference. He characterized the weakened contingent as "ballast" or excess weight. Reporting on the physical profile of the camp prisoners, he noted a marked decline: "It's clear from this data that the valuable, work-capable contingent has declined while the defective contingent has increased. This is due to the fact that, in 1945, Taishet camp gave us their entire ballast in the amount of two thousand people, which sharply altered the physical profile of our camp. Many prisoners who came to us from the Taishet camp have now recovered, but some of them are still hospitalized."[122] Thus the same individual could express feelings of sympathy and contempt for the prisoners simultaneously.

Camp officials had clearly internalized the values of the Gulag system. They focused on conserving scarce resources for work-capable prisoners and not wasting resources on the weakest group. Those present at the conference were keen to give their Gulag boss, Loidin, what he wanted. They behaved like typical bureaucrats within a hierarchical system. Their actions were motivated by a desire to comply with the rules of the system, rather than by a distinct hatred towards prisoners. The medical-sanitation department directors were preoccupied with satisfying their superiors and fulfilling their own mandate of keeping mortality and illness rates low and costs down, and simply doing more with less. The director of the medical-sanitation department in the Yakut ASSR described the job as follows: "Comrade Stalin said that without the 'small screws' we're not worth anything. We, the sanitation service, are one of the small screws of the system. The task before us is to reduce mortality, not allow escapes, and to systematically generate funds and resources for the state."[123]

CONCLUSION

The transcript of the September 1945 meeting between the Gulag medical-sanitation department chief and his camp subordinates, one of the unique documents preserved in the Gulag archive, is revealing on many levels. The discussion exposes the tensions between the center and periphery, the unrelenting pressure of the Stalinist leadership on the camps, and the expectation that the camps can do more with less. The Gulag health chief, Loidin, blames his subordinates for prisoners' poor health, and is largely unsympathetic to their legitimate complaints. For their part, the medical-sanitation department directors defend themselves vigorously, insisting that they are trying to do their jobs under impossible circumstances. As they attest, many Soviet officials—camp administrators, the Gulag leadership, civilian health institutions, even local party officials—fail to help them improve the health of prisoners. The medical-sanitation department directors describe the numerous obstacles they face in improving prisoners' physical condition, but their boss hears their concerns as excuses and largely dismisses them.

Loidin remains tough and uncompromising, and intensely pressures his staff. He is quick to cast blame.

Moreover, there is a sense of urgency in Loidin's message. For the first time in the history of Stalin's Gulag, the medical-sanitation department directors have been called together to meet with their boss. At no other point in the fifteen-year existence of Stalin's forced labor camp system had anyone gathered the camp medical professionals to discuss improvements in prisoners' physical condition. Now, suddenly, in the months after the Nazi surrender, the Gulag health chief told his subordinates that they faced many pressing tasks: "Our demand of you is to transform your hospitals [and out-patient clinics] in the shortest possible time into exemplary civilized health care institutions."[124] In closing, Loidin told his subordinates that they would meet again, and he even surprised them with a one-month bonus that had just been authorized by the Gulag leadership. He said that it demonstrated "a high regard for the work of our sanitation service and our medical cadres."[125]

Why the urgency to create "exemplary" and "civilized" health care institutions? Why did Loidin insist that the camps and colonies produce exceptionally good health data, and reduce rates of mortality and illness to levels far below those that had been tolerated in the past? Why was this meeting held in September 1945? Perhaps the liberation of the Nazi death camps in Europe prompted the Stalinist regime to intensify its efforts to camouflage the violence of its own forced labor camp system. In the years 1943–1946, the NKVD-Gulag leadership issued a series of directives aimed at improving the health and living conditions of prisoners. These directives were no doubt motivated by the Gulag's high wartime mortality, but their timing was probably no coincidence. Following the liberation of the Nazi concentration camps, the Soviets faced international scrutiny for their own forced labor camp system. As Mark Harrison noted, "The growing postwar difficulties of Stalin's penal system were not just a domestic issue. There was a global context. After World War II the victors acclaimed the outcome as a victory over fascism and exploitation."[126] The Stalinist regime was operating a vast system of human exploitation, which became increasingly costly to conceal.

8 Selection

"The More (and Less) Valuable Human Element"

THE OGPU-NKVD-MVD MANAGED its "human raw material" through an elaborate system of selection (*otbor*). This system illustrates how prisoners in different degrees of ill health were sorted and managed. In order to maximize exploitation, camp officials moved prisoners around according to their physical labor capability. As we have seen, the most weakened prisoners were released from the camps entirely. Persons sentenced under more severe counterrevolutionary statutes and prisoners capable of light labor were selected out and concentrated in regional camps and labor colonies. Prisoners categorized for heavy physical labor were assigned to the priority camps, but as their health deteriorated from working in mines or forests, they were transferred to lower levels on the Gulag pyramid. The frequent movement of prisoners and the brutality of the transport process have been well documented in the historical and memoir literature. Historians believe that the Gulag continuously moved prisoners around due to changing demands for labor and the desire to separate certain categories of prisoners. However, as I demonstrate, these transfers were predominantly motivated by the health of prisoners.

The Stalinist labor camp system relocated prisoners according to their physical labor capability. My reading of declassified Gulag archival documents suggests that Stalin's labor camps and colonies constituted a hierarchical system of human exploitation in which prisoners moved from higher priority camps to lower priority colonies as their health deteriorated. The Gulag's unrelenting transfer of prisoners reflected its management of "the inferior workforce." The Gulag's bureau that oversaw the management of the inmate population was called the Department for the Accounting and Distribution of Prisoners (*otdel ucheta i raspredeleniia zakliuchennykh*), and the word "distribution" is key here. We have long believed that the labor colonies housed short-term criminal offenders under a lighter detention regime, yet the picture is more complicated.[1] In fact, Stalin's labor colonies became the dumping ground for severely ill and emaciated prisoners.

The Gulag's management of its disabled workforce illustrates the degree to which camps, colonies, prisons, and settlements formed a single unified system. These diverse forms and locations of incarceration have often been viewed as distinct but, as Steven Barnes has demonstrated, they formed a "hierarchy of detention."[2] Prisoners perceived as more threatening to the regime were subjected to strict isolation and especially harsh conditions. One of the long-term trends in Gulag practice, according to Barnes, involved the "ever-finer sorting of the prisoner population into ever-more-specialized detention institutions."[3] I speak here of another process of prisoner sorting, one governed not by the perceived danger of prisoners, but by their health. The OGPU-NKVD-MVD leadership distributed prisoners among camps and colonies according to the inmates' health, with the ultimate goal of maximizing production and exploitation.

THE RANKING OF HUMAN VALUE

In Stalin's Gulag, camps were forced to make calculations concerning which prisoners were worthy of medical care, as hospital stays had to be strictly rationed. They based these decisions on whether or not a prisoner was expected to recover and return to work. An OGPU order of July 1934, signed by the assistant Gulag chief, Izrail Pliner, warned camp officials that they needed to improve the health of weakened prisoners because "this contingent can spread mass illness" and an epidemic would drain the existing allocation for hospital beds. Thus camps would lose their ability to hospitalize the more valuable human element (*bole tsennyi liudskoi element*).[4] Those who could be exploited further were considered "the more valuable human element."

Like medical care, food was allocated according to a hierarchy of value. Not only did more productive workers receive more food, but prisoners in priority camps and priority sectors had access to food of higher quality and quantity. Food and other resources were also routinely transferred from low- to high-priority facilities. One official complained that his camp was not allowed to consume its own harvest because it was ordered to send many of the vegetables it grew to Construction No. 500, a high-priority site.[5] Another official noted that her three agricultural colonies had to give up most of their food to supply other camps: "How much of the butter from our colonies was used by these same colonies? A negligible amount. Why? Because the camp leadership says that there's a special order on the use of food supplies internally by the colonies and that it is impossible to give the prisoner contingent the amount of food we would prefer."[6] Many of the system's weakest prisoners were concentrated in the agricultural colonies. In the Gulag's hierarchy of value, more work-capable prisoners ate better than others.

Food allocations varied across camps, but the priority camps and sectors received more than others. For example, before the war, prisoners working above the Arctic Circle were supposed to get more food, and camps carefully priced each component of every ration.[7] In December 1934, the prisoners at Bamlag OGPU (the camp of the Baikal-Amur Mainline or BAM) received a third more vegetable oil in their monthly ration than prisoners in other OGPU camps.[8] In May 1941, the NKVD chief, Lavrenty Beria, issued an order granting a 25 percent increase in the food ration for prisoners constructing a certain oil pipeline, and days after the Nazi invasion, the Gulag further raised the food allotments for these prisoners.[9] Prisoners in priority camps such as the Norilsk camp received more than the average food ration, and prisoners at Pechorlag, Vorkutlag, and those working underground or in high elevations were supposed to receive 15–25 percent more bread.[10] In May 1943, the Gulag chief, V.G. Nasedkin, instructed certain camps to organize separate well-supplied cafeterias where the truly exceptional workers or "record-breakers," who exceeded their norms by 200 percent or more, would earn better food. The order was issued during a period of severe wartime shortages and high mortality, and when a majority of prisoners ate in their barracks because camps and colonies did not have sufficient cafeteria space.[11]

At the top of the Gulag pyramid stood Stalin's priority camps, around which grew large urban centers, such as Norilsk, Vorkuta, and Magadan. The Norilsk camp or Norillag represented one of the crown jewels of the Gulag industrial machine. Hundreds of thousands of prisoners passed through the vast Norilsk complex, a remote network of camps located above the Arctic Circle, where the long winter months included violent snowstorms and temperatures as low as minus 45 degrees Fahrenheit. According to Simon Ertz, the Norilsk region possessed enormous economic and military significance for the Soviet Union, given its vast mineral deposits. The region was home to more than a third of the world's nickel and 40 percent of its platinum, plus significant reserves of cobalt, copper, and coal.[12] The camp grew exponentially, from 1200 prisoners in 1935 to 19,500 in 1940 and 68,849 in 1952.[13] The transport of these prisoners proved especially treacherous, involving weeks in a train plus a lengthy journey by ship. Many prisoners did not survive the hardships of transport. The NKVD-MVD issued strict requirements that barred prisoners with certain ailments from being transported to this high-priority facility. As Leonid Borodkin and Simon Ertz explain, the lower-than-average mortality rates at Norilsk can be attributed to the fact that "medical examinations and the selection of prisoners for Norilsk were done at the sites from which prisoners were dispatched. Prisoners deemed unable to work in the Arctic were not sent to Norilsk."[14] Thus the priority camps had less illness and mortality than the non-priority camps and colonies. Starting in the 1930s, the most able-bodied prisoners were directed to prioritized sites.[15] At the camp of the White Sea–Baltic Sea Canal (Belbaltlag) in the 1930s, mortality rates were consistently lower than the Gulag average, often by as much as 30–50 percent.[16] During the war, when total Gulag mortality rate reached nearly 25 percent, mortality at the priority camp of Norilsk averaged only 5.5 percent.[17]

Stalin's security police did not want "physically inferior people" working at the Norilsk camp and combine. In 1948, the camp's medical-sanitation department generated a list of over a hundred illnesses and conditions that would prohibit prisoners from being sent there.[18] That same year, the Norilsk camp's medical-sanitation department submitted a collection of medical studies produced by its health-care institutions.[19] In one of the studies, two medical scientists and the director of the Norilsk combine hospital described the medical selections and screenings for existing or prospective Norilsk workers.[20] They enumerated the illnesses and physical limitations that would exclude people from working at Norilsk: "The ultimate goal of our work is to establish criteria for determining the degree to which this or that physically inferior person (*fizicheski nepolnotsennoe litso*) will be work capable and useful in the conditions of the North."[21] The authors stressed that "healthy, normal, physically developed people" could handle a lengthy residence in the North, but that "people who are physically inferior . . . often get sick and, in these conditions, turn out to be defective with little work ability."[22] They argued that sick individuals were slower to recover in the conditions of the North. The freezing temperatures, dropping to minus 30 or minus 40 degrees on many days, persisted for most of the year. The brutal winds, especially strong in the winter when blizzards were common, constituted "one of the most unpleasant aspects of the Norilsk climate," yet "without a doubt, the most negative aspect of the Norilsk climate is the lack of sunlight." The authors noted difficulties with the food supply as well, as fruits and vegetables, plus meat and dairy products, were not produced locally, but shipped in from elsewhere. Residents needed vitamin supplements to compensate for nutritional deficiencies in their diet.[23]

Norilsk strove to keep its "inferior workforce" to a minimum. The authors provided a detailed list of over one hundred ailments and conditions that should prevent people from living in the North, depending on whether they were doing hard physical labor outdoors, physical labor indoors, or white-collar technical or administrative work. Moreover, they specified which people should be excluded from working in the North and which should be moved out. The following persons could not work at Norilsk: those with chronic illnesses or who were disabled or required extended hospitalization; persons with reduced hearing or vision, heart and circulatory diseases, hypertension, bronchial asthma, emphysema, gastroenteritis, stomach ulcers, kidney disease, diabetes, anemia, pulmonary tuberculosis, epilepsy, arthritis, "the absence of upper or lower extremities," glaucoma, severe eczema, and senility and decrepitude of old age (*starcheskaia driakhlost'*).[24] Various reasons were provided for these exclusions, for example, those with tuberculosis were difficult to treat and "hard to rationally situate in work," so "pulmonary tuberculosis constitutes a cause for transfer out of the Arctic."[25] The fundamental calculation of all Gulag operations was articulated in this report: "Always, what should be taken into account is the degree to which the use of physically inferior persons defrays the costs related to their maintenance and medical treatment."[26] This striking statement is highly illustrative of the Gulag mentality. Sick and weakened prisoners represented a burden because they siphoned resources away from the more physically capable laborers. One former prisoner described how those conducting the health inspection were most concerned "not to let themselves be duped into inadvertently acquiring cripples, invalids, or the sick—in short, persons who were good only for eating up bread for nothing."[27]

Moreover, the Gulag's resources went from the weakest to the strongest, from the least to the more valuable "human element." Extra food for the most productive workers often came at the expense of the weaker prisoners. Administrators, guards, and wage-laborers were often drawing from the same pool of supplies as the prisoners. As noted in an earlier chapter, the problem with food in the Gulag was not limited to shortages. The Gulag represented a pyramid of camps and colonies, where both people and sites were ranked according to their value within the production system. Camp directors, wage laborers, and their families were first in line for food. In November 1933, the Gulag chief, M.D. Berman, told the deputy OGPU chairman, G.G. Yagoda, that the Gulag made up for its shortage of flour and grain by drawing "surplus" from the fund for special settlers.[28] He also complained that food rations for prisoners were inadequate in conditions of heavy physical labor, and that they were drawing from the general fund for all prisoners in order to give higher rations to the most productive workers.[29] In fact, this allocation constituted the normal state of Gulag operations, especially in later years. The Gulag system was not designed to feed every prisoner at levels that would ensure survival.

In keeping with the values of the Gulag leadership, camp officials were more focused on production numbers than on human lives. One group of prisoners was supplied at the expense of another. In early 1941, officials at a camp in Kazakhstan diverted large sums of money that had been allocated for prisoners' food and used the funds to obtain goods and bonuses for the most productive prisoners.[30] Thus it appeared economically efficient to feed the most productive workers at the expense of the least productive. At Viatlag in January 1943, one official insisted that their situation was "catastrophic" and that unless the rations of sick prisoners were redirected to the healthier prisoners, all would die. He justified his proposal to starve the sick by suggesting that some are "saboteurs" anyway.[31] This method of rationalizing a policy of starvation was not uncommon. Camps had the option of accusing sick prisoners of faking their illnesses, which would permit time in the penalty isolator and significantly reduce ration disbursements. As a prisoner, Antoni Ekart worked in the Kotlas camp hospital, and he described these selections: "A special commission of free NKVD doctors specified certain grades of patients to whom an additional 100 or 200 grams of bread was given. These were people whose age and type of illness would permit of their recovery and return to work. Old persons and those suffering from chronic illness, such as heart disease, did not receive any extra rations, but were allowed to perish slowly of hunger."[32]

THE BASE OF THE GULAG PYRAMID

The Gulag's regional camps and labor colonies have received little attention in the historical and memoir literature. Yet recently declassified archival documents reveal that the colonies had a major role within the system. My research indicates that the Gulag concentrated its enormous population of sick and emaciated prisoners in the regional camps and colonies, especially in the vast network of labor colonies. In 1947, when the majority of Gulag prisoners were unfit for heavy or medium physical labor, there were nearly a million prisoners in the Soviet Union's labor colonies alone (984,979), and this population surpassed the total number of inmates detained in the Gulag's four Main Administrations or Glavki (GULLP, GULGMP, GULPS, GULZhDS).[33] Regional camps and colonies received unhealthy prisoners from the prisons and higher-priority camps. They were expected to improve the health of these prisoners, and then transfer them to higher-priority sites. The Gulag leadership relied on agricultural colonies, in particular, to restore the health of prisoners.[34] Once prisoners became work-capable again, they were moved out of these detention facilities at the bottom of the Gulag pyramid to higher-priority camps, factories, and construction projects.[35] In 1945, a State Defense Committee (GOKO) decree ordered the Sverdlovsk system of labor camps and colonies to send thousands of its healthier prisoners to other locations, including military factories, railroad construction sites, and the building site of the Sverdlovsk City Soviet.[36] That same year, directors of regional labor camps and colonies touted their own efforts to transfer work-capable prisoners to high-priority industrial sites.[37]

According to Solzhenitsyn, camp life involved "eternal impermanence," marked by "dark and sudden shuffling of 'contingents'—either a transfer 'in the interests of production,' or a 'commissioning' by a medical review board, or inventory of property."[38] This "dark and sudden" reshuffling of inmates began in the mid-1930s with the rapid expansion of the prisoner population, and accelerated during the war, when the Gulag faced a burgeoning population of sick, emaciated, and invalid prisoners. In the early years of Stalin's Gulag, 1930–1934, all prisoners were sent to camps, but this practice changed in 1935 when hundreds of thousands of prisoners began to be transferred to the colonies as well. Still, these numbers remained relatively small. In 1935–1937, only about 25–35 percent of Gulag prisoners were detained in colonies. This number changed dramatically in 1938, when nearly half of all prisoners were detained in colonies, a sharp increase over the previous year. In 1939–1942, about 23–29 percent of all Gulag prisoners were located in the colonies. In 1943–1945, as the number of sick and emaciated prisoners rose dramatically, the number of inmates in the colonies increased to over half of all Gulag prisoners.[39] These wartime years were also a period when NKVD-Gulag authorities began to manage their population of weak and invalid prisoners more systematically, directing some to invalid camps and others to colonies, and releasing many more.

In the late Stalin years, the Gulag's distribution system meant that the vast majority of sick prisoners resided in just four sectors of the system, about half in the colonies alone. In 1948, a Gulag chart on first-time patients, mortality, and total labor losses reported 65.5 million "labor days lost"—as if nearly 180,000 prisoners had been absent from work for an entire year.[40] Moreover, just four sectors of the system accounted for 90 percent of these "lost labor days." They included the administration of regional camps and colonies (UITLK-OITK), the main administration for forestry camps (GULLP), the main administration of camps for railroad construction (GULZhDS), and the agricultural camps. The administration of regional camps and colonies alone represented 46 percent of the total.[41] By the first quarter of 1953, the Gulag medical-sanitation department reported a dramatic decline in "lost labor days" across the system, to the equivalent of 31,000 prisoners out sick for a year, nearly a third of them from tuberculosis. However, the distribution of sick prisoners did not change. Once again, the sickest prisoners were concentrated in just a few sectors of Stalin's Gulag system. The administration of regional camps and colonies, the administration for forestry camps, the main administration of camps for railroad construction, the agricultural camps, and the main administration of camps for mining and metallurgy (GULGMP) accounted for nearly 84 percent of these "lost labor days." The UITLK-OITK system alone represented 32 percent of the total lost labor days, and the main administration for forestry camps 21 percent.[42] Two factors account for this distribution. First, certain types of work, such as logging, railroad construction and mining, were notoriously lethal. Second, the Gulag system continued to relocate its weakest prisoners into agricultural camps as well as regional camps and colonies. Data from November 1951 indicate that the UITLK-OITK system detained an enormous population of invalid prisoners. The Sverdlovsk region alone had nearly 47,000, and fewer than 20 percent of these weakened prisoners had been sentenced under harsh statutes as bandits or counterrevolutionaries.[43]

By the 1950s, Stalin's labor colonies appear to have become tantamount to invalid camps. In May 1952, the deputy director of the Stalingrad regional MVD and director of the region's labor colonies reported on a certain camp division that held 601 prisoners, only 36 percent of whom were considered work-capable, and these 218 prisoners largely performed agricultural work.[44] The deputy director of the Stalingrad region MVD did not identify this camp division as an invalid camp, but perhaps there was no need to. In the Stalingrad region's Camp Division No. 2, located in the village of Tsarev, the exceptionally poor "physical labor capability" of the 489 prisoners there was illustrated by their classification: only nine in category 1 "basically fit for physical labor"; eighty-eight classified as category 2 "physically defective prisoners;" and as many as 392 were considered "invalids." The breakdown of these same prisoners by criminal offense indicates that only 122 were sentenced for counterrevolutionary or political offenses, and only ten had committed serious crimes such as banditry, armed robbery, and premeditated murder, while as many as 469 had been sentenced for "other crimes," likely petty criminal offenses.[45] Once again, we see that ordinary criminal offenders were the principal victims of Stalinist exploitation.

In addition to the colonies, the transit camps (*peresyl'nye punkty*) also increasingly became invalid camps in the late Stalin years. As ailing and disabled prisoners were being transported between camps and colonies, they often got stuck in the transit camps, and these camps grew into gathering points for the ailing workforce. In March 1950, a Dalstroi transit camp in the Khabarovsk region housed 1590 prisoners, including 1254 men and 336 women. A Gulag sanitation inspection characterized their physical profile (*fizprofil'*) as follows: category 1 "basically fit for physical labor," 305 prisoners; category 2 "physically defective prisoners," 563; category 3 "invalids," 275; and as many as 343 hospitalized. In other words, nearly 40 percent of prisoners at this transit camp were either invalids or hospitalized, and another 35 percent were deemed "physically defective prisoners." A mere 19 percent could be identified as "basically fit for physical labor" by a system that maintained a very low bar for this classification. The prisoners in categories 1 and 2 were being "utilized" primarily in capital construction, renovating barracks and other buildings, plus railway construction.[46] This kind of work would likely prove far too strenuous for these weakened and emaciated prisoners.

The result of transferring the most sick and disabled inmates to the regional system of labor camps and colonies is reflected in the especially bleak physical labor capability of prisoners located there. For the first three months of 1948, nearly half of the over 12.5 million cases of illness in the Gulag were recorded by the regional administration of camps and colonies (UITLK), and over half of all deaths from illness.[47] The rates of illness (digestive disorders, nutritional dystrophy, malaria, pneumonia, tuberculosis, flu, even workplace accidents) for the UITLK administration far exceeded those for such main administrations as metallurgy, forestry and railroad construction (GULMPU, GULLP, GULZhDS).[48] Across all sectors of the Gulag (camps, colonies, main administrations), cases of pulmonary tuberculosis and nutritional dystrophy caused the most labor losses to the system and were most likely to result in a prisoner's death.[49] Gulag statistics for 1948 stated that, across the Gulag system, pulmonary tuberculosis constituted 0.9 percent of illness, 15.2 percent of "labor losses," and 39.9 percent of all deaths. The highest rates of illness were recorded in the regional administrations of labor camps and colonies, the main administration for forestry, and the agricultural camps.[50]

The Gulag largely concealed the fact that it dumped its weakened prisoners in the regional system of labor camps and colonies, but this systematic practice is sometimes made explicit in the archival record. For example, a 1948 narrative accompanying statistics on illness, "labor losses," and mortality noted the following: "UITLK-OITK and agricultural camps exceed the Gulag's average rate because invalids and those of limited fitness are settled mainly in these camps and colonies."[51] Occasionally, the NKVD-MVD-Gulag leadership spoke openly about the practice of shuffling prisoners around according to their health. Colonies were often explicitly identified as locations for sick and disabled prisoners. MVD Order No. 0418 of June 1949 openly referred to the hierarchy of camps and the movement of prisoners according to their physical labor capability. The strongest would be directed to the priority camps while the weakest would be concentrated in regional camps and colonies. MVD chief S.N. Kruglov affirmed that, "Henceforth, the MVD USSR camps should be filled up first with prisoners whose physical condition places them in category 1 [basically fit for] physical labor," while the directors of all other camps and colonies would be "held fully responsible" for the physical condition of their prisoners.[52] The feeder camps were responsible for getting prisoners up to the level of being "basically fit for physical labor" so that these inmates could be transported to the priority camps.

At the same time, the Gulag leadership often sent the camps mixed messages. The MVD chief expressed concern that camp officials were too readily dumping their diseased and ailing inmates onto the colonies. In MVD Order No. 0418, Kruglov scolded camp directors for failing to maintain the health of prisoners, a complaint he regularly repeated. He condemned the practice of moving unhealthy prisoners from camps into colonies because it reduced the incentive of camp directors to improve inmate health: "Directors of the corrective-labor camps must take necessary measures to improve the health of the weakened contingent. The practice to date of sending this type of contingent from the camps to the regional camps and colonies is considered "incorrect" because it absolves camp directors of responsibility for preserving the physical condition of inmates and for their correct labor utilization."[53]

KEEPING OUT THE SICKEST PRISONERS

As early as December 1933, the Procuracy, the Commissariat of Justice, and the Gulag agreed that sick prisoners and those exposed to epidemics would not be sent to the camps.[54] The Gulag leadership also denounced the practice of moving prisoners who were too weak to endure the journey. In February 1938, Gulag chief Pliner sent an angry telegram to prison and camp officials in which he denounced the practice of transporting sick prisoners to the labor camps. He gave examples such as cases where weakened prisoners with a temperature or those sick with typhus had been transported to camps. Some had even died en route. He warned that prison and camp officials would be held responsible for such "completely intolerable and disgraceful facts." Pliner stated forcefully that sick prisoners must not be loaded onto trains bound for the camps.[55]

As the Gulag leadership confronted an ever-growing population of weak and emaciated prisoners, it refined its system of selection and separation. Camp officials were required to perform selections in order to ensure that no sick and diseased prisoners were transported to the camps. In March 1938, the Gulag chief stressed the importance of proper "selection" and transport of inmates from prisons and colonies. In a lengthy circular to all prison and camp directors, he denounced "very severe violations" in the rules for transporting prisoners. Infectious diseases were entering the camps and a significant number of sick prisoners were being removed during transport. Pliner insisted that prisoners had to be subjected to thorough medical and sanitary inspections at the prisons and transit camps. Prisoners' clothing had to be disinfected and their hair cut, train cars had to be properly cleaned and disinfected, a special sanitary train car or isolator had to be assigned for long trips so that sick prisoners could be quarantined, and doctors and medical assistants should be assigned to large transports of prisoners.[56] "Low-level staff" would no longer be responsible for loading prisoners and managing deportations. Rather, these selections had to be carried out personally by the director of the prison or colony, the head of the accounting and distribution unit (URCh), and the head of the sanitation section (*sanchast'*) and they must strictly adhere to Gulag rules on prisoner convoys.[57] Memoirists have described in grisly detail the conditions of train and maritime transports that took prisoners to distant labor camps. The Gulag chiefs objected to these horrific situations too, but for different reasons.

Even before the war sharply increased the numbers of sick and disabled inmates, Gulag officials insisted that only those who were suitable for physical exploitation be selected for the camps. The medical-sanitation departments not only inspected prisoners, but were also charged with separating and isolating the weaker population. On May 17, 1941, the Gulag leadership sent instructions to the medical-sanitation department directors for all the camps and colonies regarding health provisions for prisoners at "special construction sites."[58] These sites were supposed to have an experienced doctor, the water quality at the location had to be assessed, and medical facilities located close to the site and within the civilian health system were to be made available to prisoners. All prisoners being prepared for work at the special construction sites should be subjected to careful and thorough medical inspection, and sick prisoners should not be transferred, especially those with infectious diseases, those requiring medical attention, the chronically ill, invalid and very old prisoners who were not able to work, those with a long history of frequent illness, weakened and emaciated prisoners with signs of vitamin deficiency, and those who had come into contact with persons sick with infectious diseases. Instead, prisoners in the aforementioned categories should be sent to hospitals and weakened brigades (*slabkomandy*) in a timely fashion.[59] In 1947, the Soviet government declared that MVD-Gulag enterprises in the Far North and Far East represented priority destinations for prisoners, given that these regions possessed valuable natural resources such as nickel, gold, and timber. Only the healthiest Gulag prisoners were supposed to be directed to these important sites.[60]

Moreover, camps that were faced with having to give up prisoners consistently chose to remove the "inferior contingent." The Gulag tended to contract out its less valuable workers (women, elderly, unhealthy, and unskilled prisoners) to the civilian economic ministries that clamored for penal labor.[61] Camp administrators moved out their weakest population too, whenever possible. In 1945, the Gulag medical-sanitation department chief described what he called "dangerous

phenomena." He explained that a high-priority Gulag site, Construction Site No. 500, needed doctors, so the Gulag sent an order to the
Ivdellag camp to transfer two doctors: "Who do you think Ivdellag sent
on a 10,000-kilometer trip? Two elderly doctors who were chronically
ill and bedridden and who were in no condition to work."[62]

Low-priority camps often complained that high-priority camps unloaded their least healthy prisoners onto them.[63] The medical-sanitation
department director for the Khabarovsk region complained that high-
priority camps were sending their weakened prisoners to his camp, thus
causing his own camp to miss its production targets: "Construction Site
No. 500 took advantage of its status and cleared out all of its health-
care facilities to the point where it made our work in the Khabarovsk
camp more difficult." He charged Construction Site No. 500 with using
the pretext of "providing other camps with laborers" in order simply to
unload its ailing prisoners.[64] The health director accused other camps
of dumping, too: "The Primorsky camp did the same thing. In 1945,
it freed itself of its ballast and thereby improved its statistics. [The
Primorsky camp] sent those in terrible condition with tuberculosis to
us, and thus infected other camps and camp divisions."[65]

Within the Gulag system of exploitation, physical labor capability
often mattered more than other markers of identity, such as a prisoner's sentence. The Gulag distributed prisoners among camps and
colonies according to their capacity for labor rather than their sentence
or perceived danger. For example, in February 1942, deputy NKVD
chief Kruglov informed NKVD officials that inmates in the prisons
had to be moved quickly into camps, as NKVD chief Beria had ordered that, "the most important new military building projects that the
NKVD had been assigned by the government had to be fully staffed."
The primary consideration in the transfer of prisoners from prisons to
camps and colonies would be their health. Kruglov gave no mention of
whether the prisoners were so-called counterrevolutionaries or traitors
or recidivists. He addressed only the prisoners' capacity for physical
labor: "The entire physically healthy work-capable portion of prisoners" must be sent immediately to NKVD camps and new construction sites, and "all other prisoners should be sent to colonies within
the boundaries of the region."[66] Similarly, in a November 1950 letter to his NKVD boss, Gulag chief Dobrynin indicated that the Gulag
MVD "considered it expedient" to use the categories of physical labor

capability "when deciding which prisoners to direct to new camps that needed labor."[67]

LETHAL EXPLOITATION

The Gulag also sorted prisoners according to the nature of their crime and the relative danger they were believed to pose for Soviet society.[68] Stalin established light regime and strict regime camps, and allowed some prisoners to move without convoy and others only under reinforced security. Within each camp complex, there were zones marked for the worst offenders. In 1933, the camp of Dmitlag, which built the Moscow-Volga Canal, established strict regime camp sections to house the worst criminal offenders, such as shirkers, thieves, and escapees. These camp sections were under tight security, with extra convoy guards and two layers of barbed wire instead of one. In the early 1930s, large camp complexes, such as Dmitlag, Dalstroi, and Siblag, established camp sections designed to severely punish, as much as exploit, the worst offenders. These camp sections became notorious among prisoners, who considered them tantamount to a death sentence.[69] This idea of physical labor as punishment was not introduced by the Stalinist labor camp system. As early as the 1920s, the Soviet leadership viewed heavy physical labor as a form of severe punishment. Reporting on their operations in 1926–1927, the directors of SLON noted that their "principal method" for dealing with prisoners who violated camp rules was to assign the violators to "especially heavy labor and the penalty isolator for the maximum term."[70]

During the war, hard-labor camp divisions emerged for the state's worst enemies. An April 19, 1943 decree of the Presidium of the USSR Supreme Soviet "On measures for punishing German fascist villains, spies, and traitors to the Motherland and their accomplices" established distinct camp divisions for harsh regime labor (*katorzhnye lagernye otdeleniia*).[71] The hard-labor prisoners wore distinct uniforms with a prisoner number, and were housed "separate from other camp inmates in special barracks with bars on the windows." They worked longer hours than other prisoners, and they were placed "primarily in the most strenuous work."[72] The Stalinist leadership introduced *katorga* as an alternative to capital punishment for those sentenced under any section of the criminal code.[73]

With the establishment of the *katorga* system, the NKVD-MVD acknowledged openly that heavy physical labor constituted a form of severe punishment. It was the high-priority camps of Norilsk, Vorkuta, and Kolyma that first established *katorga* camp sections.[74] In the katorga and later "special camp" system, the Gulag effectively eliminated the categories of physical labor capability. Prisoners were literally worked to death, and there was little pretense otherwise. According to Solzhenitsyn, "These were, undisguisedly, murder camps: but in the Gulag tradition murder was protracted, so that the doomed would suffer longer and put a little work in before they died."[75] On his way from Pechorlag to a Moscow prison in 1946, Antoni Ekart described meeting a Polish prisoner, a doctor who had been sentenced to *katorga*. He told Ekart that there was "no comparison" between the *katorga* regime and ordinary camps. Ekart could see that "the subject was painful to him." The Polish prisoner explained: "People who are sentenced to *katorga* receive a number on arrival at the camp, and lose their names. They work underground in the deepest mines, so that there shall not be any possibility of their escaping. On return from work they are immediately locked up in their huts . . . There are no days off from work . . . The sick and weak were taken to hospital, from which they never returned."[76] Women too could be classified as *katorzhane*, prisoners who worked twelve-hour days, and had no right to receive letters or parcels from family.[77] One woman who experienced a hard-labor regime at the Norilsk camp claimed that she was given no days off at all, during or after the war.[78] Moreover, when outdoor temperatures reached minus 40 degrees Celsius at Norilsk, work was cancelled for ordinary prisoners, but not for the hard-labor prisoners.[79] The Stalinist regime forced *katorga* prisoners to perform the harshest tasks, including mining uranium and other radioactive ore.[80]

As in the ordinary camps, the *katorga* system had its own process of selection and separation. The weakest *katorga* prisoners were supposed to be concentrated in a separate *katorga* division at Karlag, where a hard-labor division was established for *katorga* prisoners, or *katorzhane*, who had become ill and no longer work-capable. Beria declared: "All sick and not-work-capable prisoners are to be directed to the hard-labor division of Karlag."[81] Following the establishment of the "special camps" in 1948, especially dangerous state criminals were directed to special camps rather than to Karlag. Thus the composition of prisoners at Karlag began to change. Its population of counterrevolutionary offenders was 52.6 percent in January 1945, and 53.3 percent in January 1948, but 39.7 percent by January 1949 and 38.6 percent by January 1950. In a December 1950 report on Karlag, Dobrynin indicated that the remaining "especially dangerous state criminals" would be transferred from Karlag to special camps in the next two months. Moreover, "at the same time, 7876 persons who are criminal-bandit elements and fit for heavy or medium physical labor will be transferred from Karlag to places like Sevvostlag, Angarlag, and the logging camps, and also to "harsh regime camp divisions."[82] Dobrynin's words illustrate how the Gulag leadership deliberately concentrated the worst offenders in the most brutal work. Karlag transferred its healthier prisoners out to harsh labor so it now housed many sick and disabled inmates. In 1949, half of its prisoners were classified as physically weak or invalid. According to Steven Barnes, the agricultural camp Karlag was one of the largest in the Gulag, yet "it was low in the pecking order for supply of the necessities of survival, including food."[83]

In the late 1940s, Stalin's Gulag grew progressively crueler as the system of exploitation intensified. The camp population increased sharply following Stalin's theft decrees. The new List of Illnesses revised the categories of physical labor capability to force a larger population of prisoners, even those already weakened, into heavy physical labor. Moreover, separate "special camps" were created for the Soviet Union's worst criminal and political offenders. A February 21, 1948 instruction of the USSR Council of Ministers established special camps (*osobye lageria*) under the MVD USSR initially in the Kolyma and Karaganda regions, the Far North, Norilsk, and the Komi ASSR and at Temlag in the Mordova autonomous republic. These camps would detain "especially dangerous state criminals," that is, "spies, saboteurs, terrorists, Trotskyists, Rightists, Mensheviks, SRs, anarchists, nationalists, White emigrants, and participants in other anti-Soviet organizations, and other persons, who, by their anti-Soviet connections and enemy activities, pose a threat."[84] No prisoners outside these categories could be detained in the special camps. According to Anne Applebaum, "the special camps were really an extension of the *katorga* regime, and contained many of the same features: the striped uniforms; the numbers on their foreheads, backs, and chests; the barred windows; and the locking of the barracks at night."[85] However, the special camps detained many more prisoners and operated as independent camp complexes, whereas the *katorga* represented subdivisions of larger camps.[86]

Special camps were distinguished by their harsh labor regime and the fact that, as Kokurin and Petrov write, "work-capable prisoners were to be used primarily in heavy physical labor."[87] Nearly all inmates in these camps would be subjected to harsh physical exploitation. All camp inmates identified as "especially dangerous state criminals" according to the criteria above were to be directed to these newly established special camps "with the exception of prisoners with severe, incurable, or chronic illnesses and feeble invalids (*besmoshchnikh invalidov*) who should remain in their previous place of detention."[88] In large camp complexes like Vorkuta, distinct camp divisions were established as special camps for political enemies, such as arrested Germans and other foreigners. These prisoners worked in the most brutal jobs at clay and stone quarries, and quickly died given their meager rations and the lack of medical care. The Vorkuta camp medical staff was under explicit orders to allow the ailing German officers in the special camp to die, but to treat the German doctors and transfer them to other camp divisions where their medical knowledge could be utilized.[89]

The Stalinist leadership concealed the Gulag's system of lethal exploitation in various ways. One method was to give obscure names to the most brutal Gulag sites, as in the case of the independent invalid camps and the special camps. Most camps had names that reflected their location, but the special camps did not. They were deceptively named for natural elements: Mineral (*Mineral'nyi*), Mountain (*Gornyi*), Oak Forest (*Dubravnyi*), Steppe (*Stepnoi*), Coastal (*Beregovoi*), River (*Rechnoi*), Lake (*Ozernyi*), Sand (*Peschanyi*), Meadow (*Lugovoi*), Reed (*Kamyshovyi*), Distant (*Dal'nii*), and Watershed (*Vodorazdel'nyi*). Meadow combined with Sand in 1951, and three more special camps were added in the 1950s—Reed, Distant, and Watershed—to make a total of eleven special camps by the end of 1952.[90] The point of these "names derived from the landscape," Applebaum asserted, "was presumably conspiratorial—to hide the nature of the camps—since there were no oak trees at Oak camp, and certainly no seashore at Seashore camp."[91] Neither did the names of the special camps have any connection to their activities. The River special camp was involved in coal mining and the Lake special camp did railroad construction and forestry.[92] These highly secretive and lethal camps were intended primarily for political prisoners. A report of January 1951 indicated that 95 percent of prisoners in the MVD special camps were sentenced for counter-revolutionary offenses and only 5 percent were serving criminal sentences.[93] The official mortality rates also concealed the brutality of the special camps. As with the ordinary camps, the MVD recorded improbably low mortality rates in the special camps—only 0.01–0.08 percent in 1950.[94]

Within the special camp system itself, the Gulag leadership continued the practice of selecting out and concentrating invalids. According to data from 1950, many nonworking invalids were directed to two of the special camps—Oak Forest and Meadow—whose economy included agricultural work, plus garment and other consumer goods production, the typical jobs assigned to weaker prisoners. The largest number of sick and invalid prisoners was recorded for Oak Forest, which had "a separate camp division for nonworking invalids."[95] Oak Forest registered only 43 percent of its prisoners as working, and almost two-thirds as very frail. Nearly 30 percent were classified as invalids, and another 28 percent were identified as "sick" or "not working for various reasons." Overall, roughly a quarter of prisoners in special camps were designated as sick or invalid, far more than in the standard camps.[96] According to Solzhenitsyn, "sick prisoners were sent to die in the celebrated Spassk camp (near Karaganda)—the 'All-Union convalescent home' of the Special Camps."[97] As soon as these terminally ill prisoners entered the gates of Spassk camp, they ceased to be regarded as sick and were placed in various forms of work. According to Solzhenitsyn: "All one-legged men were employed on sedentary work: breaking stones for road surfacing, or grading firewood. Neither crutches nor even a missing arm was any obstacle to work in Spassk." Both men and women were forced to wield picks and hammers in stone quarries, and "all this work was done not only by sick people, not only without any mechanical aids at all, but in the harsh winter of the steppes (at temperatures as low as 30 to 35 degrees below freezing, and with a wind blowing), and what is more, in *summer clothing,* since there was no provision for the issue of warm clothing to *nonworkers,* i.e. to the unfit."[98]

In the special camps, there were no accommodations for prisoners who were sick, disabled, or weakened. All prisoners had to perform heavy physical labor. Thus, not surprisingly, some of the largest percentages of ailing prisoners appear in the special camps. An MVD report of December 1950 indicated that "especially dangerous state criminals" who were sentenced to hard-regime labor were supposed to be directed to the special camps, despite the state of their health.[99] Data from December 1950 indicated that there were 62,544 such prisoners, of which 26,307 were housed in special camps and 36,237 in basic camps. These *katorzhane* were extremely frail. At Karlag, for example, only 200 of the 1509 *katorzhane* were identified as "basically fit for physical labor." Those considered fit were supposed to be sent to Vorkutlag. The remaining 1309 invalid *katorzhane*, who had been concentrated in a special camp division for hard laborers at Karlag, were supposed to be sent to a settlement (*poselok*) that was still subordinate to a MVD special camp. As discussed in chapter 6, the Gulag probably recorded these prisoners under "losses" and persons "transferred to other places of detention." In Siblag, there were 5705 *katorzhane*, and the barely 500 who were fit for physical labor were to be sent to Vorkutlag while the remaining 5205 invalids were to be concentrated in a special camp division for *katorzhane*. The so-called "especially-dangerous state criminals who were sentenced to harsh-regime labor" were supposed to be sent to special camps "regardless of their physical condition."[100] A February 1951 instruction on the special camps treated prisoners sentenced to harsh-regime labor as either capable of physical labor or invalid.[101] There was no middle ground. These strict regime prisoners or *katorzhane* likely endured the most violent forms of human exploitation. A Gulag report on the Norilsk camp in March 1953 noted that, "in harsh-regime camp divisions the contingent is being taken to the work site with no account for their physical condition."[102]

The strict regime prisoners, like those in the special camps, were sorted and distributed according to their physical condition, as well as the severity of their crime. The *katorzhane* were moved around like other camp prisoners but they were kept within a narrow group of camps. If these *katorzhane* were "fit for physical labor," they were supposed to be sent to such high-priority camps as Vorkutlag, Norilsk, and Sevvostlag. If invalids, they were concentrated in special camp sections for penal laborers under other camps lower down the Gulag pyramid. These included, for example, Siblag, Angarlag, the White Sea camp division for *katorzhane* of the Vologoda regional colonies, located in a former monastery on an island in the White Sea, or the Oak Forest special camp.[103] The camp divisions in the general camps that detained *katorzhane* were called "special camp divisions for strict regime prisoners" and these were subordinated to the Fourth Division of the Gulag MVD USSR.[104] Thus there appear to have been two distinct groups: *katorzhane* who were "especially dangerous state criminals" and those who were not; all of the former went to special camps, while the latter were directed to camps according to their physical labor capability, whether invalid or work-capable, and detained in special camp divisions for hard laborers. Nonetheless, they never lost the designation *katorzhane,* and they were tracked separately from other prisoners.[105] The toughest labor regime within both the special camps and the hard labor divisions was reserved for "especially dangerous state criminals" who were most often politicals. In December 1950, counterrevolutionary offenders constituted 41 percent of prisoners at the Karaganda camp (19,246 out of 47,028), a camp whose population was overwhelmingly weak—nearly 69 percent of prisoners there were classified as "physically inferior" and nearly 20 percent as invalids.[106] Gulag chief Dobrynin explained that Karlag had a high percentage of counterrevolutionary offenders and harsh regime inmates.

Overall, roughly 10 percent of Stalin's Gulag prisoners resided in special camps. As of January 1951, there were 215,185 prisoners detained in nine special camps, including 38,057 women and only 11,752 prisoners sentenced for criminal offenses; and just a small fraction, 26,557, were classified as *katorzhane.*[107] These prisoners were not typically included in the total numbers on MVD prisoners. A January 1952 report (*svodka*) lists data from the special camps separately, and the data from the ten special camps, which held 258,324 prisoners, was placed at the very end of the report. As in the regular camps, the *katorzhane* in the special camps were separated from the other prisoners. The official mortality statistics for the special camps appear to be remarkably low, just 0.1 percent of all prisoners, despite the exceptionally brutal regime of exploitation and the very poor health of prisoners.[108] As of October 1952, there were about 222,900 prisoners in ten special camps (the eleventh, Watershed, had only just been established), and they were severely weakened by work.[109] Many special camp prisoners labored in the high-priority mining camps of Vorkuta, Norilsk, and Kolyma, or in the Kazakh desert and the Moldavian forests.[110]

Like the regular camps, the special camps sorted prisoners according to their health, and directed the weakest and healthiest prisoners to different locations. In a November 1952 report to MVD chief Kruglov,

Gulag chief Dolgikh offered a breakdown of special camp prisoners by physical labor ability. There were three categories at the time: category 1 "basically fit for labor," category 2 "physically defective prisoners," and category 3 "invalids." The weakest prisoners resided in Oak Forest, (category 1 "basically fit for physical labor": 14.2 percent; category 2 "physically defective": 56.4 percent; invalid: 29.4 percent) followed by Lake (category 1 "basically fit for physical labor": 25.5 percent; category 2 "physically defective": 41.8 percent; invalid: 32.7 percent). Oak Forest and Lake were likely reserved for invalids and included convalescent camp divisions. River, the largest special camp, with over 27,000 prisoners, was part of the Vokutlag camp complex in Komi ASSR, and reported the healthiest prisoners (category 1 "basically fit for physical labor": 77 percent; category 2 "physically defective": 14.6 percent; invalid: 8.4 percent). Coastal, the second largest and part of the Far North Construction complex (*Dalstroi*), included the gold mines of the Kolyma region of Magadan. It detained over 18,000 (category 1 "basically fit for physical labor": 72.5 percent; category 2 "physically defective": 24.8 percent; invalid: 2.7 percent). As in the ordinary system of camps, the healthier prisoners were selected for the priority special camps. Prisoners sentenced for the most severe offenses, such as treason and spying, were assigned the most grueling work, and concentrated in hard labor camp sections or in special camps. As they grew weaker physically, they stayed on the job, and they were not moved to lighter work. Once invalids, they were transferred to special camp sections for invalids.

The conventional image of the special camp prisoner has been informed by the strikes and uprisings at these camps after Stalin died, such as the legendary Kengir uprising.[111] These incidents call to mind an image of strong prisoners, yet the data from the special camps in the last months of Stalin's life reveal a very frail group of inmates. A report from Gulag chief Dolgikh to MVD chief Kruglov in November 1952 concerning the labor productivity of prisoners in special camps indicated that about half were classified as "basically fit for physical labor"; the other half was designated either "invalid" or "physically defective."[112] The health of prisoners in the harsh special camps was generally worse than in the Gulag at large. Throughout the special camp system, prisoners were quite weak overall (category 1 "basically fit for physical labor": 51.6 percent; category 2 "physically defective":

33.7 percent; category three "invalids": 14.7 percent). They were exploited more severely and it was more difficult for these "most dangerous state enemies" to get reclassified once they became weak.[113] Dolgikh told his MVD boss that "the unsatisfactory labor utilization of the special contingent in special camps" was due to two things: first, "the presence of a significant number of prisoners in the second category of physical labor, who, because of the state of their health, cannot be placed in the basic work (*osnovnye raboty*)" and, second, the fact that "physically healthy laborers are not directed to production jobs because of an absence of work, a shortage of building materials, or a lack of transportation vehicles and instruments." He offered several suggestions "for the purpose of more fully utilizing the labor of the special contingent." In particular, Dolgikh suggested transforming Vorkutlag, Norillag, and the Dalstroi camp complexes into special camps, and arranging real work for the category 2 "physically defective" prisoners.[114] The Gulag chief wanted the regime of physical exploitation at these top priority sites to be no less brutal than in the special camps.

The increasing harshness of the Stalinist camps from the 1930s to the 1950s as illustrated not only by the regime of exploitation but by the length of sentences. Sentences of twenty and twenty-five years became routine in the late Stalin years. According to Solzhenitsyn, the ten-year sentence or *tenner*, so common in the 1930s, was supplanted by the twenty-five year sentence in the 1940s: "This sentence, called the *quarter*, had been introduced . . . to replace the death penalty, which had been abolished as a humane act." When the harsh regime or *katorga* system was introduced in April 1943, prisoners' sentences could be up to twenty-five years. The twenty-five year sentence, rarely meted out in the prewar years, became common for counterrevolutionary offenders after the war.[115] Stalin's abolition of capital punishment in a decree of May 26, 1947 also had an effect on prisoner's sentences. Galina Ivanova identified this act as "one of the factors bringing the size of the population of the Gulag in 1949–1950 to its highest point in the whole history of its existence; that is, those who would undoubtedly have been shot before now entered the Gulag, increasing the number of its residents."[116] Sentences for other crimes increased as well. A June 4, 1947 theft decree called for sentences of up to twenty-five years, supplanting earlier theft decrees with shorter sentences. A June 9, 1947 law on "Divulging State Secrets" (which replaced an earlier wartime decree) mandated sentences of up to twenty years, for "a simple slip of the tongue, negligence, or incautious publication."[117] Even prisoners with shorter sentences could be detained longer. The Gulag frequently punished inmates with additional sentences. Former Gulag boss Mochulsky, who worked in the camps in the 1940s, wrote: "As a rule, the people who ended up in the Gulag were given long sentences (many from ten to twenty-five years), and frequently, after they had served their time, their prison sentence was for some reason extended."[118]

CONCLUSION

The Stalinist leadership selected and sorted prisoners for exploitation according to their "physical labor capability." In order to maximize the exploitation of prisoners, the Gulag moved inmates around depending on the state of their health. Sick and emaciated prisoners were relocated. Some went into the civilian health system, others to invalid camps and settlements, and most to the regional camps and colonies at the base of the Gulag pyramid. These regional camps and colonies functioned like feeder camps, taking in the system's most depleted inmates, and dispatching recovered prisoners who could be physically exploited again. High-priority camps received the "most valuable human element" or the physically strongest prisoners and did not get the "inferior workforce." Thus the rates of illness and mortality in these camps appear lower than in other camps within the Gulag pyramid. The Gulag's elaborate system of prisoner selection and distribution meant that inmates could have vastly different camp experiences. One prisoner might be a Stakhanovite in more comfortable barracks, receiving higher quality food, while another might be sleeping on bare ground and earning just a partial ration. One might be in an established camp division with a major hospital and available medicines, while another might be in a makeshift camp, lacking proper barracks or a single doctor. Resources of better quality and quantity, such as food and medical care, went to the stronger workers in the higher priority camps. Smaller camp divisions in less important industries or temporary outposts of a mine or railway site proved especially brutal as prisoners lacked proper housing and food.

Gulag survivor Jacques Rossi wrote that the camps were not unlike the larger Soviet Union—a "Stratistan" in which groups were stratified, separated, and sorted. [119] Stalin's Gulag represented a highly coordinated hierarchy of human exploitation, in which camps and colonies were deeply interconnected. Each detention facility possessed a ranking within this stratified system relative to the economic importance of the enterprise. The form and severity of human exploitation also varied. In the 1940s, Stalin created a *katorga* regime and special camp system where the Soviet state's worst enemies were subjected to especially harsh exploitation. There, all prisoners performed heavy physical labor, regardless of their health. These highly secret special camps functioned as a distinct system within a system, and they too concentrated their weakest prisoners in select locations. Human exploitation intensified from the 1930s to the 1950s, as evidenced not only by the creation of the special camps and *katorga* system, but by the longer Gulag sentences. By the late 1940s, a term of over twenty years had become increasingly common for both criminal and political offenders.

9   Exploitation
"Labor Utilization"

THE INSCRIPTION ON the gates of the Soviet camp read, "Labor is honor, glory, nobility, and heroism."[1] Everyone had to work. There would be no idlers and shirkers. Individual camps had to report to their Gulag bosses, and the Gulag bosses to their OGPU-NKVD-MVD superiors, that all prisoners were working, and most of them in heavy physical labor. Camps were required to demonstrate maximum labor utilization (*trudovoe ispol'zovanie*) of their prison workforce and minimal "lost labor days." No one could be allowed a free ride on the Gulag's scarce resources. Prisoners were the equivalent of workhorses—often literally, with a harness, pulling carts loaded with timber or coal. Memoirists characterized physical labor in the Gulag as lethal. Antoni Ekart described how "hungry, tired prisoners on general labor" were "fighting to survive, and were usually doomed to perish sooner or later."[2] For Varlam Shalamov, who experienced the gold mines of Kolyma, "Gold was death."[3] Shalamov wrote, "In camp it is the work that kills, and anyone who praises it is either a scoundrel or a fool. Twenty-year-olds, thirty-year-olds died one after another."[4]

The Gulag leadership masked the violence of physical exploitation by classifying the most brutalized inmates as "working" or "in use." The data on labor utilization concealed the decrepitude of the prison workforce and offered a relatively positive picture of Gulag operations.

As the Gulag intensified its system of exploitation, it ceased reporting data on physical labor capability to its party bosses. Documenting the labor utilization as opposed to the physical labor capability of prisoners had distinct advantages. Gulag bosses no longer had to communicate the true scale of their enfeebled and emaciated forced labor force. The Gulag's reporting system seems designed not so much to track invalids as to conceal them, to make them invisible. Camp administrators routinely hid the physical degradation of their workforce by reclassifying and moving sick prisoners. In addition, labor utilization data concealed the scale of the weakened workforce. Prisoners who had grown so weak and emaciated that they could no longer be exploited were dropped from the labor pool. Camp officials sought to make disabled inmates invisible in reports and statistics, and to demonstrate the maximum number of bodies being used in production. When individuals could no longer be utilized because of their poor health, they lost their ability to survive, for only through work could a nonhospitalized prisoner earn a ration or a salary.

THE "MAXIMUM UTILIZATION" OF PRISONERS

According to Shalamov, camp authorities were focused on one thing —getting prisoners to work: "In the eyes of the convict they are all symbols of oppression and compulsion . . . Daily, hourly, all these people repeat to the convict: 'Work! Work more!'"[5] The Soviet leadership granted prisoners few days off. The official length of the workday grew systematically from the early 1930s to the early 1940s, when the demands of wartime production led to twelve-hour days.[6] In 1947, the Gulag officially established a nine-hour workday for ordinary prisoners (with four days off per month), and a ten-hour workday for hard-labor prisoners (with three days off per month). Yet prisoners' reality often diverged from this. Gulag survivors recall very long workdays of 12–16 hours and few, if any, days off. Rest days undermined the camp's production plan so they were often cancelled, especially as camps rushed to fulfill their plan. Some prisoners were left at the worksite until the quota for the day had been fulfilled, regardless of the hours worked.[7] In response to such brutal physical exploitation, in 1936, a group of political prisoners in Vorkuta went on a hunger strike demanding improved conditions. They issued a formal statement to the camp administration in which they described Vorkuta as a "deadly place even for genuinely healthy people."[8]

Physical exploitation in Stalin's Gulag came in different forms, and certain jobs were much more taxing than others. The Stalinist leadership, however, wanted as many prisoners as possible in basic work (*osnovnaia rabota*), which involved strenuous physical labor. Prisoners unloaded bricks with their bare hands, dug clay and sand, cut coal and gold-bearing ore with a pick, cast metal, and carved out tunnels for roads and metro lines.[9] They were used in place of the heavy machinery that the Soviet Union lacked. Moreover, prisoners were expected to meet very high production targets. In the early 1930s, prisoners' work assignments were supposed to reflect their "social origin," sentence, and health.[10] Soviet regulations required that the most serious counter-revolutionary offenders be placed in the most physically taxing jobs.[11] The more comfortable work assignments were often obtained through personal ties, social networks, bribery, or luck. The most brutal, according to prisoner accounts, included mining, railroad construction, and logging. Gustaw Herling wrote: "Forest work was considered to be one of the heaviest forms of labor in the camp . . . As a rule [prisoners] left after a year, with incurable disease of the heart, and were transferred to brigades engaged at lighter work; from these they soon 'retired'—to the mortuary."[12]

The Gulag tried many different ways to get prisoners to work harder —from punishment, coercion, starvation, and terror, to higher rations and wages, even bonuses and medals. Brigade leaders and Stakhanovites could receive better rations, clothing, living conditions, and other benefits, including "workday credits" which granted reduced sentences to prisoners who overfulfilled their plan. The work credit system was abolished in 1939 but reintroduced by the end of the 1940s.[13] In the 1940s, Gulag officials used material and other incentives to increase productivity, with positive incentives targeting "those who distinguished themselves at work and systematically exceed production targets."[14] Anne Applebaum noted that, "throughout his life, [Stalin] demanded regular information about the level of 'inmate productivity' in the camps."[15]

Steven Barnes calls labor utilization "the key statistic for the Gulag bureaucracy."[16] Beginning in 1935, the Gulag tracked camps' labor utilization using four alphabetical categories: Group A: "labor force

working in industry"; Group B: "occupied in the service and maintenance of camps and colonies"; Group C: "sick"; Group D: "not working for various reasons."[17] NKVD-MVD superiors monitored whether
the Gulag was maximally exploiting its prisoners. They pored over
data on each camp's labor utilization breakdown, focusing on Group
A, that is, the percentage of inmates working in industrial jobs at the
camp (logging, mining, construction, etc.), but also on Groups C and D,
that is, inmates not working. Gulag authorities issued target figures to
the camps and colonies on the numbers that they had to maintain for
each of these groupings, and condemned their subordinates when the
data diverged from quota. For Solzhenitsyn, the "all-embracing system
of classification of camp prisoners into Groups A, B, C, D" marked
the emergence of the Stalinist camp system. These groupings "left no
leeway to the camp chiefs and even less to the prisoner: everyone not
engaged in providing essential services for the camp (B), not verified as
being ill (C), and not undergoing correction in a punishment cell (D)
must drag his workload (A) every day of his sentence."[18]

Evaluating the camps by labor utilization presented a generally positive picture of the Gulag workforce, from the perspective of the Stalinist
leadership. Huge segments of the inmate population could be depicted
as engaged in physical labor, regardless of their health. In May–July
1938, about 70 percent of prisoners were reported as working in industry, although several camps recorded well under 60 percent.[19] The
NKVD-MVD-Gulag leadership wanted to see labor utilization rates
over 70 percent. In all of 1940, roughly 80 percent of prisoners were
classified in Group A (working in industry), 7.6 percent in Group B
(camp services), 7.6 percent in Group C (sick), and only 4.6 percent
in Group D (nonworking). The war affected these numbers, especially
Group C. During the bleak war years of 1942–1944, the percentage
of prisoners working in industry dropped to 65–70 percent, while the
population of sick inmates jumped to over 20 percent.[20] Yet even during the war when prisoners' health plummeted, percentages of inmates
working in industry remained consistently high, ranging from the high
60s to the low 80s, despite lower percentages at certain colonies and
low-priority camps. There were still only 0.2–5.0 percent of Gulag prisoners classified as nonworking.[21] In 1950, about 77 percent of inmates
were classified as working in industry, 9.9 percent in camp services,
7.7 percent as sick, and 5 percent as nonworking.[22]

The Stalinist camps reported large numbers of prisoners exploited in industrial labor, yet there was considerable variation across camps and main administrations. In 1951, prisoners working in industry constituted over 85 percent in the main administration for industrial construction (*Glavpromstroi*) and in the main administration for road construction (GUShOSDOR), and over 80 percent at the high priority Dalstroi and Norilsk camps. By contrast, only 65 percent in the Gulag's Third Administration were well enough to perform industrial labor, and the low priority Borsky and Belrechlag camps reported only 56 percent of prisoners healthy enough to be working in industry.[23] While there was an incentive for camp administrators to produce favorable statistics on labor utilization—and, indeed, nearly all camps reported 60–90 percent in Group A—there were outliers on both ends.

Labor utilization figures conceal the poor health of Gulag prisoners and demonstrate that sick and emaciated inmates continued to be physically exploited in the basic work of the camps. For example, in July 1947, less than 10 percent of prisoners in MVD camps and colonies were classified as fit for heavy physical labor, while nearly 60 percent were classified for light labor or as invalids.[24] Despite the catastrophic state of their health, all of these prisoners continued to be physically exploited in basic work. The Gulag reported nearly 80 percent of prisoners in MVD camps and colonies in Group A or working in industry.[25] A February–March 1950 Gulag sanitation inspection of several camp divisions operated by the Primorsky regional MVD established that only 52.3 percent were in category 1 "basically fit for physical labor," 39.6 percent in category 2 "physically defective prisoners," and 8 percent in category 3 "invalids." Nevertheless, this poor physical profile produced a surprisingly impressive labor utilization breakdown, with 74 percent in Group A working in industry.[26] After 1948, Gulag leaders included labor utilization percentages but simply omitted data on prisoners' physical labor capability in routine reports for their MVD and party bosses. Impressive labor utilization figures concealed the ill health of exploited prisoners.

Labor utilization rates did not always successfully hide the degree of prisoners' ill health. In March 1945, the Gulag chief, V.G. Nasedkin, reported on the labor utilization of prisoners at camps, colonies, and NKVD construction sites.[27] The report explained why certain camps reported fewer prisoners working in industry and large percentages of sick inmates. He gave many reasons for the "unsatisfactory" labor utilization rates, including the poor health of prisoners: "Lately Privolzhlag has become a place for the concentration of weakened and bedridden prisoners from the NKVD northern camps, and this is why Group A never exceeds 54 percent in the camp." Illustrating how the Gulag sorted prisoners according to their health, Nasedkin indicated that with the closing of Privolzhlag, the work-capable population would be transferred to other Gulag sites, while the camp's sanatorium-towns and invalid camp sections would become part of the labor colony system of either the Saratov or Stalingrad region.[28]

Moreover, labor utilization data reveals that the special camps and the strict regime camps, whose policy was to work prisoners to death, had the highest numbers of sick and nonworking prisoners. According to a January 1948 report on labor utilization, the Siblag camp reported over 70 percent in Group A working in industry, and about 16 percent either sick or nonworking (Groups C and D); whereas Siblag-katorzhane, the camp's harsh regime division, reported a staggering 52 percent either sick or nonworking, and only 42 percent working in industry.[29] Special camps had lower rates of labor utilization, given the very poor health of their prisoners. In the MVD special camps for March 1951, about two-thirds of prisoners were working in industry (Group A) and over one quarter were either sick or nonworking (Groups C and D).[30] Some individual special camps recorded even lower rates of labor utilization. The lowest percentages of prisoners "working in industry" were recorded at camps with especially large numbers of sick and emaciated prisoners. At the Oak Forest special camp, where the special camp system concentrated its weakest prisoners, fewer than half of all inmates were Group A working in industry, and over one-third were nonworking.[31]

Gulag leaders criticized camps for "incorrect labor utilization," which meant the failure to place prisoners in jobs consistent with their health and to maintain proper food, housing, clothing, and medical care.[32] They demanded that inmate labor be "utilized" according to the List of Illnesses, that is, as dictated by a prisoner's physical labor capability. In 1945, the medical-sanitation department chief, D.M. Loidin, condemned "violations in the labor utilization of prisoners," such as the placement of light labor prisoners in heavy physical labor. At the time, weaker prisoners doing heavy labor were supposed to receive reductions in their production targets.[33] Loidin did not address the fact that prisoners classified for light labor were so weak that they could not perform heavy physical labor, even with reduced targets. Rather, the medical-sanitation department chief stressed that his subordinates had in their possession "a listing of all kinds of jobs according to their level of physical difficulty" and that they must "know this document and use it daily in their work."[34] The NKVD made it the responsibility of camp medical-sanitation department directors to ensure the "proper labor utilization of prisoners," and to punish those who violate camp rules and over-exploit prisoners.[35] Loidin told them that they "represent the front line in this matter."[36] Although camp medical-sanitation department directors were supposed to enforce labor utilization rules, in reality they held little power over camp officials.

Over the years, OGPU-NKVD-MVD instructions to the camps urging officials to improve prisoners' health did not necessarily reflect a high-level concern for the lives of inmates. Rather, as Oleg Khlevniuk explains, "Gulag planners from time to time recognized the limits of overexploitation."[37] Production plans had to be met. One need not make too much of such instructions, for during World War II, both the Nazi and Soviet leadership issued orders prohibiting the abuse of POWs, yet the brutal treatment of POWs under Stalin and Hitler is legendary.[38] In 1945, when the Gulag had an enormous number of weakened prisoners, Loidin insisted that all prisoners had to be put to work, even the weakest: "The surplus of category 3 [light labor] prisoners can be utilized normally on work that is for higher categories of labor, but with a reduction [in their production quota]. We cannot allow any other violations. If you have a surplus of category 3 [light] labor, you have to use it somehow."[39] Weakened prisoners were still marched out to perform difficult physical labor. Moreover, despite its instructions to preserve the health of prisoners, the Stalinist leadership generated production plans for the Gulag without taking into account the health of prisoners. As one health official complained: "They issue plans without considering how many prisoners are in categories 1, 2, or 3 [capable of heavy, medium, or light physical labor]. Herein lies the root of the violations of labor utilization."[40] Gulag leaders also issued instructions to camps to preserve the health of prisoners, yet such instructions must be read critically. They were not suggesting an increase in the camps' allowable quotas for sick or nonworking prisoners. Nor were they excusing the severely ill from heavy physical labor, or from a brutal regime that tied their rations to their productive output.

The Gulag maintained strict quotas that bore little relation to the realities of prisoners' health. Whether inmates were physically capable or not, they had to be marched out to work in order for the camp to meet its high quotas on "utilized" prisoners, and its low limits on sick and nonworking prisoners. The physical exploitation of extremely sick and emaciated prisoners constituted routine Gulag practice. Yet the goners, or last-leggers (*dokhodiagi*), simply could not work. Those locations at the bottom of the Gulag pyramid where the system concentrated its sickest inmates reported the smallest labor pool (*rabochii fond, trudfond*) as a percentage of total prisoners, as well as the lowest rates of working prisoners.

Not surprisingly, sick prisoners who were forced to work failed to meet their production quotas and thus received hardly any food. A Gulag report on the Norilsk camp in March 1953 indicated that nearly 90 percent of prisoners were either Group A working in industry or Group B camp services, yet nearly 20 percent of prisoners there failed to meet their plan targets, "mainly those with limited fitness for work."[41] Similarly, at the Lake special camp, more than 20 percent of prisoners failed to meet their production quotas, and in the colonies of Vladimir it was 25 percent. In Unzhlag, nearly 32 percent did not meet their targets.[42] The many frail prisoners recorded in Group A working in industry often failed to earn a standard ration. According to one Gulag survivor: "The emaciated prisoners, covered in the ulcers of scurvy, didn't have the strength to complete even half of their work norms. The administration tried another way of pushing those who didn't fulfill their norms. Prisoners who lagged behind especially badly were put right into special brigades. They were left to work all night on the road, with no sleep or rest . . . The miracle didn't happen: those on their last legs didn't find an ounce of extra strength or work any harder. They simply started bringing loads of corpses into the camp in the mornings."[43]

OFF THE BOOKS: MAKING INVALIDS INVISIBLE

The Gulag's Department for the Accounting and Distribution of Prisoners or OURZ compiled monthly reports for the Gulag chief and the NKVD-MVD leadership on the number, movement, labor utilization, and physical labor capability of inmates. In Gulag reports of the late 1940s, the labor utilization data appears more frequently than data on prisoners' health and, as noted previously, data on physical labor capability was eventually dropped entirely from external reports in 1948. Following the 1949 revision to the categories of physical labor capability, prisoners classified as category 1 "basically fit for physical labor" correlated with labor utilization Group A or the "labor force working in industry." Physical profile now overlapped with labor utilization, as the latter represented the key metric. The MVD-Gulag leadership wanted camps to report around 70–80 percent of prisoners in Group A working in industry, so camps were sure to classify this many as "basically fit for physical labor." Under the new scheme, prisoners' physical labor capability essentially became invisible and meaningless, as health data was eclipsed by data on rates of exploitation.

Internal Gulag reports indicate that even camps with many sick prisoners could report large numbers in heavy physical labor. This was done not only by forcing sick inmates into brutal work, but by removing the most emaciated prisoners from the Gulag's books. In internal reports, the Gulag made a critical and striking distinction between "prisoners on the labor rolls" (*zakliuchennye po trudfondu*) and "certified invalids off the labor rolls (*aktirovannye invalidy, otnesennye za balans rabochei sily*).[44] Only prisoners "on the labor rolls" were included in the labor utilization data that went to the party leadership. This accounting manipulation became especially significant during the war, when the Gulag experienced a sharp increase in the number of nonworking invalids "off the labor rolls" as well as Group D "not working for various reasons." In just the first few months of the war, the number of emaciated and nonworking Gulag prisoners more than doubled. From June 1941 to March 1942, nonworking prisoners grew from 10 to over 22 percent, while invalids off the labor rolls jumped from 5 to 9 percent.[45] In the first year of the war, roughly one third of the Gulag's inmates were either invalids or nonworking. Prisoners "off the labor rolls" consisted largely of the Gulag's most emaciated workforce, for example, weakened prisoners in regional hospitals and convalescent camps.[46] Also removed from the labor pool were certified, nonworking invalids, prisoners who were not working because they were being transported to another camp or colony (typically due to poor health), and inmates in transit prisons, who were typically ill as well. By the 1950s, the transit camps had become overloaded with prisoners, and evidence suggests that in this period they became tantamount to invalid camps. Prisoners "off the labor rolls" also included inmates in investigatory isolators, and those under quarantine.[47] This large inmate population did not factor into the camps' labor utilization data, which is why the Gulag was able to report large numbers of prisoners in basic work.

The prisoners included in the OURZ statistics represented the labor pool and they were divided into two broad categories—the nonworking and the "utilized" (ispol'zovano). In 1942–1943, nearly a third of all prisoners in NKVD labor camps and colonies were recorded as either "not working due to illness" or "invalids off the labor rolls," but at the Gulag's notoriously brutal logging camps (ULLP), the figure was over 40 percent.[48] The Gulag reported in June 1950 over one million prisoners in regional labor camps and colonies, but only 82 percent of them were actually included in the labor pool and placed within one of the four labor utilization groupings. Of this 82 percent, over three quarters were reported in Group A (working in industry), and roughly 10 percent each in Group B (camp services) and in Groups C and D (sick or not working for various reasons). The 18 percent of prisoners excluded from these statistics represented emaciated prisoners "off the labor rolls," and these largely included invalids (77 percent), but also prisoners under quarantine or in transit prisons.[49] Nearly identical statistics were reported the following year.[50] The Gulag met the Stalinist leadership's highly demanding labor utilization quotas by concealing the ill health of its workforce.

The goners or dokhodiagi were largely dropped from Gulag reports. The dokhodiagi who were "off the books" or "off the labor rolls" (za balansom) were typically isolated in separate camp sections and deprived of resources. Camps also isolated other severely ill and dying prisoners, as many had infectious diseases like tuberculosis. The Gulag wanted these prisoners transferred out of camp hospitals and clinics so that they would not occupy hospital beds over the long term.[51] One camp official boasted that these prisoners "nonetheless work and provide some profit for the state."[52] If they were in a hospital or working, then they could be fed. The Gulag allocated funds for working prisoners, but not necessarily for low priority, unproductive inmates.

Prisoners "off the labor rolls" were essentially left to starve. According to one camp official, "in the first quarter of 1945, we received nothing in the [Gulag] plan for prisoners off the labor rolls."[53]

The number of prisoners "off the labor rolls" was much greater in the colonies and lower priority camps where the Gulag concentrated its *dokhodiagi*. In 1951–1952, the MVD camps detained over 1.5 million prisoners. About 8 percent of registered prisoners were "off the labor rolls" and of this group, roughly three quarters were invalids and another 15 percent in transit prisons.[54] In June 1950, at camps like Karlag and Siblag, where large numbers of sick and emaciated prisoners were concentrated, prisoners "off the labor rolls" represented over 20 percent of all inmates.[55] The same pattern is evident in the colonies, where the Gulag located many of its invalids. The Vologoda regional labor colonies detained over eight thousand prisoners and as many as a third were "off the labor rolls." Nearly 90 percent of its "off the labor rolls" prisoners were invalids, but invalids could also be registered in the labor pool. Large numbers of prisoners in the Vologoda colonies worked in industrial labor and in camp services.[56] Moreover, the MVD special camps reported large numbers of prisoners "off the labor rolls." In 1951, the special camps had 242,871 registered prisoners but only 202,129 or 83 percent of this total were actually included in the labor pool and placed within one of the four labor utilization groups. Prisoners identified as "off the labor rolls" numbered 40,742, 17 percent of special camp prisoners; and this population consisted mostly of invalids (70 percent), but also included prisoners under quarantine (13 percent).[57]

The Gulag's deceptive method of reporting labor utilization data reveals that the four alphabetical groupings did not capture all prisoners. More research needs to be done before we fully understand what happened to prisoners "off the labor rolls." However, it appears unlikely that they continued to be fed since they were no longer working. The Gulag only fed nonworking prisoners in hospitals and convalescent camps. Nonetheless, it manufactured mortality data consistent with party quotas. In the 1950s, despite the enormous population of *dokhodiagi* in both its regular camps and special camps, the Gulag reported the lowest mortality rates in its history, less than 1 percent of all inmates.[58]

PAID WORK AND INTENSIFIED EXPLOITATION

To improve prisoners' labor productivity, the Gulag employed coercion and hunger, as well as propaganda and material incentives. The Stalinist leadership tried to motivate camp prisoners and staff by promoting the glory, heroism, and the redeeming value of labor. As Steve Barnes has shown, "economic productivity was always at the forefront of cultural-educational activity," and camp newspapers engaged in "propagandizing for high labor productivity."[59] The Gulag also relied on incentives. In the late 1940s, after a decade long ban, the system of workday credits was gradually reintroduced for privileged workers, first at select camps and sectors and eventually system-wide.[60] In 1947, Gulag chief Nasedkin noted that, "Wherever workday credits were introduced, the fulfillment of production plans improved considerably."[61] A system of wages was introduced too, which would have far-reaching impact on the deterioration of prisoners' health and the Gulag's failure to assume any responsibility for it.

The MVD lobbied hard for the right to introduce wages as an incentive for prison-laborers. Wages for prisoners were first introduced on a limited basis in a few camps in 1940, but significantly expanded in 1948, until the reform became system-wide in 1950.[62] A March 1950 decree of the Soviet Council of Ministers and subsequent MVD decree of April 1950 established a system of pay for prisoners in camps and colonies. Initially, the special camps were exempted, but later salaries were introduced there too. In general, salaries paid to Gulag prisoners were 30–50 percent lower than those of workers in civilian industries, but varied across different camps and economic sectors.[63] Prisoners with the highest wages included skilled workers and those in priority sectors such as coal and mining.

The introduction of wages did not translate into more money for the camps or the prisoners. Cash wages had to be derived from existing allocations, so camps would cut back on food and clothing allowances to help pay for wages.[64] In 1953, the average prisoner salary across all camps and colonies was 324 rubles per month, but prisoners had to pay for their upkeep, so they only received 129 rubles in hand. Within this average, over 40 percent of prisoners received less than 100 rubles, and another 25 percent received 100–200 rubles. Just over 10 percent of working prisoners earned 200–300 rubles, while a prisoner aristocracy of about six thousand received 750 rubles and higher.[65] Even at the priority camp of Norilsk, as Borodkin and Ertz write, "inmates received about one-third the pay of the lowest-paid civilian workers and about 15 percent of the pay of workers in comparable jobs."[66] Moreover, camp officials routinely stole from prisoners' salaries, and about one-third of all prisoners, including nonworking invalids and condemned "work refusers" (otkazchiki), received no salary at all.[67]

The introduction of wages made the Gulag's redistribution system more brutal, as the bottom of the pyramid was left further behind. Certified invalids were paid in accordance with regular piecework rates for work they actually completed.[68] In 1951–1952, as many as 26–28 percent of working prisoners doing piecework failed to meet their production targets.[69] A December 1950 Gulag report on the Kursk regional labor colonies, where three quarters of the prisoners were category two "physically defective" or "invalids," as many as 27.2 percent of working prisoners were not fulfilling their production norms. They received very low pay, only the 10 percent minimum salary.[70] At the Mineral special camp in 1950, over 40 percent of inmates received a salary under seventy-five rubles.[71] Prisoners who were too frail to work were often grouped together with shirkers, and could not earn enough money for their own survival. Not surprisingly, in 1952 the Gulag reported that prisoners' health had deteriorated sharply, especially in the logging camps, but also at camps in metallurgy, railroad construction, and other industrial sectors.[72]

With the introduction of the salary system, the Gulag leadership ruthlessly abandoned any accommodations for weaker prisoners. In a November 1950 letter to Kruglov, the Gulag chief, G.P. Dobrynin, argued that the categories of physical labor capability should be largely discarded, and considered only when transferring prisoners to other camps.[73] He believed that it was no longer necessary for the Gulag to continue the practice of giving weaker prisoners less strenuous work and lower quotas. Dobrynin told his MVD boss that as a result of the introduction of paid work for prisoners, "prisoners' interest in the results of their labor has increased significantly. Thus the need to divide prisoners into categories according to their physical condition has diminished. Therefore, the Gulag considers it expedient to eliminate the division of prisoners according to the categories of physical condition . . . and to stop applying any kind of discount for the less physically capable contingent that is being utilized in work in camps and colonies."[74] The Gulag chief indicated that even frail and emaciated prisoners would be placed in basic work rather than in lighter labor. In July 1951, the Gulag stressed this point when it told the medical-sanitation department to ensure that prisoners were "maximally drawn into the labor process" in basic industrial work.[75]

The new salary system essentially represented a defunding of weaker prisoners. Prisoners had to earn their food through work. If they failed to do so, then their declining health should not result in easier work, according to Dobrynin. In 1950, the Gulag chief told his MVD boss that the new system of salaries for prisoners effectively enabled them to buy food when they earned their pay. No allowances would be made for prisoners who could not support themselves. Together with the end to light labor and other accommodations for weak prisoners, the new policy intensified Gulag exploitation. At Karlag the number of prisoners in Group A industrial labor increased, but the overall health of prisoners deteriorated. In March 1951, Karlag reported that, "the labor utilization of prisoners significantly increased" following the introduction of wages, while prisoners' physical condition declined.[76] Given that roughly 80 percent of Karlag's prisoners carried the "physically defective" or "invalid" classifications, it is striking that so many of them were reported working. In the late 1940s and early 1950s, as exploitation intensified, the Gulag generated an ever-larger population of sick and emaciated prisoners. Stalin's policies were undermining his own objectives, for brutal physical exploitation only reduced camp productivity.

THE LATE STALIN YEARS: CRISIS IN THE GULAG

During the war, the NKVD argued for the release of prisoners "who do not pose a threat to state security." The security police wanted to concentrate its limited resources on policing and isolating the most dangerous state enemies. This desire was articulated again in the years before Stalin died, as the Gulag began to transform a significant number of prisoners into wage laborers. Prior to Stalin's death in March 1953, Gulag leaders again voiced the opinion that it made financial sense to concentrate scarce resources on the most serious offenders, rather than squander funds detaining petty criminals. The gradual transformation of the system, to one in which more dangerous prisoners remained under guard and less dangerous inmates were freed early to be wage laborers, appears strikingly similar to the change that the NKVD had advocated during the war.

By the early 1950s, the MVD-Gulag leadership acknowledged either that free labor was more productive than slave labor, or that it was at least less costly, and authorized large groups of prisoners at some priority camps to become free workers.[77] In 1950, MVD chief Kruglov reported to Beria that the cost of camp detention exceeded the salary of wage laborers, when one considered the MVD's additional expenses in armed guards and secure compounds.[78] This cost comparison made a great impression on both Kruglov and Beria, and in 1951, Kruglov asked for permission to grant thousands of prisoners early release and to turn them into wage laborers, on the grounds that certain construction sites had a shortage of qualified workers. As Marta Craveri and Oleg Khlevniuk explain, prior to Stalin's death in 1953, the foundation of the Stalinist forced labor camp system was being undermined by several practices—the introduction of salaries for prisoners, the early release and transfer of prisoners into paid labor, and the widespread practice of employing deconvoyed prisoners. Moreover, the fact that many Gulag construction projects appeared wasteful and useless "provided an additional blow to the system of forced labor" by convincing many around Stalin that the system no longer made economic sense. The Gulag had grown increasingly inefficient, economic plans were not being fulfilled, and expenses exceeded income.[79]

Prisoner strikes and large numbers of condemned "work refusers" contributed to the increasing inefficiency of the camps in the late Stalin years. It is likely that many of those labeled as "work refusers" were sick and emaciated prisoners, as this practice of relabeling was not uncommon.[80] One high-level Gulag report indicated that, "sick, emaciated, unclothed, shoeless prisoners, prisoners in transit, etc., are automatically branded as [refusers]."[81] Refusal to work in Stalin's Gulag constituted an anti-Soviet or counterrevolutionary act. A 1947 Gulag report stressed the importance of the "struggle against work resisters, especially in cases of organized refusal to work by violators of Soviet legality."[82] Not all "work refusers" were sick. In the late Stalin years, Gulag inmates included opponents of the regime and prisoners of war who had military experience. Many formed underground organizations, murdered guards and inmate-informers, staged large riots and escapes, and generally undermined camp control. In May 1947, the various crimes and "antigovernmental activity" by camp prisoners cataloged by the Gulag leadership included the following: an armed uprising planned by former Latvian soldiers, an armed uprising planned by the "Russian Society for Revenge against the Bolsheviks," an anti-Soviet organization led by German intelligence officers that planned to seize arms and free prisoners, an Estonian military-fascist rebel organization, and other groups of prisoner "bandits" who planned armed escapes.[83]

Although camp uprisings took place before the 1950s, including a 1942 uprising at Ust-Usa, prisoner unrest became more frequent in the 1950s.[84] A former Gulag official noted that one of the "most serious allegations against a foreman and boss at a camp unit would be to have 'refusers' in their unit, that is, prisoners who refused to go out and work."[85] Gulag leaders detailed these menaces and appealed to Soviet leaders for a tougher camp regime and more armed guards, as guards constituted only 8–9 percent of the prisoner population.[86] In the late 1940s, the camps and colonies did not have enough guards, and about 10 percent of the armed guards they did have were prisoners. About a third of the over seven thousand escapees were never caught.[87] The sharp increase in Gulag prisoners in the late 1940s and early 1950s also contributed to disorder in the camps. A 1951 report to MVD chief Kruglov indicated that the camp population at the Dalstroi camps had doubled since 1947, resulting in a large population of "criminal-bandit recidivists," severe overcrowding, and shortages in housing and guards.[88]

The Gulag's armed guards were tasked with marching prisoners to work and back. They stood in the watchtowers with their rifles and possessed a great deal of power over prisoners. Letters from prisoners denouncing camp administrators and guards were taken seriously, for such abuse was seen as obstructing the system of exploitation.[89] The profile of camp guards varied greatly in the Stalin years. In the prewar period, the guards were described as young, "physically healthy," and with Red Army experience. But during the war, the young cohort was replaced by men who were elderly, repatriated, or had passed through filtration camps, and who had little experience in military matters.[90] The Gulag leadership wanted to improve the recruitment and retention of guards through increased pay, improved status and rank, and better living conditions. It feared that aggressive prisoners could overwhelm less attentive escorts, seize their weapons, and execute armed escapes. Camp authorities told party leaders that the job of isolating and guarding prisoners "has become more complicated in recent years" not only because of the profile of the guards themselves but "also by the fact that the proportion of especially dangerous counterrevolutionary and criminal elements among prisoners has significantly increased."[91] Camp survivors describe a wide variety of guards, from thugs, sadists, murderers, and merciless slave drivers, to nonmalicious, lazy bureaucrats and decent human beings, although acts of kindness appear exceptional.[92] Many guards were themselves prisoners or former prisoners, or could become prisoners. Like their inmates, they often had to deal with malnutrition and lice, food shortages, long workdays, poor housing, and Arctic temperatures.

The party leadership was always obsessed with labor productivity in the camps, but these concerns became especially acute in the late 1940s and 1950s. Increasingly large numbers of prisoners were identified as not working, an act tantamount to sabotage, at a time when the role and responsibilities of the Gulag had increased. The MVD doubled capital construction in 1949–1952 alone.[93] Historians describe a "crisis" in the Gulag economy in the early 1950s, due to prisoner unrest and the large numbers of nonworking prisoners. The MVD-Gulag leadership was alarmed by the sharp rise in strikes, work refusals, and attendant "lost labor days."[94] Labor utilization rates and plan fulfillment were in decline, and the Stalinist leadership initiated a series of investigations to determine why. According to Nicolas Werth, "In 1951 General Kruglov, the minister of internal affairs, was worried about the constant decline in productivity among penal workers" and "began a vast inspection campaign to assess the state of the Gulags." The conclusions of the 1951–1952 inspection reports underscored the fact that "the Gulag had become a much harder mechanism to control."[95] Many inmates refused to work, were not given work, or could not go to work because of a shortage of guards; some were confined to punishment cells for violating camp rules.[96] According to Galina Ivanova, "In 1951–1952, not a single major camp production administration completed its plan," and the camps' poor economic performance continued into 1953.[97]

Even camps with a history of poor labor utilization rates witnessed further declines. Camps like Pechorlag that had chronically experienced low labor productivity for decades did even worse in the 1950s. In May–July 1938, Pechorlag's earlier incarnations, Ukhtpechlag and Sevzheldorlag, had attracted the attention of Gulag officials for their strikingly low rates of labor utilization—59.6 percent and 54.8 percent respectively, well below the camp average of about 70 percent at the time.[98] In August 1938, the director of Sevzheldorlag asked the Gulag medical-sanitation department to assist the camp in exploiting its "significantly large number of weak and invalid prisoners."[99] Over a decade later, Pechorlag's plan called for 65.5 percent in Group A "working in industry," but the camp reported 57.4 percent, and the number of prisoners in Group D "not working for various reasons" was double the maximum set by the plan.[100] Like many other camps, Pechorlag also reported a dramatic spike in the number of prisoners refusing to work, from 14,154 incidents in 1951 to as many as 39,745 in 1952.[101] Historians have attributed the decline in the number of working prisoners in the early 1950s to sharp increases in prisoners classified as "work refusers." From 1951 to 1952, the number of reported incidents of work refusal doubled, while in 1952 as many as 32 percent of prisoners failed to meet their production quotas.[102]

In my view, the increasing brutality of camp exploitation in the late Stalin years contributed greatly to the "crisis" of the Gulag. I believe that it was the extremely poor health of prisoners, more than camp unrest or strikes, that caused labor utilization rates to decline and hindered the Gulag's ability to meet production targets. From this perspective, the crisis in the Gulag in the early 1950s was not the result of greater numbers of emboldened prisoners willfully refusing to work. Evidence suggests that many prisoners classified as "work refusers" or under Group D "not working for various reasons" were in fact severely weakened inmates. Camps often concealed their population of sick and emaciated prisoners by classifying them as "work refusers," violators of labor discipline, or inmates who were nonworking for lack of supplies or convoy. Gulag officials routinely engaged in creative reclassifications, for example, listing prisoners as refusing to work when they actually lacked shoes and clothing.[103] Similarly, a 1950 Gulag sanitation inspection of the Primorsky regional MVD camps attributed the large number of nonworking prisoners to the fact that there was "no work available" for the roughly two thousand prisoners "with physical deficiencies."[104]

Prior to Stalin's death, the problem of the increasing population of sick and disabled prisoners consumed the Gulag leadership. A November 1952 letter from Dolgikh to MVD chief Kruglov reported on efforts to improve the labor utilization of prisoners and reduce the number of "lost labor days." He wanted camps and colonies to punish those who "allowed massive idleness in the labor force and the resulting material losses for the government."[105] Dolgikh noted that the number of prisoners "not working for various reasons" had more than doubled at many camps, and only a few of those prisoners were work refusers. Most were identified as nonworking due to "lack of a work assignment." The Gulag chief also highlighted the "labor days lost" due to "indiscriminate detention in penalty isolators" and camp transfers. In addition, he indicated that nearly a third of all prisoners doing piecework across the MVD system had not fulfilled their plan targets.

Dolgikh did not explicitly address the destruction of prisoners' health, but this fact is unmistakably evident in his data. If inter-camp transfers had increased, it was likely due to the routine relocation of severely ill prisoners. If nearly a third of prisoners doing piecework were failing to meet their production targets (classified invalids typically performed such work), then they were likely very ill and, given their decreased ration for underperformance, would only get sicker. An increase in "indiscriminate detention in penalty isolators" may have been due to the Gulag's criminalization of underperforming, emaciated prisoners, who were routinely denounced as shirkers and "work refusers." If a rising number of prisoners lacked work assignments, this was likely due to the fact that they were too sick and weak to perform physical labor. Camp officials routinely complained about their inability to find suitable work for severely ill prisoners. Moreover, the Gulag chief noted that the very same camps that reported large numbers of nonworking prisoners had issued requests for additional workers. Once their prisoners had become thoroughly "wrung out" by the Gulag's brutal system of physical exploitation, camp officials sought replacement workers. The poor health of prisoners appears to be the underlying problem throughout Dolgikh's memo. In the late Stalin years, the "crisis in the Gulag" was essentially a monumental health crisis.

SURVIVAL: AVOIDING PHYSICAL EXPLOITATION

According to Solzhenitsyn, there were two types of prisoners—the sloggers (*rabotiagi*) who performed heavy physical labor and the trusties (*pridurki*) who did not.[106] As we have seen, many of the sloggers were petty criminal offenders, the so-called *bytoviki* and *ukazniki*. Of the Gulag's four labor utilization categories, the vast majority of prisoners were supposed to be Group A or, in Solzhenitsyn's words, "sloggers," working in industry or doing general-assignment work. Memoirists describe such work in the camps as tantamount to a death sentence. Ekart asserted that, "most prisoners died within the first few months."[107] The physical destruction in the camps was even more dreadful than the mass slaughter of war, according to Shalamov: "Experience on the front cannot prepare a man for the sight of death in the camps."[108] He noted that, "out of the entire brigades which began the gold-mining season, not a single person would survive, except the brigadier himself, the brigade orderly, and a few of the brigadier's personal friends."[109]

Yet people did survive the Gulag and, according to memoir accounts, they were overwhelmingly the "trusties" represented by Group B "occupied in the service and maintenance of camps and colonies." They largely worked indoors, often behind a desk or in a clinic, spared the heavy physical labor of the "sloggers." Group B prisoners sometimes included invalids who performed maintenance jobs around the camp.[110] Many were political prisoners, who tended to be better educated, despite official regulations that, for many years, prohibited them from such privileged jobs.[111] According to Solzhenitsyn: "The genuine compound trusties were: cooks, bread cutters, stock clerks, doctors, medical assistants, barbers, instructors of the Cultural and Educational Section, bath managers, bakery managers, storeroom managers, parcel room managers, senior barracks orderlies, superintendents of quarters, work assigners, accountants, clerks of the headquarters barracks, engineers of the camp compound and of the camp workshops."[112] Some were musicians, actors, and artists.[113]

"Survivors wrote memoirs, not victims," as Alexander Etkind reminds us, and "survivors did not share the most extreme experiences of the life in the camp, such as scapegoating or terminal illness, because these experiences made survival impossible."[114] What made survival possible was the avoidance of physical exploitation. The authors of our most valued accounts of the Gulag experience, people like Shalamov, Solzhenitsyn, Ginzburg, Scholmer, Razgon and Ekart, had all somehow avoided many years of harsh physical labor in the camps.[115] A veteran prisoner gave the following advice to Solzhenitsyn, a new arrival at the transit camp: "The main thing is: avoid *general-assignment work* . . . General-assignment work—that is the main and basic work performed in any given camp. Eighty percent of the prisoners work at it, and they all die off. All. And then they bring new ones in to take their places and they again are sent to general-assignment work. Doing this work, you expend the last of your strength . . . The only ones who *survive* in camps are those who try at any price not to be put on general as-signment work."[116] According to memoir accounts, survival was the result of luck, good fortune, and the avoidance of general work. Thus emerged in the 1930s, as Leona Toker writes, "the concept *vytashchit'*, "to drag someone out" from general duties into easier work.[117] Accord-ing to Toker, "Gulag survivor memoirs rehabilitate chance as an inte-gral aspect of human life. Behind this attitude lies an awareness that statistical odds are strongly against individual survival and that ill for-tune is not something that 'can' happen but the general state of affairs . . . The chance in question was that of being 'dragged out' from the general duties."[118] Being "dragged out" from general work represented another form of Gulag selection, but it was the most fortunate kind. Antoni Ekart, a Polish engineer who spent seven and a half years in the camps, survived by working as an engineer and later in a hospital. The latter position, he wrote, "saved me from death by starvation."[119]

Indoor jobs often required certain skills, so more educated political prisoners may have had an advantage. Some political prisoners had been allowed to work as engineers or other professionals in the camps, but this changed with the Great Terror when all counterrevolutionaries had to be used in general work or physical labor.[120] Political prison-ers with technical expertise and education could no longer hope to be singled out, and were assigned to manual physical labor. Geologists, doctors, and engineers, imprisoned in the Great Terror, mined gold and felled trees. By the 1940s, camp officials realized that they needed the knowledge and expertise of trained professionals, even if they were political prisoners.[121] This explains Varlam Shalamov's assertion that service or staff positions, such as "bookkeeper, orderly, doctor, labora-tory assistant . . . were filled by persons sentenced under Article 58 of the Criminal Code."[122] One Gulag prisoner in a camp near Norilsk attributed his survival to his knowledge of Latin. Severely weakened from malnutrition after several months of working in a rock quarry, and weighing only 46 kilograms, he was able to acquire privileged jobs with the medical-sanitation department, as a nurse and pharmacist.[123] Sometimes prisoners' stature or connections rather than education helped to free them from heavy physical labor. Alexander Svanidze, the oldest brother of Stalin's first wife, lived as a privileged Gulag prisoner exempt from general work after his arrest in 1936. He had the soft job of watchman in the zone for prisoners with pellagra, until the outbreak of the war.[124] Memoirs of camp survivors indicated that the way to avoid premature death was through nonphysical labor. As Solzhenitsyn wrote, "Almost every long-term *zek* you congratulate on having survived was a trusty. Or had been one for a large part of his term."[125]

Gulag prisoners so associated general work with death that they took desperate measures to maintain their trusty positions. Gustaw Herling spent eighteen months between 1940 and 1942 in the Kargopol camp near Arkhangelsk, and was finally released with scurvy sores all over his body, swelling from malnutrition, and on the verge of death. He concluded his memoir with the gripping testimony of another survivor who, after less than two years of grueling labor in a timber camp, was saved when he was dragged out of general work and sent to the technical barrack. Soon after, NKVD officials told him that he should denounce four ethnic German prisoners. The man explained his actions: "The NKVD did not conceal from me that I would be sent back to the forest if I refused . . . I had to choose between my own death and that of those four . . . I chose. I had had enough of the forest, and of that terrible daily struggle with death—I wanted to live. I testified. Two days later they were shot beyond the zone."[126] Some trusties were deeply ashamed by their moral comprises and complicity with a violent system, and felt a "sense of wrongdoing" for their collaboration.[127] Gulag survivors often expressed sentiments similar to those of Holocaust survivors such as Primo Levi and Eli Wiesel, who speak of the shame, embarrassment, and guilt of survival, and the idea that others died in one's place.[128]

The trusties were designated Group B "occupied in the service and maintenance of camps and colonies." Due to the Gulag's strict quotas, typically fewer than 10 percent of prisoners could be so classified. If, as memoirs indicate, prisoners could only live out their sentence through a trusty work assignment, then the number of prisoners who survived the Stalinist camps would have been small indeed.

CONCLUSION

A fellow prisoner told Varlam Shalamov, "The only ones who call for honest work are the bastards who beat and maim us, eat our food, and force us living skeletons to work to our very deaths."[129] The Stalinist regime may have touted labor as heroic and redemptive, but work in the Gulag proved lethal. Most inmates performed exhausting physical labor. To survive, a prisoner had to avoid physical labor and seek work at a desk instead. Prisoners skilled as artists or accountants might have the good fortune of working indoors in jobs that were not physically depleting. However, quotas governed these comfortable positions, and camps were required to maintain low percentages of inmates in non-physical labor. The maximum utilization of prisoners constituted one of the core principles of the Gulag, but inmates could hardly survive the system of extreme physical exploitation. As their health declined, they were moved to light manufacturing and agriculture—making shoes, sewing clothes, weaving baskets, tending to chickens, or growing potatoes. But they had to work. Only through work could they eat.

In the early 1950s, the Gulag system experienced a crisis. Many more camps—as well as individual prisoners—failed to meet production targets. Large numbers of prisoners were identified as "work refusers." Labor utilization rates plummeted. Historians have interpreted this crisis of productivity as a consequence of prisoner unrest in the camps, as well as mounting economic inefficiencies. I believe that the enormous population of severely ill prisoners contributed no less to this crisis. In the late 1940s, the Gulag population expanded greatly and the regime of exploitation intensified. The introduction of paid work in 1950 brutalized the majority of prisoners further, by heightening the Gulag's systemic transfer of resources from the weakest to the strongest inmates. Frail and emaciated prisoners were often criminalized for their failure to meet production quotas. The most severely ill prisoners who could not work received no salary at all. Herein lies the crisis in the Gulag: Stalin's forced labor camp system destroyed its own capital.

When the Gulag's destructive capacity reached its zenith, the system was dismantled. The process of dismantling began almost immediately following the death of Joseph Stalin in March 1953. As Hannah Arendt famously wrote, de-Stalinization was motivated by the realization among "Stalinist functionaries themselves that a continuation of the regime would lead, not to an insurrection, against which terror is indeed the best safeguard, but to paralysis of the whole country."[130] When the dictator died, the Gulag lost its most powerful advocate. Stalin's entourage had realized years earlier that merciless physical exploitation in the Gulag had become self-defeating. Gulag violence came to an end not because it was perceived as inhumane, but rather because it was inefficient.

Epilogue
Deaths and Deceptions

SOLZHENITSYN USED METAPHOR to illustrate the destructive capacity of the system, calling the Gulag "a meat grinder for the worthless millions" (*miasorubka dlia negodnykh millionov*).[1] In the present work I have explored this metaphor, examining the systemic violence of camp life, including the punitive rationing system that starved millions, and the brutalizing system of "physical labor capability" classifications and merciless "labor utilization" quotas that worked to death millions more. The Gulag represented the Stalinist state's redistributive power at its most extreme. Punitive redistribution involved the planned transfer of resources from weak to strong prisoners, and from the base of the Gulag pyramid of camps and colonies to the pinnacle, as well as the systematic starvation of inmates considered "useless." I have also underscored the institutionalized dehumanization of inmates, which made the mass killing possible. The Stalinist camps viewed prisoners as "human raw material" for the state's profit, considered sick and emaciated inmates "defective," "inferior," and "ballast" to be discarded, and showed concern for prisoners' illnesses and mortality only as these related to "lost labor days." The Gulag represented the essential Stalinist institution, where individuals were dehumanized and violence was normalized, and where the few survived at the expense of the many.

In Stalin's Gulag, the masses of "human raw material" had to work in order to eat. Failures to produce at levels demanded by the party were punished by starvation. Prisoners suffered from various untreated illnesses that were largely induced by nutritional deficiency. Starvation diseases such as pellagra were commonplace. Indeed, vitamin deficiency was the predominant underlying illness of prisoners. The Gulag system purposefully withdrew food from inmates who could not work up to the levels mandated by the party. Resources denied to nonworking emaciated prisoners were systematically transferred to stronger prisoners. Prisoners were exploited to the point of thorough depletion, at each stage of their declining health. The Stalinist leadership expected camps to achieve "maximum labor utilization," Gulag-speak for the extreme exploitation of prisoners. It established strict limits on the number of prisoners who could be hospitalized or nonworking. Virtually all prisoners were supposed to perform basic industrial work. The Gulag's medical establishment served the system of violent exploitation and was tasked with ensuring the maximum possible number of working inmates. Doctors had to conform to strict quotas on illness and hospitalizations, even in the face of rising numbers of incapacitated inmates. Lacking voice in major health decisions, they largely remained powerless before the camp production managers.

The destructive nature of the Gulag system forced the Stalinist leadership to manage an enormous population of sick and emaciated prisoners. It did so by organizing the vast Gulag system as a pyramid of camps and colonies, in which camps in priority sectors received more than camps in lower-priority sectors. The Gulag pyramid transferred stronger prisoners to the high-priority camps and relocated depleted prisoners to low-priority regional camps and colonies. The Gulag selected and sorted its prisoners according to their "physical labor capability," within a highly coordinated system of human exploitation. As this study has demonstrated, the system's more than four hundred labor colonies served a critical function. Stalin's labor colonies have been largely overlooked in the historical literature, yet they constituted the enormous base of the Gulag pyramid, the vast dumping ground for depleted and dying prisoners.

The Stalinist Gulag's exploitation of prisoners generated an enormous population of sick and disabled people, because it required that prisoners be thoroughly "wrung out" for the state's profit. Nonhospitalized prisoners who were emaciated and unable to work were a burden to the camp economy. Vilified as "idlers" and "ballast," these last-leggers or *dokhodiagi* were systematically discarded beyond the barbed wire. Routine releases of depleted prisoners artificially reduced mortality rates and concealed the destructive nature of the camps. The Stalinist leadership considered it preferable to work prisoners to death and replace them, rather than allocate sufficient resources to keep everyone alive. Yet it remained highly secretive about this calculation. The archival evidence suggests that NKVD-Gulag and Soviet justice officials worked hard to convince Stalin and the party leadership to release many starving prisoners during the war, and even advocated restructuring the Gulag into a more limited forced labor camp system. Stalin apparently did not want to reduce the size and scale of the Gulag, to limit detention to the state's most dangerous offenders. He wanted to maintain a Gulag for the masses. Thus the system became even more massive and cruel in the postwar period. Human exploitation in the Gulag intensified over the years and peaked in the late 1940s and early 1950s, during the years of High Stalinism. More physically weakened prisoners were forced to perform heavy physical labor in camps and colonies with fewer resources per prisoner. Ultimately, the Gulag's violence undermined its economic ambitions. A depleted, sickened, and starving workforce could generate little profit for the state.

Merciless exploitation and punitive starvation rations killed millions in Stalin's Gulag. Yet how did this vast system of destructive labor camps persist for nearly a quarter of a century? Many factors contributed to the Gulag's longevity, including the compelling ideology of redemptive labor, the obsessive national security concerns of the Soviet state, and Stalin's belief in both the economic efficiency of penal labor and the political efficacy of mass terror. No less important to the system's longevity, however, was the Gulag's highly developed regime of secrecy. Silence, concealment, and distortions enabled this violent institution to function for decades.

KEEPING THE GULAG SECRET

Nearly seventy years ago, David Dallin and Boris Nicolaevsky published the first major scholarly study of the Stalinist camps. Among other things, they noted that Soviet citizens confronted "myriad internal curtains" that concealed the nature of the camps.[2] For most of its existence, the Gulag operated under a heavy veil of secrecy. One former prisoner recalled the long rail journey "taking us deep into Russia, to Siberia" to the camp destination: "The train never stopped at stations, only in open areas. The NKVD probably didn't want ordinary citizens to see these densely packed cages [of people]."[3] Similarly, another Gulag survivor noted the secrecy of the prisoners' three-week train journey to their camp: "There were some stations where they took us to the bathhouse. And at one of the stations they take you to a transfer prison, and it's important that no one sees this. At night, with dogs, well, you can imagine."[4] Solzhenitsyn described the fundamental paradox of an "amazing country of Gulag" that, like a gigantic patchwork of "islands," cut into cities and hovered over streets, and yet remained "almost invisible, almost imperceptible."[5] Recent scholarship has challenged the image of isolated and invisible camps. We now know that many Gulag prisoners regularly interacted with the local civilian population, and that prisoners could be seen working on construction projects in major Soviet cities.[6] Nonetheless, distrust and fear likely played a role in these encounters, and limited what ordinary civilians could learn about the labor camps. Antoni Ekart described being marched through the town of Vladimir in the late 1930s with a group of prisoners: "They did not see us, simply by pretending that we were not there. I did not see a single glance in our direction. Men, women, and even children walked along looking straight ahead or turning their heads away. Now I understand that it was fear that obliged them not to notice us: fear of being accused of too much sympathy for the 'enemies of the people': fear that they might know too much, for one may never speak aloud of prisons and camps in the USSR. The NKVD are on the watch to make sure that all this remains a mystery, even while masses of human beings from the camps are being driven in broad daylight through the streets."[7]

Routine silences and distortions made it possible for the violent exploitation to persist for decades. When the "corrective labor camps" were first established, the Stalinist regime publicly acknowledged their existence. Yet it never publicized OGPU-NKVD-MVD regulations on routine camp operations, such as the system of physical exploitation, the punitive ration schedules, or the brutal List of Illnesses. In the 1930s, Soviet propaganda merely touted the camps as sites of re-form and rehabilitation. Maxim Gorky's famous collection of essays on the building of the White Sea-Baltic Sea Canal praised the way it re-deemed prisoners through physical labor.[8] Former kulaks touted their work achievements in the camps and how they had been rehabilitated through labor.[9] As Anne Applebaum explains, the widespread public-ity ended quickly with Stalin's purges in the late 1930s. A heavy veil of secrecy descended on the Gulag, and the Soviet public no longer read about the Gulag's "corrective labor" in the official press. This message was now limited to the Gulag newspapers, which could not be taken out of the camps. Gorky's collection was banned.[10] The secrecy that had once involved only internal Gulag operations now extended to the very mention of the camps.

There are many mysteries surrounding the Gulag, making scholarly investigation more difficult. We may never know the size of the Gu-lag, not only because camp locations remained highly secret, but also because many camps were only temporary. Some of the most brutal camps, where prisoners endured extreme conditions with only tempo-rary shelter, were also the most short-lived.[11] The Gulag's own regime of secrecy prohibited the production of printed maps. As Mark Har-rison explains, "If the *Gulag* had no printed maps, it is because the production and distribution of printed maps could only have widened the circle of people with access to the identity and location of camps. Printed maps were not wanted because the information they would have carried was among the top state secrets of the Soviet era."[12] Se-crecy was an essential element of the Gulag enterprise. According to Steven Barnes, "Prisoner transports were hidden as 'special equipment.' Prisoner correspondence was severely restricted. Released prisoners signed secrecy agreements forbidding them to talk about the camps. Nobody could enter regions like Kolyma without special entrance per-mits."[13] A Gulag survivor explained that in prisoners' letters to fam-ily members "no criticism of the camp administration or conditions in camp was allowed. You couldn't . . . well, no one would have written that he was starving for instance."[14] An MVD official instructed Antoni Ekart, upon his 1947 release as an invalid, "to undertake in writing to observe complete secrecy about everything I had seen in Soviet camps and prisons."[15]

The Stalinist regime kept the mass executions of the late 1930s secret by lying to relatives and generating false death certificates to the effect that arrestees had died in confinement.[16] It no less brazenly concealed the destructive nature of the camps. The regime used veiled language to obscure the location and nature of routine camps, invalid camps, and special camps. In telegram communications, any mention of prisoners' illnesses, deaths, or physical labor capabilities had to be masked using code words.[17] Prisoners were allowed to write to their family members, but they could not mention anything about the camp—its economic tasks, regimen, or everyday life.[18] During the reforms of the MVD following Stalin's death, when it was suggested that prisoners should be detained in the places where they lived and worked and not shipped to distant locations, MVD boss I.A. Serov protested that the establishment of colonies in practically every region of the USSR would "make visible the presence in the USSR of an enormous number of places of detention."[19] This was unacceptable. Those who managed the Stalinist camps could hardly imagine making the system visible.

The regime concealed the Gulag not only from the larger Soviet public, but from the international community as well. The official Soviet narrative concerning benign camps for the rehabilitation and reeducation of criminal offenders was critical to the country's favorable image abroad. In the 1920s, the Soviet Union faced international accusations of forced labor. Camp memoirs published abroad described the conditions of brutality and starvation at Solovki. According to Michael David-Fox, this criticism prompted a Soviet "counter-campaign that brazenly denied all evidence of forced labor."[20] International condemnation culminated in a Western campaign against Soviet slave labor in 1930–1931. The resulting boycott of Soviet timber threatened the country's ability to acquire hard currency for industrial development. The regime feared that the boycott might spread to other commodities that relied on slave labor, such as Kolyma's gold. Even more than the timber boycott, a Western ban on imports of Soviet gold would have had a negative impact on the regime's industrialization drive.[21] Stalinist propaganda claimed that unemployed people in capitalist countries "would envy the work and living conditions of prisoners in our northern regions."[22] The party covered up the reality of the Gulag to protect its commodity exports and the Soviet Union's image.

In the postwar years, with international attention focused on human rights, war crimes, and genocide, the Stalinist regime intensified its efforts to conceal the destructive capacity of the camps. The Gulag could not appear to be in any way similar to the Nazi camps, for international critics were now pointing to the Soviets' hypocrisy in passing judgment on the Nazis for war crimes. As Tony Judt wrote: "To have the Soviets sitting in judgment on the Nazis—sometimes for crimes they had themselves committed—devalued the Nuremberg and other trials."[23] Not coincidentally, it was at this very time that the Soviets began talking about the "humane treatment" and "dignity" of prisoners. In the years that coincided with the liberation of the Nazi camps and the Nuremberg trials, the Gulag leadership issued several directives on the need to improve the health of prisoners and to punish "violations of labor utilization." In 1947, the Gulag chief V.G. Nasedkin made repeated references to "humanism," a word that appeared in MVD Order No. 165 of 1946. The decree called upon the camps and colonies to improve living conditions, to become models of corrective labor, and to "fully meet the demands of socialist legality and humanism." Workers at corrective labor camps and colonies had to be taught a "humane attitude towards prisoners" and to "decisively end all acts that decreased the human dignity of prisoners."[24] Such references to humanism are very unusual, if not completely absent, in the periods before and after the mid-1940s, prompting one to suspect that they were inspired by international events. As Amir Weiner has shown, the Soviets possessed an acute sensitivity over being equated with the Nazis.[25]

SYSTEMIC DECEPTION INSIDE THE GULAG

Although scholars were aware that the Gulag was shrouded in secrecy during its existence, they expected that the history of the camps could be revealed once the archives were declassified. However, we have learned in recent years that declassified Gulag archival documents fail to tell the whole story. In the official record, there is evidence of irregular reporting, poor record-keeping, omissions, distortions, and falsifications. Camp officials often falsified economic data to make their operations appear profitable. Camp administrators padded statistics and manipulated their data to conform to the mandated quotas on such matters as illness, mortality, labor utilization, and productive output. The fact that camps and colonies were often located far from urban centers enabled such deceptive practices. It was difficult for Moscow to verify reports, so distant camps freely fudged their numbers.[26] At the same time, distance and isolation alone do not fully explain the massive systemic deceptions. Police and judicial organs responded to various incentives to underreport some issues (such as illness and death in the Gulag) and to ratchet up the numbers on arrests and executions during campaigns against various state enemies.[27] Camps maintained poor records on prisoners and deliberately concealed mortality, often recording deaths as escapes or under "departed for various reasons."[28] Gulag officials did not openly acknowledge the destructive nature of their enterprise, even in highly classified reports. According to Oleg Khlevniuk, "In the documents of the Stalinist repressive apparatus one can find not only inaccuracies but outright falsifications made with criminal intent."[29]

Routine silences and deceptions are especially pronounced in official records related to prisoners' health. While the camps used various reporting methods to conceal the destructive nature of exploitation, the Gulag leadership did the same to show party bosses that they were successfully exploiting prisoners' labor for profit. Soviet doctors and officials were constrained in their ability to speak about the realities of famine and chronic malnutrition under Stalin. According to Veniamin Zima, "Even the word 'famine' was at this time [during the 1946–1947 famine] under strict prohibition and was not used in the most secret reports of the government."[30] Similarly, Rebecca Manley describes how doctors were forbidden to discuss the 1932–1933 famine, just as during World War II "mainstream medical literature passed over starvation in the rear in silence."[31] In the Gulag, authorities and doctors likewise remained silent about the deliberately insufficient rations and starving prisoners. They concealed the reality of mass starvation in the camps by classifying the symptoms of vitamin deficiency diseases in various ways. The enormous starving population of Gulag prisoners was divided up among many categories of ailments. The Gulag routinely recorded persons with pellagra and other starvation diseases as suffering from skin disorders and digestive problems. Medical-sanitation department officials differentiated people, separated them into distinct boxes, and adopted multiple classifications as a way of masking or hiding underlying phenomena. They used multiple categories of illness to conceal widespread malnutrition and starvation. They used multiple categories of physical labor capability to conceal ill health and disability on a massive scale. They reported high rates of labor utilization, even when most prisoners were so frail they could hardly work.

The Gulag carefully instructed doctors on how to complete death certificates in a way that would conceal the fact that prisoners were dying of starvation. In May 1941, Gulag chief Nasedkin complained to the heads of labor camps and colonies that on documents concerning the cause of a prisoner's death, many medical-sanitation departments were writing emaciation and exhaustion (*istoshchenie*). These documents, he wrote, have been going not only to the courts that sentenced the prisoner, but to the relatives of the dead, where "they prompt undesirable judgments about the cause of death." Notably, he described the judgments of these family members as "undesirable" and not "incorrect." To combat this bad publicity, Nasedkin instructed his subordinates to report not only the "basic diagnosis" of exhaustion and emaciation, but also an "accompanying ailment" such as paralysis of the heart, weakened heart activity, tuberculosis, etc. The former would remain on internal documents reserved for the eyes of medical-sanitation department officials. Only the accompanying diagnosis, he stressed, should go on death notices to relatives or on documents being circulated to other organizations, like the civilian courts.[32] Prisoner doctors confirm that following the obligatory autopsy of the dead, the only permissible final diagnosis that could be noted on camp death certificates was "weakness of the heart muscles."[33] The Stalinist leadership enforced a policy of camouflage to conceal the Gulag's system of lethal exploitation.

The OGPU-NKVD-MVD constantly berated the Gulag leadership for problems at the camps (which its investigators regularly uncovered) and Gulag officials in turn criticized camps for their operational failures. Given the climate of accusation and blame, there was a good deal of misinformation in communications between the Gulag administration, the OGPU-NKVD-MVD, and the party leadership. Gulag bosses tried to keep unfavorable information from the OGPU-NKVD-MVD, and the latter, from the party leadership.[34] Since the Gulag leadership was always blamed for the weakness of the labor force, it generally avoided the subject of prisoners' physical labor capability when talking to MVD superiors. References to the dismal state of the Gulag labor force appear distinctly understated. In May 1947, the Gulag chief Nasedkin euphemistically told his MVD bosses that in the first months of the war, when large numbers of prisoners were being evacuated to the Soviet interior, at times on foot and over vast terrain, "some worsening in the physical condition of prisoners occurred."[35] The Gulag archival record constitutes a riddle of representation, and the task of understanding the reality of the camps can be immensely challenging.

THE PROBLEM OF KNOWING

Although numerous published memoirs have shed light on Gulag operations, individual testimonies do not tell the whole story. There are the silences and distortions in the memoir literature as well. Some Gulag survivors who worked "trusty jobs" as doctors and cooks likely experienced a degree of survivors' guilt, which may have led to testimonies that failed to mention the worst horrors of the camps. Others may have implicitly justified the camps by focusing attention on the violent criminal recidivists. The impression they give is that although the Gulag may have been inappropriate for political prisoners, it was not so for many other inmates. Moreover, even memoirists like Solzhenitsyn did not have access to official Gulag documents. It would have been difficult for them to differentiate anecdotal information from formal Gulag instruction, or to understand the system as a whole. Each individual prisoner possessed a limited perspective on the vast Gulag pyramid. Individual camp experiences might not reveal that the colonies and camps were fundamentally linked, or that sick and emaciated prisoners were concentrated in certain locations. Prisoners at one camp or camp section knew little about the experiences of their fellow inmates elsewhere. Historical analysis might also be complicated by the pride of prisoners and nonprisoners alike in the work of the camps. Eugenia Ginzburg recalled her release from the camps at Kolyma and her residency in the city of Magadan, a city built by prisoners. She took pride in the fact that a city had been built from nothing.[36] Many felt similar pride in helping to create cities, factories, medical research, and a military superpower.

The Soviet regime devoted a great deal of attention to bureaucratic recordkeeping, a sign of socialist modernity. V.I. Lenin famously said that "socialism is accounting and control."[37] On the ground, however, socialist accounting was far from satisfactory. There were striking deficiencies in the case of Gulag health records, as medical workers complained repeatedly about the shortage of paper, especially during the war and postwar years. In 1945, the medical-sanitation department director for the Turkmen SSR camps and colonies described how hard it was for his staff to maintain records: "There's no paper," he said, "they write on newspapers and on torn scraps of paper." The Gulag medical-sanitation department chief, Loidin, asked, "Don't they write on plywood?" He answered, "They also write on plywood. There is no precise documentation, no proper accounting. What are they supposed to write on when there's no paper?"[38] Another health official described her camps' documentary system as "extremely primitive." Her attempt to establish uniform recordkeeping across all camp sections failed, she said, due to lack of paper.[39] The medical-sanitation department director of the Buriat-Mongolia system of camps and colonies complained: "We have no paper. We don't give prisoners medical certificates because there are no forms and no paper. There are only ID cards (*kartochki*) for prisoners, but they're filled out using paper from books."[40]

Historians cannot trust the veracity of Gulag records, not only because they were often falsified and manipulated, but because even earnest camp officials did not have the resources to maintain proper recordkeeping. According to the medical-sanitation department chief for the Kazakh SSR camps and colonies: "The issue of medical statistics is a question of paper, and there is no paper. We have no primary documentation anywhere, so data does not always reflect the actual situation on the ground."[41] Another described how they kept medical records on scraps of paper or on boards and walls: "Sometimes at a colony you learn that the history of illness has been written on plywood and that it disappeared somewhere, or a nurse erased a decade and started to record another."[42] A great deal of information was simply lost. The medical-sanitation department director of the Altai regional system of labor camps and colonies admitted, "the lack of documentation—that's everywhere."[43] He described how prior to 1944 his staff maintained a card catalogue to record prisoners' health, medical history, and treatment in a hospital or clinic. The card catalogue helped the camp staff to assess their work and determine whether a prisoners' health was improving or deteriorating. But the staff eventually had to stop maintaining these records due to lack of paper. "With no catalog," he lamented, "it is extremely difficult to work."[44] The Gulag medical chief, Loidin, agreed "we have no paper," but stubbornly insisted that the problem of paper shortages was no excuse for poor documentation.[45]

The silences, omissions, and distortions in memoir accounts and Gulag archival records suggest that we may never be able to completely
ascertain the human cost of Stalin's forced labor camp system. As Alexander Etkind explained, "The time, place, and circumstances of deaths
in the camp remained unknown, as if such deaths were simultaneously
both a state secret and a matter of mere detail, not even worth men-
tioning."[46] Many deaths were unrecorded. The bodies of dead prisoners
were thrown overboard from transport ships. Corpses were secretly
moved at night, bodies dumped into mass graves in random locations.
Personal case files of prisoners were often lost.[47] Gulag survivor Gustaw
Herling wrote: "Death in the camp possessed another terror: its anonymity. We had no idea where the dead were buried, or whether, after
a prisoner's death, any kind of death certificate was ever written . . .
I twice saw a sledge taking bodies out beyond the camp . . . probably
making for some abandoned forest clearing, whose whereabouts no
one in the camp knew."[48]

Despite the many problems of knowing, I believe that it is possible
to offer an estimation (however incomplete) of Gulag mortality. Given
the archival record on "physical labor capability," it is reasonable to
conclude that at least a third of the eighteen million people who were
condemned to Gulag detention in the Stalin years perished as a result of their experience. This represents the population of prisoners
who received a health classification of "invalid," "light physical labor,"
"light individualized labor," or "physically defective." The archives
reveal that in practice these health classifications described prisoners
with extremely severe or terminal illnesses. In the postwar years, the
proportion of prisoners thus classified far exceeded one-third and was
often as high as two-thirds. Therefore, deaths that resulted from Gulag
detention may be estimated very conservatively at around six million.
Some might object to the six million figure, and argue that some prisoners who were classified as severely ill or released from the camps as
invalids eventually recovered their health. Although it is often difficult
to know for certain whether a particular individual's death resulted
from time in the camps, the tremendously harmful impact of Gulag
detention on prisoners' health is plainly evident. Would we include a
prisoner like Gustaw Herling, who was released from the Gulag as an
invalid, but whose ailment did not quickly end his life, even if it shortened his years? The problem of knowing lies not just in the inadequacy

of the official record and the testimonies of Gulag survivors. It also derives from problems of definition, and whether we are counting deaths in the camps, deaths that occurred shortly after release, or simply what demographers refer to as "excess mortality" resulting from Gulag detention. I believe that we must count not just deaths that were officially recorded within the barbed wire of the camps, but the severely damaged bodies and shortened lives as well.[49]

Despite the many problems of knowing, there is now a good deal that we do know. We know that the official Gulag mortality rate was artificially suppressed in various ways. We know that hundreds of labor colonies were not simply used for short-term offenders, as Soviet officials claimed, but for physically weakened and "defective" prisoners who had been "unloaded" from the camps after they became incapable of heavy physical labor. We know that many did not survive the journey to distant camps, or their first winter, or their first couple of years. We know that prisoners were greatly devalued and dehumanized. We know that, with the constant stream of new prisoners, camp officials did not need to be concerned about labor shortages, and had little incentive to care for individual prisoners. As the historian of slavery, David Brion Davis, wrote: "Chattel slaves at least represented a valuable investment, an investment of rising value in much of the New World, but that slightly protective aspect of chattel slavery was absent from twentieth-century 'state slavery.'"[50] Indeed, Stalin's state slaves lacked every protection. The Gulag routinely discarded its weakened population, whether they were transferred to settlements and colonies or freed, and many died shortly after their release. The Gulag system thoroughly depleted and then discarded its commodified prisoners or, as Varlam Shalamov wrote, its "human waste, remnants, trash."[51]

THE BEGINNING OF THE END

Stalin's labor camp system began with the mass arrests and deportations of the so-called rich peasants or kulaks.[52] In many ways, it ended as it had begun, with the mass release of ordinary Russian workers and peasants. As an institution of production, the Gulag was sustained by Stalin's unrelenting arrests of various categories of political and criminal offenders. The largest group of inmates, the petty criminal offenders, was the first to be released. After Stalin died, Nikita Khrushchev and the party leadership freed most of the Gulag's prisoners and gradually dismantled the Stalinist machinery of forced labor. The dismantling of Stalin's Gulag took place over the course of much of the 1950s. A number of historians have analyzed various aspects of this long and complex process.[53] I would like to underscore simply that the process began with the large-scale release of the Gulag's majority prisoner population.

The demise of the system began in 1953, when the party freed the largest segment of the Gulag workforce. In 1949–1951, the MVD sought a reorganization that would have allowed camps to more effectively meet their production goals while continuing to isolate only the most dangerous political and criminal offenders.[54] The MVD leadership believed it was unnecessary for all their prison laborers to be detained in high-security camps. According to Aleksei Tikhonov, deputy MVD minister S.S. Mamulov supported the conversion of petty criminal offenders from camp inmates into an exile labor force. These individuals would be forced to work at MVD production sites and receive lower wages than other exiles. However, the new status would allow them to be joined by their families in exile settlements. This fundamental restructuring would have converted nearly 70 percent of Gulag prisoners into exile laborers.[55] To Stalin's security police, the reform was highly appealing. The state would save eight billion rubles per year in the cost of detaining petty offenders, and the Gulag could focus its resources on the worst criminal offenders, recidivists, and counterrevolutionaries. As described in chapter 6, the Gulag-NKVD leadership, as well as the Soviet Procuracy and the Commissariat of Justice, had advocated a very similar restructuring during the war.

Similar to its original wartime proposal, the MVD plan targeted the Gulag's majority population—petty criminal offenders. Nearly 60 percent of the camp inmates whose status would convert to exiles under the proposed changes were convicted under the June 7, 1947 theft decrees, but also included were persons sentenced for white collar and economic crimes, hooliganism, property offenses, and violations of the passport law. This enormous population of prisoners, as we have seen, swelled the Gulag ranks in the 1940s. By turning petty offenders into exiles, the MVD would eliminate the responsibility and cost of detaining them in camps. Discussions over the proposal took place internally between MVD and Gulag leaders. Interestingly, the Gulag leadership objected. Gulag chief Dolgikh believed that such a disruptive reorganization would compromise the camps' ability to meet production goals. He also rejected the idea of an automatic and blanket conversion of all prisoners sentenced under certain articles of the criminal code. Consistent with Gulag practice, he preferred to use exile status as a work incentive or to reward prisoners who met their production quotas.[56] The 1951 MVD proposal largely revived ideas that Lavrenty Beria had expressed during the war, but the proposed camp reform failed this time too. It was filed away for two years until Stalin's death, when it served as the model for the 1953 amnesty.

The 1953 amnesty, which was introduced days after Stalin died, marked the beginning of the end of the Gulag system.[57] The amnesty targeted prisoners that represented the largest segment of the prison workforce, poorly educated Russian workers and peasants who had been sentenced under Stalin's harsh labor laws and theft decrees. In a June 16, 1953 memo to the USSR Council of Ministers and the Presidium of the Party Central Committee, Beria urged his colleagues "to abolish the existing system of forced labor due to its economic inefficiency and lack of potential."[58] During the period from March 18 to March 28, 1953, the government either abandoned or sharply reduced MVD capital projects, reassigned responsibility for camps and colonies to the Ministry of Justice, and transferred MVD economic functions to the appropriate civilian economic ministries.[59] In a memo to the Presidium of the Central Committee, Beria stated openly that "dangerous state criminals" made up fewer than 10 percent of the Gulag population.[60] These prisoners were largely confined in the special camps, and they remained under the jurisdiction of the MVD.

Enormous numbers of prisoners left the camps and began the painful transition back to a world that had abandoned them. Over the next three months, roughly 1.5 million prisoners, or 60 percent of all Gulag inmates, were freed from detention.[61] The dismantling of the Gulag also involved the wholesale transfer of entire camp sections and divisions for invalids and weakened prisoners from the MVD to the USSR Ministry for Social Security.[62] The MVD had tried for years to place invalid ex-prisoners in civilian invalid homes, but it had routinely encountered resistance from the Soviet Ministry of Social Security.[63] Following the amnesty, the Gulag's "inferior workforce" became the responsibility of Soviet civilian health institutions, and many invalid prisoners were released into the care of family members. Nonetheless, their neglect often continued. Exhausted and depleted from Gulag exploitation, former prisoners were not easily accepted back into Soviet society.

In the post-Stalin years, the Gulag production system was dismantled, and its slave laborers released or reassigned. The Soviet camps became concentration camps once again, for the isolation and detention of perceived state enemies or counterrevolutionaries. Stalin derived his prison labor force largely from the masses of Russian workers and peasants, who were able-bodied and could perform heavy physical labor. This "human raw material" performed the brutal work of mining coal and gold, cutting timber, and laying railroad tracks. The Stalinist forced labor camp system depleted and destroyed them by design and by the millions. As the writer Joseph Brodsky noted in his Nobel lecture: "In the real tragedy, it is not the hero who perishes, it is the chorus."[64] Such was the Gulag tragedy.

Notes

INTRODUCTION

1. For a history of the Soviet forced labor camp system, see Anne Applebaum. *Gulag: A History* (New York: Doubleday, 2003). On the special settlements, see Lynne Viola, *The Unknown Gulag: The Lost World of Stalin's Special Settlements* (Oxford: Oxford University Press, 2007); Lynne Viola, "Stalin's Empire: The Gulag and Police Colonization in the Soviet Union in the 1930s," in Timothy Snyder and Ray Brandon, eds., *Stalin and Europe: Imitation and Domination, 1928–1953* (New York: Oxford University Press, 2014), 18–43.

2. On kinship and terror under Stalin, see Golfo Alexopoulos, "Stalin and the Politics of Kinship: Practices of Collective Punishment, 1920s–1940s." *Comparative Studies in Society and History* 50 (January, 2008): 91–117; Sheila Fitzpatrick, *On Stalin's Team: The Years of Living Dangerously in Soviet Politics* (Princeton, NJ: Princeton University Press, 2015).

3. Oleg V. Khlevniuk, *History of the Gulag: From Collectivization to the Great Terror* (New Haven, CT: Yale University Press, 2004), 161; Steven A. Barnes, *Death and Redemption: The Gulag and the Shaping of Soviet Society* (Princeton, NJ: Princeton University Press, 2011), 7–8.

4. A.I. Kokurin and N.V. Petrov, *Gulag (glavnoe upravlenie lagerei), 1918–1960* (Moscow, 2000), 725; GARF f. 9414, op. 1, d. 374, l. 4–5.

5. Quoted in Barnes, *Death and Redemption,* 163.

6. Applebaum, *Gulag;* Khlevniuk, *History of the Gulag;* Viola, *Unknown Gulag;* Nicolas Werth, *Cannibal Island: Death in a Siberian Gulag* (Princeton, NJ: Princeton University Press, 2007); James R. Harris, "The Growth of the Gulag: Forced Labor in the Urals Region, 1929–1931," *Russian Review* 56 (April 2007):

265–280; Michael Jakobson, *Origins of the Gulag: The Soviet Prison Camp System, 1917–1934* (Lexington: University Press of Kentucky, 2014).

7. See, for example, Alan Barenberg, *Gulag Town, Company Town: Forced Labor and Its Legacy in Vorkuta* (New Haven, CT: Yale University Press, 2014); Paul R. Gregory and Valery Lazarev, eds., *The Economics of Forced Labor: The Soviet Gulag* (Stanford, CA: Hoover Institution Press, 2003); Oleg Khlevniuk, "The Economy of the Gulag," in Paul R. Gregory, ed., *Behind the Façade of Stalin's Command Economy: Evidence from the Soviet State and Party Archives* (Stanford, CA: Hoover Institution Press, 2001), 111–129; Simon Ertz, *Zwangsarbeit im stalinistischen Lagersystem: Eine Untersuchung der Methoden, Strategien und Ziele ihrer Ausnutzung am Beispiel Norilsk, 1935–1953* (Berlin: Duncker & Humblot, 2006).

8. The Gulag's ideological-cultural project is explored in Barnes, *Death and Redemption;* Julie S. Draskoczy, *Belomor: Criminality and Creativity in Stalin's Gulag* (Brighton, MA: Academic Studies Press, 2014); Michael David-Fox, *Showcasing the Great Experiment: Cultural Diplomacy and Western Visitors to the Soviet Union, 1921–1941* (Oxford: Oxford University Press, 2012); Maxim Gorky, L. Auerbach and S.G. Firin, *Belomor: An Account of the Construction of the New Canal between the White Sea and the Baltic Sea* (New York: Harrison Smith and Robert Haas, 1935); Stephen Kotkin, *Magnetic Mountain: Stalinism as a Civilization* (Berkeley: University of California Press, 1997); Cynthia A. Ruder, *Making History for Stalin: The Story of the Belomor Canal* (Gainesville: University of Florida Press, 1998); Cristina Vatulescu, *Police Aesthetics: Literature, Film, and the Secret Police in Soviet Times* (Stanford, CA: Stanford University Press, 2010).

9. On biopolitics, see Dan Healey, "Lives in the Balance: Weak and Disabled Prisoners and the Biopolitics of the Gulag," in *Kritika: Explorations in Russian and Eurasian History* 16:3 (Summer 2015): 527–556. On prisoner correspondence, see Arsenii Formakov, *Gulag Letters,* ed. Emily D. Johnson (New Haven, CT: Yale University Press, 2017).

10. See, for example, Edwin Bacon, *The Gulag at War: Stalin's Forced Labour System in the Light of the Archives* (New York: New York University Press, 1994); Christian Gerlach and Nicolas Werth, "State Violence—Violent Societies," in Michael Geyer and Sheila Fitzpatrick, eds., *Beyond Totalitarianism: Stalinism and Nazism Compared* (Cambridge: Cambridge University Press, 2009); On the experiences of women and children in the camps, see Cathy A. Frierson and Semyon Vilensky, *Children of the Gulag* (New Haven, CT: Yale University Press, 2010); Paul R. Gregory, ed., *Women of the Gulag: Portraits of Five Remarkable Lives* (Stanford, CA: Hoover Institution Press, 2013; Simeon Vilensky, ed., *Till My Tale Is Told: Women's Memoirs of the Gulag* (Bloomington: Indiana University Press, 1999).

11. Barenberg, *Gulag Town;* Miriam Dobson, *Khrushchev's Cold Summer: Gulag Returnees, Crime, and the Fate of Reform after Stalin* (Ithaca, NY: Cornell University Press, 2011); Amir Weiner, "The Empires Pay a Visit: Gulag Returnees, East European Rebellions, and Soviet Frontier Politics," *Journal of Modern History* 78:2 (June 2006): 333–376.

12. Applebaum, *Gulag;* Barnes, *Death and Redemption;* Robert Conquest, *Kolyma: The Arctic Death Camps* (New York: Viking Press, 1978); Galina Mikhai-

lovna Ivanova, *Labor Camp Socialism: The Gulag in the Soviet Totalitarian System* (New York: M.E. Sharpe, 2000); Khlevniuk, *History of the Gulag;* Aleksandr I. Solzhenitsyn, *The Gulag Archipelago, 1918–1956: An Experiment in Literary Investigation,* vols. 1–2 (New York: Harper & Row, 1973).

13. Aleksandr I. Solzhenitsyn, *The Gulag Archipelago, 1918–1956: An Experiment in Literary Investigation,* vols. 3–4 (New York: Harper & Row, 1974), 49.

14. Solzhenitsyn, *Gulag Archipelago,* vols. 3–4, 49.

15. A.B. Bezborodov and V.M. Khrustalev, eds., *Istoriia stalinskogo Gulaga: konets 1920-kh–pervaia polovina 1950-kh godov, tom 4: naselenie Gulaga* (Moscow, 2004), 352–353.

16. Khlevniuk, *History of the Gulag,* 337. See also Viola, *Unknown Gulag,* 187.

17. Giorgio Agamben, *State of Exception,* trans. Kevin Attell (Chicago: University of Chicago Press, 2005).

18. Slavoj Zizek, *Violence: Six Sideways Reflections* (New York: Picador, 2008), 2, 12–13. See also Zygmunt Bauman, *Modernity and the Holocaust* (Ithaca, NY: Cornell University Press, 1991).

19. In the 1930s and much of the 1940s, the Gulag health service was referred to as the sanitation department (*sanitarnyi otdel*). In the late 1940s and early 1950s, it took the name medical-sanitation department (*meditsinskii-sanitarnyi otdel*) or simply medical department (*meditsinskii otdel*). Throughout this work, I use medical-sanitation department to remind contemporary readers that this was a health service.

20. Applebaum, *Gulag,* 276; David Nordlander, "Magadan and the Economic History of Dalstroi in the 1930s," in *Economics of Forced Labor,* 124–125.

21. Varlam Shalamov, *Kolyma Tales* (New York: Penguin Books, 1994), 184. See also Victor Kravchenko, *I Choose Freedom: The Personal and Political Life of a Soviet Official* (London: Robert Hale Limited, 1947), 279, 295–297.

22. See, for example, Barnes, *Death and Redemption;* Amir Weiner, *Making Sense of War: The Second World War and the Fate of the Bolshevik Revolution* (Princeton, NJ: Princeton University Press, 2002).

23. On the contemporary legacies of the Gulag see, for example, Marjorie Mandelstam Balzer, "Local Legacies of the GULag in Siberia: Anthropological Reflections," *Focaal: Journal of Global and Historical Anthropology* 73 (2015): 99–113; Judith Pallot, "The Gulag as the Crucible of Russia's 21st-Century System of Punishment," *Kritika: Explorations in Russian and Eurasian History* 16:3 (Summer 2015): 681–710; David Remnick, *Lenin's Tomb: The Last Days of the Soviet Empire* (New York: Vintage, 1994).

24. Katherine Verdery, *What Was Socialism, and What Comes Next* (Princeton, NJ: Princeton University Press, 1996), 23–26.

25. Timothy Snyder, *Bloodlands: Europe Between Hitler and Stalin* (New York: Basic Books, 2012), 42.

26. Simon Ertz, "Building Norilsk," in *Economics of Forced Labor;* Ertz, *Zwangsarbeit im stalinistischen Lagersystem.*

27. Julie Hessler, *A Social History of Soviet Trade: Trade Policy, Retail Practices, and Consumption, 1917–1953* (Princeton, NJ: Princeton University Press, 2004);

Elena Osokina, *Our Daily Bread: Socialist Distribution and the Art of Survival in Stalin's Russia, 1927–1941* (New York: M.E. Sharpe, 2000).

28. Aleksandr Solzhenitsyn, *Arkhipelag Gulag* (Al'fa-Kniga: Moscow, 2009), 385.

29. Solzhenitsyn, *Arkhipelag Gulag,* 386.

30. Barnes, *Death and Redemption,* 2.

31. Oleg V. Khlevniuk, *Stalin: New Biography of a Dictator* (New Haven, CT: Yale University Press, 2015), 38.

32. Applebaum, *Gulag,* xxxix.

33. The exception here would be the earlier work on the Gulag. See Conquest's *Kolyma;* David J. Dallin and Boris I. Nicolaevsky, *Forced Labor in Soviet Russia* (New Haven, CT: Yale University Press, 1947).

34. See, for example, Viola, *Unknown Gulag,* 9; Donald Filtzer, "Starvation Mortality in Soviet Home-Front Industrial Regions during World War II," in Wendy Z. Goldman and Donald Filtzer, eds., *Hunger and War: Food Provisioning in the Soviet Union during World War II* (Bloomington: Indiana University Press, 2015), 330.

35. See, for example, Gerlach and Werth, "State Violence—Violent Societies," 171.

36. On the differences between the Nazi and Soviet concentration camps, see Applebaum, *Gulag,* Barnes, *Death and Redemption,* and Snyder, *Bloodlands.* Many Gulag survivors and dissidents make analogies between the two camp systems. For example, Elena Bonner stated not long ago: "[Nazi] Death camps and the Gulag. Gas was used in the former. The latter didn't need to waste money on it—hunger and cold did the job." Elena Bonner, "The Remains of Totalitarianism," in *The New York Review of Books* (March 8, 2001). See also Dimitri Panin, *The Notebooks of Sologdin* (New York: Harcourt Brace Jovanovich, 1976), 66–68.

37. The question of genocide seems implied in any comparison of the two camp systems and, here again, scholars resist drawing analogies. Norman Naimark did not include a discussion of the Gulag in his study of Stalinist genocide, and no comparison of the two camp systems appears in Michael Geyer and Sheila Fitzpatrick's examination of the two regimes. See Norman M. Naimark, *Stalin's Genocides* (Princeton, NJ: Princeton University Press, 2011); Michael Geyer and Sheila Fitzpatrick, eds., *Beyond Totalitarianism: Stalinism and Nazism Compared* (Cambridge: Cambridge University Press, 2008). On the distinctions between Nazi and Soviet state violence, see Peter Holquist, "State Violence as Technique: The Logic of Violence in Soviet Totalitarianism," in Amir Weiner, ed., *Landscaping the Human Garden: Twentieth-Century Population Management in a Comparative Framework* (Stanford, CA: Stanford University Press, 2003); Snyder, *Bloodlands;* Weiner, *Making Sense of War;* Amir Weiner, "Nothing But Certainty," *Slavic Review* 61 (Spring 2002): 44–53.

38. On the Nazi forced labor camp, see Christopher R. Browning, *Remembering Survival: Inside a Nazi Slave-Labor Camp* (New York: W.W. Norton, 2010).

39. See, for example, Eugenia Ginzburg, *Within the Whirlwind* (New York: Harvest Books, 1982); Shalamov, *Kolyma Tales;* Solzhenitsyn, *Gulag Archipelago.* On Gulag narratives, see Leona Toker, *Return from the Archipelago: Narratives*

of Gulag Survivors (Bloomington: Indiana University Press, 2000); Anne Applebaum, *Gulag Voices: An Anthology* (New Haven, CT: Yale University Press, 2011); Jehanne M. Gheith and Katherine R. Jolluck, *Gulag Voices: Oral Histories of Soviet Incarceration and Exile* (New York: Palgrave Macmillan, 2011); Jehanne M. Gheith, "'I Never Talked': Enforced Silence, Non-narrative Memory, and the Gulag," *Mortality* 12 (April 2007): 159–175; Catherine Merridale, *Night of Stone: Death and Memory in Twentieth Century Russia* (New York: Viking, 2001).

40. See, for example, Nanci Adler, *The Gulag Survivor: Beyond the Soviet System* (New Brunswick, NJ: Transaction Publishers, 2002); Nanci Adler, *Keeping Faith with the Party: Communist Believers Return from the Gulag* (Bloomington: Indiana University Press, 2012); Stephen F. Cohen, *The Victims Return: Survivors of the Gulag after Stalin* (New York: I.B. Tauris, 2012).

41. Robert Jay Lifton, *The Nazi Doctors: Medical Killing and the Psychology of Genocide* (New York: Basic Books, 1988), 30. See also Robert Proctor, *Racial Hygiene: Medicine under the Nazis* (Cambridge, MA: Harvard University Press, 1988).

42. Applebaum, *Gulag,* 285.

43. Antoni Ekart, *Vanished Without Trace: The Story of Seven Years in Soviet Russia* (London: Max Parrish, 1954), 56.

44. Viola, *Unknown Gulag,* 91.

45. Snyder, *Bloodlands,* 11, 177. On the use of food as a weapon in Russia, see also Peter Holquist, *Making War, Forging Revolution: Russia's Continuum of Crisis, 1914–1921* (Cambridge, MA: Harvard University Press, 2002).

46. Alexander Etkind, *Warped Mourning: Stories of the Undead in the Land of the Unburied* (Stanford, CA: Stanford University Press, 2013), 27.

47. Boris Nakhapetov, *Ocherki istorii sanitarnoi sluzhby gulaga* (Moscow 2009), 119–131; Bezborodov and Khrustalev, *Istoriia stalinskogo gulaga,* 363–364; Kokurin and Petrov, *Gulag,* 480–481.

48. Giorgio Agamben, *Remnants of Auschwitz: The Witness and the Archive* (New York: Zone Books, 2002), 82–83. See also Michel Foucault, *"Society Must Be Defended": Lectures at the Collège de France, 1975–76* (New York: Picador, 1997), 239–265.

49. See, for example, Daniel Beer, "Penal Deportation to Siberia and the Limits of State Power, 1801–81," *Kritika: Explorations in Russian and Eurasian History* 16 (Summer 2015): 621–650; Andrew A. Gentes, *Exile to Siberia, 1590–1822: Corporeal Commodification and Administrative Systemization in Russia* (New York: Palgrave Macmillan, 2008); Richard Hellie, *Slavery in Russia, 1450–1725* (Chicago: University of Chicago Press, 1982); George Kennan, *Siberia and the Exile System* (Chicago: University of Chicago Press, 1958); Abby M. Schrader, *Languages of the Lash: Corporal Punishment and Identity in Imperial Russia* (DeKalb: Northern Illinois University Press, 2002).

50. Kokurin and Petrov, *Gulag,* 62.

51. Khlevniuk, *History of the Gulag;* Viola, *Unknown Gulag.* Later, when officials told the story of the Gulag, they began their narrative in 1930 with the establishment of the OGPU's GULAG administration. See GARF f. 9414, op. 1, d. 374, l. 1–2.

52. On Gulag exploitation of prisoners' intellectual capital, see Golfo Alexopoulos, "Medical Research in Stalin's Gulag," *Bulletin of the History of Medicine* 90:3 (Fall 2016): 363–393; Asif Siddiqi, "Scientists and Specialists in the Gulag: Life and Death in Stalin's *Sharashka*" *Kritika: Explorations in Russian and Eurasian History* 16:3 (Summer 2015): 557–588.

53. See for example, Barenberg, *Gulag Town, Company Town;* Wilson Bell, "Was the Gulag an Archipelago? De-Convoyed Prisoners and Porous Borders in the Camps of Western Siberia," *Russian Review* 72:1 (2013): 116–141; Oleg Khlevniuk, "The Gulag and the Non-Gulag as One Interrelated Whole," *Kritika: Explorations in Russian and Eurasian History* 16:3 (Summer 2015): 479–498.

54. Paul Gregory, "Introduction," in *Economics of Forced Labor*, 5, 21.

55. Jan Plamper, "Foucault's Gulag," *Kritika: Explorations in Russian and Eurasian History* 3 (Spring 2002): 255–280. See also Holquist, "State Violence as Technique"; David L. Hoffmann, "The Conceptual and Practical Origins of Soviet State Violence," in James Harris, ed., *The Anatomy of Terror: Political Violence under Stalin* (Oxford: Oxford University Press, 2013), 89–104.

56. GARF f. 9414, op. 1, d. 2743, l. 6.

57. GARF f. 9414, op. 1, d. 144, l. 1.

58. GARF f. 9414, op. 1, d. 374, l. 43; Applebaum, *Gulag*, 231–232; Barnes, *Death and Redemption;* Nordlander, "Magadan," 112–113; Viola, *Unknown Gulag*, 102–104.

59. Oleg Khlevniuk, "The Economy of the OGPU, NKVD, and MVD of the USSR, 1930–1953: The Scale, Structure, and Trends of Development," in *Economics of Forced Labor*, 58; Stephen Kotkin, *Armageddon Averted: The Soviet Collapse, 1970–2000* (New York: Oxford University Press, 2008), 32.

60. Gregory, "Introduction," 8, 19–20.

61. Simon Ertz, "Building Norilsk," in *Economics of Forced Labor*, 127–150; Applebaum, *Gulag*, 471.

62. Paul R. Gregory, *Terror by Quota: State Security from Lenin to Stalin* (New Haven, CT: Yale University Press, 2009), 283.

63. Yoram Gorlizki and Oleg Khlevniuk, *Cold Peace: Stalin and the Soviet Ruling Circle, 1945–1953* (Oxford: Oxford University Press, 2004), 125.

64. The words of Olga Vasileevna, an engineer and inspector for the Gulag, quoted in Applebaum, *Gulag*, 113.

65. Vladimir Voinovich, *Moscow 2042* (New York: Harcourt Brace Jovanovich, 1987), 220.

66. Kokurin and Petrov, *Gulag*, 441–442; Applebaum, *Gulag*, 582–583; Barnes, *Death and Redemption*, 76, 116.

67. J. Arch Getty, Gabor T. Rittersporn, and Viktor N Zemskov, "Victims of the Soviet Penal System in the Pre-war Years: A First Approach on the Basis of Archival Evidence," *American Historical Review* 98 (October 1993): 1017–1049.

68. Golfo Alexopoulos, "Amnesty 1945: The Revolving Door of Stalin's Gulag," *Slavic Review* 64 (Summer, 2005): 274–306; Barnes, *Death and Redemption;* Getty, Rittersporn and Zemskov, "Victims of the Soviet Penal System"; Snyder, *Bloodlands*.

69. Khlevniuk, "The Gulag and the Non-Gulag."

70. See, for example, Sheila Fitzpatrick, *Everyday Stalinism: Ordinary Life in Extraordinary Times: Soviet Russia in the 1930s* (New York: Oxford University Press, 2000); James Heinzen, "The Art of the Bribe: Corruption and Everyday Practice in the Late Stalinist USSR," *Slavic Review* 66 (Fall 2007): 389–412; Alena V. Ledeneva, *Russia's Economy of Favours: Blat, Networking, and Informal Exchange* (Cambridge: Cambridge University Press, 1998).

71. See Applebaum, *Gulag,* 582–583; Barnes, *Death and Redemption,* 76–77, 116; Bezborodov and Khrustalev, *Istoriia stalinskogo gulaga,* 54–55; Getty, Rittersporn, and Zemskov, "Victims of the Soviet Penal System," 1017–1049; Khlevniuk, "The Gulag and the Non-Gulag"; Khlevniuk, *History of the Gulag,* 320–327; Kokurin and Petrov, *Gulag,* 441–442.

72. See, for example, Bezborodov and Khrustalev, *Istoriia stalinskogo gulaga,* 139–140 (1930); Kokurin and Petrov, *Gulag,* 278, 318, 425–426 (1940s); GARF f. 9414, op. 1, d. 378, l. 157 (1942); GARF f. 9414, op. 1, d. 395, l. 128 (1943); GARF f. 9414, op. 1, d. 446, l. 32–34, 138–141 (1946); GARF f. 9414, op. 1, d. 459, l. 59–62, 89–90 (1947); GARF f. 9414, op. 1, d. 492, l. 111 (January 1953).

73. Jacques Rossi. *The Gulag Handbook: An Encyclopedia Dictionary of Soviet Penitentiary Institutions and Terms Related to the Forced Labor Camps* (New York: Paragon House, 1989), 107, 476. See also Applebaum. *Gulag,* 334–335; Aleksandr I. Solzhenitsyn, *The Gulag Archipelago, 1918–1956: An Experiment in Literary Investigation,* vols. 3–4, trans. Thomas P. Whitney (New York: Harper & Row, 1975), 530–531.

74. Agamben, *Remnants of Auschwitz;* Etkind, *Warped Mourning,* 26.

75. See, for example, Etkind, *Warped Mourning;* Healey, "Lives in the Balance."

76. Etkind, *Warped Mourning,* 85.

77. Applebaum, *Gulag,* xxxix.

78. Barnes, *Death and Redemption,* 51.

79. Solzhenitsyn, *Gulag Archipelago,* vols. 3–4, 86, 104; Solzhenitsyn, *Arkhipelag Gulag,* 436, 450. The writer draws attention to the dehumanizing term "human raw material," which Maxim Gorky used to describe penal laborers on the White Sea canal project. Referring to the process of rehabilitation through labor, Gorky wrote: "Human raw material is infinitely harder to work with than wood, stone, or metal (*Chelovecheskoe syr'e obrabatyvaetsia neizmerimo trudnee, chem derevo, kamen', metall*)." See M. Gor'kii, L. Averbakh, and S. Firin, *Belomorsko-Baltiiskii kanal imemi Stalina: istoriia stroitel'stva, 1931–1934* (Moscow, 1934), 609. The analogous term "human material" (*chelovecheskii material*) also appears in a similar context. See, for example: idem, 248.

80. Solzhenitsyn, *Arkhipelag Gulag,* 355.

81. Yehoshua A. Gilboa, *Confess! Confess! Eight Years in Soviet Prisons* (Boston: Little, Brown, 1968), 68.

82. Viktor Berdinskikh, *Istoriia odnogo lageria–Viatlag* (Moscow, 2001), 14.

83. On the Bolsheviks' new and highly symbolic language, see Kotkin, *Magnetic Mountain;* Michael S. Gorham, *Speaking in Soviet Tongues: Language Culture and the Politics of Voice in Revolutionary Russia* (DeKalb: Northwestern Illinois University Press, 2003).

CHAPTER 1. FOOD

1. *Konstitutsii i konstitutsionnye akty RSFSR, 1918–1937* (Moscow, 1940), 24. The phrase originates in the biblical saying from Thessalonians. In his 1917 masterwork, *State and Revolution,* Lenin called this a fundamental socialist principle. For Stalin, as Norman Naimark noted, "those who did not work—the so-called idlers—deserved to starve." See his *Stalin's Genocides* (Princeton, NJ: Princeton University Press, 2010), 72–73.

2. Aleksandr. I Solzhenitsyn, *The Gulag Archipelago, 1918–1956: An Experiment in Literary Investigation,* vols. 3–4, trans. Thomas P. Whitney (New York: Harper & Row, 1975), 173–174. Naimark, *Stalin's Genocides,* 72–73.

3. A.I. Kokurin and N.V. Petrov, *Gulag (glavnoe upravlenie lagerei), 1918–1960* (Moscow, 2000), 667.

4. Antoni Ekart, *Vanished Without Trace: The Story of Seven Years in Soviet Russia* (London: Max Parrish, 1954), 60. See also Leona Toker, *Return from the Archipelago: Narratives of Gulag Survivors* (Bloomington: Indiana University Press, 2000), 21.

5. See, for example, Steven A. Barnes, *Death and Redemption: The Gulag and the Shaping of Soviet Society* (Princeton, NJ: Princeton University Press, 2011); Leonid Borodkin and Simon Ertz, "Coercion versus Motivation," in Paul R. Gregory and Valery Lazarev, eds., *The Economics of Forced Labor: The Soviet Gulag* (Stanford, CA: Hoover Institution Press, 2003), 85–89.

6. Quoted in Solzhenitsyn, *Gulag Archipelago,* vols. 3–4, 265.

7. GARF f. 9414, op. 1, d. 1913, l. 21–22; GARF f. 9414, op. 2, d. 169, l. 33.

8. Paul Gregory, "An Introduction to the Economics of Forced Labor," in Paul R. Gregory and Valery Lazarev, eds., *The Economics of Forced Labor: The Soviet Gulag* (Stanford, CA: Hoover Institution Press, 2003), 4.

9. GARF f. 9414, op. 1, d. 1913, l. 2–4.

10. GARF f. 9414, op. 1, d. 1913, l. 5.

11. GARF f. 9414, op. 1, d. 1913, l. 5.

12. Wendy Z. Goldman, "Not by Bread Alone: Food, Workers, and the State," in Wendy Z. Goldman and Donald Filtzer, eds., *Hunger and War: Food Provisioning in the Soviet Union during World War II* (Bloomington: Indiana University Press, 2015), 56–61.

13. In the 1930s, prisoners' daily ration depended on their performance the previous day, but in 1940 this changed to a system where rations were based on ten-day production averages. See A.B. Bezborodov and V.M. Khrustalev, eds., *Istoriia stalinskogo Gulaga: konets 1920-kh–pervaia polovina 1950-kh godov, tom 4: naselenie Gulaga* (Moscow, 2004), 351. On Gulag food rations, see also Barnes *Death and Redemption,* 41–43, 69.

14. Anne Applebaum, *Gulag: A History* (New York: Doubleday, 2003), 104.

15. Bezborodov and Khrustalev, *Istoriia stalinskogo Gulaga,* 591 (fn. 188); see also Oleg V. Khlevniuk, *History of the Gulag: From Collectivization to the Great Terror* (New Haven, CT: Yale University Press, 2004), 201.

16. On the system of prisoners' rank (*razriad*), see Jacques Rossi, *The Gulag Handbook: An Encyclopedia Dictionary of Soviet Penitentiary Institutions and Terms Related to the Forced Labor Camps* (New York: Paragon House, 1989), 360–361.

17. Bezborodov and Khrustalev, *Istoriia stalinskogo Gulaga*, 351–352.

18. Applebaum, *Gulag,* 206.

19. Rossi, *Gulag Handbook,* 12.

20. GARF f. 9401, op. 1, d. 713, l. 218.

21. GARF f. 9414, op. 2, d. 169, l. 11.

22. S.F. Sapolnova, T.A. Vekshina, F.G. Kanev, eds., *Liudi v belykh khalatakh* (Syktyvkar: Komi respublikanskaia tipografiia, 2009), 28; Applebaum, *Gulag,* 213; Aleksandr I. Solzhenitsyn, *The Gulag Archipelago, 1918–1956: An Experiment in Literary Investigation,* vols. 1–2 (New York: Harper & Row, 1973), 533.

23. GARF f. 9414, op. 1, d. 1923, l. 189; GARF f. 9414, op. 1, d. 1925, l. 209–210.

24. Bezborodov and Khrustalev, *Istoriia stalinskogo Gulaga,* 402.

25. GARF f. 9414, op. 1, d. 4, l. 33.

26. This across-the-board reduction came shortly after a January 1940 memo from the deputy NKVD chief in which he demanded that all camps intensify their efforts to obtain local food sources. He insisted that no additional food allocations would be issued centrally, so it was no use sending in requests. See GARF f. 9414, op. 1, d. 1916, l. 2–3.

27. If in 1939 inmates received 1200 grams (2.6 lbs.) for meeting their norm, they would now need to fulfill their production targets by 125 percent or higher in order to receive the same amount, and 300 of these grams could only be obtained through purchase. Bezborodov and Khrustalev, *Istoriia stalinskogo Gulaga,* 351.

28. Bezborodov and Khrustalev, *Istoriia stalinskogo Gulaga,* 352.

29. Applebaum, *Gulag,* 209; Barnes, *Death and Redemption,* 116; Bezborodov and Khrustalev, *Istoriia stalinskogo Gulaga,* 358–359.

30. GARF f. 9414, op. 1, d. 1919, l. 17; Bezborodov and Khrustalev, *Istoriia stalinskogo Gulaga,* 355–357.

31. GARF f. 9414, op. 1, d. 1919, l. 17–18.

32. Bezborodov and Khrustalev, *Istoriia stalinskogo Gulaga,* 355–357. See also GARF f. 9414, op. 1, d. 1919, l. 18–19.

33. Bezborodov and Khrustalev, *Istoriia stalinskogo Gulaga,* 357; GARF f. 9414, op. 1, d. 1919, l. 20–25.

34. Bezborodov and Khrustalev, *Istoriia stalinskogo Gulaga,* 354. See also David J. Dallin and Boris I. Nicolaevsky, *Forced Labor in Soviet Russia* (New Haven, CT: Yale University Press, 1947), 9–11.

35. Ekart, *Vanished Without Trace,* 59–60.

36. GARF f. 9414, op. 1, d. 1919, l. 23.

37. GARF f. 9414, op. 1, d. 1919, l. 24.

38. GARF f. 9414, op. 1, d. 1919, l. 25.

39. Donald Filtzer, "Starvation Mortality in Soviet Home-Front Industrial Regions during World War II," in Wendy Z. Goldman and Donald Filtzer, eds., *Hunger and War: Food Provisioning in the Soviet Union during World War II* (Bloomington: Indiana University Press, 2015), 265–335.

40. Varlam Shalamov, *Kolyma Tales* (New York: Penguin Books, 1994), 126. Solzhenitsyn agreed. See Solzhenitsyn, *Gulag Archipelago,* vols. 3–4, 203, 218, 512.

41. Lev Razgon, *True Stories* (Dana Point, CA: Ardis Publishers, 1997), 155.

42. Bezborodov and Khrustalev, *Istoriia stalinskogo Gulaga,* 351, 368–369.

43. On wartime rations, see Wendy Z. Goldman and Donald Filtzer, eds., *Hunger and War: Food Provisioning in the Soviet Union during World War II* (Bloomington: Indiana University Press, 2015); John Barber and Mark Harrison, *The Soviet Home Front, 1941–1945: A Social and Economic History of the USSR in World War II* (London: Longman, 1991).

44. Barnes, *Death and Redemption,* 116.

45. GARF f. 9401, op. 1, d. 713, l. 210; Kokurin and Petrov, *Gulag,* 542. Soviet health authorities used soap in the late 1940s, for example, to reduce the death rate from parasitic typhus. See Veniamin F. Zima, "Medical Expertise and the 1946–47 Famine: The Identification and Treatment of a State-Induced Illness," in Frances L. Bernstein, Christopher Burton, and Dan Healy, eds., *Soviet Medicine: Culture, Practice, and Science* (Dekalb: Northern Illinois University Press, 2010), 180.

46. Bezborodov and Khrustalev, *Istoriia stalinskogo Gulaga,* 393–394.

47. Gulag chief Nasedkin boasted that, "In 1946, 36.5 percent of working prisoners fulfilled their work norms by 150 to 200 percent and more." See GARF f. 9414, op. 1, d. 374, l. 53.

48. Bezborodov and Khrustalev, *Istoriia stalinskogo Gulaga,* 393–394.

49. GARF f. 9414, op. 1, d. 366, l. 1.

50. Bezborodov and Khrustalev, *Istoriia stalinskogo Gulaga,* 351–352.

51. Bezborodov and Khrustalev, *Istoriia stalinskogo Gulaga,* 363, 373; GARF f. 9401, op. 1, d. 713, l. 210.

52. GARF f. 9414, op. 1, d. 1925, l. 229–230.

53. GARF f. 9414, op. 2, d. 169, l. 17.

54. GARF f. 9414, op. 1, d. 1920, l. 21.

55. Bezborodov and Khrustalev, *Istoriia stalinskogo Gulaga,* 426–436.

56. Bezborodov and Khrustalev, *Istoriia stalinskogo Gulaga,* 429–430.

57. Bezborodov and Khrustalev, *Istoriia stalinskogo Gulaga,* 431–433.

58. Bezborodov and Khrustalev, *Istoriia stalinskogo Gulaga,* 427.

59. Kokurin and Petrov, *Gulag,* 541–552. These came following MVD Order No. 0418 that revised the categories of physical labor capability, and forced weaker prisoners into heavy physical labor.

60. Kokurin and Petrov, *Gulag,* 543–546, 551; GARF f. 9401, op. 1a, d. 313, l. 13.

61. Kokurin and Petrov, *Gulag,* 541–542.

62. Kokurin and Petrov, *Gulag,* 543.

63. Kokurin and Petrov, *Gulag,* 544–546.

64. Bezborodov and Khrustalev, *Istoriia stalinskogo Gulaga,* 441–443.

65. Bezborodov and Khrustalev, *Istoriia stalinskogo Gulaga,* 444.

66. Bezborodov and Khrustalev, *Istoriia stalinskogo Gulaga,* 444–446.

67. GARF f. 9414, op. 1, d. 2737, l. 1.

68. GARF f. 9414, op. 1, d. 2739, l. 1.

69. GARF f. 9414, op. 2, d. 169, l. 4.

70. Kokurin and Petrov, *Gulag,* 480–481.

71. Kokurin and Petrov, *Gulag,* 480–481.

72. GARF f. 9414, op. 1, d. 1919, l. 27; GARF f. 9401, op. 1, d. 713, l. 213.

73. GARF f. 9414, op. 1, d. 1919, l. 26.

74. Bezborodov and Khrustalev, *Istoriia stalinskogo Gulaga*, 366–367, 393–394.

75. Sheila Fitzpatrick, *Everyday Stalinism: Ordinary Life in Extraordinary Times: Soviet Russia in the 1930s* (Oxford: Oxford University Press, 2000); Julie Hessler, *A Social History of Soviet Trade: Trade Policy, Retail Practices, and Consumption, 1917–1953* (Princeton, NJ: Princeton University Press, 2004); Janos Kornai, *Economics of Shortage* (New York: North-Holland, 1980).

76. GARF f. 9414, op. 1, d. 1920, l. 87.

77. GARF f. 9401, op. 1, d. 713, l. 213.

78. GARF f. 9401, op. 1, d. 713, l. 213.

79. GARF f. 9401, op. 1, d. 713, l. 222.

80. GARF f. 9414, op. 2, d. 169, l. 27.

81. GARF f. 9414, op. 2, d. 169.

82. GARF f. 9414, op. 2, d. 169, l. 15.

83. GARF f. 9414, op. 2, d. 169, l. 25.

84. Bezborodov and Khrustalev, *Istoriia stalinskogo Gulaga*, 431.

85. Bezborodov and Khrustalev, *Istoriia stalinskogo Gulaga*, 431–435.

86. GARF f. 9401, op. 1a, d. 313, l. 12.

87. GARF f. 9401, op. 1a, d. 313, l. 13.

88. GARF f. 9414, op. 2, d. 169, l. 24–25.

89. Kokurin and Petrov, *Gulag*, 546–547.

90. Kokurin and Petrov, *Gulag*, 551.

91. GARF f. 9414, op. 1, d. 1909, l. 144.

92. The other prisoners took pity and shared their own meagerly rations with her. See Memorial Archive, St. Petersburg, Russia. Uncatalogued case file of M.K. Sandratskaia, memoir manuscript, page 50.

93. Applebaum, *Gulag*, 77.

94. Fedor V. Mochulsky, *Gulag Boss: A Soviet Memoir*, trans. and ed. Deborah Kaple (New York: Oxford University Press, 2011), 80.

95. Quoted in Applebaum, *Gulag*, 355.

96. Golfo Alexopoulos, "A Torture Memo: Reading Violence in the Gulag," in *Writing the Stalin Era: Sheila Fitzpatrick and Soviet Historiography* (New York: Palgrave Macmillan, 2011), 157–176. On the penalty isolators or punishment cells, see Applebaum, *Gulag*, 242–247; Barnes, *Death and Redemption*, 19, 68–69; Rossi, *Gulag Handbook*, 374; Solzhenitsyn, *Gulag Archipelago*, vols. 3–4, 420.

97. Bezborodov and Khrustalev, *Istoriia stalinskogo Gulaga*, 346; GARF f. 9414, op. 1, d. 1919, l. 30.

98. GARF f. 9401, op. 1, d. 713, l. 223; Bezborodov and Khrustalev, *Istoriia stalinskogo Gulaga*, 434.

99. Kokurin and Petrov, *Gulag*, 550.

100. Sapolnova, Vekshina, and Kanev, *Liudi v belykh khalatakh*, 30.

101. GARF f. 9401, op. 1, d. 713, l. 215.

102. GARF f. 9414, op. 1, d. 366, l. 13.

103. GARF f. 9414, op. 1, d. 86, l. 131.

104. GARF f. 9414, op. 1, d. 2741, l. 49.

105. GARF f. 9414, op. 2, d. 169, l. 9.

106. GARF f. 9414, op. 2, d. 169, l. 4.

107. James Heinzen, "Corruption in the Gulag: Dilemmas of Officials and Prisoners," *Comparative Economic Studies* 47 (2005): 456–475.

108. GARF f. 9414, op. 1, d. 1925, l. 215, 230.

109. GARF f. 9414, op. 1, d. 2741, l. 46.

110. Problems of theft, food shortages, and spoiled supplies are described in many Gulag documents. See, for example, GARF f. 9414, op. 1, d. 1923, l. 179–194; GARF f. 9414, op. 1, d. 1925, l. 191–234; GARF f. 9414, op. 1, d. 39, l. 158–160; Bezborodov and Khrustalev, *Istoriia stalinskogo Gulaga*, 439–440.

111. L.I. Gvozdkova, *Stalinskie lageria na territorii Kuzbassa, 30–40-e gg* (Kemerovo, 1994), 90.

112. Khlevniuk, "Economy of the OGPU, NKVD, and MVD," 54.

113. See, for example, a 1947 speech by Nasedkin in GARF f. 9414, op. 1, d. 374, l. 44–45.

114. GARF f. 9414, op. 1, d. 1913, l. 41.

115. Solzhenitsyn, *Gulag Archipelago*, vols. 3–4, 202.

116. GARF f. 9414, op. 1, d. 2756, l. 492.

117. GARF f. 9414, op. 1, d. 1918, l. 105–106.

118. Hoover Institution Archives, Anne Applebaum Collection, box 1, folder 5.

119. He described how from January to June prisoners received 10,000 food packages weighing 69,928 kilograms, and they purchased 2,955,549 rubles of food for prisoners through the local vendors. GARF f. 9414, op. 2, d. 169, l. 8.

120. GARF f. 9414, op. 1, d. 1925, l. 202.

121. GARF f. 9414, op. 2, d. 169, l. 12.

122. GARF f. 9414, op. 2, d. 169, l. 26.

123. Shalamov, *Kolyma Tales,* 114.

124. Shalamov, *Kolyma Tales,* 115.

125. Yehoshua A. Gilboa, *Confess! Confess! Eight Years in Soviet Prisons* (Boston: Little, Brown, 1968), 61.

126. Shalamov, *Kolyma Tales,* 114.

127. Shalamov, *Kolyma Tales,* 115.

128. Applebaum, *Gulag,* 308. See also Solzhenitsyn, *Gulag Archipelago*, vols. 3–4, 230. Similarly, Soviet doctors noted during the wartime siege of Leningrad that women's bodies did not succumb as easily to the sustained lack of food. See Rebecca Manley, "Nutritional Dystrophy: The Science and Semantics of Starvation in World War II," in Wendy Goldman and Donald Filtzer, eds., *Hunger and War: Food Provisioning in the Soviet Union During World War II* (Bloomington: Indiana University Press, 2015), 225–227.

129. This is according to the Harvard School of Public Health. See www.health.harvard.edu/healthbeat/HEALTHbeat_092706.htm#art1

130. A. N. Kustyshev, *Evropeiskii Sever Rossii v repressivnoi politike XX veka* (Ukhta, 2003), 58.

131. Bezborodov and Khrustalev, *Istoriia stalinskogo Gulaga*, 358, 383; GARF f. 9414, op. 2, d. 169, l. 90.

132. Bezborodov and Khrustalev, *Istoriia stalinskogo Gulaga*, 352–353.

133. Ekart, *Vanished Without Trace*, 60–61.

134. Bezborodov and Khrustalev, *Istoriia stalinskogo Gulaga*, 377.

135. GARF f. 9414, op. 2, d. 169, l. 2.
136. GARF f. 9414, op. 1, d. 366, l. 81–84.

CHAPTER 2. PRISONERS

1. Nicolas Werth, "A State against its People: Violence, Repression, and Terror in the Soviet Union," in Mark Kramer, ed., *The Black Book of Communism: Crimes, Terror, Repression* (Cambridge, MA: Harvard University Press, 1999), 206. See also Nicolas Werth, *Cannibal Island: Death in a Siberian Gulag* (Princeton, NJ: Princeton University Press, 2007).

2. David R. Shearer, *Policing Stalin's Socialism: Repression and Social Order in the Soviet Union, 1924–1953* (New Haven, CT: Yale University Press, 2009); Paul Hagenloh, *Stalin's Police: Public Order and Mass Repression in the USSR, 1926–1941* (Washington, DC: Johns Hopkins University Press, 2009); Peter H. Solomon, Jr., *Soviet Criminal Justice under Stalin* (Cambridge: Cambridge University Press, 1996); Christian Gerlach and Nicolas Werth, "State Violence—Violent Societies," in Michael Geyer and Sheila Fitzpatrick, eds., *Beyond Totalitarianism: Stalinism and Nazism Compared* (Cambridge: Cambridge University Press, 2009).

3. Oleg V. Khlevniuk, *The History of the Gulag: From Collectivization to the Great Terror* (New Haven, CT: Yale University Press, 2004), 314.

4. See, for example, Kees Boterbloem, *The Life and Times of Andrei Zhdanov, 1896–1948* (Montreal: McGill-Queens University Press, 2004); Jonathan Brent and Vladimir P. Naumov, *Stalin's Last Crime: The Plot against the Jewish Doctors, 1948–1953* (New York: HarperCollins, 2003); Joshua Rubenstein and Vladimir P. Naumov, *Stalin's Secret Pogrom: The Postwar Inquisition of the Jewish Anti-Fascist Committee* (New Haven, CT: Yale University Press, 2001).

5. GARF f. 9414, op. 1, d. 378, l. 155–158.
6. GARF f. 9414, op. 1, d. 446, l. 139–141; GARF f. 9414, op. 1, d. 459, l. 59–62.

7. See, for example, Mark Kramer, "Stalin, Soviet Policy, and the Establishment of a Communist Bloc in Eastern Europe, 1941–1948," in Timothy Snyder and Ray Brandon, eds., *Stalin and Europe: Imitation and Domination, 1928–1953* (Oxford: Oxford University Press, 2014), 264–294; Amir Weiner, *Making Sense of War: The Second World War and the Fate of the Bolshevik Revolution* (Princeton, NJ: Princeton University Press, 2001).

8. These three categories of prisoners were assigned to one of three camp regimes: primary (*pervonachal'nyi*), lightened (*oblegchennyi*), and privileged (*l'gotnyi*), which governed, for example, whether inmates could work outside the camp zone, or whether they could hold administrative positions or receive awards. See A.I. Kokurin and N.V. Petrov, *Gulag (glavnoe upravlenie lagerei), 1918–1960* (Moscow, 2000), 67–68.

9. Kokurin and Petrov, *Gulag,* 68.
10. GARF f. 9414, op. 1, d. 374, l. 49.
11. After the 1941 Nazi invasion of the USSR, juveniles over 16 were transferred from prisons to corrective-labor colonies. A.B. Bezborodov and V.M. Khrustalev, eds., *Istoriia stalinskogo Gulaga: konets 1920-kh–pervaia polovina 1950-kh godov, tom 4: naselenie Gulaga* (Moscow, 2004), 84.

12. Varlam Shalamov, *Kolyma Tales* (New York: Penguin Books, 1994), 24.

13. Bezborodov and Khrustalev, *Istoriia stalinskogo gulaga,* 64, 75–76.

14. Anne Applebaum. *Gulag: A History* (New York: Doubleday, 2003), 292.

15. Khlevniuk, *History of the Gulag,* 91–93.

16. Aleksandr I. Solzhenitsyn, *The Gulag Archipelago, 1918–1956: An Experiment in Literary Investigation,* vols. 1–2 (New York: Harper & Row, 1973), 60; Aleksandr I. Solzhenitsyn, *The Gulag Archipelago, 1918–1956: An Experiment in Literary Investigation,* vols. 3–4 (New York: Harper & Row, 1974), 297–298.

17. GARF f. 9414, op. 1, d. 446, l. 139–141; GARF f. 9414, op. 1, d. 459, l. 59–62.

18. Applebaum, *Gulag,* 294–295; Aleksandr I. Solzhenitsyn, *The Gulag Archipelago, 1918–1956: An Experiment in Literary Investigation,* vols. 5–7 (New York: Harper & Row, 1978), 34–35.

19. GARF f. 9414, op. 1, d. 469, l. 71–74; GARF f. 9414, op. 1, d. 471, l. 154–159; GARF f. 9414, op. 1, d. 478, l. 1–6; GARF f. 9414, op. 1, d. 492, l. 1–6; GARF f. 9414, op. 1, d. 492, l. 106–111.

20. Applebaum, *Gulag,* 463–465.

21. References to these hardened criminals are numerous in Shalamov, *Kolyma Tales.* See, for example, pages 5–10, 124–125, 143, 159–160, 228–231, 347–354, 384, 409–431. On the "thieves in law" see also Steven A. Barnes, *Death and Redemption: The Gulag and the Shaping of Soviet Society* (Princeton, NJ: Princeton University Press, 2011), 173–179.

22. Adi Kuntsman, "'With a Shade of Disgust': Affective Politics of Sexuality and Class in Memoirs of the Stalinist Gulag," *Slavic Review* 68 (Summer, 2009): 308–328.

23. Shalamov, *Kolyma Tales,* 411; Solzhenitsyn, *Gulag Archipelago,* vols. 1–2, 501–504. See also Barnes, *Death and Redemption,* 89–90.

24. Galina Mikhailovna Ivanova, *Labor Camp Socialism: The Gulag in the Soviet Totalitarian System* (New York: M.E. Sharpe, 2000), 188. See also Pohl, *Stalinist Penal System,* 24–25.

25. Bezborodov and Khrustalev, *Istoriia stalinskogo gulaga,* 64–65, 75–77.

26. GARF f. 9414, op. 1, d. 378, l. 155–158; GARF f. 9414, op. 1, d. 446, l. 32–34. Persons sentenced for armed robbery, possession of illegal arms, murder, or as "socially-harmful elements" and "thieves-recidivists" constituted 12 percent of all prisoners in camps and colonies in 1947. As petty criminal offenders flooded into the camps, the criminal recidivists declined as a proportion of inmates, dropping steadily to 8 percent in 1948, 6–7 percent in 1949, and roughly 5 percent in 1950–1953. See GARF f. 9414, op. 1, d. 459, l. 59–62; GARF f. 9414, op. 1, d. 469, l. 71–74; GARF f. 9414, op. 1, d. 471, l. 47–52, 154–159; GARF f. 9414, op. 1, d. 478, l. 1–6; GARF f. 9414, op. 1, d. 492, l. 1–6, 106–111.

27. Solzhenitsyn, *Gulag Archipelago,* vols. 1–2, 86, 595.

28. Bezborodov and Khrustalev, *Istoriia stalinskogo gulaga,* 36–37; Applebaum, *Gulag,* 282–283. See also Jörg Baberowski, *Der rote Terror* (Deutsche Verlags-Anstalt, 2003).

29. Khlevniuk, *History of the Gulag,* 305–306. See also Barnes, *Death and Redemption,* 91–92.

30. Golfo Alexopoulos, *Stalin's Outcasts: Aliens, Citizens, and the Soviet State, 1926–1936* (Ithaca, NY: Cornell University Press, 2003).

31. Lynne Viola, *The Unknown Gulag: The Lost World of Stalin's Special Settlements* (Oxford: Oxford University Press, 2007), 162–166.

32. A 1935 report noted that 60 percent of labor camp prisoners had been sentenced by the Commissariat of Justice courts, and 40 percent by OGPU-NKVD organs. See Bezborodov and Khrustalev, *Istoriia stalinskogo gulaga*, 64.

33. GARF f. 9414, op. 2, d. 169, l. 13.

34. Lev Razgon, *True Stories* (Dana Point, CA: Ardis Publishers, 1997), 155.

35. Shalamov, *Kolyma Tales,* 305.

36. Applebaum, *Gulag,* 306. See also Solzhenitsyn, *Gulag Archipelago,* vols. 3–4, 264; Applebaum, *Gulag,* 302–303.

37. David Nordlander, "Magadan and the Economic History of Dalstroi in the 1930s," in Paul R. Gregory and Valery Lazarev, eds., *The Economics of Forced Labor: The Soviet Gulag* (Stanford, CA: Hoover Institution Press, 2003), 108.

38. Bezborodov and Khrustalev, *Istoriia stalinskogo gulaga*, 64–65.

39. Shearer, *Policing Stalin's Socialism*, 210–211.

40. Bezborodov and Khrustalev, *Istoriia stalinskogo gulaga*, 91.

41. GARF f. 9414, op. 1, d. 378, l. 155–158. In 1942–1944, they made up 60–70 percent of the nearly half million prisoners in regional labor colonies. See GARF f. 9414, op. 1, d. 391, l. 20–21; GARF f. 9414, op. 1, d. 409, l. 20.

42. GARF f. 9414, op. 1, d. 459, l. 59–60, 89–90; GARF f. 9414, op. 1, d. 446, l. 32–33; GARF f. 9414, op. 1, d. 446, l. 139–141.

43. He also noted that many of these short-term offenders were eligible for release under the terms of the 1945 amnesty. GARF f. 9414, op. 2, d. 169, l. 27.

44. Barnes, *Death and Redemption,* 113–115, 125; Khlevniuk, *History of the Gulag,* 237, 244–245.

45. Khlevniuk, *History of the Gulag,* 9, 245.

46. *Ugolovnyi kodeks RSFSR* (Moscow, 1950), 142–143. On the 1947 theft decrees, see Barnes, *Death and Redemption,* 159–160; Donald Filtzer, *Soviet Workers and Late Stalinism: Labour and the Restoration of the Stalinist System after World War II* (Cambridge: Cambridge University Press, 2007), 28–29, 251–256; Paul R. Gregory, *Lenin's Brain and Other Tales from the Secret Soviet Archives* (Stanford, CA: Hoover Institution Press, 2008); Yoram Gorlizki, "Rules, Incentives and Soviet Campaign Justice after World War II," *Europe-Asia Studies* 51 (1999): 1245–1265; Yoram Gorlizki and Oleg Khlevniuk, *Cold Peace: Stalin and the Soviet Ruling Circle, 1945–1953* (Oxford: Oxford University Press, 2004), 125; James Heinzen, "Corruption in the Gulag: Dilemmas of Officials and Prisoners," *Comparative Economic Systems* 47 (2005): 456–475; Solomon, *Soviet Criminal Justice under Stalin.*

47. Ivanova, *Labor Camp Socialism,* 49.

48. V.N. Zemskov, "Gulag (istoriko-sotsiologicheskii aspect)" *Sotsiologicheskie issledovaniia* 7 (1991): 10.

49. Solzhenitsyn, *Gulag Archipelago,* vols. 1–2, 88–89.

50. Kramer, "Stalin, Soviet Policy"; Mark Kramer, "Stalin, the Split with Yugoslavia, and Soviet-East European Efforts to Reassert Control, 1948–1953," in Snyder and Brandon, *Stalin and Europe,* 295–315.

51. GARF f. 9414, op. 1, d. 459, l. 59–60, 89–90; GARF f. 9414, op. 1, d. 471, l. 47–50, 154–157.

52. GARF f. 9414, op. 1, d. 478, l. 1–6, 76–79; GARF f. 9414, op. 1, d. 492, l. 1–6; GARF f. 9414, op. 1, d. 492, l. 106–108.

53. Bezborodov and Khrustalev, *Istoriia stalinskogo gulaga,* 64–65; Applebaum, *Gulag,* 291–292; Khlevniuk, *History of the Gulag,* 315–320; Kokurin and Petrov, *Gulag,* 416–419.

54. GARF f. 9414, op. 1, d. 378, l. 155–158; GARF f. 9414, op. 1, d. 391, l. 20–23, 112–115; GARF f. 9414, op. 1, d. 395, l. 121–129.

55. GARF f. 9414, op. 1, d. 446, l. 32–34; GARF f. 9414, op. 1, d. 471, l. 47–52.

56. GARF f. 9414, op. 1, d. 478, l. 1–6, 76–81; GARF f. 9414, op. 1, d. 492, l. 1–6.

57. Kokurin and Petrov, *Gulag,* 429.

58. Werth, *Cannibal Island,* 157.

59. Camps sometimes housed the "not-work-capable" or the invalids together with the children. See T.E. Vasil'chenko, *Pol'skie grazhdane na Evropeiskom Severe SSSR: ot deportatsii k amnistii i repatriatsii (1939–1946 gg),* tom 4 (Arkhangel'sk, 2010), 138, 143.

60. GARF f. 9414, op. 2, d. 169, l. 34.

61. Applebaum, *Gulag,* 320–325; Barnes, *Death and Redemption,* 98–106, 150–153; Khlevniuk. *History of the Gulag,* 123–129; Cathy A. Frierson and Semyon Vilensky, *Children of the Gulag* (New Haven, CT: Yale University Press, 2010).

62. Bezborodov and Khrustalev, *Istoriia stalinskogo gulaga,* 53.

63. Applebaum, *Gulag,* 325.

64. GARF f. 9414, op. 2, d. 169, l. 17.

65. Bezborodov and Khrustalev, *Istoriia stalinskogo gulaga,* 82–83, 89, 91–93; Khlevniuk, *History of the Gulag,* 37, 108, 133

66. Bezborodov and Khrustalev, *Istoriia stalinskogo gulaga,* 37–38, 113.

67. Bezborodov and Khrustalev, *Istoriia stalinskogo gulaga,* 113.

68. Bezborodov and Khrustalev, *Istoriia stalinskogo gulaga,* 124.

69. Memorial Archive, St. Petersburg, Russia. Uncatalogued case file of M.K. Sandratskaia, memoir manuscript, page 26, 44, 46–47.

70. Bezborodov and Khrustalev, *Istoriia stalinskogo gulaga,* 127; Barnes, *Death and Redemption,* 104.

71. Eugenia Ginzburg, *Within the Whirlwind* (New York: Harcourt Brace Jovanovich, 1979), 106.

72. Jacques Rossi, *The Gulag Handbook: An Encyclopedia Dictionary of Soviet Penitentiary Institutions and Terms Related to the Forced Labor Camps* (New York: Paragon House, 1989), 228.

73. Fedor V. Mochulsky, *Gulag Boss: A Soviet Memoir,* trans. and ed. Deborah Kaple (New York: Oxford University Press, 2011), 147.

74. Jehanne M. Gheith and Katherine R. Jolluck, eds., *Gulag Voices: Oral Histories of Soviet Incarceration and Exile* (New York: Palgrave Macmillan, 2011), 93–94.

75. Solzhenitsyn, *Gulag Archipelago*, vols. 3–4, 234.

76. Solzhenitsyn, *Gulag Archipelago*, vols. 3–4, 246–247.

77. Applebaum, *Gulag;* Paul R. Gregory, ed., *Women of the Gulag: Portraits of Five Remarkable Lives* (Stanford, CA: Hoover Institution Press, 2013; Simeon Vilensky, ed., *Till My Tale Is Told: Women's Memoirs of the Gulag* (Bloomington: Indiana University Press, 1999).

78. Applebaum, *Gulag,* 322.

79. GARF f. 9414, op. 1, d. 2756, l. 222–223. On abortion deaths, see also GARF f. 9414, op. 1, d. 2743, l. 6; Applebaum, *Gulag,* 319.

80. Golfo Alexopoulos, "Stalin and the Politics of Kinship: Practices of Collective Punishment, 1920s–1940s." *Comparative Studies in Society and History* 50 (January, 2008): 91–117; Solzhenitsyn, *Gulag Archipelago*, vols. 5–7, 67; Golfo Alexopoulos, *Stalin's Outcasts: Aliens, Citizens, and the Soviet State, 1926–1936* (Ithaca, NY: Cornell University Press, 2003).

81. Bezborodov and Khrustalev, *Istoriia stalinskogo gulaga,* 37, 64–65, 75, 85, 91, 98–99, 114.

82. Ginzburg, *Within the Whirlwind,* 218–219.

83. From Elinor Lipper, *Seven Years in Soviet Prison Camps* (London and Chicago, 1951), quoted in Conquest, *Kolyma,* 193–194.

84. Mochulsky, *Gulag Boss,* 148.

85. Solzhenitsyn, *Gulag Archipelago*, vols. 3–4, 225.

86. Solzhenitsyn, *Gulag Archipelago*, vols. 3–4, 149.

87. Yehoshua A. Gilboa, *Confess! Confess! Eight Years in Soviet Prisons* (Boston: Little, Brown, 1968), 72–73.

88. See, for example, Barnes, *Death and Redemption,* 35–36; Khlevniuk, *History of the Gulag,* 24, 331–333; Oleg Khlevniuk, "The Economy of the OGPU, NKVD, and MVD of the USSR, 1930–1953: The Scale, Structure, and Trends of Development," in Paul R. Gregory and Valery Lazarev, eds., *The Economics of Forced Labor: The Soviet Gulag* (Stanford, CA: Hoover Institution Press, 2003), 49; David Nordlander, "Magadan and the Economic History of Dalstroi in the 1930s," in Gregory and Lazarev, *Economics of Forced Labor,* 114–115.

89. Khlevniuk, "Economy of the OGPU," 45–46, 52–53.

90. Khlevniuk, "Economy of the OGPU," 66.

91. Mikhail Morukov, "The White Sea-Baltic Sea Canal," in Gregory and Lazarev, *Economics of Forced Labor,* 158. See also Applebaum, *Gulag,* 55–56; Khlevniuk, *History of the Gulag,* 333.

92. Khlevniuk, *History of the* Gulag, 332–333.

93. Khlevniuk, *History of the* Gulag, 243–246; See Paul Gregory, "Introduction," in Gregory and Lazarev, *Economics of Forced Labor,* 16.

94. GARF f. 9414, op. 1, d. 371, l. 75–79; *Sistema ispravitel'no-trudovykh lagerei v SSSR, 1923–1960: Spravochnik* (Moscow, 1998), 329.

95. Khlevniuk. *History of the Gulag,* 202.

96. Andrei Sokolov, "Forced Labor in Soviet Industry: The End of the 1930s to the Mid-1950s: An Overview," in Paul R. Gregory and Valery Lazarev, eds., *The Economics of Forced Labor: The Soviet Gulag* (Stanford, CA: Hoover Institution Press, 2003), 25.

97. N. Vert and S.V. Mironenko, eds., *Istoriia stalinskogo gulaga, konets 1920-kh–pervaia polovina 1950-kh godov,* tom 1: Massovye repressii v SSSR (Moscow, 2004), 603.

98. Vert and Mironenko, *Istoriia stalinskogo gulaga,* 611.

99. Sokolov, "Forced Labor," 28.

100. Sokolov, "Forced Labor," 32; A. N. Kustyshev, *Evropeiskii Sever Rossii v repressivnoi politike XX veka* (Ukhta, 2003), 15–16.

101. Sokolov, "Forced Labor," 25.

102. Sokolov, "Forced Labor," 31.

103. Antoni Ekart, *Vanished Without Trace: The Story of Seven Years in Soviet Russia* (London: Max Parrish, 1954), 286–287.

104. Mochulsky, *Gulag Boss,* 170.

105. Solzhenitsyn, *Gulag Archipelago,* vols. 3–4, 578.

106. Shalamov, *Kolyma Tales,* 34.

CHAPTER 3. HEALTH

1. Varlam Shalamov, *Kolyma Tales* (New York: Penguin Books, 1994), 406–407.

2. Simon Ertz, "Building Norilsk," in Paul R. Gregory and Valery Lazarev, eds., *The Economics of Forced Labor: The Soviet Gulag* (Stanford, CA: Hoover Institution Press, 2003), 147–148.

3. GARF f. 9414, op. 1, d. 2737, l. 1.

4. OGPU-NKVD-MVD internal documents reveal frequent complaints about the misuse of skilled workers in unskilled manual labor. See Oleg Khlevniuk, "The Economy of the OGPU, NKVD, and MVD of the USSR, 1930–1953: The Scale, Structure, and Trends of Development," in Paul R. Gregory and Valery Lazarev, eds., *The Economics of Forced Labor: The Soviet Gulag* (Stanford, CA: Hoover Institution Press, 2003), 64.

5. Anne Applebaum. *Gulag: A History* (New York: Doubleday, 2003), 176–178, 202.

6. GARF f. 9414, op. 1, d. 2743, l. 3.

7. Applebaum, *Gulag,* 178. See also Antoni Ekart, *Vanished Without Trace: The Story of Seven Years in Soviet Russia* (London: Max Parrish, 1954), 188; Margarete Buber, *Under Two Dictators* (London: Victor Gollancz Ltd., 1949), 72.

8. GARF f. 9414, op. 1, d. 2737, l. 2; GARF f. 9414, op. 2, d. 169, l. 158. The continuous movement of prisoners often meant that inmates were not always adequately documented. See, for example, GARF f. 9414, op. 1, d. 61, l. 46.

9. GARF f. 9414, op. 1, d. 2737, l. 1–2.

10. Regulations on the corrective labor camps from April 1930 did not mention the documenting of bodies, and the revised regulations of October 1934 stated only that, "a doctor's opinion concerning a prisoner's health is considered when work assignments are made." Camp regulations of July 1949 indicated that labor brigades would be organized according to prisoners' gender, age, and sentence, and that the work should be appropriate to a prisoner's physical condition. See A.I. Kokurin and N.V. Petrov, *Gulag (glavnoe upravlenie lagerei), 1918–1960* (Moscow, 2000), 67–68, 82, 141–142.

11. The April 1930 investigation of the Solovetsky camps stated that prisoners were assigned to their category of labor capability by "a special commission" comprised of camp administrators and doctors and that "until this year, this determination had been the sole responsibility of the doctor." See A.B. Bezborodov and V.M. Khrustalev, eds., *Istoriia stalinskogo Gulaga: konets 1920-kh–pervaia polovina 1950-kh godov, tom 4: naselenie Gulaga* (Moscow, 2004), 139, 31.

12. The VTEK introduced in 1949 also included someone from the production section and a civilian doctor. GARF f. 9401, op. 1a, d. 313, l. 10.

13. GARF f. 9414, op. 1, d. 2737, l. 1.

14. Leona Toker, *Return from the Archipelago: Narratives of Gulag Survivors* (Bloomington: Indiana University Press, 2000), 88–90. See also Jehanne M. Gheith, "'It's Difficult to Convey': Oral History and Memories of Gulag Survivors," *Gulag Studies* 2–3 (2009–2010): 37–53.

15. Quoted in Applebaum, *Gulag,* 180.

16. Aleksandr I. Solzhenitsyn, *The Gulag Archipelago, 1918–1956: An Experiment in Literary Investigation*, vols. 1–2 (New York: Harper & Row, 1973), 583. See also Steven A. Barnes, *Death and Redemption: The Gulag and the Shaping of Soviet Society* (Princeton, NJ: Princeton University Press, 2011), 170–171.

17. G.I. Kasabova, ed., *O vremeni, o Noril'ske, o sebe . . . Kniga 6* (Moscow, 2005), 550–551.

18. Quoted in Applebaum, *Gulag,* 180.

19. Gustaw Herling, *A World Apart* (New York: Penguin Books, 1986), 41.

20. Solzhenitsyn, *Gulag Archipelago*, vols. 1–2, 562. The emphasis on the words "buyer" and "merchandise" is in Solzhenitsyn's text.

21. Prior to that, in 1930, new arrivals in the Solovetsky labor camps were assigned to one of the following four categories: category 4: capable of all forms of labor; category 3: capable of labor, except especially heavy labor; category 2: capable of light labor; category 1: invalid. See Bezborodov and Khrustalev, *Istoriia stalinskogo gulaga,* 139–140.

22. GARF f. 9414, op. 1, d. 2737, l. 1.

23. The special settlers were divided into five labor groupings: group A: able to perform any kind of physical work; group B: able to perform light physical work; group C: incapable of physical work but able to work in and around the special settlement in various seasonal activities (gathering mushrooms, berries, etc.) and in handicrafts; group D: incapable of work; group E: children under sixteen. See Lynne Viola, *The Unknown Gulag: The Lost World of Stalin's Special Settlements* (Oxford: Oxford University Press, 2007), 98.

24. Oleg V. Khlevniuk, *History of the Gulag: From Collectivization to the Great Terror* (New Haven, CT: Yale University Press, 2004), 72–73.

25. Shalamov, *Kolyma Tales,* 406–407.

26. The earliest reference that I have seen to the List of Illnesses is from April 1930, and it suggests that the Solovetsky camps had just begun to use the list on orders of the administration of the northern camps (USLON). See Bezborodov and Khrustalev, *Istoriia stalinskogo gulaga,* 139.

27. GARF f. 9414, op. 1, d. 2737, l. 3–10.

28. GARF f. 9414, op. 1, d. 2737, l. 3–11.

29. GARF f. 9414, op. 1, d. 2737, l. 4.

30. GARF f. 9414, op. 1, d. 2737, l. 11.

31. Fedor V. Mochulsky, *Gulag Boss: A Soviet Memoir*, trans. and ed. Deborah Kaple (New York: Oxford University Press, 2011), 83.

32. Kokurin and Petrov, *Gulag,* 866.

33. Kokurin and Petrov, *Gulag,* 425–426; GARF f. 9414, op. 1, d. 378, l. 157; GARF f. 9414, op. 1, d. 395, l. 124.

34. L.I. Gvozdkova, *Stalinskie lageria na territorii Kuzbassa, 30–40-e gg.* (Kemerovo, 1994), 86.

35. GARF f. 9414, op. 1, d. 366, l. 12.

36. GARF f. 9414, op. 1, d. 366, l. 80.

37. Kokurin and Petrov, *Gulag,* 278.

38. GARF f. 9414, op. 2, d. 165, l. 39–45.

39. GARF f. 9414, op. 2, d. 169, l. 19.

40. GARF f. 9414, op. 2, d. 165, l. 40.

41. The goiter included the note "subject to surgical intervention." GARF f. 9414, op. 2, d. 165, l. 40.

42. GARF f. 9414, op. 2, d. 165, l. 40–44.

43. GARF f. 9414, op. 1, d. 2737, l. 4.

44. GARF f. 9414, op. 2, d. 165, l. 39.

45. GARF f. 9414, op. 1, d. 2737, l. 4–5; GARF f. 9414, op. 2, d. 165, l. 39–40; GARF f. 9414, op. 1, d. 2737, l. 7; GARF f. 9414, op. 2, d. 165, l. 42 GARF f. 9414, op. 1, d. 2737, l. 11; GARF f. 9414, op. 2, d. 165, l. 44.

46. Shalamov, *Kolyma Tales,* 165. Sick prisoners would be subject to re-examination to determine whether they had recovered enough strength to be fit for manual labor once again. In theory, inmates who wished to challenge their assigned category of physical labor ability could petition the medical-sanitation department chief for a re-examination. GARF f. 9414, op. 1, d. 2737, l. 2.

47. Viktor Samsonov, *Parus Podnimaiu: zapiski lishentsa* (Petrozavodsk: Kareliia, 1993), 74.

48. Donald Filtzer, *Soviet Workers and Late Stalinism: Labour and the Restoration of the Stalinist System after World War II* (Cambridge: Cambridge University Press, 2002), 101.

49. Doctors had to sign all medical-labor commission protocols of inspection. GARF f. 9414, op. 1, d. 2737, l. 2.

50. Aleksandr I. Solzhenitsyn, *The Gulag Archipelago, 1918–1959: An Experiment in Literary Investigation,* vols. 3–4 (New York: Harper & Row, 1975), 216; Aleksandr Solzhenitsyn, *Arkhipelag Gulag* (Moscow: Al'fa-Kniga, 2009), 517.

51. GARF f. 9414, op. 2, d. 169, l. 18.

52. GARF f. 9414, op. 2, d. 165, l. 39–45. In the stenogram, the assigned category is given as 4, which is likely a misprint.

53. GARF f. 9414, op. 2, d. 165, l. 39–45.

54. GARF f. 9414, op. 2, d. 169, l. 22.

55. GARF f. 9414, op. 2, d. 169, l. 22.

56. GARF f. 9414, op. 2, d. 165, l. 39–45.

57. GARF f. 9414, op. 2, d. 169, l. 22.

58. GARF f. 9414, op. 2, d. 169, l. 113.

59. GARF f. 9414, op. 2, d. 169, l. 57.

60. GARF f. 9414, op. 2, d. 169, l. 19–20.

61. GARF f. 9414, op. 2, d. 169, l. 126.

62. GARF f. 9414, op. 1, d. 374, l. 46–47.

63. GARF f. 9414, op. 1, d. 374, l. 47.

64. Solzhenitsyn, *Gulag Archipelago*, vols. 3–4, 556.

65. Khlevniuk, *History of the Gulag,* 37.

66. Bezborodov and Khrustalev, *Istoriia stalinskogo Gulaga,* 591 (fn. 188); see also Khlevniuk, *History of the Gulag,* 201.

67. Kokurin and Petrov, *Gulag,* 419–420.

68. Kokurin and Petrov, *Gulag,* 278.

69. Kokurin and Petrov, *Gulag,* 425–426; GARF f. 9414, op. 1, d. 378, l. 157; GARF f. 9414, op. 1, d. 395, l. 124.

70. GARF f. 9414, op. 1, d. 1139, l. 131, 192.

71. GARF f. 9414, op. 1, d. 53, l. 6.

72. GARF f. 9414, op. 1, d. 1925, l. 241–242.

73. Bezborodov and Khrustalev, *Istoriia stalinskogo gulaga,* 399.

74. Viktor Berdinskikh, *Viatlag* (Kirov, 1998), 28.

75. GARF f. 9414, op. 1, d. 446, l. 34; GARF f. 9414, op. 1, d. 443, l. 32; GARF f. 9414, op. 1, d. 446, l. 138–141.

76. GARF f. 9414, op. 1, d. 459, l. 59–62, 89–90.

77. Kokurin and Petrov, *Gulag,* 318.

78. GARF f. 9414, op. 1, d. 446, l. 34.

79. Golfo Alexopoulos, "Amnesty 1945: The Revolving Door of Stalin's Gulag," *Slavic Review* 64 (Summer 2005): 274–306.

80. GARF f. 9414, op. 1, d. 446, l. 138. The labor colonies of the fourteen republics (excluding the RSFSR) reflected similar data. See GARF f. 9414, op. 1, d. 443, l. 32.

81. GARF f. 9414, op. 1, d. 459, l. 59–62; GARF f. 9414, op. 1, d. 459, l. 89–90. See also GARF f. 9414, op. 1, d. 86, l. 129. This breakdown was reviewed by the MVD chief, Kruglov, and it prompted him to lambast Dobrynin for failing to attend to the physical condition of prisoners. It is possible that Kruglov's severe reaction discouraged Gulag officials from regularly generating physical profile statistics and/or showing these figures to their MVD bosses.

82. Samsonov, *Parus Podnimaiu,* 77.

83. See, for example, GARF f. 9414, op. 1, d. 378, l. 155–158; GARF f. 9414, op. 1, d. 446, l. 138; GARF f. 9414, op. 1, d. 390, l. 81–84; GARF f. 9414, op. 1, d. 446, l. 32–34; GARF f. 9414, op. 1, d. 459, l. 89–90; GARF f. 9414, op. 1, d. 459, l. 59–62; GARF f. 9414, op. 1, d. 446, l. 139–141; GARF f. 9414, op. 1, d. 443, l. 1–32.

84. See, for example, the 1948–1953 quarterly reports on the composition of prisoners in labor camps and colonies that were compiled by central Gulag authorities: GARF f. 9414, op. 1, d. 469, l. 71–74; GARF f. 9414, op. 1, d. 471, l. 47–52, 152–159; GARF f. 9414, op. 1, d. 478, l. 1–6, 76–81; GARF f. 9414, op. 1, d. 484, l. 79–104; GARF f. 9414, op. 1, d. 492, l. 1–6, 177–181.

85. Kokurin and Petrov, *Gulag,* 726–727.

86. GARF f. 9414, op. 1, d. 409, l. 20–21.

87. GARF f. 9414, op. 1, d. 86, l. 127.

88. GARF f. 9401, op. 1a, d. 313, l. 7.

89. GARF f. 9401, op. 1a, d. 313, l. 7.

90. GARF f. 9401, op. 1a, d. 313, l. 8. The three-tiered system was supposed to take effect August 1, 1949. GARF f. 9414, op. 1, d. 2854, l. 82–83.

91. GARF f. 9401, op. 1a, d. 313, l. 8. The introduction of this practice appears to have been a 1947 MVD order that approved the use of category 3 light labor prisoners in medium labor with a 25 percent reduction in their work quota. See Bezborodov and Khrustalev, eds., *Istoriia stalinskogo gulaga, tom 4,* 426.

92. GARF f. 9401, op. 1a, d. 313, l. 10.

93. GARF f. 9401, op. 1a, d. 313, l. 8.

94. GARF f. 9401, op. 1a, d. 313, l. 10. They would only be reexamined twice a year, in January and July.

95. GARF f. 9401, op. 1a, d. 313, l. 14–15.

96. GARF f. 9401, op. 1a, d. 313, l. 14–18.

97. GARF f. 9401, op. 1a, d. 313, l. 8–9.

98. GARF f. 9401, op. 1a, d. 313, l. 8–9.

99. GARF f. 9401, op. 1a, d. 313, l. 9.

100. GARF f. 9401, op. 1a, d. 313, l. 8–9.

101. Officials included the note: "Beginning in September, the physical profile is given in two categories consistent with MVD USSR Order No. 0418." See GARF f. 9414, op. 1, d. 372, l. 110. See also GARF f. 9414, op. 1, d. 371, l. 120.

102. GARF f. 9414, op. 1, d. 378, l. 322; GARF f. 9414, op. 1, d. 492, l. 106–111.

103. GARF f. 9414, op. 1, d. 2854, l. 33.

104. GARF f. 9414, op. 1, d. 492, l. 106–111. The January 1953 report "on the composition of prisoners detained in MVD USSR camps and colonies" had omitted physical profile data, but it was written in by hand at the very end of the report. A scribbled note on the face of the report with the date of April 1 suggests that prisoners' physical profile data was added by hand after Stalin's death, when party leaders were preparing for the large amnesty of Gulag prisoners that released many sick and emaciated prisoners.

105. Yehoshua A. Gilboa, *Confess! Confess! Eight Years in Soviet Prisons* (Boston: Little, Brown, 1968), 60.

106. Mark Mazower, *Hitler's Empire: How the Nazis Ruled Europe* (New York: Penguin Books, 2008), 306–307.

CHAPTER 4. ILLNESS AND MORTALITY

1. Varlam Shalamov, *Kolyma Tales* (New York: Penguin Books, 1994), 107–110.

2. Quoted in Anne Applebaum, *Gulag: A History* (New York: Doubleday, 2003), 370.

3. Shalamov, *Kolyma Tales,* 405–406.

4. Aleksandr I. Solzhenitsyn, *The Gulag Archipelago, 1918–1959: An Experiment in Literary Investigation,* vols. 3–4 (New York: Harper & Row, 1975), 215–216.

5. GARF f. 9414, op. 1, d. 4, l. 58–62.

6. Applebaum, *Gulag,* 377.

7. Letter entitled "Don't listen to Rumor Mongers" published in *Perekovka: na stroitel'stvo kanala Moskva-Volga,* no. 36 (129), May 23, 1934. The letter was placed below a piece urging prisoners to protect themselves against typhus "for our Soviet government." See GARF f. 9414, op. 4, d. 1, l. 334.

8. Oleg V. Khlevniuk, *The History of the Gulag: From Collectivization to the Great Terror* (New Haven, CT: Yale University Press, 2004), 39.

9. GARF f. 9414, op. 1, d. 2745, l. 1, 8; GARF f. 9414, op. 1, d. 2749, l. 1, 4.

10. Khlevniuk, *History of the Gulag,* 210. See also Dan Healey, "Lives in the Balance: Weak and Disabled Prisoners and the Biopolitics of the Gulag," in *Kritika: Explorations in Russian and Eurasian History* 16:3 (Summer 2015): 528–529.

11. Christopher Joyce, "The Gulag in Karelia: 1929–1941," in Paul R. Gregory and Valery Lazarev, eds., *The Economics of Forced Labor: The Soviet Gulag* (Stanford, CA: Hoover Institution Press, 2003), 184.

12. GARF f. 9414, op. 1, d. 621, l. 2, 5.

13. GARF f. 9414, op. 1, d. 621, l. 5.

14. GARF f. 9414, op. 1, d. 2753, l. 158–159.

15. GARF f. 9414, op. 1, d. 2753, l. 159.

16. Ads had to be sent to the Gulag medical-sanitation department for approval. GARF f. 9414, op. 1, d. 2753, l. 142–144.

17. GARF f. 9414, op. 1, d. 2739, l. 3.

18. GARF f. 9414, op. 2, d. 169, l. 6.

19. GARF f. 9414, op. 1, d. 2753, l. 142.

20. Antoni Ekart, *Vanished Without Trace: The Story of Seven Years in Soviet Russia* (London: Max Parrish, 1954), 275, 291.

21. In the post-Stalin years, Kharechko was rehabilitated and became a well-known physician in the Komi republic, where he was honored for his medical accomplishments. S.F. Sapolnova, T.A. Vekshina, F.G. Kanev, eds., *Liudi v belykh khalatakh* (Syktyvkar: Komi respublikanskaia tipografiia, 2009), 66–70.

22. Alexander Dolgun with Patrick Watson, *Alexander Dolgun's Story: An American in the Gulag* (New York: Alfred A. Knopf, 1975), 251.

23. GARF f. 9414, op. 2, d. 169, l. 25.

24. G.I. Kasabova, ed., *O vremeni, o Noril'ske, o sebe . . . Kniga 6* (Moscow, 2005), 552. See also V. A. Samsonov, *Zhizn' prodolzhitsia: zapiski lagernogo legpoma* (Petrozavodsk: Kareliia, 1990), 227–229.

25. Lev Kopelev, *To Be Preserved Forever* (Philadelphia: J.B. Lippincott Company, 1977), 217–218. See also Joseph Scholmer, *Vorkuta* (New York: Henry Holt and Company, 1955), 155–156.

26. GARF f. 9414, op. 1, d. 2743, l. 6–7.

27. Memorial Archive, St. Petersburg, Russia. Uncatalogued case file of M.K. Sandratskaia, memoir manuscript, page 50.

28. GARF f. 9414, op. 1, d. 2737, l. 2.

29. On the advice of another prisoner, Ekart successfully bribed the doctor to release him from general work. Ekart, *Vanished Without Trace,* 60.

30. Eugenia Ginzburg, *Journey into the Whirlwind* (New York: Houghton Mifflin Harcourt, 2002), 335. See also David J. Dallin and Boris I. Nicolaevsky, *Forced Labor in Soviet Russia* (New Haven, CT: Yale University Press, 1947), 241.

31. Kopelev, *To Be Preserved Forever,* 218.

32. GARF f. 9414, op. 2, d. 169, l. 13.

33. GARF f. 9414, op. 1, d. 39, l. 2–4.

34. Steven A. Barnes, *Death and Redemption: The Gulag and the Shaping of Soviet Society* (Princeton, NJ: Princeton University Press, 2011), 118–121.

35. The Gulag followed up on some of these letters and confirmed their contents. GARF f. 9414, op. 1, d. 2753, l. 145 (April 1938).

36. GARF f. 9414, op. 1, d. 2753, l. 366–367.

37. GARF f. 9414, op. 1, d. 2756, l. 222–223.

38. Sapolnova, et al, *Liudi v belykh khalatakh,* 27; Applebaum, *Gulag,* 374–375; Kasabova, *O vremeni, o Noril'ske,* 555. A medical worker even admitted to giving one gang of prisoners drugs as a form of protection against another gang.

39. Solzhenitsyn, *Gulag Archipelago,* vols. 3–4, 612–613.

40. Ekart, *Vanished Without Trace,* 239.

41. Ekart, *Vanished Without Trace,* 240–241.

42. Applebaum, *Gulag,* 163–173, 195–198. See also GARF f. 9414, op. 2, d. 169, l. 18, 150.

43. Khlevniuk, *History of the Gulag,* 37.

44. Shalamov, *Kolyma Tales,* 31, 135.

45. Sapolnova, et al., *Liudi v belykh khalatakh,* 30. See also A. I. Kaufman, *Lagernyi vrach* (Tel Aviv: AM OVED, 1973), 55.

46. Kasabova, *O vremeni, o Noril'ske,* 554.

47. Kasabova, *O vremeni, o Noril'ske,* 550–554.

48. N.A. Morozov, *Osobye lageria MVD SSSR v Komi ASSR (1948–1954)* (Syktyvkar, 1998), 111.

49. Morozov, *Osobye lageria,* 111–112.

50. Memorial Archive, St. Petersburg, Russia, f. B-1, op. 1, d. Anatolii Fedorovich Chernusov, l. 3.

51. Sapolnova, et al., *Liudi v belykh khalatakh,* 22.

52. Memorial Archive, St. Petersburg, Russia, f. B-1, op. 1, d. Iakov Davydovich Zultan, l. 2–1, 4–1.

53. GARF f. 9414, op. 2, d. 169, l. 2, 13–14, 60, 88, 94.

54. GARF f. 9414, op. 2, d. 169, l. 21.

55. GARF f. 9414, op. 2, d. 169, l. 101.

56. GARF f. 9414, op. 2, d. 169, l. 138.

57. Quoted in Applebaum, *Gulag,* 199; GARF f. 9414, op. 2, d. 169, l. 9–10.

58. GARF f. 9414, op. 2, d. 169, l. 88.

59. Applebaum, *Gulag,* 24.

60. GARF f. 9414, op. 2, d. 169, l. 139.

61. GARF f. 9414, op. 2, d. 169, l. 6.

62. GARF f. 9414, op. 2, d. 169, l. 6.

63. GARF f. 9414, op. 2, d. 169, l. 21.

64. GARF f. 9414, op. 2, d. 169, l. 13.

65. GARF f. 9414, op. 2, d. 169, l. 19.

66. GARF f. 9414, op. 2, d. 169, l. 2.

67. GARF f. 9414, op. 2, d. 169, l. 2, 5, 15.

68. GARF f. 9414, op. 2, d. 169, l. 5.

69. GARF f. 9414, op. 2, d. 169, l. 5.

70. GARF f. 9414, op. 2, d. 169, l. 115.

71. Applebaum, *Gulag*, 97.

72. GARF f. 9414, op. 1, d. 3, l. 60; GARF f. 9414, op. 1, d. 4, l. 42–43.

73. Kokurin, A.I. and N.V. Petrov, *Gulag (glavnoe upravlenie lagerei), 1918–1960* (Moscow, 2000), 508.

74. GARF f. 9414, op. 1, d. 374, l. 45–46.

75. See Mark G. Field, "Dissidence as Disability: The Medicalization of Dissidence in Soviet Russia," in William O. McCagg and Lewis Siegelbaum, eds., *The Disabled in the Soviet Union: Past and Present, Theory and Practice* (Pittsburgh, PA: University of Pittsburgh Press, 1989), 253–275.

76. GARF f. 9414, op. 1, d. 2737, l. 2.

77. Kasabova, *O vremeni, o Noril'ske*, 555; Applebaum, *Gulag*, 378–379; Khlevniuk, *History of the Gulag*, 40–41, 219–220.

78. GARF f. 9414, op. 1, d. 2743, l. 6.

79. GARF f. 9414, op. 1, d. 2741, l. 21.; Khlevniuk, *History of the Gulag*, 74.

80. Jacques Rossi, *The Gulag Handbook: An Encyclopedia Dictionary of Soviet Penitentiary Institutions and Terms Related to the Forced Labor Camps* (New York: Paragon House, 1989), 227–228.

81. Kasabova, *O vremeni, o Noril'ske*, 555; Khlevniuk, *History of the Gulag*, 74, 108, 220–221; Shalamov, *Kolyma Tales*, 320–324.

82. Solzhenitsyn, *Gulag Archipelago*, vols. 3–4, 219–220.

83. GARF f. 8131, op. 13, d. 28, l. 24–25.

84. Solzhenitsyn, *Gulag Archipelago*, vols. 3–4, 599.

85. GARF f. 9414, op. 1, d. 2756, l. 64–65.

86. GARF f. 9414, op. 1, d. 2756, l. 66–69.

87. Sapolnova, et al., *Liudi v belykh khalatakh*, 70.

88. Jörg Baberowski and Anselm Doering-Manteuffel, "The Quest for Order and the Pursuit of Terror: National Socialist Germany and the Stalinist Soviet Union as Multiethnic Empires," in Michael Geyer and Sheila Fitzpatrick, eds., *Beyond Totalitarianism: Stalinism and Nazism Compared* (Cambridge: Cambridge University Press, 2009), 224.

89. See, for example, Golfo Alexopoulos, "A Torture Memo: Reading Violence in the Gulag," in Golfo Alexopoulos, Julie Hessler and Kiril Tomoff, eds., *Writing the Stalin Era: Sheila Fitzpatrick and Soviet Historiography* (New York: Palgrave Macmillan, 2011), 159–178; V.A. Samsonov, *Preodoleniia: v nelegkom puti v nauku ot medbrata-zakliuchennogo do professora universiteta* (Petrozavodsk: PetrGU, 2004), 57.

90. GARF f. 9414, op. 1, d. 374, l. 27–37.

91. GARF f. 9414, op. 1, d. 374, l. 35–36.

92. Kasabova, *O vremeni, o Noril'ske*, 555. Another former prisoner explained, "Self-mutilation was punished viciously, like for sabotage." Quoted in Applebaum, *Gulag*, 378.

93. GARF f. 9414, op. 2, d. 175, l. 1–72. Bogolepov was identified as a sixty-year-old sentenced under Article 58-10-2, located in a camp system of the Smolensk region. The report was a publication of the medical division of the MVD USSR Main Administration of Corrective-Labor Colonies.

94. GARF f. 9414, op. 2, d. 175, l. 1.

95. GARF f. 9414, op. 2, d. 175, l. 69–70.

96. GARF f. 9414, op. 2, d. 175, l. 1.

97. GARF f. 9414, op. 2, d. 175, l. 3.

98. GARF f. 9414, op. 2, d. 175, l. 70–71.

99. Sapolnova, et al., *Liudi v belykh khalatakh*, 28–31.

100. Quoted in Applebaum, *Gulag,* 373. A similar case was reported at Pechor-lag, where ailing prisoners were condemned as bandits and work-refusers. See Alexopoulos, "Torture Memo."

101. Applebaum, *Gulag,* 375.

102. Alexander Solzhenitsyn, *One Day in the Life of Ivan Denisovich* (New York: Bantam Classics, 2005), 17.

103. GARF f. 9414, op. 2, d. 169, l. 142. On "labor therapy" in the Gulag, see also Healey, "Lives in the Balance," 550–551.

104. GARF f. 9414, op. 2, d. 169, l. 113.

105. Simeon Vilensky, ed., *Till My Tale Is Told: Women's Memoirs of the Gulag* (Bloomington: Indiana University Press, 1999), 258.

106. GARF f. 9414, op. 2, d. 169, l. 25.

107. GARF f. 9414, op. 2, d. 169, l. 23.

108. GARF f. 9414, op. 2, d. 169, l. 36.

109. Golfo Alexopoulos, "Medical Research in Stalin's Gulag," *Bulletin of the History of Medicine* 90:3 (Fall, 2016): 363–393.

110. GARF f. 9414, op. 2, d. 169, l. 80.

111. GARF f. 9414, op. 2, d. 169, l. 25.

112. GARF f. 9414, op. 2, d. 169, l. 57.

113. GARF f. 9414, op. 1, d. 621, l. 127.

114. Ekart, *Vanished Without Trace,* 281.

115. GARF f. 9414, op. 1, d. 621, l. 19.

116. GARF f. 9414, op. 2, d. 169, l. 31.

117. GARF f. 9414, op. 1, d. 621, l. 127.

118. GARF f. 9414, op. 1, d. 621, l. 1–43. The pattern is also evident in regional camps, as indicated by 1949–1950 data from the Novosibirsk region in GARF f. 9414, op. 1, d. 371, l. 217.

119. Solzhenitsyn, *Gulag Archipelago*, vols. 3–4, 235–236.

120. GARF f. 9414, op. 2, d. 169, l. 108.

121. Shalamov, *Kolyma Tales,* 149.

CHAPTER 5. INVALIDS

1. GARF f. 9414, op. 1, d. 1909, l. 126.

2. Varlam Shalamov, *Kolyma Tales* (New York: Penguin Books, 1994), 126.

3. Oleg V. Khlevniuk, *History of the Gulag,* (New Haven, CT: Yale University Press, 2004), 37.

4. Anne Applebaum, *Gulag: A History* (New York: Doubleday, 2003), 373.

5. Khlevniuk, *History of the Gulag,* 42–43.

6. GARF f. 9414, op. 1, d. 2737, l. 1.

7. GARF f. 9414, op. 1, d. 4, l. 58.

8. A.B. Bezborodov and V.M. Khrustalev, eds., *Istoriia stalinskogo Gulaga: ko-nets 1920-kh–pervaia polovina 1950-kh godov, tom 4: naselenie Gulaga* (Moscow, 2004), 353–354; Lynne Viola, *The Unknown Gulag: The Lost World of Stalin's Special Settlements* (Oxford: Oxford University Press, 2007); 152.

9. Some would regain their health at agricultural colonies or in jobs fishing. GARF f. 9414, op. 2, d. 169, l. 18, 33–34.

10. GARF f. 9414, op. 1, d. 14, l. 140.

11. Applebaum, *Gulag,* 373.

12. GARF f. 9414, op. 1, d. 491, l. 113.

13. *Sistema ispravitel'no-trudovykh lagerei v SSSR, 1923–1960: Spravochnik* (Moscow, 1998), 320–321. An enormous exodus of prisoners, probably invalids, occurred in 1940. The camp reported 31,087 prisoners in January 1940, but only 12,034 in January 1941. Afterwards, the population increased steadily again, reaching 36,125 in January 1943, the year that the camp was dissolved. On Sazlag, see also Khlevniuk, *History of the Gulag,* 359.

14. *Sistema ispravitel'no-trudovykh lagerei v SSSR,* 190–191. See also Marga-rete Buber, *Under Two Dictators* (London: Victor Gollancz Ltd., 1949), 73.

15. GARF f. 9414, op. 1, d. 164, l. 1; GARF f. 9414, op. 1, d. 366, l. 162.

16. GARF f. 9414, op. 1, d. 2782, l. 3.

17. GARF f. 9414, op. 1, d. 40, l. 41–46.

18. V.M. Poleshchikov, *Ot Vorkuty do Syktyvkara: sud'by evreev v Respublike Komi: Sbornik* (Syktyvkar: Eskom, 2003), 246.

19. GARF f. 9414, op. 1, d. 39, l. 94.

20. GARF f. 9414, op. 1, d. 39, l. 62.

21. GARF f. 9414, op. 1, d. 366, l. 162.

22. GARF f. 9414, op. 1, d. 366, l. 118, 124.

23. V.N. Zemskov, "Gulag," 6 *Sotsiologicheskie issledovaniia* (1991), 14.

24. GARF f. 9414, op. 1, d. 366, l. 14.

25. GARF f. 9414, op. 1, d. 366, l. 124–128.

26. GARF f. 9414, op. 1, d. 366, l. 118.

27. GARF f. 9414, op. 1, d. 366, l. 127.

28. GARF f. 9414, op. 1, d. 366, l. 128.

29. Dan Healey, "Lives in the Balance: Weak and Disabled Prisoners and the Biopolitics of the Gulag," in *Kritika: Explorations in Russian and Eurasian History* 16:3 (Summer 2015): 553–554.

30. Applebaum, *Gulag,* 200–201.

31. See, for example, GARF f. 9414, op. 1, d. 2743, l. 11.

32. GARF f. 9414, op. 2, d. 169, l. 18, 21.

33. Paul Gregory, "Introduction," in Paul R. Gregory and Valery Lazarev, eds., *The Economics of Forced Labor: The Soviet Gulag* (Stanford, CA: Hoover Institu-tion Press, 2003), 17–18.

34. S.F. Sapolnova, T.A. Vekshina, and F.G. Kanev, eds., *Liudi v belykh khala-takh* (Syktyvkar: Komi respublikanskaia tipografiia, 2009), 22–23.

35. Quoted in Khlevniuk, *History of the Gulag,* 37–39.

36. GARF f. 9414, op. 2, d. 169, l. 13.

37. Orlando Figes, *The Whisperers: Private Life in Stalin's Russia* (New York: Picador, 2007), 430.

38. *Sistema ispravitel'no-trudovykh lagerei v SSSR,* 476–477.

39. At the end of the poem, the barrel of a gun emerges from the watch tower, crushing the prisoners' will to revolt. See Memorial Archive, St. Petersburg, Russia, f. B-1, op. 1, d. Gordon, Lev Semenovich, l. 5. Gordon was rearrested in 1949 and sentenced under Article 58-10. He was detained in the Taishet camp, eventually released in 1956, and later worked as a history professor until his death in 1973.

40. GARF f. 9414, op. 1, d. 1913, l. 5.

41. GARF f. 9414, op. 1, d. 4, l. 22.

42. Aleksandr I. Solzhenitsyn, *The Gulag Archipelago, 1918–1956: An Experiment in Literary Investigation,* vols. 3–4 (New York: Harper & Row, 1974), 126–127. On the mistreatment of the goners by other prisoners, see also Applebaum, *Gulag,* 273, 278, 337.

43. GARF f. 9414, op. 1, d. 2741, l. 47.

44. GARF f. 9414, op. 1, d. 2741, l. 47.

45. GARF f. 9414, op. 1, d. 12, l. 261.

46. GARF f. 9414, op. 1, d. 2756, l. 219.

47. GARF f. 9414, op. 1, d. 2763, l. 1–2.

48. Bezborodov and Khrustalev, *Istoriia stalinskogo gulaga,* 382.

49. GARF f. 9414, op. 2, d. 169, l. 20.

50. GARF f. 9414, op. 2, d. 169, l. 3.

51. GARF f. 9414, op. 2, d. 169, l. 3.

52. GARF f. 9414, op. 2, d. 169, l. 8.

53. GARF f. 9414, op. 2, d. 169, l. 21.

54. GARF f. 9414, op. 2, d. 169, l. 3.

55. GARF f. 9414, op. 1, d. 12, l. 261; GARF f. 9414, op. 1, d. 14, l. 140.

56. GARF f. 9414, op. 1, d. 39, l. 125–126; GARF f. 9414, op. 2, d. 169, l. 52.

57. GARF f. 9414, op. 1, d. 61, l. 46; GARF f. 9414, op. 2, d. 169, l. 40.

58. GARF f. 9414, op. 2, d. 169, l. 34.

59. Shalamov, *Kolyma Tales,* 320–321. According to Solzhenitsyn, "they will send out a three-man gang of armless men to stamp down the foot-and-a-half snow." See Solzhenitsyn, *Gulag Archipelago,* vols. 3–4, 199.

60. Applebaum, *Gulag,* 198.

61. Memorial Archive (Moscow), file of Marianna Lazarevna Antsis: f. 2, op. 1, d. 5, l. 129–130.

62. The food allotment for invalid prisoners and others who did not meet their production norms was anywhere from 25–50 percent less. Hoover Archive, Anne Applebaum collection, box 1, file 1 (1940–1941); GARF f. 9414, op. 1, d. 1919, l. 18–19.

63. See Alan Barenberg, *Gulag Town, Company Town: Forced Labor and its Legacy in Vorkuta* (New Haven, CT: Yale University Press, 2014); Wilson T. Bell, "Was the Gulag an Archipelago? De-Convoyed Prisoners and Porous Borders in the Camps of Western Siberia," *The Russian Review* 72 (January 2013): 116–141.

64. GARF f. 9414, op. 2, d. 169, l. 11, 30.

65. Fedor V. Mochulsky, *Gulag Boss: A Soviet Memoir,* trans. and ed. Deborah Kaple (New York: Oxford University Press, 2011), 42.

66. Leona Toker, *Return from the Archipelago: Narratives of Gulag Survivors* (Bloomington: Indiana University Press, 2000), 146.

67. Shalamov, *Kolyma Tales,* 28. See also Bell, "Was the Gulag an Archipelago? 128–129.

68. Shalamov, *Kolyma Tales,* 307–308.

69. See, for example, Solzhenitsyn, *Gulag Archipelago,* vols. 3–4, 220.

70. Bezborodov and Khrustalev, *Istoriia stalinskogo gulaga,* 392; Buber, *Under Two Dictators,* 86–87.

71. GARF f. 9414, op. 2, d. 169, l. 16–17.

72. Quoted in Applebaum, *Gulag,* 168.

73. GARF f. 9414, op. 2, d. 169, l. 20.

74. GARF f. 9414, op. 1, d. 2737, l. 1–2. A doctor would have to approve any release from work that exceeded 14 days.

75. See, for example, GARF f. 9414, op. 1, d. 2743, l. 11.

76. GARF f. 9414, op. 1, d. 2743, l. 11.

77. GARF f. 9414, op. 1, d. 2782, l. 101.

78. GARF f. 9414, op. 1, d. 2762, l. 18.

79. GARF f. 9414, op. 1, d. 2762, l. 97–98.

80. GARF f. 9414, op. 1, d. 2762, l. 97–98.

81. GARF f. 9414, op. 1, d. 2762, l. 98. Nasedkin mentioned the need to execute the instructions of a Gulag circular of December 16, 1940 on improving the health of prisoners. Monthly reports on the work and effectiveness of the "group 1" and "group 2" brigades for the weak had to be submitted to the medical-sanitation department of the Gulag NKVD USSR.

82. GARF f. 9414, op. 1, d. 1919, l. 27.

83. Bezborodov and Khrustalev, *Istoriia stalinskogo gulaga,* 366.

84. Bezborodov and Khrustalev, *Istoriia stalinskogo gulaga,* 386, 509–512. What I translate as "convalescent camps" other scholars have translated as "recovery *lagpunkts*" and "recovery camps." See Applebaum, *Gulag,* 371–373; Healey, "Lives in the Balance."

85. Bezborodov and Khrustalev, *Istoriia stalinskogo gulaga,* 394.

86. GARF f. 9414, op. 2, d. 169, l. 149.

87. GARF f. 9414, op. 2, d. 169, l. 149.

88. GARF f. 9414, op. 2, d. 169, l. 150.

89. Applebaum, *Gulag,* 277–278.

90. GARF f. 9414, op. 2, d. 169, l. 25.

91. GARF f. 9414, op. 2, d. 169, l. 145–146.

92. GARF f. 9414, op. 2, d. 169, l. 23.

93. GARF f. 9414, op. 2, d. 169, l. 25.

94. GARF f. 9414, op. 2, d. 169, l. 146.

95. GARF f. 9414, op. 2, d. 169, l. 147.

96. GARF f. 9414, op. 2, d. 169, l. 148.

97. GARF f. 9414, op. 2, d. 169, l. 148.

98. GARF f. 9414, op. 1, d. 374, l. 44.

99. GARF f. 9401, op. 1, d. 713, l. 214; Bezborodov and Khrustalev, *Istoriia stalinskogo gulaga,* 387, 411.

100. Bezborodov and Khrustalev, *Istoriia stalinskogo gulaga,* 432; A.I. Kokurin and N.V. Petrov, *Gulag (glavnoe upravlenie lagerei), 1917–1960* (Moscow, 2000), 548.

101. GARF f. 9414, op. 1, d. 446, l. 34. No prisoners in the colonies were recorded as located in a camp section for prophylactic rest, which suggests that these convalescent institutions were limited to the camps.

102. Kokurin and Petrov, *Gulag*, 318.

103. GARF f. 9414, op. 1, d. 621, l. 42–43.

104. Kokurin and Petrov, *Gulag*, 536–537.

105. Kokurin and Petrov, *Gulag*, 536–537.

106. Kokurin and Petrov, *Gulag*, 536.

107. Bezborodov and Khrustalev, *Istoriia stalinskogo gulaga*, 411–412.

108. Solzhenitsyn, *Gulag Archipelago*, vols. 3–4, 218–219.

109. GARF f. 9401, op. 1a, d. 313, l. 13–14.

110. GARF f. 9414, op. 2, d. 169, l. 32.

111. L.I. Gvozdkova, *Stalinskie lageria na territorii Kuzbassa, 30-40-e gg* (Kemerovo, 1994), 90.

112. GARF f. 9414, op. 2, d. 169, l. 87.

113. GARF f. 9414, op. 2, d. 169, l. 87.

114. GARF f. 9414, op. 1, d. 369, l. 1–5.

115. GARF f. 9414, op. 1, d. 2854, l. 38.

116. Giorgio Agamben, *Remnants of Auschwitz: The Witness and the Archive* (New York: Zone Books, 2002), 52.

117. Shalamov, *Kolyma Tales,* 116–117, 127. See also Solzhenitsyn, *Gulag Archipelago*, vols. 3–4, 213.

118. GARF f. 9414, op. 2, d. 169, l. 21.

119. Solzhenitsyn, *Gulag Archipelago*, vols. 3–4, 208.

CHAPTER 6. RELEASES

1. Christian Gerlach and Nicolas Werth, "State Violence—Violent Societies," in Michael Geyer and Sheila Fitzpatrick, eds., *Beyond Totalitarianism: Stalinism and Nazism Compared* (Cambridge: Cambridge University Press, 2009), 168–169.

2. Michael Ellman, "Soviet Repression Statistics: Some Comments," *Europe-Asia Studies* 54 (2002): 1153.

3. Alexander Etkind, *Warped Mourning: Stories of the Undead in the Land of the Unburied* (Stanford, CA: Stanford University Press, 2013), 112.

4. The Russian is as follows: "*Po aktirovkam—vrachei putovkam; Rodnoi ia lager' pokidal.*" I thank Arseny Roginsky for bringing this to my attention.

5. Oleg V. Khlevniuk, *History of the Gulag: From Collectivization to the Great Terror* (New Haven, CT: Yale University Press, 2004), 368; *Kodeksy RSFSR, Ugolovno-protsessual'nyi kodeks, s izmeneniiami na 1 dekabria 1938 g.* (Moscow, 1938), Article 457–8, p. 108. See also Varlam Shalamov, *Kolyma Tales* (New York: Penguin Books, 1994), 406.

6. GARF f. 9414, op. 1, d. 2737, l. 1, 11.

7. GARF f. 9414, op. 1, d. 2737, l. 11.

8. Oleg V. Khlevniuk, *History of the Gulag: From Collectivization to the Great Terror* (New Haven, CT: Yale University Press, 2004), 37.

9. GARF f. 9414, op. 1, d. 2747, l. 1.

10. GARF f. 9414, op. 1, d. 2741, l. 21.

11. Khlevniuk, *History of the Gulag,* 37, 108.

12. GARF f. 9414, op. 1, d. 1229, l. 6; GARF f. 9414, op. 1, d. 1228, l. 39; GARF f. 9414, op. 1, d. 1246, l. 222.

13. Oleg Volkov, *Pogruzhenie vo t'mu* (Moscow, 2000), 366.

14. Khlevniuk, *History of the Gulag,* 201–203.

15. Khlevniuk, *History of the Gulag,* 45–46, 202. On workday credits and early release, see also Simon Ertz, "Trading Effort for Freedom: Workday Credits in the Stalinist Camp System," *Comparative Economic Studies* 47 (June 2005): 476–491.

16. Khlevniuk, *History of the Gulag,* 207.

17. A.I. Kokurin and N.V. Petrov, *Gulag (glavnoe upravlenie lagerei), 1917–1960* Moscow, 2000), *Gulag,* 116–117.

18. GARF f. 9414, op. 1, d. 366, l. 158.

19. GARF f. 9414, op. 1, d. 366, l. 156; Anne Applebaum, *Gulag: A History* (New York: Doubleday, 2003), 112, 372; Steven A. Barnes, *Death and Redemption: The Gulag and the Shaping of Soviet Society* (Princeton, NJ: Princeton University Press, 2011), 75–76.

20. Barnes, *Death and Redemption,* 136.

21. A.B. Bezborodov and V.M. Khrustalev, eds., *Istoriia stalinskogo gulaga: konets 1920-kh–pervaia polovina 1950-kh godov, tom 4: naselenie gulaga* (Moscow, 2004), 82–83.

22. Bezborodov and Khrustalev, *Istoriia stalinskogo gulaga,* 82–83, 664–665.

23. Applebaum, *Gulag,* 417–418; Barnes, *Death and Redemption,* 114–115.

24. GARF f. 9414, op. 1, d. 366, l. 152–155. The memo noted that the release was per Article 457 of the Criminal Procedural Code that allowed for the early release of prisoners who are suffering from "a psychological illness or a serious, incurable ailment."

25. GARF f. 9414, op. 1, d. 366, l. 154–155.

26. N. Vert and S.V. Mironenko, eds., *Istoriia stalinskogo gulaga, konets 1920-kh–pervaia polovina 1950-kh godov, tom 1: Massovye repressii v SSSR* (Moscow, 2004), 424–425.

27. GARF f. 9414, op. 1, d. 366, l. 136.

28. Bezborodov and Khrustalev, *Istoriia stalinskogo gulaga,* 79, 85; Barnes, *Death and Redemption,* 115.

29. GARF f. 9414, op. 1, d. 366, l. 91.

30. GARF f. 9414, op. 1, d. 366, l. 89–90.

31. GARF f. 9414, op. 1, d. 366, l. 135.

32. Bezborodov and Khrustalev, *Istoriia stalinskogo gulaga,* 575.

33. Vert and Mironenko, *Istoriia stalinskogo gulaga,* 424–425.

34. Amir Weiner, *Making Sense of War: The Second World War and the Fate of the Bolshevik Revolution* (Princeton, NJ: Princeton University Press, 2001), 148–149.

35. Bezborodov and Khrustalev, *Istoriia stalinskogo gulaga,* 424–425.

36. Vert and Mironenko, eds., *Istoriia stalinskogo gulaga,* 434.

37. Bezborodov and Khrustalev, *Istoriia stalinskogo gulaga,* 92–93, 575. The data on conscriptions as a percentage of World War II Gulag releases appears imprecise. A 1942 letter to Stalin and Molotov from NKVD chief Beria, the USSR

Procurator and the Commissar of Justice indicated that the November 24, 1941 amnesty resulted in the release of 386,000 prisoners, of which 122,000 were conscripted into the Red Army. See GARF f. 9414, op. 1, d. 366, l. 13. Basically, however, only a fraction of those released were ever conscripted.

38. The ban was lifted after the war. See *Sbornik zakonodatel'nykh i normativnykh aktov o repressiiakh i reabilitatsii zhertv politicheskikh repressii* (Moscow: Respublika, 1993), 158, 163–165.

39. GARF f. 9414, op. 1, d. 366, l. 82.

40. GARF f. 9414, op. 1, d. 366, l. 38.

41. GARF f. 9414, op. 1, d. 366, l. 39.

42. GARF f. 9414, op. 1, d. 366, l. 15.

43. GARF f. 9414, op. 1, d. 366, l. 15.

44. GARF f. 9414, op. 1, d. 366, l. 41.

45. GARF f. 9414, op. 1, d. 366, l. 10.

46. GARF f. 9414, op. 1, d. 366, l. 13. On Beria's 1940 assertion that the Gulag paid for itself, see Robert Service, *Stalin: A Biography* (Cambridge, MA: Harvard University Press, 2006), 374.

47. J. Arch Getty, Gàbor T. Rittersporn, and Viktor N. Zemskov, "Victims of the Soviet Penal System in the Pre-war Years: A First Approach on the Basis of Archival Evidence," *The American Historical Review* 98 (October 1993): 1019.

48. Khlevniuk, *History of the Gulag*, 245.

49. On noncustodial sentences see, for example, Getty, Rittersporn, and Zemskov, "Victims of the Soviet Penal System"; Oleg Khlevniuk, "The Gulag and the Non-Gulag as One Interrelated Whole," *Kritika: Explorations in Russian and Eurasian History* 16, 3 (Summer 2015): 479–498.

50. GARF f. 9414, op. 1, d. 366, l. 16.

51. GARF f. 9414, op. 1, d. 366, l. 57–59.

52. GARF f. 9414, op. 1, d. 366, l. 17–18, 78–80.

53. GARF f. 9414, op. 1, d. 366, l. 57–59. See also GARF f. 9414, op. 1, d. 366, l. 17–18.

54. GARF f. 9414, op. 1, d. 366, l. 57–59.

55. Ertz, "Trading Effort for Freedom," 480.

56. GARF f. 9414, op. 1, d. 366, l. 124–128.

57. *Sbornik zakonodatel'nykh i normativnykh aktov*, 159; on the application of this directive to so-called "family members of traitors to the motherland," see Bezborodov and Khrustalev, *Istoriia stalinskogo gulaga*, 106.

58. *Sbornik zakonodatel'nykh i normativnykh aktov*, 159.

59. Bezborodov and Khrustalev, *Istoriia stalinskogo gulaga*, 507–509.

60. See GARF f. 9414, op. 1, d. 366, l. 84. See also *Sbornik zakonodatel'nykh i normativnykh aktov*, 160–161.

61. Bezborodov and Khrustalev, *Istoriia stalinskogo gulaga*, 106–107.

62. Bezborodov and Khrustalev, *Istoriia stalinskogo gulaga*, 226.

63. Bezborodov and Khrustalev, *Istoriia stalinskogo gulaga*, 92–93, 107, 577–578.

64. GARF f. 9414, op. 1, d. 366, l. 1–3, 7–8.

65. Kokurin and Petrov, *Gulag*, 275.

66. GARF f. 9414, op. 1, d. 366, l. 7–8.

67. GARF f. 9414, op. 1, d. 366, l. 1–2, 7. He argued for the release of caregivers and heads of households as well. See also Golfo Alexopoulos, "Exiting the Gulag after War: Women, Invalids, and the Family," *Jahrbücher für Geschichte Osteuropas* 57:4 (2009): 563–579.

68. GARF f. 9414, op. 1, d. 366, l. 7.

69. Khlevniuk, *History of the Gulag*, 37, 78.

70. Aleksandr I. Solzhenitsyn, *The Gulag Archipelago, 1918–1956: An Experiment in Literary Investigation*, vols. 3–4, trans. Thomas P. Whitney (New York: Harper & Row, 1975), 650–651.

71. Golfo Alexopoulos, "Amnesty 1945: The Revolving Door of Stalin's Gulag," *Slavic Review* 64 (Summer 2005): 274–306.

72. Bezborodov and Khrustalev, *Istoriia stalinskogo gulaga*, 401–404.

73. GARF f. 9414, op. 2, d. 169, l. 20–21, 30, 46–47.

74. GARF f. 9414, op. 2, d. 169, l. 66.

75. GARF f. 9414, op. 2, d. 169, l. 35.

76. GARF f. 9414, op. 2, d. 169, l. 22.

77. Bezborodov and Khrustalev, *Istoriia stalinskogo gulaga*, 107.

78. Kokurin and Petrov, *Gulag*, 274–275, 278.

79. GARF f. 9414, op. 2, d. 169, l. 155. See also GARF f. 9414, op. 2, d. 169, l. 124–125.

80. See, for example, GARF f. 9414, op. 1, d. 395, l. 124, 128.

81. GARF f. 9414, op. 1, d. 459, l. 59–62.

82. Invalids and other not-work-capable prisoners who lacked relatives to care for them lived in separate sections of these special settlements. See Barnes, *Death and Redemption*, 21–23.

83. GARF f. 9414, op. 1, d. 469, l. 71–74.

84. GARF f. 9414, op. 1, d. 471, l. 47–52.

85. GARF f. 9414, op. 1, d. 365, l. 56.

86. GARF f. 9414, op. 1, d. 144, l. 2, 9–10, 87, 91.

87. GARF f. 9414, op. 1, d. 478, l. 76–81.

88. GARF f. 9414, op. 1, d. 492, l. 1–6.

89. GARF f. 9414, op. 1, d. 492, l. 106–111.

90. William Moskoff, *The Bread of Affliction: The Food Supply in the USSR During World War II* (Cambridge: Cambridge University Press, 1990), 226–227.

91. Rebecca Manley, "Nutritional Dystrophy: The Science and Semantics of Starvation in World War II," in Wendy Goldman and Donald Filtzer, eds., *Hunger and War: Food Provisioning in the Soviet Union During World War II* (Bloomington: Indiana University Press, 2015), 211.

92. Veniamin F. Zima, "Medical Expertise and the 1946–1947 Famine: The Identification and Treatment of a State-Induced Illness," in Frances L. Bernstein, Christopher Burton, and Dan Healey, eds., *Soviet Medicine: Culture, Practice, and Science* (DeKalb: Northern Illinois University Press, 2010), 182.

93. Donald Filtzer, "Starvation Mortality in Soviet Home-Front Industrial Regions during World War II," in Wendy Z. Goldman and Donald Filtzer, eds., *Hunger and War: Food Provisioning in the Soviet Union during World War II* (Bloomington: Indiana University Press, 2015), 268, 272.

94. Applebaum, *Gulag*, 88, 228; Mikhail Morukov, "The White Sea-Baltic Sea Canal," in Paul R. Gregory and Valery Lazarev, eds., *The Economics of Forced Labor: The Soviet Gulag* (Stanford, CA: Hoover Institution Press, 2003), 160.

95. Shalamov, *Kolyma Tales*, 174.

96. There was a good deal of variation, with camps in the republics of Turkmenistan and Uzbekistan reporting over 11 percent and Ukraine and Kazakhstan reporting 2–3 percent. See GARF f. 9414, op. 1, d. 2740, l. 1, 51. See also Kokurin and Petrov, *Gulag*, 441–442.

97. Khlevniuk, *History of the Gulag*, 321–327.

98. On the official Gulag mortality data, see Applebaum, *Gulag*, 582–583; Barnes, *Death and Redemption*, 76–77, 116; Bezborodov and Khrustalev, *Istoriia stalinskogo gulaga*, 54–55; Getty, Rittersporn, and Zemskov, "Victims of the Soviet Penal System," 1017–1049; Khlevniuk, *History of the Gulag*, 320–327; Kokurin and Petrov, *Gulag*, 441–442.

99. GARF f. 9414, op. 1, d. 2741, l. 7; Khlevniuk, *History of the Gulag*, 323–324.

100. GARF f. 9414, op. 1, d. 2745, l. 1.

101. GARF f. 9414, op. 2, d. 169, l. 125–127; GARF f. 9401, op. 1a, d. 313, l. 11; Khlevniuk, *History of the Gulag*, 322.

102. GARF f. 9414, op. 2, d. 169, l. 11.

103. GARF f. 9414, op. 1, d. 2741, l. 7; Khlevniuk, *History of the Gulag*, 323–324.

104. GARF f. 9414, op. 1, d. 39, l. 62.

105. GARF f. 9401, op. 1a, d. 313, l. 11.

106. GARF f. 9414, op. 2, d. 169, l. 13.

107. GARF f. 9414, op. 1, d. 2743, l. 6.

108. GARF f. 8131, op. 12, d. 38, l. 2.

109. The USSR Procuracy stressed that according to the Criminal code, the early release of sick prisoners was to be reviewed by the courts. GARF f. 8131, op. 12, d. 38, l. 4. In fact, however, these cases were reviewed by many different organs. See GARF f. 8131, op. 12, d. 38, l. 9.

110. G.I. Kasabova, ed., *O vremeni, o Noril'ske, o sebe . . . Kniga 6* (Moscow, 2005), 553.

111. GARF f. 9414, op. 2, d. 169, l. 93. In the special settlements too, officials used the term "ballast" to refer to the non-able-bodied population. See Lynne Viola, *The Unknown Gulag: The Lost World of Stalin's Special Settlements* (New York: Oxford University Press, 2007), 110, 144.

112. GARF f. 9414, op. 2, d. 169, l. 31.

113. GARF f. 9414, op. 2, d. 169, l. 13.

114. She continued, "But in fact, [this makeshift regional hospital] didn't even resemble an OP. It was an OK, because an OP has food." GARF f. 9414, op. 2, d. 169, l. 13.

115. Solzhenitsyn, *Gulag Archipelago*, vols. 3–4, 220.

116. Khlevniuk, *History of the Gulag*, 78, 108.

117. Applebaum, *Gulag*, 583.

118. V.A. Isupov, *Demograficheskie katastrofy i krizisy v Rossii v pervoi polovine XX veka* (Novosibirsk, 2000), 164.

119. M. Iu. Nakonechnyi, "Sazlag OGPU-NKVD kak lager' permanentnoi katastrofy so smertnost'iu zakliuchennykh: sravnenie s Bukhenval'dom SS," in K.M. Aleksandrov, S.V. Sheshunova, eds., *Trudy III istoricheskikh chtenii pamiati generala N.N. Golovina*. (Saint Petersburg, 2013): 337–380.

120. Etkind, *Warped Mourning,* 44–59.

121. Bezborodov and Khrustalev, *Istoriia stalinskogo gulaga,* 89; GARF f. 9414, op. 1, d. 366, l. 91.

122. Orlando Figes, *The Whisperers: Private Life in Stalin's Russia* (New York: Picador, 2007), 424–425.

123. Solzhenitsyn, *Gulag Archipelago,* vols. 3–4, 561.

124. Leona Toker, *Return from the Archipelago: Narratives of Gulag Survivors* (Bloomington: Indiana University Press, 2000), 54.

125. Memorial, St. Petersburg, f. B-1, op. 1, d. Gol'ts, Ekaterina Pavlovna, interview with Niki Georgievna Gol'ts in Moscow on October 13, 2010, conducted by Irina Suslova of Memorial in St. Petersburg. From pages 3 and 4 of the transcribed interview, which is item 10 in the file.

CHAPTER 7. POWER

1. Robert Jay Lifton, *The Nazi Doctors: Medical Killing and the Psychology of Genocide* (New York: Basic Books, 1988), 425. See also Fedor V. Mochulsky, *Gulag Boss: A Soviet Memoir,* trans. and ed. Deborah Kaple (New York: Oxford University Press, 2011); Lynne Viola, "The Question of the Perpetrator in Soviet History," *Slavic Review* 72 (Spring 2013): 1–23.

2. GARF f. 9414, op. 2, d. 169, l. 6.

3. A.B. Bezborodov and V.M. Khrustalev, eds., *Istoriia stalinskogo gulaga: konets 1920-kh–pervaia polovina 1950-kh godov, tom 4: naselenie gulaga* (Moscow, 2004), 373.

4. GARF f. 9414, op. 2, d. 169, l. 157.

5. GARF f. 9414, op. 2, d. 169, l. 157.

6. The transcript of this meeting is located in GARF f. 9414, op. 2, d. 169.

7. A.I. Kokurin and N.V. Petrov, *Gulag (glavnoe upravlenie lagerei), 1917–1960* Moscow, 2000), 272. In 1947, there were 54 centrally controlled camps and camp divisions and 79 labor camps and colonies that were administered at the republic, regional, and provincial levels, UITLK (OITK MVD) UMVD. See Kokurin and Petrov, *Gulag,* 318.

8. Oleg V. Khlevniuk, *The History of the Gulag: From Collectivization to the Great Terror* (New Haven, CT: Yale University Press, 2004), 244–245.

9. GARF f. 9414, op. 2, d. 169, l. 96, 123.

10. GARF f. 9414, op. 2, d. 169, l. 17.

11. GARF f. 9414, op. 2, d. 169, l. 15.

12. GARF f. 9414, op. 2, d. 169, l. 92.

13. GARF f. 9414, op. 2, d. 169, l. 108.

14. GARF f. 9414, op. 2, d. 169, l. 26, 130–132.

15. GARF f. 9414, op. 2, d. 169, l. 132–135.

16. GARF f. 9414, op. 2, d. 169, l. 132–133.

17. GARF f. 9414, op. 2, d. 169, l. 120.

18. GARF f. 9414, op. 2, d. 169, l. 129–130.

19. GARF f. 9414, op. 2, d. 169, l. 104–106.

20. GARF f. 9414, op. 2, d. 169, l. 101.

21. GARF f. 9414, op. 2, d. 169, l. 30.

22. GARF f. 9414, op. 2, d. 169, l. 113–114.

23. GARF f. 9414, op. 2, d. 169, l. 108–110.

24. GARF f. 9414, op. 2, d. 169, l. 150.

25. GARF f. 9414, op. 2, d. 169, l. 128.

26. GARF f. 9414, op. 2, d. 169, l. 153.

27. GARF f. 9414, op. 2, d. 169, l. 9.

28. See, for example, Sheila Fitzpatrick, "Signals from Below: Soviet Letters of Denunciation," *Journal of Modern History* 68 (December 1996): 831–866; Sheila Fitzpatrick, *Stalin's Peasants: Resistance and Survival in the Russian Village After Collectivization* (Oxford: Oxford University Press, 1996); Golfo Alexopoulos, "Exposing Illegality and Oneself: Complaint and Risk in Stalin's Russia," in Peter Solomon, ed., *Reforming Justice in Russia, 1864–1994: Power, Culture, and the Limits of Legal Order,* (Armonk, NY: M.E. Sharpe, 1997): 168–190; Golfo Alexopoulos, *Stalin's Outcasts: Aliens, Citizens, and the Soviet State, 1926–1936* (Ithaca, NY: Cornell University Press, 2003).

29. GARF f. 9414, op. 2, d. 169, l. 154.

30. GARF f. 9414, op. 2, d. 169, l. 154–155.

31. GARF f. 9414, op. 2, d. 169, l. 87.

32. GARF f. 9414, op. 2, d. 169, l. 8, 66.

33. GARF f. 9414, op. 2, d. 169, l. 11.

34. GARF f. 9414, op. 2, d. 169, l. 19, 28.

35. GARF f. 9414, op. 2, d. 169, l. 2.

36. GARF f. 9414, op. 2, d. 169, l. 2.

37. GARF f. 9414, op. 2, d. 169, l. 44.

38. GARF f. 9414, op. 2, d. 169, l. 3.

39. GARF f. 9414, op. 2, d. 169, l. 10.

40. GARF f. 9414, op. 2, d. 169, l. 36.

41. GARF f. 9414, op. 2, d. 169, l. 5.

42. GARF f. 9414, op. 2, d. 169, l. 5. Little changed after the war. A 1948 inspection of twenty-three camps revealed extreme shortages of clothing, undergarments, and shoes, even at the high-priority camps such as Norilsk, where as many as a quarter of prisoners lacked warm boots, and Vorkuta, where the number was over half. See Anne Applebaum, *Gulag: A History* (New York: Doubleday, 2003), 225.

43. This order is cited in Bezborodov and Khrustalev, *Istoriia stalinskogo gulaga,* 384; GARF f. 9414, op. 2, d. 169, l. 9, 18, 22.

44. GARF f. 9414, op. 2, d. 169, l. 9.

45. GARF f. 9414, op. 2, d. 169, l. 9.

46. GARF f. 9414, op. 2, d. 169, l. 12.

47. GARF f. 9414, op. 2, d. 169, l. 58.

48. GARF f. 9414, op. 2, d. 169, l. 24.

49. GARF f. 9414, op. 2, d. 169, l. 24. See also Applebaum, *Gulag,* 200.

50. GARF f. 9414, op. 2, d. 169, l. 24.

51. GARF f. 9414, op. 2, d. 169, l. 12.

52. GARF f. 9414, op. 2, d. 169, l. 28.

53. Varlam Shalamov, *Kolyma Tales* (New York: Penguin Books, 1994), 37. See also Applebaum, *Gulag*, 202.

54. Judith Pallot, "The Topography of Incarceration: The Spatial Continuity of Penality and the Legacy of the Gulag in Twentieth and Twenty-First Century Russia, *Laboratorium: Russian Review of Social Research* (2015): 35–36.

55. GARF f. 9414, op. 2, d. 169, l. 22.

56. GARF f. 9414, op. 2, d. 169, l. 50.

57. GARF f. 9414, op. 2, d. 169, l. 15.

58. GARF f. 9414, op. 2, d. 169, l. 27.

59. GARF f. 9414, op. 2, d. 169, l. 38.

60. GARF f. 9414, op. 2, d. 169, l. 57.

61. GARF f. 9414, op. 2, d. 169, l. 37.

62. GARF f. 9414, op. 2, d. 169, l. 85.

63. GARF f. 9414, op. 2, d. 169, l. 20.

64. GARF f. 9414, op. 2, d. 169, l. 27.

65. GARF f. 9414, op. 2, d. 169, l. 9.

66. GARF f. 9414, op. 2, d. 169, l. 9–10.

67. GARF f. 9414, op. 2, d. 169, l. 161–162.

68. GARF f. 9414, op. 2, d. 169, l. 14.

69. GARF f. 9414, op. 2, d. 169, l. 16.

70. GARF f. 9414, op. 2, d. 169, l. 28.

71. GARF f. 9414, op. 2, d. 169, l. 19.

72. GARF f. 9414, op. 2, d. 169, l. 10.

73. GARF f. 9414, op. 2, d. 169, l. 25.

74. GARF f. 9414, op. 2, d. 169, l. 6.

75. GARF f. 9414, op. 2, d. 169, l. 6.

76. GARF f. 9414, op. 2, d. 169, l. 14.

77. GARF f. 9414, op. 2, d. 169, l. 25.

78. GARF f. 9414, op. 2, d. 169, l. 16.

79. GARF f. 9414, op. 2, d. 169, l. 14.

80. GARF f. 9414, op. 2, d. 169, l. 3.

81. GARF f. 9414, op. 2, d. 169, l. 156–157.

82. Viktor Bulgakov, "Nauka v Vorkutlage—'Chernoe piatno' v otechestvennoi istorii" in E.V. Markova, V.A. Volkov, A.N. Rodnyi, and V.K. Iasnyi, eds., *Gulagovskie tainy osvoeniia severa* (Moscow, 2002), 45–46. For example, scientific research laboratories operated under the medical-sanitation department of the Northern Railway camp or Sevzheldorlag. See GARF f. 9414, op. 2, d. 168.

83. See, for example, Robert Jay Lifton, *The Nazi Doctors: Medical Killing and the Psychology of Genocide* (New York: Basic Books, 1986); Robert N. Proctor, *Racial Hygiene: Medicine under the Nazis* (Cambridge, MA: Harvard University Press, 1988).

84. GARF f. 9414, op. 2, d. 168, l. 23.

85. Golfo Alexopoulos, "Medical Research in Stalin's Gulag," *Bulletin of the History of Medicine* 90:3 (Fall 2016): 363–393.

86. Shalamov, *Kolyma Tales*, 406–407.

87. Aleksandr I. Solzhenitsyn, *The Gulag Archipelago, 1918–1959: An Experiment in Literary Investigation*, 3–4 (New York: Harper & Row, 1975), 201, 217–218.

88. GARF f. 9414, op. 2, d. 169, l. 2.

89. GARF f. 9414, op. 2, d. 169, l. 15.

90. GARF f. 9414, op. 2, d. 169, l. 9.

91. Solzhenitsyn, *Gulag Archipelago*, vols. 3–4, 215.

92. GARF f. 9414, op. 2, d. 169, l. 26. See also, GARF f. 9414, op. 2, d. 169, l. 8, 11.

93. GARF f. 9414, op. 2, d. 169, l. 15.

94. Applebaum, *Gulag*, 149.

95. GARF f. 9414, op. 2, d. 169, l. 16, 29.

96. GARF f. 9414, op. 2, d. 169, l. 19.

97. GARF f. 9414, op. 2, d. 169, l. 27.

98. Shalamov, *Kolyma Tales*, 161.

99. Applebaum, *Gulag*, 147.

100. GARF f. 9414, op. 2, d. 169, l. 22.

101. GARF f. 9414, op. 2, d. 169, l. 16.

102. GARF f. 9414, op. 2, d. 169, l. 100.

103. GARF f. 9414, op. 2, d. 169, l. 17.

104. GARF f. 9414, op. 2, d. 169, l. 17.

105. GARF f. 9414, op. 2, d. 169, l. 17.

106. GARF f. 9414, op. 2, d. 169, l. 20.

107. GARF f. 9414, op. 2, d. 169, l. 24.

108. GARF f. 9414, op. 2, d. 169, l. 30.

109. GARF f. 9414, op. 2, d. 169, l. 27.

110. GARF f. 9414, op. 2, d. 169, l. 32.

111. GARF f. 9414, op. 2, d. 169, l. 30.

112. GARF f. 9414, op. 2, d. 169, l. 28. The wage scales of various camp authorities depended on the relative rank of their camp; and within the camp, they were ranked by priority as well. See GARF f. 9401, op. 1a, d. 189, l. 13–17. In 1935, the head and assistant head of a camp's medical-sanitation department were supposed to be physicians and paid 750 rubles per month, but the heads of sanitation sections (*sanchasti*) for the camp's divisions could be doctors or not (if doctors, they received 650 per month; if not, 450). See GARF f. 9414, op. 1, d. 2753, l. 11.

113. Aleksandr Solzhenitsyn, *Arkhipelag Gulag* (Moscow: Al'fa-Kniga, 2009), 517.

114. GARF f. 9414, op. 2, d. 169, l. 6.

115. GARF f. 9414, op. 2, d. 169, l. 58.

116. Solzhenitsyn, *Gulag Archipelago*, vols. 3–4, 556.

117. GARF f. 9414, op. 2, d. 169, l. 3.

118. GARF f. 9414, op. 2, d. 169, l. 11.

119. GARF f. 9414, op. 2, d. 169, l. 21.

120. GARF f. 9414, op. 2, d. 169, l. 24.

121. Applebaum, *Gulag*, 196–197.

122. GARF f. 9414, op. 2, d. 169, l. 25. In a similar use of the term, Solzhenitsyn described his malignant tumor as a "piece of ballast." See *Gulag Archipelago*, vols. 3–4, 614.

123. GARF f. 9414, op. 2, d. 169, l. 80.

124. GARF f. 9414, op. 2, d. 169, l. 143.

125. GARF f. 9414, op. 2, d. 169, l. 122.

126. Mark Harrison, "Coercion, Compliance, and the Collapse of the Soviet Command Economy," *Economic History Review* 55 (2002): 404.

CHAPTER 8. SELECTION

1. According to Soviet law, prisoners with shorter sentences (under three years) were to be detained in labor colonies, while the camps would be reserved for more serious offenders. In practice, most prisoners in the colonies had sentences of over three years. The Soviet state's most important economic projects were not assigned to the colonies. See Paul Gregory, "An Introduction to the Economics of Forced Labor," in Paul R. Gregory and Valery Lazarev, eds., *The Economics of Forced Labor: The Soviet Gulag* (Stanford, CA: Hoover Institution Press, 2003), 14. There is little historical research on the labor colonies, but one exception is Stephen Kotkin's *Magnetic Mountain: Stalinism as a Civilization* (Berkeley: University of California Press, 1997).

2. Steven A. Barnes, *Death and Redemption: The Gulag and the Shaping of Soviet Society* (Princeton, NJ: Princeton University Press, 2011), 16–17.

3. Barnes, *Death and Redemption,* 184.

4. GARF f. 9414, op. 1, d. 2743, l. 11. See also GARF f. 9414, op. 1, d. 2753, l. 134–135.

5. GARF f. 9414, op. 2, d. 169, l. 33.

6. GARF f. 9414, op. 2, d. 169, l. 4.

7. Hoover Institution Archives, Anne Applebaum, box no. 1, file no. 1, general supply department of the Vorkutpechlag camp administration, 1940–1941.

8. GARF f. 9414, op. 1, d. 1913, l. 14.

9. GARF f. 9414, op. 1, d. 1919, l. 16.

10. A.B. Bezborodov and V.M. Khrustalev, eds., *Istoriia stalinskogo gulaga: konets 1920-kh–pervaia polovina 1950-kh godov, tom 4: naselenie gulaga* (Moscow, 2004), 370.

11. Bezborodov and Khrustalev, *Istoriia stalinskogo gulaga,* 372, 407.

12. Simon Ertz, "Building Norilsk," in Paul R. Gregory and Valery Lazarev, eds., *The Economics of Forced Labor: The Soviet Gulag* (Stanford, CA: Hoover Institution Press, 2003), 127–150. See also Simon Ertz, *Zwangsarbeit im stalinistischen Lagersystem. Eine Untersuchung der Methoden, Strategien und Ziele ihrer Ausnutzung am Beispiel Norilsk, 1935–1953* (Berlin: Duncker & Humblot, 2006).

13. Anne Applebaum, *Gulag: A History* (New York: Doubleday, 2003), 113.

14. Leonid Borodkin and Simon Ertz, "Coercion versus Motivation," in Paul R. Gregory and Valery Lazarev, eds., *The Economics of Forced Labor: The Soviet Gulag* (Stanford, CA: Hoover Institution Press, 2003), 80.

15. Oleg V. Khlevniuk, *History of the Gulag: From Collectivization to the Great Terror* (New Haven, CT: Yale University Press, 2004), 108.

16. Christopher Joyce, "The Gulag in Karelia: 1929–1941," in Paul R. Gregory and Valery Lazarev, eds., *The Economics of Forced Labor: The Soviet Gulag* (Stanford, CA: Hoover Institution Press, 2003), 185.

17. Borodkin and Ertz, "Coercion versus Motivation," 78–79.

18. GARF f. 9414, op. 2, d. 175, l. 28–40.

19. GARF f. 9414, op. 2, d. 175, l. 1–119.

20. GARF f. 9414, op. 2, d. 175, l. 18–40.

21. GARF f. 9414, op. 2, d. 175, l. 28.

22. GARF f. 9414, op. 2, d. 175, l. 23.

23. GARF f. 9414, op. 2, d. 175, l. 19–23.

24. GARF f. 9414, op. 2, d. 175, l. 28–40.

25. GARF f. 9414, op. 2, d. 175, l. 25–27.

26. GARF f. 9414, op. 2, d. 175, l. 27.

27. Quoted in Applebaum, *Gulag*, 180.

28. GARF f. 9414, op. 1, d. 1913, l. 2.

29. GARF f. 9414, op. 1, d. 1913, l. 2.

30. GARF f. 9414, op. 1, d. 39, l. 76–78.

31. Viktor Berdinskikh, *Viatlag* (Kirov, 1998), 28.

32. Antoni Ekart, *Vanished Without Trace: The Story of Seven Years in Soviet Russia* (London: Max Parrish, 1954), 254.

33. At the time, nearly 60 percent of all Gulag prisoners were classified as either category 3 light labor, category 3 individualized labor, or invalids. A.I. Kokurin and N.V. Petrov, *Gulag (glavnoe upravlenie lagerei), 1917–1960* Moscow, 2000), 318.

34. GARF f. 9414, op. 2, d. 169, l. 3.

35. See, for example, GARF f. 9414, op. 2, d. 169, l. 12.

36. GARF f. 9414, op. 2, d. 169, l. 7.

37. See, for example, GARF f. 9414, op. 2, d. 169, l. 28.

38. Aleksandr I. Solzhenitsyn, *The Gulag Archipelago, 1918–1959: An Experiment in Literary Investigation*, vols. 3–4 (New York: Harper & Row, 1975), 207.

39. Bezborodov and Khrustalev, *Istoriia stalinskogo gulaga*, 109.

40. GARF f. 9414, op. 1, d. 621, l. 39.

41. GARF f. 9414, op. 1, d. 621, l. 39.

42. GARF f. 9414, op. 1, d. 2878, l. 1–2.

43. GARF f. 9414, op. 1, d. 488, l. 55–60.

44. GARF f. 9414, op. 1, d. 167, l. 42.

45. In Agricultural Camp Section No. 1, there were 112 de-convoyed female prisoners who were sentenced for "everyday crimes" (*bytovye prestupleniia*), and their physical profile was as follows: 30 "basically fit for physical labor"; 69 "physically defective"; and 13 invalids. See GARF f. 9414, op. 1, d. 167, l. 42.

46. GARF f. 9414, op. 1, d. 2854, l. 20.

47. GARF f. 9414, op. 1, d. 621, l. 2.

48. GARF f. 9414, op. 1, d. 621, l. 2–5.

49. GARF f. 9414, op. 1, d. 621, l. 6.

50. GARF f. 9414, op. 1, d. 621, l. 34.

51. GARF f. 9414, op. 1, d. 621, l. 36.

52. GARF f. 9401, op. 1a, d. 313, l. 8.

53. GARF f. 9401, op. 1a, d. 313, l. 8.

54. GARF f. 8131, op. 11, d. 109, l. 163–165.

55. GARF f. 9414, op. 1, d. 2753, l. 48.

56. GARF f. 9414, op. 1, d. 2753, l. 117–119.

57. GARF f. 9414, op. 1, d. 2753, l. 117.

58. GARF f. 9414, op. 1, d. 2762, l. 93.

59. GARF f. 9414, op. 1, d. 2762, l. 93.

60. Gregory, "Introduction," 14, 19.

61. Gregory, "Introduction," 15.

62. GARF f. 9414, op. 2, d. 169, l. 164.

63. GARF f. 9414, op. 2, d. 169, l. 92.

64. Not coincidentally, the Gulag chief had praised Construction No. 500 for the fact that its convalescent camps (OP) "systematically generated entirely satisfactory results." Perhaps such success was due in no small measure to the practice of moving the weakest prisoners out. GARF f. 9414, op. 2, d. 169, l. 146.

65. GARF f. 9414, op. 2, d. 169, l. 93.

66. GARF f. 9414, op. 1, d. 45, l. 114.

67. GARF f. 9414, op. 1, d. 2854, l. 82–83. See also GARF f. 9414, op. 1, d. 1347, l. 5–6.

68. Barnes, *Death and Redemption*, 16–17.

69. Applebaum, *Gulag*, 246–247. Strict regime camp sections were also established in late 1948 as punishment camps for the worst criminal offenders. See Applebaum, *Gulag*, 468.

70. Iu. A. Brodskii, *Solovki: dvadtsat' let Osobogo Naznacheniia* (Moscow, 2009), 206.

71. N.V. Petrov, *Istoriia stalinskogo gulaga, tom 2: karatel'naia sistema* (Moscow, 2004), 220.

72. Petrov, *Istoriia stalinskogo gulaga*, 220–221.

73. Barnes, *Death and Redemption*, 140–143.

74. Applebaum, *Gulag*, 438.

75. Aleksandr I. Solzhenitsyn, *The Gulag Archipelago, 1918–1956: An Experiment in Literary Investigation*, vols. 5–7 (New York: Harper & Row, 1978), 8.

76. Ekart, *Vanished Without Trace*, 295–296.

77. Solzhenitsyn, *Gulag Archipelago*, vols. 5–7, 8–10.

78. Borodkin and Ertz, "Coercion versus Motivation," 87.

79. Borodkin and Ertz, "Coercion versus Motivation," 87–88.

80. Barnes, *Death and Redemption*, 141; Applebaum, *Gulag*, 439.

81. Petrov, *Istoriia stalinskogo gulaga*, 220; Barnes, *Death and Redemption*, 143.

82. GARF f. 9414, op. 1, d. 164, l. 1–3.

83. Barnes, *Death and Redemption*, 117, 183.

84. Kokurin and Petrov, *Gulag*, 135.

85. Applebaum, *Gulag*, 466–467. See also Barnes, *Death and Redemption*, 164–174, 182–185; Solzhenitsyn, *Gulag Archipelago*, vols. 5–7, 34–35.

86. Barnes, *Death and Redemption*, 184.

87. Kokurin and Petrov, *Gulag*, 135.

88. Kokurin and Petrov, *Gulag*, 135.

89. N.A. Morozov, *Osobye lageria MVD SSSR v Komi ASSR (1948–1954)* (Syktyvkar, 1998), 110–111.

90. GARF f. 9414, op. 1, d. 1347, l. 26.

91. Applebaum, *Gulag*, 467.

92. GARF f. 9414, op. 1, d. 1350, l. 66.

93. GARF f. 9414, op. 1, d. 1350, l. 61. Mortality in these camps was listed mostly at 1–2 percent but sometimes as high as 8 percent. See GARF f. 9414, op. 1, d. 1350, l. 65–66. Across the Gulag, mortality in March–April and June–July was listed at 7–8 percent. See GARF f. 9414, op. 1, d. 1344, l. 15–17, 27–29. It seems inconceivable that mortality rates in the special camps were lower than other camps. See GARF f. 9414, op. 1, d. 1921, l. 1–6, 12, 21.

94. GARF f. 9414, op. 1, d. 1350, l. 65–66.

95. GARF f. 9414, op. 1, d. 1350, l. 68.

96. GARF f. 9414, op. 1, d. 1350, l. 66.

97. Solzhenitsyn, *Gulag Archipelago*, vols. 5–7, 62.

98. Solzhenitsyn, *Gulag Archipelago*, vols. 5–7, 62–63.

99. GARF f. 9414, op. 1, d. 1350, l. 36.

100. GARF f. 9414, op. 1, d. 1350, l. 34–37; 71–74.

101. Steven A. Barnes, "All for the Front, All for Victory! The Mobilization of Forced Labor in the Soviet Union during World War Two," *International Labor and Working Class History* 58 (Fall 2000): 251–253.

102. GARF f. 9414, op. 1, d. 1909, l. 201.

103. GARF f. 9414, op. 1, d. 1350, l. 34–37; 71–74.

104. GARF f. 9414, op. 1, d. 1350, l. 37.

105. GARF f. 9414, op. 1, d. 1350, l. 37.

106. GARF f. 9414, op. 1, d. 164, l. 1–3.

107. GARF f. 9414, op. 1, d. 1350, l. 61.

108. GARF f. 9414, op. 1, d. 495, l. 7.

109. GARF f. 9414, op. 1, d. 1347, l. 26.

110. Applebaum, *Gulag*, 467.

111. See, for example, Barnes, *Death and Redemption*, 211–232; Andrea Graziosi, "The Great Strikes of 1953 in Soviet Labor Camps in the Accounts of their Participants: A Review," *Cahiers du Monde russe et soviétique* 33:4 (October–December, 1992): 419–446; V.A. Kozlov, ed., *Istoriia stalinskogo gulaga: konets 1920-kh–pervaia polovina 1950-kh godov, tom 6: vosstaniia, bunty i zabastovki zakliuchennykh* (Moscow, 2004).

112. GARF f. 9414, op. 1, d. 1347, l. 26–28.

113. GARF f. 9414, op. 1, d. 1347, l. 26.

114. GARF f. 9414, op. 1, d. 1347, l. 27.

115. Aleksandr I. Solzhenitsyn, *The Gulag Archipelago, 1918–1956: An Experiment in Literary Investigation*, vols. 1–2 (New York: Harper & Row, 1973), 89; Applebaum, *Gulag*, 438; Kokurin and Petrov, *Gulag*, 433–434.

116. Galina Mikhailovna Ivanova, *Labor Camp Socialism: The Gulag in the Soviet Totalitarian System* (New York: M.E. Sharpe, 2000), 58–59.

117. Ivanova, *Labor Camp Socialism*, 52.

118. Fedor V. Mochulsky, *Gulag Boss: A Soviet Memoir*, trans. and ed. Deborah Kaple (New York: Oxford University Press, 2011), xxxv–xxxvi. See also Barnes, *Death and Redemption*, 73–75.

119. Jacques Rossi and Michèle Sarde, *Jacques le Français: pour mémoire du Goulag* (Paris: Cherche midi, 2002), 83.

CHAPTER 9. EXPLOITATION

1. Varlam Shalamov, *Kolyma Tales* (New York: Penguin Books, 1994), 330. On Gulag labor and Bolshevik ideology, see Steven A. Barnes, *Death and Redemption: The Gulag and the Shaping of Soviet Society* (Princeton, NJ: Princeton University Press, 2011), 36–41, 128–134, 162–163.

2. Antoni Ekart, *Vanished Without Trace: The Story of Seven Years in Soviet Russia* (London: Max Parrish, 1954), 291.

3. Shalamov, *Kolyma Tales*, 156.

4. Shalamov, *Kolyma Tales*, 326.

5. Shalamov, *Kolyma Tales*, 405.

6. Anne Applebaum, *Gulag: A History* (New York: Doubleday, 2003), 192–194; Oleg V. Khlevniuk, *The History of the Gulag: From Collectivization to the Great Terror* (New Haven, CT: Yale University Press, 2004), 246–247.

7. Leonid Borodkin and Simon Ertz, "Coercion versus Motivation," in Paul R. Gregory and Valery Lazarev, eds., *The Economics of Forced Labor: The Soviet Gulag* (Stanford, CA: Hoover Institution Press, 2003), 85–89; Applebaum, *Gulag,* 192–194. A 1949 camp report indicated that valued prison laborers went three months without a rest day. See GARF f. 9414, op. 1, d. 371, l. 76–77.

8. Alan Barenberg, *Gulag Town, Company Town: Forced Labor and its Legacy in Vorkuta* (New Haven, CT: Yale University Press, 2014), 26.

9. Aleksandr I. Solzhenitsyn, *The Gulag Archipelago, 1918–1959: An Experiment in Literary Investigation*, vols. 3–4 (New York: Harper & Row, 1975), 161.

10. Applebaum, *Gulag,* 179.

11. Applebaum, *Gulag,* 294.

12. Gustaw Herling, *A World Apart* (New York: Penguin Books, 1986), 41.

13. Simon Ertz, "Trading Effort for Freedom: Workday Credits in the Stalinist Camp System," *Comparative Economic Studies* 47 (June 2005): 476–491; Borodkin and Ertz, "Coercion versus Motivation," 75–104.

14. GARF f. 9414, op. 1, d. 374, l. 44–45.

15. Applebaum, *Gulag,* 54.

16. Barnes, *Death and Redemption,* 39.

17. Borodkin and Ertz, "Coercion versus Motivation," 80.

18. Solzhenitsyn, *Gulag Archipelago*, vols. 3–4, 78.

19. GARF f. 9414, op. 1, d. 1139, l. 132, 190–191.

20. Oleg Khlevniuk, "The Economy of the OGPU, NKVD, and MVD of the USSR, 1930–1953: The Scale, Structure, and Trends of Development," in Paul R. Gregory and Valery Lazarev, eds., *The Economics of Forced Labor: The Soviet Gulag* (Stanford, CA: Hoover Institution Press, 2003), 51; A.B. Bezborodov and V.M. Khrustalev, eds., *Istoriia stalinskogo gulaga: konets 1920-kh–pervaia polovina 1950-kh godov, tom 4: naselenie gulaga* (Moscow, 2004), 99–100.

21. GARF f. 9414, op. 1, d. 329, l. 193–194.

22. Bezborodov and Khrustalev, *Istoriia stalinskogo gulaga,* 123.

23. GARF f. 9414, op. 1, d. 489, l. 1–9, 111–118. The Borsky camp was closed in October 1951. There is evidence that camps with high concentrations of invalid prisoners were often liquidated, thus removing these prisoners from Gulag statistics altogether. See *Sistema ispravitel'no-trudovykh lagerei v SSSR, 1923–1960: Spravochnik* (Moscow, 1998), 175.

24. GARF f. 9414, op. 1, d. 459, l. 59–62.

25. GARF f. 9414, op. 1, d. 455, l. 106. This report (*svodka*) on labor utilization in MVD camps and colonies omitted the dismal figures on prisoners' physical profile. Whoever read the report made markings only around the figures on the total prisoner population and its labor utilization.

26. GARF f. 9414, op. 1, d. 2854, l. 24, 27.

27. GARF f. 9414, op. 1, d. 329, l. 192–194.

28. GARF f. 9414, op. 1, d. 329, l. 192.

29. GARF f. 9414, op. 1, d. 466, l. 15–18. At the high-priority Norilsk camp, which was supposed to have fewer emaciated prisoners, the data appeared more favorable, even in the hard-regime camp divisions.

30. GARF f. 9414, op. 1, d. 485, l. 87–88.

31. GARF f. 9414, op. 1, d. 489, l. 111–118.

32. GARF f. 9414, op. 1, d. 329, l. 192.

33. GARF f. 9414, op. 2, d. 169, l. 143–144.

34. GARF f. 9414, op. 2, d. 169, l. 144. I have not seen such a document, and camp officials often complained that they lacked specific instructions concerning what jobs constituted heavy, medium, and light labor.

35. GARF f. 9414, op. 2, d. 169, l. 144–145.

36. GARF f. 9414, op. 2, d. 169, l. 118.

37. Khlevniuk, *History of the Gulag,* 42.

38. See Christian Gerlach and Nicolas Werth, "State Violence—Violent Societies," in Michael Geyer and Sheila Fitzpatrick, eds., *Beyond Totalitarianism: Stalinism and Nazism Compared* (Cambridge: Cambridge University Press, 2009), 168–171.

39. GARF f. 9414, op. 2, d. 169, l. 118.

40. GARF f. 9414, op. 2, d. 169, l. 6.

41. GARF f. 9414, op. 1, d. 1909, l. 201.

42. GARF f. 9414, op. 1, d. 1909, l. 206, 209–210.

43. Simeon Vilensky, ed., *Till My Tale Is Told: Women's Memoirs of the Gulag* (Bloomington: Indiana University Press, 1999), 258.

44. See, for example, GARF f. 9414, op. 1, d. 387, l. 15, 22, 29, 43; GARF f. 9414, op. 1, d. 366, l. 19. On prisoners "off the labor rolls" or "off the labor balance" see Dan Healey, "Lives in the Balance: Weak and Disabled Prisoners and the Biopolitics of the Gulag," in *Kritika: Explorations in Russian and Eurasian History* 16:3 (Summer 2015): 527–556.

45. GARF f. 9414, op. 1, d. 366, l. 10.

46. In the May 1946 MVD order that established the convalescent camps, MVD chief S.N. Kruglov specified that "prisoners located in the convalescent camp sections and camps are to be registered as off the labor rolls." See A.I. Kokurin and N.V. Petrov, *Gulag (glavnoe upravlenie lagerei), 1917–1960* Moscow, 2000), 536.

47. Documents of the mining camp Kedrovyi Shor. Hoover Institution Archives, Anne Applebaum Collection, box 1, folder 2.

48. GARF f. 9414, op. 1, d. 388, l. 1–4; GARF f. 9414, op. 1, d. 390, l. 81–84.

49. GARF f. 9414, op. 1, d. 1341, l. 31–36. As Shalamov describes, typhoid quarantine took place in the transit prison. See *Kolyma Tales,* 149.

50. GARF f. 9414, op. 1, d. 495, l. 1–7.

51. GARF f. 9414, op. 2, d. 169, l. 25.
52. GARF f. 9414, op. 2, d. 169, l. 29.
53. GARF f. 9414, op. 2, d. 169, l. 13.
54. GARF f. 9414, op. 1, d. 489, l. 1–9, 61–69, 111–118.
55. GARF f. 9414, op. 1, d. 1340, l. 47.
56. GARF f. 9414, op. 1, d. 491, l. 23.
57. GARF f. 9414, op. 1, d. 485, l. 87–88.
58. J. Arch Getty, Gàbor T. Rittersporn, and Viktor N. Zemskov, "Victims of the Soviet Penal System in the Pre-war Years: A First Approach on the Basis of Archival Evidence," *The American Historical Review* 98 (October 1993): 1017–1049; Kokurin and Petrov, *Gulag,* 441–442; Applebaum, *Gulag,* 582–583; Barnes, *Death and Redemption,* 76, 116; Bezborodov and Khrustalev, *Istoriia stalinskogo gulaga,* 54–55; Khlevniuk, *History of the Gulag,* 320–327.
59. Barnes, *Death and Redemption,* 161–162.
60. Ertz, "Trading Effort for Freedom"; Borodkin and Ertz, "Coercion versus Motivation," 75–104; Khlevniuk, "Economy of the OGPU, NKVD, and MVD," 55.
61. GARF f. 9414, op. 1, d. 374, l. 54.
62. Borodkin and Ertz, "Coercion versus Motivation," 95–97; Marta Craveri and Oleg Khlevniuk, "Krizis ekonomiki MVD (konets 1940-kh–1950-e gody)," *Cahiers du Monde russe,* 36:1–2 (janvier–juin 1995), 184; Barnes, *Death and Redemption,* 163–164.
63. N.A. Morozov, *Osobye lageria MVD SSSR v Komi ASSR, 1948–1954* (Syktyvkar, 1998), 45–46; Andrei Sokolov, "Forced Labor in Soviet Industry: The End of the 1930s to the Mid-1950s: An Overview," and Khlevniuk, "Economy of the OGPU, NKVD, and MVD," in *Economics of Forced Labor,* 40, 57.
64. Borodkin and Ertz, "Coercion versus Motivation," 100.
65. Kokurin and Petrov, *Gulag,* 669.
66. Borodkin and Ertz, "Coercion versus Motivation," 101.
67. Applebaum, *Gulag,* 473; Sokolov, "Forced Labor," 40.
68. Borodkin and Ertz, "Coercion versus Motivation," 99–100.
69. Khlevniuk, "Economy of the OGPU, NKVD, and MVD," 54–55.
70. GARF f. 9414, op. 1, d. 369, l. 93–95.
71. Morozov, *Osobye lageria,* 45–46.
72. GARF f. 9414, op. 1, d. 2877, l. 7–8.
73. GARF f. 9414, op. 1, d. 2854, l. 82–83.
74. GARF f. 9414, op. 1, d. 2854, l. 82–83.
75. GARF f. 9414, op. 1, d. 621, l. 46–47.
76. GARF f. 9414, op. 1, d. 164, l. 36–40.
77. Applebaum, *Gulag,* 473–474.
78. Craveri and Khlevniuk, "Krizis ekonomiki," 186.
79. Craveri and Khlevniuk, "Krizis ekonomiki," 185, 187. See also Barenberg, *Gulag Town, Company Town.*
80. Khlevniuk, *History of the Gulag,* 247–248. See also the case described in Golfo Alexopoulos "A Torture Memo: Reading Violence in the Gulag," in Golfo Alexopoulos, Julie Hessler and Kiril Tomoff, eds., *Writing the Stalin Era: Sheila Fitzpatrick and Soviet Historiography* (New York: Palgrave Macmillan, 2011), 159–178.

81. Khlevniuk, *History of the Gulag*, 250.

82. GARF f. 9414, op. 1, d. 374, l. 27.

83. GARF f. 9414, op. 1, d. 374, l. 27–37.

84. Barenberg, *Gulag Town, Company Town*, 43–52; Craveri and Khlevniuk, "Krizis ekonomiki," 182–183.

85. Fedor V. Mochulsky, *Gulag Boss: A Soviet Memoir*, trans. and ed. Deborah Kaple (New York: Oxford University Press, 2011), 78.

86. V.A. Kozlov, ed., *Istoriia stalinskogo gulaga, konets 1920-kh–pervaia polovina 1950-kh godov, tom 6: vosstaniia, bunty i zabastovki zakliuchennykh* (Moscow: Rosspen, 2004); Craveri and Khlevniuk, "Krizis ekonomiki," 183.

87. GARF f. 9414, op. 1, d. 86, l. 130.

88. GARF f. 9414, op. 1, d. 160, l. 79–80.

89. Craveri and Khlevniuk, "Krizis ekonomiki," 183–184; Alexopoulos "A Torture Memo."

90. GARF f. 9414, op. 1, d. 374, l. 38–39.

91. GARF f. 9414, op. 1, d. 374, l. 39–42; Applebaum, *Gulag*, 261.

92. Applebaum, *Gulag*, 270–272; Leona Toker, *Return from the Archipelago: Narratives of Gulag Survivors* (Bloomington: Indiana University Press, 2000); Solzhenitsyn, *Gulag Archipelago*, vols. 3–4, 556–560.

93. Khlevniuk, "Economy of the OGPU," 53.

94. Applebaum, *Gulag*, 472; Craveri and Khlevniuk, "Krizis ekonomiki," 182.

95. Nicolas Werth, "A State against Its People: Violence, Repression, and Terror in the Soviet Union," in Stephane Courtois, Nicolas Werth, et al., *The Black Book of Communism: Crimes, Terror, Repression* (Cambridge, MA: Harvard University Press, 1999), 238, 241.

96. GARF f. 9414, op. 1, d. 1909, l. 99–128.

97. G.M. Ivanova, *Istoriia GULAGa, 1918–1958: sotsial'no-ekonomicheskii i politiko-pravovoi aspect* (Moscow: Nauka, 2006), 385; Sokolov, "Forced Labor," 40.

98. GARF f. 9414, op. 1, d. 1139, l. 131–132, 191.

99. GARF f. 9414, op. 1, d. 14, l. 154.

100. GARF f. 9414, op. 1, d. 1908, l. 166.

101. GARF f. 9414, op. 1, d. 1908, l. 163, 167; Alexopoulos, "A Torture Memo."

102. Craveri and Khlevniuk, "Krizis ekonomiki," 183.

103. GARF f. 9414, op. 1, d. 164, l. 38.

104. GARF f. 9414, op. 1, d. 2854, l. 24, 27.

105. GARF f. 9414, op. 1, d. 1347, l. 16–18.

106. Aleksandr Solzhenitsyn, *Arkhipelag Gulag* (Moscow: Al'fa-Kniga, 2009), 538–562. For contemporary usage of the term, which can also mean "morons," see Alexei Yurchak, *Everything was Forever, Until it was No More: The Last Soviet Generation* (Princeton, NJ: Princeton University Press, 2005), 234.

107. Ekart, *Vanished Without Trace*, 61.

108. Shalamov, *Kolyma Tales*, 174.

109. Quoted in Applebaum, *Gulag*, 104.

110. For example, of the 7350 prisoners who performed camp maintenance jobs at the White Sea-Baltic Sea Canal project (BBLag) in 1938, fewer than 20 percent

were classified invalids. Many secured these privileged jobs through bribery and connections. See Christopher Joyce, "The Gulag in Karelia: 1929–1941," in Paul R. Gregory and Valery Lazarev, eds., *The Economics of Forced Labor: The Soviet Gulag* (Stanford, CA: Hoover Institution Press, 2003), 184.

111. Solzhenitsyn, *Gulag Archipelago*, vols. 3–4, 254; Applebaum, *Gulag*, 364–365.

112. Solzhenitsyn, *Gulag Archipelago*, vols. 3–4, 252–253. See also Applebaum, *Gulag*, 218; Toker, *Return from the Archipelago*, 17, 21, 51, 91.

113. Alexander Etkind, *Warped Mourning: Stories of the Undead in the Land of the Unburied* (Stanford, CA: Stanford University Press, 2013), 64, 89–90; Solzhenitsyn, *Gulag Archipelago*, vols. 3–4, 604; Tim Tzouliadis, *The Forsaken: An American Tragedy in Stalin's Russia* (New York: Penguin Books, 2009).

114. Etkind, *Warped Mourning*, 85.

115. Applebaum, *Gulag*, 367–368; Barnes, *Death and Redemption*, 77–78, 121.

116. Aleksandr I. Solzhenitsyn, *The Gulag Archipelago, 1918–1956: An Experiment in Literary Investigation*, vols. 1–2 (New York: Harper & Row, 1973), 564. The emphasis is in Solzhenitsyn's text.

117. Toker, *Return from the Archipelago*, 17.

118. Toker, *Return from the Archipelago*, 90–91.

119. Ekart, *Vanished Without Trace*, 194. See also Dimitri Panin, *The Notebooks of Sologdin* (New York: Harcourt Brace Jovanovich, 1973), 213.

120. Applebaum, *Gulag*, 104.

121. David Nordlander, "Magadan and the Economic History of Dalstroi in the 1930s," in Paul R. Gregory and Valery Lazarev, eds., *The Economics of Forced Labor: The Soviet Gulag* (Stanford, CA: Hoover Institution Press, 2003), 119–120. See also Applebaum, *Gulag*, 110, 212.

122. Shalamov, *Kolyma Tales*, 222–223.

123. G.I. Kasabova, ed., *O vremeni, o Noril'ske, o sebe . . . Kniga 6* (Moscow, 2005), 526.

124. After the Nazis invaded, Svanidze was taken away and shot, together with other high-profile political prisoners. See S.F. Sapolnova, T.A. Vekshina, F.G. Kanev, eds., *Liudi v belykh khalatakh* (Syktyvkar: Komi respublikanskaia tipografiia, 2009), 22, 32–33.

125. Solzhenitsyn, *Gulag Archipelago*, vols. 3–4, 252.

126. Herling, *A World Apart*, 247.

127. Solzhenitsyn, *Gulag Archipelago*, vols. 3–4, 562–563; Applebaum, *Gulag*, 368.

128. Giorgio Agamben, *Remnants of Auschwitz: The Witness and the Archive* (New York: Zone Books, 2002), 87–91.

129. Shalamov, *Kolyma Tales*, 40–41.

130. Hannah Arendt, *On Violence* (New York: Harcourt, 1969), 55–56.

EPILOGUE

1. Aleksandr Solzhenitsyn, *Arkhipelag Gulag* (Moscow: Al'fa-Kniga, 2009), 769.

2. David J. Dallin and Boris I. Nicolaevsky, *Forced Labor in Soviet Russia* (New Haven, CT: Yale University Press, 1947), xii.

3. S.F. Sapolnova, T.A. Vekshina, and F.G. Kanev, eds., *Liudi v belykh khalatakh* (Syktyvkar: Komi respublikanskaia tipografiia, 2009), 26.

4. Jehanne M. Gheith and Katherine R. Jolluck, eds., *Gulag Voices: Oral Histories of Soviet Incarceration and Exile* (New York: Palgrave Macmillan, 2011), 105.

5. Aleksandr I. Solzhenitsyn, *The Gulag Archipelago, 1918–1956: An Experiment in Literary Investigation*, vols. 1–2, trans. Thomas P. Whitney (New York: Harper & Row, 1973), x, 489; Alexander Schmemann, "Reflections on *The Gulag Archipelago*," in John B. Dunlop, Richard Haugh, and Alexis Klimoff, eds., *Aleksandr Solzhenitsyn: Critical Essays and Documentary Materials* (New York: Macmillan, 1975), 516–517.

6. Alan Barenberg, *Gulag Town, Company Town: Forced Labor and its Legacy in Vorkuta* (New Haven, CT: Yale University Press, 2014); Wilson T. Bell, "Was the Gulag an Archipelago? De-Convoyed Prisoners and Porous Borders in the Camps of Western Siberia," *Russian Review* 72 (January 2013): 116–141; Anne Applebaum, *Gulag: A History* (New York: Doubleday, 2003), 114.

7. Antoni Ekart, *Vanished Without Trace: The Story of Seven Years in Soviet Russia* (London: Max Parrish, 1954), 76.

8. See Steven A. Barnes, *Death and Redemption: The Gulag and the Shaping of Soviet Society* (Princeton, NJ: Princeton University Press, 2011); Michael David-Fox, *Showcasing the Great Experiment: Cultural Diplomacy and Western Visitors to the Soviet Union, 1921–1941* (Oxford: Oxford University Press, 2012).

9. Golfo Alexopoulos, *Stalin's Outcasts: Aliens, Citizens, and the Soviet State, 1926–1936* (Ithaca, NY: Cornell University Press, 2003).

10. Applebaum, *Gulag*, 67, 233.

11. Applebaum, *Gulag*, 113–114; Aleksandr I. Solzhenitsyn, *The Gulag Archipelago, 1918–1959: An Experiment in Literary Investigation*, vols. 3–4 (New York: Harper & Row, 1975), 594.

12. Mark Harrison, "Secrecy, Fear and Transaction Costs: The Business of Soviet Forced Labour in the Early Cold War," *Europe-Asia Studies* 65 (August 2013): 1115.

13. Barnes, *Death and Redemption*, 256.

14. Emily D. Johnson, "Interview with Nikolai Ivanovich Lileev," *Gulag Studies* 1 (2008): 124.

15. Ekart, *Vanished Without Trace*, 311. See also Janusz Bardach and Kathleen Gleeson, *Surviving Freedom: After the Gulag* (Berkeley: University of California Press, 2003), 11; Jacques Rossi and Michèle Sarde, *Jacques le Français: pour mémoire du Goulag (Paris: Cherche midi, 2002), 181–182.

16. Paul R. Gregory, *Lenin's Brain and Other Tales from the Secret Soviet Archives* (Stanford, CA: Hoover Institution Press, 2008), 73–79.

17. For Gulag instructions dated January 1935, see GARF f. 9414, op. 1, d. 2744, l. 4. NKVD order of August 20, 1940 included an elaborate listing of code words that had to be used in all telegraphic communications concerning

prisoners. See Kokurin, A.I. and N.V. Petrov, *Gulag (glavnoe upravlenie lagerei), 1918–1960* (Moscow, 2000), 866.

18. Applebaum, *Gulag,* 248; Arsenii Formakov, *Gulag Letters,* ed. Emily D. Johnson, (New Haven, CT: Yale University Press, 2017).

19. Marta Craveri and Oleg Khlevniuk, "Krizis ekonomiki MVD (konets 1940-kh–1950-e gody)," *Cahiers du Monde russe,* XXXVI (1–2), janvier–juin 1995: 189.

20. David-Fox, *Showcasing the Great Experiment,* 143. See also Oleg V. Khlevniuk, *The History of the Gulag: From Collectivization to the Great Terror* (New Haven, CT: Yale University Press, 2004), 29–30.

21. Applebaum, *Gulag,* 61–62, 87.

22. Khlevniuk, *History of the Gulag,* 30.

23. Tony Judt, *Postwar: A History of Europe since 1945* (New York: Penguin, 2005), 54.

24. GARF f. 9414, op. 1, d. 374, l. 48–49.

25. Amir Weiner, *Making Sense of War: The Second World War and the Fate of the Bolshevik Revolution* (Princeton, NJ: Princeton University Press, 2001), 38–39.

26. Khlevniuk, *History of the Gulag,* 287, 292, 338; Simon Ertz, "Building Norilsk," in Paul R. Gregory and Valery Lazarev, eds., *The Economics of Forced Labor: The Soviet Gulag* (Stanford, CA: Hoover Institution Press, 2003), 137; Oleg Khlevniuk, "The Economy of the OGPU, NKVD, and MVD of the USSR, 1930–1953: The Scale, Structure, and Trends of Development," in Paul R. Gregory and Valery Lazarev, eds., *The Economics of Forced Labor: The Soviet Gulag* (Stanford, CA: Hoover Institution Press, 2003), 64–65; Viola, *Unknown Gulag,* 106–108.

27. Paul R. Gregory, *Terror by Quota: State Security from Lenin to Stalin* (New Haven, CT: Yale University Press, 2009); Norman M. Naimark, *Stalin's Genocides* (Princeton, NJ: Princeton University Press, 2010), 11–12.

28. Khlevniuk, *History of the Gulag,* 179, 321–322.

29. Khlevniuk, *History of the Gulag,* 7.

30. Veniamin F. Zima, "Medical Expertise and the 1946–47 Famine: The Identification and Treatment of a State-Induced Illness," in Frances L. Bernstein, Christopher Burton, and Dan Healy, eds., *Soviet Medicine: Culture, Practice, and Science* (Dekalb: Northern Illinois University Press, 2010), 182.

31. Rebecca Manley, "Nutritional Dystrophy: The Science and Semantics of Starvation in World War II," in Wendy Z. Goldman and Donald Filtzer, eds., *Hunger and War: Food Provisioning in the Soviet Union during World War II* (Bloomington: Indiana University Press, 2015), 211–215.

32. GARF f. 9414, op. 1, d. 2782, l. 103.

33. Isaac J. Vogelfanger, *Red Tempest: The Life of a Surgeon in the Gulag* (Montreal: McGill-Queen's University Press, 1996), 80, 144.

34. Craveri and Khlevniuk, "Krizis ekonomiki," 182–183.

35. GARF f. 9414, op. 1, d. 374, l. 43.

36. Eugenia Ginzburg, *Within the Whirlwind* (New York: Harcourt Brace Jovanovich, 1979). See also Judith Pallot, Laura Piacentini and Dominique Moran,

"Patriotic Discourses in Russia's Penal Peripheries: Remembering the Mordovan Gulag," *Europe-Asia Studies* 62 (January 2010):1–33.

37. Evgeny Dobrenko, *Political Economy of Socialist Realism* (New Haven, CT: Yale University Press, 2007), 31.

38. GARF f. 9414, op. 2, d. 169, l. 11.

39. GARF f. 9414, op. 2, d. 169, l. 12.

40. GARF f. 9414, op. 2, d. 169, l. 32.

41. GARF f. 9414, op. 2, d. 169, l. 15.

42. GARF f. 9414, op. 2, d. 169, l. 17.

43. GARF f. 9414, op. 2, d. 169, l. 19.

44. GARF f. 9414, op. 2, d. 169, l. 19.

45. GARF f. 9414, op. 2, d. 169, l. 116, 142.

46. Alexander Etkind, *Warped Mourning: Stories of the Undead in the Land of the Unburied* (Stanford, CA: Stanford University Press, 2013), 47–48.

47. Applebaum, *Gulag,* 171–172, 336, 343.

48. Gustaw Herling, *A World Apart* (New York: Penguin Books, 1996), 148–149.

49. Memorial, St. Petersburg, f. B-1, op. 1, d. Gol'ts, Ekaterina Pavlovna, interview with Niki Georgievna Gol'ts in Moscow on October 13, 2010, conducted by Irina Suslova of Memorial in St. Petersburg. The transcribed interview is item ten of the file, and the quote appears on pages three and four.

50. David Brion Davis, *Inhuman Bondage: The Rise and Fall of Slavery in the New World* (Oxford: Oxford University Press, 2006), 330.

51. Varlam Shalamov, *Kolymskie rasskazy: kniga pervaia* (Moscow: Sovetskaia Rossiia, 1992), 115.

52. Khlevniuk, *History of the Gulag;* Lynne Viola, *The Unknown Gulag: The Lost World of Stalin's Special Settlements* (New York: Oxford University Press, 2007).

53. See, for example, Nanci Adler, *The Gulag Survivor: Beyond the Soviet System* (London: Transaction Publishers, 2004); Alan Barenberg, *Gulag Town, Company Town: Forced Labor and its Legacy in Vorkuta* (New Haven, CT: Yale University Press, 2014); Stephen F. Cohen, *The Victim's Return: Survivors of the Gulag after Stalin* (Exeter, NH: PublishingWorks, Inc., 2010); Miriam Dobson, *Khrushchev's Cold Summer: Gulag Returnees, Crime, and the Fate of Reform after Stalin* (Ithaca, NY: Cornell University Press, 2009); Marc Elie, "Khrushchev's Gulag: The Soviet Penitentiary System after Stalin's Death, 1953–1964," in Denis Kozlov and Eleonory Gilburd, eds., *The Thaw: Soviet Society and Culture during the 1950s and 1960s* (Toronto: University of Toronto Press, 2013), 109–142.

54. Aleksei Tikhonov, "The End of the Gulag," in Paul R. Gregory and Valery Lazarev, eds., *The Economics of Forced Labor: The Soviet Gulag* (Stanford, CA: Hoover Institution Press, 2003), 68–69.

55. Tikhonov, "End of the Gulag," 70–71.

56. Tikhonov, "End of the Gulag," 70–71.

57. On the March 1953 amnesty, see Dobson, *Khrushchev's Cold Summer;* Tikhonov, "End of the Gulag," in *Economics of Forced Labor,* 71–73; Barenberg, *Gulag Town, Company Town,* 200–201; Barnes, *Death and Redemption,* 205–206.

58. Galina Mikhailovna Ivanova, *Labor Camp Socialism: The Gulag in the Soviet Totalitarian System* (New York: M.E. Sharpe, 2000); 124.

59. Khlevniuk, "Economy of the OGPU," 54–55; Applebaum, *Gulag,* 478–479; Ivanova, *Labor Camp Socialism,* 124.

60. Applebaum, *Gulag,* 478–479.

61. Aleksei Tikhonov, "The End of the Gulag," 67.

62. GARF f. 9414, op. 1, d. 1909, l. 235, 237–241.

63. For example, in 1951, the Gulag leadership indicated that, "the Ministry of Social Security of the republics systematically refuses to allocate space for invalid prisoners who have completed their sentence." See GARF f. 9414, op. 1, d. 621, l. 45–49.

64. Quoted in Etkind, *Warped Mourning,* 101.

Index

Illnesses *(continued)*
    frostbite, 94, 100; gastrointestinal, 91,
    94, 97, 101, 106–107, 187, 192, 239;
    glaucoma, 187; gonorrhea, 67; heart
    disease, 67, 70–71, 94, 189; hernias,
    34, 36, 73, 81, 136; inflammation, 81,
    94; influenza, 80, 92; kidney disease,
    101, 187; List of, 66–75, 79–82, 135,
    150, 199, 213, 235; malaria, 97, 107,
    172, 192; mental, 134, 138, 145;
    neurodegenerative, 80; pneumonia,
    54, 80, 92, 94, 97, 107, 192; senil-
    ity, 70, 81, 187; schizophrenia, 70;
    scurvy, 22, 31–33, 93–96, 104, 158,
    177, 215, 229; silicosis, 80–81; skin,
    94–95, 106–107, 149, 156, 168, 187,
    239; syphilis, 99; typhus, 27, 92–94,
    97, 149, 194; ulcers, 187, 215. *See also*
    blindness; deafness; dystrophy; hospi-
    tals; malnutrition; medical treatment;
    pellagra; starvation; surgery; tuberculo-
    sis; vitamin deficiency
Invalid camps, 110–116, 190–192; condi-
    tions, 115–116; costs, 112–115, 200,
    206, 217, 237; isolation of prisoners,
    110–111, 129, 132, 144; numbers
    of prisoners, 111–112, 114; quotas,
    111; work in, 110–111, 114, 122. *See
    also* agricultural camps; convalescent
    camps; invalids; transit camps
Invalids, 14, 53, 66, 115–116, 188, 246;
    certification, 69, 73, 135, 148, 169;
    concealment, 149–150, 209, 212; costs,
    111–112; isolation and separation,
    110–112, 132, 193; jobs for, 25, 30–31,
    68, 117, 226–227; labor category, 16,
    67–74, 79–81, 109; laws and direc-
    tives on, 98, 117, 128, 136, 139; living
    conditions, 115–116, 148; and mortal-
    ity, 110, 115–116, 142, 157, 243;
    not-working, 25, 29–30, 69, 123, 201,
    216–217, 220; numbers of, 69, 75–77,
    83, 111–112, 126, 135–138, 143, 146,
    191–192, 204–205, 212, 217–218; "off
    the labor rolls," 141, 155, 215–218;
    production norms, 10, 25, 123, 220,
    226; quotas, 120, 160; rations, 25–26,
    123; releases, 54, 67, 74, 80, 99–100,
    133–146, 151, 157; special camps,
    200–205; wages and salaries, 220;
    wartime, 112–114, 138–140; as work

refusers, 220, 226. *See also* illnesses;
    invalid camps
Irkutsk regional camps, 89, 116

Juvenile offenders, 52–53, 76, 137–138,
    143, 179. *See also* children; criminal
    offenders; prisoners; theft

Karelia republic camps, 112
Karlag camp, 92, 112–113, 198–199,
    201–203, 218, 221
Katorga, 13, 197–200, 205, 207. *See also*
    camps: harsh-regime
Kazakh republic camps, 112, 162, 169–172,
    188, 203, 242
Kengir uprising, 204
Khabarovsk regional camps, 83, 131, 192,
    196
Kogan, L.I., 66
Kolyma: illnesses in, 119–120, 134, 158;
    secrecy, 236–237; special camps, 199,
    203–204; women, 57; work, 198, 208,
    241. *See also* Magadan
Komi republic camps, 95, 158, 199, 204
Krasnoiarsk regional camps, 34, 125, 163,
    167, 180
Kruglov, S.N.: on invalids, 113, 117; on
    labor, 19, 193, 196, 203–204, 222–224,
    226; on health, 78–82, 127–128, 193,
    220
Kulaks, 2, 9, 11, 45, 49–50, 56, 58, 67, 139,
    158, 236, 244

Labor. *See* exploitation; labor utilization;
    work refusers
Labor productivity, 1, 12, 19, 21, 31, 204;
    declining, 224–225, 230; and food,
    27, 36; incentives, 3, 8, 132, 143–144,
    210, 219; and mechanization, 59; and
    releases, 133, 144; and self-mutilation,
    102; Stalin on, 210; and weakened
    prisoners, 123, 131–132, 221. *See also*
    exploitation; labor utilization
Labor therapy, 86, 103–105, 121, 128. *See
    also* illnesses; medical treatment
Labor utilization, 12, 62, 108, 194, 227,
    232–233; declining and poor, 82,
    169–170, 205, 224–225, 230; efforts
    to improve, 75, 78–80, 175, 221, 226,
    238; rates of, 155, 163, 165, 208–218,
    238–239; weakened prisoners, 71, 80,